The Contested Lands of Laikipia

African Social Studies Series

VOLUME 42

The titles published in this series are listed at *brill.com/afss*

The Contested Lands of Laikipia

Histories of Claims and Conflict in a Kenyan Landscape

By

Marie Ladekjær Gravesen

BRILL

LEIDEN | BOSTON

Library of Congress Cataloging-in-Publication Data

Names: Gravesen, Marie Ladekjær, author.
Title: The contested lands of Laikipia : histories of claims and conflict in a Kenyan landscape / by Marie Ladekjær Gravesen.
Description: Leiden ; Boston : Brill, [2021] | Series: African social studies series, 1568-1203 ; volume 42 | Includes bibliographical references and index.
Identifiers: LCCN 2020029838 (print) | LCCN 2020029839 (ebook) | ISBN 9789004435193 (paperback ; alk. paper) | ISBN 9789004435209 (ebook)
Subjects: LCSH: Land tenure--Kenya--Laikipia District--History. | Land use--Kenya--Laikipia District--History. | Social conflict--Kenya--Laikipia District--History. | Violence--Kenya--Laikipia District--History. | Laikipia District (Kenya)--Politics and government.
Classification: LCC HD983.Z8 L3544 2021 (print) | LCC HD983.Z8 (ebook) | DDC 333.3/167627--dc23
LC record available at https://lccn.loc.gov/2020029838
LC ebook record available at https://lccn.loc.gov/2020029839

Typeface for the Latin, Greek, and Cyrillic scripts: "Brill". See and download: brill.com/brill-typeface.

ISSN 1568-1203
ISBN 978-90-04-43519-3 (paperback)
ISBN 978-90-04-43520-9 (e-book)

This book is printed on acid-free paper and produced in a sustainable manner.

Contents

Acknowledgements

In many ways, this book has been a collaborative project despite it being a single-author piece. Many have offered their support to me, without whom I would not have been able to carry this project through – at least, the product would have been markedly different.

I would therefore like to extent a note of gratitude to the people in Laikipia who kindly opened their homes to me and entrusted me with their stories. This project would not have been possible without your trust and generosity. To my two brilliant research assistants, 'E' and 'H,' for giving me invaluable support – helping me to make sense of the things we saw and heard. To all the colleagues with whom I shared the joys and frustrations of doing fieldwork. A special thanks to Anna for being such an inspiration with your dedication and persistence.

To my friends and colleagues at the University of Cologne for creating such a safe space in which to share and challenge each other's ideas – a space for being colleagues rather than competitors. To Michael Bollig and David Anderson for giving me the opportunity to come under their supervision. Thank you for challenging me to think in new directions, for confronting my weaknesses, for opening doors for me and for trusting me to figure things out for myself after giving me a hint. To the University of Cologne, the a.r.t.e.s. Graduate School and the EU Commission under Framework 7 for financial support. To my colleagues in the Resilience in East African Landscapes (REAL) project for sharing the adventure with me and for making the many meetings and workshops enjoyable. Thanks for meeting our inter-disciplinary collaboration with curiosity rather than opposition. To the people at the Centre of African Studies (CAS) in Copenhagen for offering me a place to work. A special thanks to Amanda Hammar and Stig Jensen for making me feel welcome, and to Hannah and Julie for sharing the long working days along the way.

To my family for being compassionate. To my grandmother, who passed away while I was in Northern Kenya. Thank you for always being generous and kind, for believing in me even when my decisions to move in different directions have not always been understandable. To my wonderful friends in Copenhagen for reminding me where and who I ought to be when I occasionally drifted away. And lastly, to Joshua for enriching my life with so much love, joy and relentless encouragement. Thank you for inspiring me to be the best version of myself every single day.

Figures and Tables

Figures

Tables

CHAPTER 1

Introduction

As a precursor to the Kenyan general election in 2017, a year-long wave of uncertainty hit Laikipia County in the autumn of 2016. Thousands of armed pastoralists invaded ranches and large-scale farms, authorities refrained from intervening with adequate measures, and political opportunists took sides to exchange their support for political votes.[1] If this is approached as a singular event, one can easily be convinced that the crisis transpired due to drought, or that all the pastoralists are ungovernable, do not understand the principles of private-property rights and should be punished for illegal practices. Laikipia has seen land invasions, rebellious killing of wildlife and political incitements to violence before, although they have never previously escalated to this level.[2] However, broadening the context around the 2016–2017 events reveals a much more complex line of precursors. I argue that the historical development and influence of political and ethnic factors, along with issues of land distribution, are among the main ignition points for the general tension on the plateau, and are what ultimately led to the 2016 and 2017 state of emergency. This book explains the situation with a point of departure before violent eruption occurred. It interrogates the different types of changes that Laikipia has undergone over the past 150 years. This is done using a string of thematic components, since no singular theoretical approach can adequately explain the dynamics at play. This study does not focus on one group and one place by looking at only the larger landholdings, the smallholder livelihoods or the changes in the pastoral communities. Rather, it takes a regional approach to explore the long-term changes in the social, ecological and political dynamics of this area.

I combine oral histories with data from archives, aerial photographs and newspapers to look at environmental, political and social change, with a focus on the most recent temporal scale of the post-Independence years leading up to the present. I use three smaller areas in western Laikipia as case studies to illustrate the variety in the ways that land and political resources are, and have been, claimed. In this way, we can come to understand Laikipia's

1 *The Star*, 'Land Invasion Wrecks Laikipia,' 19 January 2017, http://www.the-star.co.ke/news/2017/01/19/land-invasion-wrecks-laikipia_c1489820, accessed 30 January 2017.

2 Parselelo Kantai, 'In the Grip of the Vampire State: Maasai Land Struggles in Kenyan Politics,' *Journal of Eastern African Studies* 1, no. 1 (2007), pp. 107–22; Michelle E. Gadd, 'Conservation outside of Parks: Attitudes of Local People in Laikipia, Kenya,' *Environmental Conservation* 32, no. 1 (March 2005), pp. 50–63.

 | DOI:10.1163/9789004435209_002

2016–2017 crisis in the context of social, political, historical and environmental fragmentation.

Whereas episodes of emergency are most often understood and explored retrospectively once the crisis has already started or even passed, this study interrogates the time and setting before the conflict broke out. The bulk of the data collection was carried out between the years of 2014 and 2016, making the study into an ethnography of a place before the flames were lit – the story of the gusts of wind that led to the storm. The study therefore occupies a unique position from which to explain the present-day social-ecological dynamics in Laikipia generally, and the 2016–2017 state of emergency specifically.

1.1 The State of Emergency in Laikipia, 2016–17

Before we go into the details of the study, let us first take a closer look at the emergency itself.

At the time of the first invasion, the Kenyan newspaper *The Star* reported: 'there have been numerous attacks in the drought-stricken region of Laikipia in recent months as armed cattle herders searching for scarce grazing have driven tens of thousands of cattle onto private farms and ranches. At least a dozen people have been killed.'[3] Although some of the numbers presented in the media were exaggerated, the attacks and invasions did lead to instances of wildlife killings,[4] looting of houses,[5] burning of tourist lodges,[6] livestock rustling[7] and forced grazing.[8]

All ranches and conservancies had security staff present on site, often including both Kenya Wildlife Service (KWS) rangers and Anti-Stock Theft Unit

3 *The Star*, 'British Father of Two Shot Dead at Sosian Ranch in Laikipia,' 3 June 2017, http://www.the-star.co.ke/news/2017/03/06/british-father-of-two-shot-dead-at-sosian-ranch-in-laikipia_c1518914, accessed 2 August 2016.

4 *The Star*, 'Pokot Gunmen Invade Laikipia Conservancy, Kill Wild Animals,' 10 January 2017, http://www.the-star.co.ke/news/2017/01/10/pokot-gunmen-invade-laikipia-conservancy-kill-wild-animals_c1485383, accessed 30 January 2017.

5 *The Star*, 'The Diary of Seven Months of Attacks on Kifuku Farm in Laikipia,' 1 February 2017, http://www.the-star.co.ke/news/2017/02/01/the-diary-of-seven-months-of-attacks-on-kifuku-farm-in-laikipia_c1498811, accessed 2 February 2017.

6 BBC Africa, 'Kuki Gallmann's Kenya Safari Lodge Burned Down,' 30 March 2017, http://www.bbc.com/news/world-africa-39442270, accessed 29 September 2017.

7 *The Star*, 'Land Invasion Wrecks Laikipia.'

8 *The Star*, 'MP Lempurkel Denies Involvement in Suyian Ranch Invasion on Sunday,' 30 January 2017, http://www.the-star.co.ke/news/2017/01/30/mp-lempurkel-denies-involvement-in-suyian-ranch-invasion-on-sunday_c1496907, accessed 30 January 2017.

police. However, the security personnel were overwhelmed by the intensity of the attacks. The ranches and conservancies targeted included Segera Conservancy,[9] Sosian Game Ranch,[10] Mugie Conservancy,[11] Laikipia Nature Conservancy[12] and Kifuku Ranch.[13] But Ol Maisor Ranch, Ngorare Ranch and Suyian Ranch were also under strong continuous pressure.[14] On Lombara Ranch, the owner was shot and his family abandoned the farm, which was subsequently taken over by Samburu herders. Not far from there, on Jennings Ranch, Samburu *morans*[15] attacked and shot the owner.[16] On Sosian, the British-born owner was shot dead when he attempted to inspect one of his tourist lodges that had been burned down.[17] Laikipia Nature Conservancy experienced attacks from Pokot when six Dutch tourists were attacked by armed Pokot youth at a roadblock inside the conservancy on New Year's Eve 2016.[18] The owner herself was shot while patrolling the conservancy.[19] Mugie Conservancy was also heavily attacked by Pokot herders.[20] According to *The Star*,

> the Pokot broke the Mugie fences and stole kilometres of wire. The herdsmen have been shooting elephant, buffalo, eland and zebra. Property was looted from houses and workshops at Mugie. An estimated 500 cattle were stolen from Mugie by the Pokot, although 290 were recovered with the help of the police.[21]

9 *The Star*, 'Laikipia Clashes Persist as MPs, Cops, Barons Blamed,' 17 November 2016, http://www.the-star.co.ke/news/2016/11/17/laikipia-clashes-persist-as-mps-cops-barons-blamed_c1456695, accessed 2 August 2017.

10 *The Star*, 'British Father of Two Shot Dead at Sosian Ranch in Laikipia.'

11 *The Star*, 'Land Invasion Wrecks Laikipia.'

12 BBC Africa, 'Kuki Gallmann's Kenya Safari Lodge Burned Down.'

13 *The Star*, 'The Diary of Seven Months of Attacks on Kifuku Farm in Laikipia.'

14 *The Star*, 'Laikipia Invasions Are Political, Governor Hopeful Says after Kifuku Ranch Raid,' 21 May 2017, http://www.the-star.co.ke/news/2017/05/21/laikipia-invasions-are-political-governor-hopeful-says-after-kifuku_c1564943, accessed 2 August 2017.

15 Young Samburu warriors.

16 *The Star*, 'Laikipia Farm Invasions Continue,' 15 November 2016, http://www.the-star.co.ke/news/2016/11/15/laikipia-farm-invasions-continue_c1456484, accessed 2 August 2017.

17 *The Star*, 'British Father of Two Shot Dead at Sosian Ranch in Laikipia.'

18 *The Star*, 'Land Invasion Wrecks Laikipia.'

19 *The Daily Nation*, 'Conservationist Shot at Her Laikipia Conservancy,' 23 April 2017, http://www.nation.co.ke/news/Kuki-Gallman-shot-and-injured/1056-3900476-2jo62v/index.html, accessed 2 August 2017.

20 *The Star*, 'Pokot Gunmen Invade Laikipia Conservancy, Kill Wild Animals.'

21 *The Star*, 'Land Invasion Wrecks Laikipia.'

Ten days after the attack on Mugie, Suyian was attacked. *The Star* reported:

> armed attackers burned down the main tourist lodge at the 44,000 acre Suyian conservancy on Sunday. Stores and garages were looted and international visitors staying there evacuated. The five Anti-Stock Theft policemen guarding the lodge were overwhelmed by scores or hundreds of attackers.[22]

Also, the chairman of the Commission on National Cohesion and Integration, Francis ole Kaparo, was attacked and his farm invaded.[23] Moreover, the communities of smallholder farmers settled in the areas between the ranches were affected, as large numbers of livestock crossed the boundaries to these farms as well.[24] These smallholders feared that the uprising signalled conflict between the ranchers and the pastoralists.[25]

Many pointed towards Pokot and Samburu politicians, claiming that they were inciting the violence and that they were using the attackers as 'useful idiots' to scare off the landowners so that they themselves could grab the land.[26] In fact, then MP for Laikipia North Lempurkel was spotted on Suyian at the time of the attack,[27] and was charged with being involved in the murder of Sosian Game Ranch's owner.[28] According to a moderate Samburu *moran*, William, this attempt to incite violence and bring support from the counties of Samburu and Isiolo should be seen as efforts to gather enough votes for Lempurkel to keep his seat in Parliament in the 2017 election.[29]

The onset of the uncertainties was grounded in the frustration of being marginalised and misrepresented by politicians and government institutions. One research participant stated that these frustrations intensified due to the proximity of the next election, and that many of the settled pastoralists complained time and again about the police taking bribes and never returning confiscated

22 *The Star*, 'MP Lempurkel Denies Involvement in Suyian Ranch Invasion on Sunday.'
23 *The Star*, 'Land Invasion Wrecks Laikipia.'
24 *The Star*, 'Laikipia Farm Invasions Continue.'
25 Field notes, email correspondence with research participant, Laikipia, 14 December 2016.
26 *The Star*, 'Pokot Gunmen Invade Laikipia Conservancy, Kill Wild Animals.'
27 *The Star*, 'Armed Herders Invade Laikipia Ranch, Harass Elephants as Tourists Watch,' 30 January 2017, http://www.the-star.co.ke/news/2017/01/30/armed-herders-invade-laikipia-ranch-harass-elephants-as-tourists-watch_c1496603, accessed 2 August 2017.
28 *The Star*, 'MP Lempurkel Denies Involvement in Suyian Ranch Invasion on Sunday.'
29 Field notes, email correspondence with research participant, Laikipia, 30 January 2017.

livestock.[30] Indeed, one could often 'smell roasted meat from the police compounds after cattle had been confiscated,' he stated.[31]

For the first six months of gradual intensification of attacks, the situation was explained with reference to the context of drought and the attendant lack of water and grazing, making people desperate to access resources.[32] Even though there have been droughts before, the scale of these events seems unprecedented. After the death of George Aggett in September 2016, his sister Maria Dodds took over the family business at Kifuku Ranch. Following six months of continuous attacks on the previously well-managed ranch, she professed: 'I would love to believe that this is just a drought and pastoralists are desperate for grass but this is far more sinister and the government seems unable or unwilling to stop it.'[33]

The position that the invasions were structured became more widely held as the election neared. In June 2017, a detailed report entered the public debates, written by an anonymous British anthropologist. The report was based on more than 100 interviews among herders and other implicated parties between January and April 2017. According to the author, the upcoming election in August 2017 had caused a power vacuum that inhibited authorities from acting, while drought had driven pastoralist elites to form a network to claim access to resources. The author stated that the invasions were:

> choreographed through meetings and mobile phones, and supported with active armament of weapons, ammunitions, cash payments and other material support from the elite cartel. Accordingly, the invaders [operated] in a militia-like formation.[34]

There are thus grounds for considering the conflict to be rooted far deeper than in the simple fault lines driving one ethnic group against another, turning blacks against whites or igniting animosity between the privileged and the marginalised. Rather, the conflict stood between 'those whose interests are in stability and the rule of law, and those who profit from its absence.'[35] The former, protectionist group attempted to safeguard their right to resources,

30 Field notes, email correspondence with research participant, Laikipia, 30 January 2017.

31 Interview with research participant, Nyahururu, 21 March 2016.

32 *The Star*, 'Laikipia Farm Invasions Continue.'

33 *The Star*, 'The Diary of Seven Months of Attacks on Kifuku Farm in Laikipia.'

34 *The Star*, 'Is Rebellion the Next Phase of Laikipia Violence?' 5 June 2017, http://www.the-star.co.ke/news/2017/06/05/is-rebellion-the-next-phase-of-laikipia-violence_c1574344, accessed 2 August 2017.

35 *The Star*, 'Is Rebellion the Next Phase of Laikipia Violence?'

instated through state legislation, including land-tenure structures and political dominance. The latter, opportunist group took advantage of the absence of authorised regulation to pursue their own interests, including trade in land, votes, firearms and livestock. This understanding of the social-ecological landscape in Laikipia bears historical resonance, which will be exemplified throughout this book in the fluctuating power balance between those who have had the capacity to take advantage of a political situation, and those who have been excluded from influence and power.

As such, the 2016–2017 wave of attacks is reminiscent of colonial Laikipia, when Samburu entered from the north to target Kikuyu farm labourers as an act of protest against the colonial holders of the resources.[36] Although the rebellion should not be considered only as a racial uprising between the pastoralists and the white community, as portrayed by the media,[37] the racial element does remain a very real part. The white community were painfully aware of this. As a resident at Suyian Ranch stated to *The New York Times*:

> For the first time ever, you get that vibe that you're a *mzungu*[38] – what are you doing here? [...] It's a bit grandiose to think we can continue to live like this when thousands of people out there don't have any land. [...] It is Zimbabwe-esque. [...] We're white people in a black country. If we're not welcome, what's the point?[39]

On the other side of the conflict, the constitution of pastoralists was no less complex. According to William, one Samburu research participant, there were two main groups contributing to the fights among the pastoralists. The incomers from Samburu, Isiolo and Baringo were the main forces behind the attacks. Yet, while the settled Samburu and Pokot in Laikipia were also responsible for some of the violence, they may not have been as active in the invasions. Being settled in the area, they were aware that they had to endure the consequences of ranchers' terminated grazing agreements once the emergency had passed.[40]

The concept of grazing agreements has long been an essential living condition for the Samburu in Laikipia, who have extensively settled and lived on

36 Elliot Fratkin, 'The Samburu Laibon's Sorcery and the Death of Theodore Powys in Colonial Kenya,' *Journal of Eastern African Studies* 9, no. 1 (2 January 2015), pp. 35–54.

37 Field notes, email correspondence with research participant, Laikipia, 30 January 2017.

38 Kiswahili for 'a white person.'

39 Jeffrey Gettleman, 'Loss of Fertile Land Fuels "Looming Crisis" Across Africa,' *The New York Times*, 29 July 2017, https://www.nytimes.com/2017/07/29/world/africa/africa-climate-change-kenya-land-disputes.html, accessed 29 September 2017.

40 Field notes, email correspondence with research participant, Laikipia, 30 January 2017.

other people's land, making them dependent on resources that belong to others. William, explained that the frustrations increased when Vice President William Ruto took over the government farm ADC Mutara and terminated the existing grazing agreements, which were held almost exclusively by Samburu herders.[41]

The 2016–2017 events were also significant in terms of the political strategy of arming certain communities in exchange for votes, while simultaneously weakening others. Interestingly, the bullets used by the invading pastoralists bore the stamp 'KOFC,' denoting that they were produced at the Kenya Ordinance Factories Corporation – the same factory that produces ammunition for the Kenyan police force.[42] Moreover, during the siege of Kifuku Ranch, a ranch resident explained how a mysterious truck came by at regular intervals to provide tea and refreshments for the invading herders. Later on, ownership of this truck was traced to a paramilitary police officer.[43] These elements contribute to the speculation that this wave of invasions and claims to the land and its resources may have signified that the political situation was now ripe for a further step towards the exclusion of remaining white landowners in the highlands.

Indeed, the political reaction, or rather the lack thereof, was astonishing. Several orders to disarm the area and neighbouring counties proved inefficient. The police were understaffed and disorganised, and did not show adequate willingness to deal with the situation.[44] Furthermore, the willingness to act was compromised by the fact that political figures owned much of the cattle that already grazed illegally in Laikipia.[45] As Laikipia-based scholar John explained:

> I was in a security meeting in Loisaba [Ranch] and they could pinpoint that these animals belong to Leshol, these to Letimalo, these belong to the governor Lenolkulal and they are being herded by paid herders. So, in most cases, even during drought, people do illegal grazing but they do it with fear and in a dynamic way that you even invade the security of the farm. Those guys are grazing in broad daylight and they don't care![46]

41 Interview with research participant, Nyahururu, 21 March 2016.

42 *The Star*, 'Laikipia Invasions Are Political, Governor Hopeful Says after Kifuku Ranch Raid.'

43 Gettleman, 'Loss of Fertile Land Fuels "Looming Crisis" Across Africa.'

44 *The Star*, 'Land Invasion Wrecks Laikipia.'

45 *The Star*, 'Laikipia Clashes Persist as MPs, Cops, Barons Blamed.'

46 Interview with research participant, Nanyuki, 16 August 2016.

In the absence of a strong political voice, local leaders in Laikipia County called for more resources to support the security situation, evict the thousands of herders and drive them back to Samburu, Isiolo and Baringo.[47] In this regard, *The Star* stated:

> The extraordinary passivity of the government in the face of the Laikipia invasion is partly due to the reluctance of the police to confront the armed pastoralists. In July last year, Deputy President William Ruto promised to restore law and order in Laikipia through disarmament of the pastoralists. [...] The Interior CS [cabinet secretary] Joseph Nkaissery was directed to immediately remove all illegal herders in private land and ranches [...]. Yet virtually nothing has happened, giving the impression to residents that there is a breakdown of government and a power vacuum.[48]

What both William and the broader media agreed upon was that the wave of attacks would not have become so intense without incitement by MPs representing Samburu County.[49] These incitements were driven by the prospects of personal gain, in particular in the 2017 election, and were undertaken in part by building on the already existing narrative that the Samburu had a right to 'claim back the land' in Laikipia. Some held that MP Lempurkel's mission was to displace people in Laikipia who were not from his ethnic group so that he could bring Samburu people into his voting area and be re-elected.[50]

The 2016–2017 state of emergency in Laikipia is significant because of the wider complex context of which it is a product. Laikipia is a contested environment, prone to tension and conflict – characteristics that have not lessened over time – and therefore the 2016–17 events cannot be analysed in isolation. That said, there is no single historical occurrence to which the tensions can be traced. Rather, it is important to underline that neither can tension and violence in Laikipia be determined to have arisen solely in relation to post-Independence settlements, and nor was it always initiated based on anti-colonial sentiments, even though these elements weigh strongly among the different groups' historical experiences. What is critical is that the field of power and the environmental conditions in Laikipia have always been shifting and hard to navigate for anyone who was ever dependent on a presence there.

47 Kenya NTV, 'What is Ailing Laikipia: Death and Destruction Visits Ranches in Laikipia,' 12 February 2017, https://www.youtube.com/watch?v=2JrOuhmEoMk, accessed 29 September 2017; interview with research participant, Nyahururu, 21 March 2016.

48 *The Star*, 'Land Invasion Wrecks Laikipia.'

49 *The Star*, 'MP Lempurkel Denies Involvement in Suyian Ranch Invasion on Sunday.'

50 Gettleman, 'Loss of Fertile Land Fuels "Looming Crisis" Across Africa.'

That historical grievances continue to be unresolved has only contributed to the propensity for tension and conflict. This is exactly what the 2016–2017 state of emergency indicated.

1.2 Organisation of Chapters

The complexity of this conflict eruption calls for an interrogation of how the social dynamics have evolved historically in and around Laikipia. Much scholarly work has dealt with this social-ecological context over the past decades. However, while they posed a valuable resource for this study, it is common to many of these works that they do not go much into detail on the historical experiences of the mixed groups of smallholders, pastoralists and other smaller groups who use the same resources outside of the larger ranches and conservancies; nor do they provide adequate detail on what, politically, has motivated people to settle in Laikipia and stay there. While some studies have examined the instances of ethnic and political conflict, few have focused directly on the context in Laikipia. And few analyses have managed to link the fragmentation of land-use systems and land-tenure systems and the lack of government support with the wider historical context.

However, the variety of scholarly works has made it possible to draw on the detailed findings of each of them. Building on the richness of studies done over the years, I identified four overarching and interrelating types of changes that have had great significance for how the Laikipia landscape has transformed: the shift in the types of claims to land and their manifestation; the increasing tendency to enclose resources; land redistribution and the creation of land-buying companies; and changing land-use fragmentation. I deal with each of these types of changes in separate chapters.

Chapter 2 presents some of the reflections behind the academic inquiry, along with introducing the setting and the case study areas – each with their specific conflict descriptions. The thematic components are also presented here, as the study's silver lining. These include ethnicity as a tool to mobilise political movements; autochthony as a legitimising factor for a claim to resources; land as both a material and a symbolic space in which control of the environment can be used to control people; and the connection between processes of fragmentation and the position of Laikipia in a frontier zone.

The study area is situated historically in Chapter 3. Here, the wider social and political dynamics are unfolded in an examination of the historical context, traversing the pre-colonial presence in the landscape, through colonial times, with the significance of regulation according to land use and ethnicity, to the Independence years and redistributions of land, and the recent decades of escalating grievances and acted-out claims to resources. In this way, the chapter situates the focus areas within the wider historical context of which the present situation is a product.

Chapter 4 investigates the various attempts to control land and resources as they have been practised in Laikipia since colonial times. Social and ethnic categories denoting affiliation and rights to resources have been constructed, reproduced, politicised and played out in relation to one another. By focusing on the different types of claims to resources that have been constructed, and by whom, this chapter establishes a set of group categorisations that can be used to navigate the social diversity in the area and to understand what motivates the different types of claims.

Chapter 5 goes more into detail about what happens when a landscape is marked by contesting claims to its resources. Therefore, this chapter focuses on the tendency to create enclosures – physical as well as symbolic. The Laikipia landscape consists of a fragmented whole of such islands. The chapter interrogates how enclosing a place by fencing or naming can support a claim to access and reserve use of a resource for a certain individual or group, while excluding others.

Chapter 6 investigates the link between land and politics by taking as its point of departure the land-buying companies that emerged in the post-Independence years, where land redistribution became a driver for the mobilisation of landless people as well as for the new Kenyan political elite. By establishing a link between the motivations for constructing these collateral companies and the political climate and the sentiment among the 'land-hungry' population at the time, a line of correlation is drawn with the different types of conflicts prevalent today.

Land use and different opinions on what a quality landscape consists of are at the heart of the discussion in Chapter 7. As the political landscape changed, people adapted by expanding or minimising different land-management practices. For instance, the fact that pastoral groups have settled in Laikipia has brought a range of implications for other actors, where ideas of what legitimises one's rights to use land resources oppose the pastoralists' moral norms. These changing perceptions of the landscape are set against a diachronic land-use analysis visualising the physical landscape change in the three case study areas.

Finally, in the concluding Chapter 8, I sum up the overall development of Laikipia as a post-colonial landscape and trace a line up to the 2016–2017 state of emergency. Here, the way the emergency transpired, with violence and an absence of authorities, is considered in the light of the social, economic and political dynamics that have transformed Laikipia over the past 150 years.

CHAPTER 2

Setting and Thematic Components

> In diversity there is beauty and there is strength.
>
> MAYA ANGELOU[1]

Laikipia is defined by division and diversity, where one moves along extreme scales of social dynamics and ethnic ideologies, as well as landscape features and land use. For this reason, the definition of the place under study is based on the politically defined area of the colonial district and present-day county of Laikipia; but the area as defined in ways other than by its political boundaries also constitutes an ecological space in its own right. As a highland area it is positioned directly east of the Rift Valley lowlands, south of the Samburu plains, and north-west of more fertile and productive farmland. Depending on the analytical context, I will therefore refer interchangeably to Laikipia District, Laikipia County, the Laikipia plateau and simply Laikipia.

Experiencing this landscape led me on a journey across time and space, combining and making sense of various types of data that were as fragmented as the landscape and its diverse features: from exploring the history of the place through old rat-eaten documents in dusty, cramped archives, to the bodily experience of traversing between Nairobi's busy atmosphere of street hawkers, white-collar workers and Java House coffee shops mushrooming on every corner; and the wide-open dusty spaces of northern Laikipia with only the sound of a motorbike emerging in the distance to interrupt the sound of the wind in the trees and the goats' bleating.[2]

This chapter introduces the setting of the study, the case studies at the heart of it, the considerations and impressions that met me there, and the theoretically anchored themes used to provide a sense of the dynamics observed.

1 Maya Angelou, *Rainbow in the Cloud: The Wit and Wisdom of Maya Angelou* (London: Hachette UK, 2014), p. 9.

2 Field notes, Nyahururu, 21 February 2015.

 | DOI:10.1163/9789004435209_003

2.1 Setting the Scene

Laikipia's diversity and fragmentation became clear to me on my first visit to the region, from the agricultural hub of Nyahururu in the south to the dusty town of Rumuruti – the last stop before the end of the tarmac road for people going to Maralal. Further to the north the landscape became even bushier and dustier, to the point where the Kikuyu farmers had given up on the possibility of making a profit from agriculture.

On the other hand, upon arriving in Nyahururu for the first time in March 2014, what first struck me was how much of a farming town it seemed to be. Dirt covered the concrete streets, and were it not for the distinct features of the potholes it would have been impossible to tell the difference between concrete and dirt roads. Countless tractors and trucks ready to be loaded barred the streets and slowed the traffic through town to the point where you might as well take the dirt road west of town when passing through during rush hour. Barrels of potatoes, cabbage, carrots and tomatoes narrowed the main streets into a one-car-at-a-time passage, and rubber boots seemed to be one of the favourite types of footwear. In sharp contrast to Nairobi, one hardly ever saw any of the glittering and shining outfits worn by the trendy young people there, except on Sundays, when the stiff and colourful dresses and the freshly polished men's shoes would sweep attention away from the muddy streets and the sharp tones of voices singing 'Amazing Grace.' The sound landscape was transformed into a camouflaged version of its usual muddy self as electronic keyboards and loudspeakers pushed to their limit went on non-stop from 5 am until late into the afternoon. Accepted by everyone present, to me the routines of the town were strikingly homogeneous. At times, it seemed the only noticeable distinction between people there was which of the churches one belonged to and which sermon one attended.[3] Notwithstanding that the town's name was said to be a Maa onomatopoeia denoting the sound of the Thomson's Falls, this was clearly a Kikuyu town. I had the impression that any non-Kikuyu person entering would immediately be singled out as someone who did not belong.[4]

Travelling further north to Rumuruti, the landscape changed. Here it did not rain as much, and what was mud in Nyahururu was dust in Rumuruti – and what an unstoppable dust it was. It would creep in everywhere through every little detectable crack. Here the colourful and proud Samburu *morans* would stand next to Somali cattle herders when the Kikuyu traders, with sunglasses and shoes shining through the dust, visited the town on the market days. Every

3 Field notes, Nyahururu, 15 February 2015.

4 Field notes, conversation with research participant, Nyahururu, 2 March 2015.

Thursday, they would come to fill a lorry with cattle bought from the pastoralists and transport it to Central Province for meat production.[5] As varied as the social scene was, so too, it seemed, were opinions about what the name of the town denoted. Some declared it to be the Africanised version of the colonial term 'remote route,' while others thought it was Maa for 'mosquito.'[6] Their town a place of diversity and mobility, Laikipians identified with places they had come from – Central Province south of the plateau, the lowland in Baringo to the west or the vast acacia grasslands of Samburu towards the north. In this regard, the naming of places is significant both as a denominator of the people present and as an active practice of territorialisation.[7] For instance, the names of the settlements Gatundia, Thome and Sipili are references to Kikuyu residence, with equivalent versions of the settlements in Central Province, whereas places such as Ewaso Narok, Suguroi and Ol Aro Nyiro have names denoting a Maa-speaking presence.[8]

Visiting the ranches in the interior of the plateau was again a completely singular experience, where I felt I once again entered another 'island.' For instance, visiting Kifuku Ranch gave me the feeling of stepping out of the chaos and into complete order, in the colonial romantic sense of the term.[9] I often went to visit the owner as a Sunday activity, partly because I found his stories from the family history of settlement in Laikipia over a hundred years and his extreme anti-conservation opinions much more fascinating than being forcefully tranquillised by the loudspeakers blaring out church music; and partly because the 40-minute drive was enough to change the weather from the cloudy cold of Nyahururu, which makes you wonder what you are doing wearing socks and sweaters in Africa. At Kifuku Ranch the wind was warm and fresh – surely suiting a Sunday mood better.[10]

2.2 Notes on the Sensitivity to Voices in a Fragmented Setting

Upon taking up the challenge to study issues around land resources and territories in such a diverse place as Laikipia, I anticipated simultaneously having to grasp the sense of time through considerations of history; space through

5 Field notes, Nyahururu, 15 March 2014.

6 Interview with research participant, Nyahuruhu, 31 March 2016; interview with research participant, south-western Laikipia, 6 March 2015.

7 Gabrielle Lynch, 'What's in a Name? The Politics of Naming Ethnic Groups in Kenya's Cherangany Hills,' *Journal of East African Studies* 10, no. 1 (2 January 2016), pp. 208–27.

8 Field notes, Nyahururu, 15 March 2015.

9 Field notes, south-western Laikipia, 10 March 2015.

10 Field notes, south-western Laikipia, 3 May 2015.

considerations of geography; and social and political perspectives through anthropological approaches to going about the inquiry. All of these disciplines engage with the concept of land as something one can control, fight over, live off and feel connected to. I then dived into considering the emotions behind the wish to control or belong, because this is where the connection to power emerges – the power of owning or controlling property as well as the power in identity, the power that forms identity and resistance to power.[11] In that sense, owning or controlling land or property can function as a reference point for identity.[12] The question 'Where are you from?' refers to a person's connectivity to a place. The question 'How old are you?' refers to a person's place in time. Both questions can anchor identity. However, the answers to both questions are simultaneously full of possibilities for manipulation. One can reply 'I was born in that place but grew up in this place,' or 'I was born in that place, but that was a place of exile and my father was from this place.' The question 'Where do you belong?' is even more open to interpretations with regard to connectivity. It can be used to imply belonging to a place on a wider scale – for instance, by replying 'This place was taken from us although it still bears our name,' or 'My father legally bought this place and I inherited it from him.'

The term *to belong* is central to this study because it denotes the abovementioned complexity in linking place with a person and a person's history. Exploring this term can potentially assist in understanding the general tension linked with questions of land and land control in Kenya and illustrate the importance of controlling land. It was therefore central to this study to explore understandings of land through different pathways. As Shipton notes: 'Truly, this topic is no discipline's territory, and the fences that divide it cannot endure long without gateways through.'[13]

Notwithstanding that I approached the dynamics from different perspectives, I could not escape certain epistemological challenges that come with the gathering of knowledge. All knowledge, including scholarly research, is considered political, situated and partial – at least according to social constructivism.[14] Triangulating knowledge from qualitative data together with archival

11 Michel Foucault, *The History of Sexuality, Vol. 1, An Introduction* (New York: Pantheon, 1978).

12 Gabrielle Lynch, 'Negotiating Ethnicity: Identity Politics in Contemporary Kenya,' *Review of African Political Economy* 33, no. 107 (1 March 2006), pp. 49–65; Parker Shipton, *Mortgaging the Ancestors: Ideologies of Attachment in Africa* (New Haven, CT: Yale University Press, 2009).

13 Shipton, *Mortgaging the Ancestors*, p. 5.

14 Andrea Nightingale, 'A Feminist in the Forest: Situated Knowledges and Mixed Methods in Natural Resource Management,' *ACME* 1, no. 2 (2003), pp. 77–90; Donna Haraway,

data and remote-sensing data does not remove that partiality. It merely minimises it or questions it.[15] However, triangulation 'allows for the notion that such knowledges are partial and that different vantage points [...] will produce different views of particular processes and events,'[16] as Nightingale states. As such, putting together these different views would, like pieces in a puzzle, provide a fuller picture of the reality under study, although it would not make it more objective in the positivist sense of the term.[17]

Moreover, certain aspects of the landscape dynamics in Laikipia are invariably real rather than constructed. For instance, a fence remains a fence to, from or between something regardless of the social constructions evolving around it. Similarly, a social constructivist understanding of the world is not useful for investigating power relations. When these are excluded from the equation, one can merely confirm the situation's complexity rather than improve one's understanding of it. Given the complexity of the social dynamics, I needed to examine how the different voices in Laikipia related to one another through the opinionated and political positioning that each individual would represent.[18] My search for different voices, carrying different perceptions and different agendas, therefore illustrates a postmodern perspective that offers voice and value to multiple truths.[19] As such, it was never my intention with this study to make any judgement about whom I considered right or wrong in the multidimensional conflicts – I rather intended to represent what had shaped the various voices and how the context had grown into a place of multidimensional conflicts.

As I set out to find voices of people with various ethnic affiliations, wealth standards, degrees of influence and livelihood practices, what I sought was life stories. Life stories that could illustrate how the landscape was lived in and perceived in different ways, but also how the act of telling these stories might carry a political agenda intended to support the narrators' presence there. As Louise Fortmannn states, telling stories is a way to act, and not merely a way to describe or account:

'Situated Knowledges: The Science Question in Feminism and the Privilege of Partial Perspective,' *Feminist Studies* 14, no. 3 (1988), pp. 575–99.

15 Haraway, 'Situated Knowledges,' pp. 575–99.

16 Nightingale, 'A Feminist in the Forest,' p. 80.

17 H. Russell Bernard, *Research Methods in Anthropology: Qualitative and Quantitative Approaches* (Lanham, MD: Rowman Altamira, 2011).

18 John W. Creswell, *Research Design: Qualitative, Quantitative, and Mixed Methods Approaches* (Thousand Oaks, CA: SAGE, 2014).

19 H. Russell Bernard and Clarence Gravlee, *Handbook of Methods in Cultural Anthropology* (Lanham, MD: Rowman & Littlefield, 2014).

> Stories have the power to frame and create understanding, [...] to create and maintain moral communities; to validate current actions; and to empower, encourage and relieve their tellers. The understanding of past and current events shaped by stories forms a discursive strategy through which struggles are waged.[20]

My travels through people's personal histories captured perceptions of long-term landscape change, different individuals' connectedness to the place, and relational positions shaping the landscape. The people I interviewed represented different positions in relation to the case study areas. Similar interviews were conducted with external experts such as local politicians or authorities, as well as people representing the other types of landholdings in Laikipia, including ranch owners, people from families with a long-term presence there and representatives of other ethnic groups in the area. Along with the informants' histories, I gathered information about livelihood strategies and motivations for migrating to this place and for continuing to stay.

Yet the study included not only a variety of voices but also different temporalities of voices. I included archival material and aerial photographs to produce more insights and greater transparency than would be possible through a short-term study exclusively collecting ethnographic material. When using data from archives and newspapers, the general social constructivist position is that no document is written from a neutral position to a neutral recipient.[21] I therefore considered each type of data fragment as a separate voice, be it a newspaper article covering the distribution of title deeds, a colonial file on grazing control, an aerial photograph of newly ploughed fields from 1967 or a biographical interview with an old labourer on a colonial cattle ranch. Such voices represent personal records and discursive tales and thus become both *definers* and *defined* for the data collection – *defined* by the context in which the voice is represented, and *definer* of the particular representation of information offered.[22]

However, inasmuch as I made an effort to get to know the area or topic of research, I would only ever be able to *understand* based on what is reported to

20 Louise Fortmann, 'Talking Claims: Discursive Strategies in Contesting Property,' *World Development* 23, no. 6 (June 1995), pp. 1053–63.

21 S.B. Wenneberg, *Socialkonstruktivisme – Positioner, Problemer og Perspektiver*, first edition (Copenhagen: Samfundslitteratur, 2000); L. Phillips and M.W. Jørgensen, *Discourse Analysis as Theory and Method* (London: SAGE, 2002).

22 Steinar Kvale and Svend Brinkmann, *Interview – Introduktion til et Håndværk*, second edition (Copenhagen: Hans Reitzels Forlag, 2009); Kirsten Hastrup, *A Passage to Anthropology – Between Experience and Theory* (London: Routledge, 1995), p. 149.

me by voices. In that sense, I would never be able to fully understand what it means to have one's life defined by 30 years of court cases to settle whether you have the right to the land you live on. Neither would I be able to completely comprehend the significance of having a year's stable income disappear if my cattle were stolen. There are limits to empathy, as Hastrup would say.[23] However, what I could do was to approximate these experiences by conveying as many parts of the context as possible.

The data for this study were collected during a long-term stay in western Laikipia between October 2014 and August 2015, along with trips to the area in 2014 and 2016. Interviewees' names have been anonymised or omitted throughout the book, except in some cases where they represent an institution or organisation. I have also generalised the location of the interview where more specific information would allow individuals to be identified. The historical and anthropological data are supplemented by remote-sensing data in order to triangulate the oral histories of long-term landscape and land-use change with visual verification. I collected the archival material and aerial photographic material from the National Archive in Kew and the Rhodes House and Weston Library in Oxford between May and August 2014 and in November 2015.

2.3 Case Selection and Ecological Overview

The ecological dynamics of the Laikipia plateau have been a determining factor for many shifting power dynamics over the past 150 years. It was never a well-watered place in the sense that rain patterns are unpredictable and there are few stable water sources, making for challenging conditions for all who have historically attempted to make use of the land, whether for grazing, large-scale agricultural production or subsistence farming.[24]

Specifically, a report on rainfall and agro-climatology from 1989 concluded that the plateau had not seen any significant change in rainfall in the years between 1946 and 1980 as a whole. Nevertheless, there was evidence of systematic fluctuations. Depending on the particular place on the Laikipia plateau, some areas would have three-year cycles while others would have 16-year cycles, without the specific locations necessarily being far apart.[25] More recent studies have confirmed these systematic fluctuations while underlining the

23 Hastrup, *A Passage to Anthropology*.
24 R. van Zwanenberg, *The Agricultural History of Kenya to 1939* (Nairobi: East African Pub. House, 1972).
25 Berger, *Rainfall and Agroclimatology of the Laikipia Plateau, Kenya*.

general difficulty in predicting the cycles. Between 1961 and 1982, there were four seasons with complete rain failure, whereas for the period 1986–2000 that number went up to six.[26] This evidence illustrates the complexity of the ecological dynamics on the Laikipia plateau, and goes to show that one cannot simply speak of one climatic condition or one cycle of rainfall. So, while an evaluation of the plateau's farming potential would show extensive abundance if done in a good year, conclusions would be adversely grim if based on a bad year. The high uncertainty around water access determined pastoralists' navigation of the area according to water points, as well as being reflected in the underlying attitudes of colonial settler politics. Both are issues that will be considered in the coming chapters.

In addition to the unreliable water conditions, the area can be divided into a generally wetter and more fertile south-west and a semi-arid centre that gradually turns more arid towards the north. These ecological conditions have remained largely the same over a long period, constraining pre-colonial pastoralists, colonial ranchers and post-colonial settlers alike. This is also the reason why the argument that one land-use type is better suited to these temporal and spatial variations can be deemed invalid.

The distinct ecological conditions are represented in my selection of three case study areas from three distinct ecological conditions on the Laikipia plateau. In conjunction with the inclusion of different parts of the challenging environment, I was interested in examining the range of historical experiences found there. Such a regional approach to studying the landscape could illustrate the diversity in how claims to land and perceptions of conflict were embodied. In conjunction with the distinct ecological conditions in the three areas, this diversity represents the wider fragmentation and complexities in the Laikipia landscape.

The first case study area, Lorien, is a green and hilly 9,700-acre former ranch situated in the south of the county.[27] With poor infrastructure combined with trees, bushes and rocky hills, it is challenging to move around unless on foot or by motorbike. For farmers, the distance to the Ewaso Narok river and the stony soil make farming difficult even though the soil is relatively rich. Lorien is sparsely populated, with a striking homogeneity of the Kalenjin presence

---

26 F. Gichuki et al., 'Scarce Water: Exploring Resource Availability, Use and Improved Management,' *Eastern and Southern Africa Geographical Journal* 8 (special issue) (1998), pp. 15–28; CETRAD (Centre for Training and Integrated Research in Arid and Semi-Arid Land Development, Nanyuki, Kenya) and CDE (Centre for Development and Environment, University of Bern, Switzerland), Socio-Ecological Database (2007).

27 Evidence from the High Court of Kenya, Civil Suit (HCCC), Nyeri, No. 248 of 1998: Title deed of David Partridge, The Agricultural Finance Corporation, 1 July 1963.

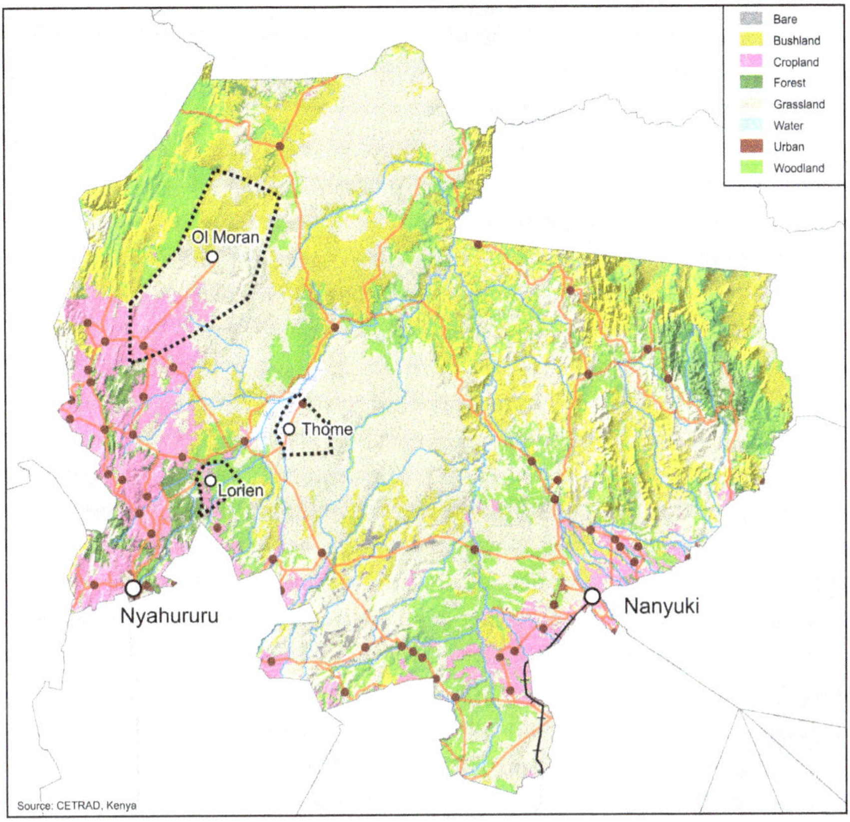

FIGURE 1 Land cover in Laikipia in 2015
© CETRAD 2015

bearing witness to a history of exclusion resulting from fights for the resources.[28] After clashes in 1993 among the post-colonial shareholders, the Kikuyu group that was settled there was evicted, and today the vast majority of the farm's population are Kalenjin, along with very few Turkana.[29] Although the situation has not been violent since 1993, the conflict has continued in a never-ending string of court cases. To the west, Lorien borders Rumuruti Forest, a government forest area, from which elephants are common visitors. To the south and south-east, Lorien borders Salama, another former settler farm, which is now populated almost exclusively by Kikuyu. Towards the north, Lorien borders the ranch of the late senator for Laikipia County, G.G. Kariuki.

28 Field notes, Lorien, 30 January 2015.
29 Interview with research participant, Lorien, 30 January 2015.

To the north-east lies Kifuku Ranch, run by the Aggett family through three generations since early colonial times. And towards the north-west on the Rumuruti–Nyahururu road lies the town Gatundia, where many of the Kikuyu who fled Lorien after clashes in 1993 now reside.[30]

In contrast to Lorien's green lands, the second case study area, Thome, is categorised as semi-arid. A 17,000-acre former ranch, it has been converted into shares of smallholder land plots by a land-buying company. It holds the presence of Kikuyu, Nandi, Samburu and Turkana alike.[31] The dry, bare land of Thome has enclosures only around the scattered homesteads. Upon my first visit, these areas appeared not to be claimed by anyone other than the herding boys with their goats gnawing on the dry acacia bushes.[32] I later discovered that many smallholders chose not to settle upon acquiring a share in the land-buying company, because of the dry conditions. This has created vast areas of seemingly vacant lands that have attracted pastoralists to occupy areas illegally. To the west and north-west, Thome meets the Rumuruti swamp. It was once a rich water resource, but has now been reduced to a small stream due to clearing of the bush and trees that shielded the sandy soil from the sun, combined with heavy irrigation to feed the agricultural production of chilli, tobacco and tomato.[33] To the north-east and east, Thome borders the almost 38,000-acre Ngorare Ranch. Ngorare is managed as a cattle ranch by a family of white Kenyans who are tolerant of wild animals. Grazing by the neighbouring pastoralists is organised under strict terms – although the pastoralists often compromise those terms.[34] Towards the south and south-west, Thome borders another private ranch, referred to as 'Jennings.' This ranch lacks good management and enforcement of its grazing licences and therefore rather functions as an open-access resource for whoever wishes to graze there.[35]

Ol Moran town, in the third case study area, is situated on the border between the land of two extensive land-buying companies that together comprises a 100,000-acre former ranch. This area encompasses a great variety in settlement density, homogeneity and agricultural potential. The northern part of the area around Ol Moran town fits the nature of this study's focus on mixed areas of lower agricultural potential which have experienced land-related conflicts. When the companies were formed, the shareholders who managed to get their share in the southern part were able to invest in farming even if they

30 Interview with research participant, Nyahururu, 30 May 2015.

31 Field notes, Thome, 16 May 2015.

32 Field notes, Thome, 21 February 2015.

33 Boniface Kiteme and Thuita Thenya, 'Assessment of Ecological Status and Socio-Economic Dynamics of Upper Ewaso Ng'iro Basin Wetlands' (Working paper CETRAD, 2011).

34 Interview with research participant, central Laikipia, 8 June 2015.

35 Interview with research participant, Marura, 6 May 2015.

were smallholders, because the land here was fertile. Contrastingly, the land around Ol Moran town towards the north is dry, with scattered bushes and poor infrastructure. Much of the land in Ol Moran is absentee landholdings – owned by people who are not there. The farmers who are present are those who have few alternatives to farm elsewhere. Similarly to Thome, it is due to their seeming vacancy that these lands have come to be settled by pastoralists. Towards the north-west of Ol Moran lies an area commonly known as Survey. Following the Pokot–Samburu war in the early 2000s the Samburu moved most of their settlements from Ol Moran to this place, whereas the Pokot stayed in Ol Moran.[36] Towards the west lies the wider Rumuruti area, with various smallholdings and pastoralist settlements. Ol Moran is situated between two large-scale landholdings. To the north is Mugie Conservancy, which is run as a conservation site and a cattle ranch. It maintains organised leases of grazing, although the Samburu and Pokot herders often violate these agreements.[37] Towards the west, Ol Moran borders the 98,000-acre Laikipia Nature Conservancy, which is run exclusively as a conservation area with no organised leases of grazing to surrounding herders. However, the land plot is so vast that it is impossible to control illegal grazing. Hence, it is widely known among both Pokot and Samburu that forced grazing is possible here.[38]

The complexity in the types of conflict in these case study areas and the different ways they play out is an element distinguishing each case from the other. While the physical conflict in Lorien ended in the early 1990s when the Kalenjin population evicted the Kikuyu, the conflict has since then taken place in courthouses by way of court cases – filed, disputed and appealed by both sides. In Thome, the conflict is also not immediately visible, because it occurs between the land-buying company which owns the land and the settled shareholders who bought their shares in the 1970s but continue to struggle to get them converted into proper title deeds today. The lack of tenure security of the settled shareholders is complicated by absentee shareholder investments and pastoralist encroachment. In Ol Moran, the absence of many landlords complicates the livelihoods of the settled smallholders. Here, the seemingly vacant lands have attracted Pokot and Samburu alike, who have continuously competed for the grazing areas.

The physical appearance and qualities of the three areas also differ. While Lorien appears as a hilly, green, relatively fertile area with many trees, the land in Thome is more bare, with larger distance between the trees. The farming in Lorien is less demanding than in Thome. However, irrigation agriculture can

36 Field notes, conversation with research participant, Laikipia, 2 August 2015.

37 Interview with research participant, northern Laikipia, 14 April 2015.

38 Interview with research participant, north of Ol Moran town, 21 July 2015.

still be sustained on a small-scale basis in Thome, whereas it is even more rare to find this in Ol Moran. There, absentee landlords own almost all of the land, and one is only able to make a sustainable living from the land if one buys enough shares from neighbours to run a medium- or large-scale farm. Even then, it has a relatively high risk of failure if the weather is not right.[39]

On the other hand, the three case study areas also have many features in common. They share a history of transitioning from being utilised as pre-colonial pastoral grazing areas, to colonial Crown Land, to post-colonial subdivided lands. All three areas were acquired by land-buying companies after Independence, and they share a position within the wider Laikipia landscape, in that their subdivided farmlands border large-scale farms or ranches (Kifuku Ranch, Mugie Ranch and Ngorare Ranch) on one side and protected areas (Ewaso Narok swamp, Laikipia Nature Conservancy and Rumuruti Forest) on the other. This is illustrated in figures 11, 13 and 15.

As for the nature of conflicts, the three areas share two common denominators. Firstly, the nature of the conflicts relates to land or a lack of tenure security. Secondly, the different sides of the conflicts are marked by ethnic differences. Different ethnic groups assume the different positions in the conflicts, so that individuals tend to take a stand according to their ethnic affiliation.[40]

It should be mentioned that the contexts of the case studies have offered different possibilities for data collection. In Ol Moran, both land-buying companies have now been closed for years and proceedings taken over by government. There has therefore not been the same amount of documentation available for this case, and therefore I rely more on oral sources to reconstruct the dynamics and history here. As for Lorien, there are opposing accounts regarding what happened in the 1980s and early 1990s, and people on the ground in Lorien offered me a myriad of highly opinionated accounts, specifically when it came to the court cases. Therefore, the bulk of the data relating to the court cases are built more on legal documentation and archival material than on oral accounts – although oral accounts of the violent conflict remained vital for discursive analyses.

2.4 Thematic Components

It is the purpose of this study not to generate new theory but rather to shed light on political processes and social dichotomies using a variety of theoretical

39 Field notes, conversation with research participant, Nyahururu, 2 March 2015.

40 Field notes, conversation with research participant, Nyahururu, 2 March 2015.

perspectives. Because the setting studied is fragmented, the theoretical approach cannot draw on one single coherent theory. Rather, it makes use of a range of theoretically anchored themes. Many of these thematic components draw links to the broad framework of political ecology, whereby concepts of nature, culture and politics are considered and valued on equal terms. The term coined in the 1970s, political ecology combines social and physical considerations of environmental degradation.[41] More recently, political ecology research has focused on cultural mobilisation in relation to increased sensitivity to environmental politics, and 'the ways in which such cultural practices – whether science, or "traditional" knowledge, or discourses, or risk, or property rights – are contested, fought over and negotiated,' as Peet and Watts note.[42] In this study, political ecology has allowed for a plural approach to exploring the manifold realities intersecting the social, political and ecological spheres in Laikipia. This section presents these themes, connecting them to the Laikipia context as well as to the theoretical discussions of which they are part. As topical undercurrents for the study, these themes assist in making sense of the type of place that Laikipia is.

2.4.1 *Contested Lands*

Land has been a hot topic in Laikipia for generations. Going 150 years back, the area was used and controlled by different pastoral groups, mainly for grazing.[43] During the colonial era the land was made property of the British Crown and was exclusively controlled by the colonial power.[44] After Independence many Kenyans were interested in gaining access to the land in Laikipia that became available with the colonial exit. Many bought land in Laikipia, whether through the government settlement schemes, through individual transfers or as groups via private land-buying companies.[45] However, rather than resolve grievances over land, the initiatives to Africanise it fed the tension and deepened the power struggle between groups to control land. This continued throughout the

41 Richard Peet and Michael Watts (eds), *Liberation Ecologies*, second edition (Abingdon, Oxon: Routledge, 2004); Piers M. Blaikie and Harold Brookfield, *Land Degradation and Society*, new edition (London and New York: Routledge, 1991).

42 Peet and Watts, *Liberation Ecologies*, p. 6.

43 Paul Lane (ed.), *Landscape and Environmental Change in Semi-Arid Regions of East and Southern Africa: Developing Interdisciplinary Approaches* (Nairobi: British Institute of Eastern Africa, 2005).

44 M.P.K. Sorrenson, *Origins of European Settlement in Kenya* (New York: Oxford University Press, 1968); Christopher Leo, *Land and Class in Kenya* (Harare: Nehands, 1989).

45 Thomas Kohler, *Land Use in Transition : Aspects and Problems of Small-Scale Farming in a New Environment: The Example of Laikipia District, Kenya* (Berne: Institute of Geography, University of Berne, 1987).

Independence years and produced the highly complex fragmentation of the physical, social and political landscape that all Laikipians must navigate today.

Conceptually, the term *land* and the term *landscape* differ. *Land* can imply many things with fundamental importance for people's livelihoods and futures. Land is a space for national and ethnic belonging; it can be imaginative in terms of memory and dreaming, or it can be material in terms of borders, resources or environmental objects; it can be bought, sold, leased or occupied.[46] Land can be discursively produced with rhetoric and terminologies, and it can be financially productive in itself; it is a space for political rules and it is subject to strife; it can hold different systems of governance – whether local or national, statutory or customary – and the effects of the types of governance can be profound in the determination of who controls and who is excluded.[47]

Similarly, *landscapes* cannot be fully described by what one sees on a map. Rather, as Moore, Kosek and Pandian state: 'landscapes articulate both culture and nature, seer and scene. But equally at stake in landscapes are the embodied practices that transform the objects of a proprietary gaze.'[48] Following Bollig, landscapes can be considered as 'the building blocks' of 'imagined worlds,' where a multitude of experience-based imaginations of life worlds flow together.[49] The actors present and their contrasting opinions about what constitutes a productive landscape and who has the user rights to it therefore define understandings of a landscape as something always under construction in a never-ending process of reproduction. In this reproduction, struggles to control take place at a specific place with specific actors, while the motivations for these struggles can differ.[50]

---

46 Berry, 'Debating the Land Question in Africa,' *Comparative Studies in Society and History* 44, no. 4 (2002), pp. 638–68; Shipton, *Mortgaging the Ancestors*; Mary Louise Pratt, *Imperial Eyes: Travel Writing and Transculturation* (London and New York: Routledge, 1992); Tania Murray Li, *Land's End, Capitalist Relations on an Indigenous Frontier* (Durham, NC: Duke University Press, 2014).

47 Pratt, *Imperial Eyes*; Berry, 'Debating the Land Question in Africa'; Li, *Land's End*; Shipton, *Mortgaging the Ancestors*.

48 Donald S. Moore, Jake Kosek and Anand Pandian (eds), *Race, Nature, and the Politics of Difference* (Durham, NC: Duke University Press, 2003), p. 11.

49 Michael Bollig, 'Visions of Landscapes: An Introduction,' in *African Landscapes: Interdisciplinary Approaches*, ed. Michael Bollig and Olaf Bubenzer (New York: Springer Science & Business Media, 2009), p. 14.

50 Pauline Peters, 'Inequality and Social Conflict over Land in Africa,' *Journal of Agrarian Change* 4, no. 3 (2004), pp. 269–314; Berry, 'Debating the Land Question in Africa'; Kristine

Besides distinguishing between land and landscape, the concept of *territoriality* is relevant for the meaning of land in Laikipia. This can be defined as the process through which institutions, groups or individuals seek to control the access and use by certain others of a geographical space through the drawing of boundaries.[51] Thereby, boundaries as well as the resources that the boundaries are intended to protect become the spatial focus of legal enforcement. Territoriality is part and parcel of Laikipia's smallholder lands, ranching lands and conservancy lands. All holders enforce their boundaries with reference to their private-property rights, while defining rules of actions and use within their boundaries, whether that implies prioritising wildlife and biodiversity or farming activities.

One method for enforcing control of land is to gain tenure security. The concept of land tenure is derived from the Latin term *tenere*, meaning *to hold*.[52] Semantically, tenure refers to methods for acquisition, holding and transference of property rights. In Kenya there are three overall types of land-tenure system: customary land tenure, applying to most land in the northern regions, where it is more relevant to speak of rules for accessing rather than property rights; modern land tenure, referring to the private-property rights of land held by an individual or a company; and government land, including forests, protected areas and urban areas.[53] In Laikipia there is an additional tenure system – a hybrid of the customary and the private tenure systems, exemplified by the group ranches and the cooperative land categories.[54] This complexity underlines the importance of legal pluralism which people have to navigate in order to hold or access land resources.

This legal pluralism also means that the law on land matters does not necessarily reflect the reality of how that law operates on the ground.[55] For instance,

Juul, Christian Lund and Christopher Lund (eds), *Negotiating Property in Africa* (Portsmouth, NH: Heinemann, 2002).

51 Peter Vandergeest, 'Mapping Nature: Territorialization of Forest Rights in Thailand,' *Society and Natural Resources: An International Journal* 9, no. 2 (1996), pp. 159–75; Nancy Lee Peluso, 'Coercing Conservation: The Politics of State Resource Control,' *Global Environmental Change* 3 (1993), pp. 199–217.

52 Merriam-Webster, 'Definition of Tenure,' https://www.merriam-webster.com/dictionary/tenure, accessed 9 August 2017.

53 Martin Huber and Chrisostom J. Opondo, *Land Use Change Scenarios for Subdivided Ranches in Laikipia District, Kenya* (Berne: Institute of Geography, University of Berne, 1995).

54 Huber and Opondo, *Land Use Change Scenarios for Subdivided Ranches in Laikipia District, Kenya.*

55 Sally Falk Moore, 'Law and Social Change: The Semi-Autonomous Social Field as an Appropriate Subject of Study,' *Law & Society Review* 7, no. 4 (Summer 1973), pp. 719–46.

state institutions in Laikipia are often experienced as absent. Consequently, one must take the law into one's own hands, to make up for the state's lacking authority.[56] Regardless of whether initiatives are sanctioned according to state law, they do not function unless state institutions in rural areas enforce them. In situations where state institutions are not present, Lund's concept of twilight institutions become relevant to consider. According to Lund, the authority of public institutions can fluctuate and be in a constant process of (re)formation. In contexts not exclusively controlled by government institutions, it follows that institutions come to operate in a twilight zone between state and society, public and private. In this zone, institutional competition is intensified, and situations that could otherwise be apolitical become politicised.[57] In Laikipia, such descriptions of fluctuating institutional authority are highly applicable, as is discussed in Chapter 6.

Specific to this study is the understanding that land as property and land as territory are conflicting notions. For the European settlers, user rights went together with private-property rights. Contrary to this, for many pastoralists the ownership of land was less meaningful because the essential factor had to do with access.[58] Claims to land are therefore not exclusively made based on private-property rights. Ribot and Peluso speak of a control of resources through modes of property as well as access.[59] Access can be defined as 'the ability to benefit from things – including material objects, persons, institutions, and symbols.'[60] The property terminology is tied to an understanding of access as rights, but as this is misleading for approaches opposing private property, it is more useful to talk of ability to access. This enables a focus on interrelations between people and not merely between people and land.

For many Laikipians, their access to land cannot be categorised simply as one of legal or physical control either. To them, access to land exists in a

56 Sandra F. Joireman, *Where There Is No Government: Enforcing Property Rights in Common Law Africa* (Oxford: Oxford University Press, 2011).

57 Christian Lund, 'Twilight Institutions: Public Authority and Local Politics in Africa,' *Development and Change* 37, no. 4 (2006), pp. 685–705.

58 Berry, 'Debating the Land Question in Africa.'

59 Nancy Lee Peluso, 'Fruit Trees and Family Trees in an Anthropogenic Forest: Ethics of Access, Property Zones, and Environmental Change in Indonesia,' *Comparative Studies in Society and History* 38, no. 3 (July 1996), pp. 510–48; Jesse Ribot, 'Theorizing Access: Forest Profits along Senegal's Charcoal Commodity Chain,' *Development and Change* 29, no. 2 (1 April 1998), pp. 307–41.

60 Jesse Ribot and Nancy Lee Peluso, 'A Theory of Access,' *Rural Sociology* 68, no. 2 (2003), pp. 153–81.

somewhat grey zone, its maintenance dependent on other actors or factors.[61] This is where land relations in Laikipia relate to the 'bundle of rights' approach, because there can be multiple access relations for the same piece of land besides those legally authorised.[62] As such, squatters on absentee land, managers on ranches and children with informally transferred rights to their father's land exemplify how parts of the bundles of rights have been transferred.

Access also differs from property, as the latter denotes social agreement by focusing on the right to control. While this agreement often takes place within the support of statutory law with private-property rights, it does not have to, as such socially agreed-upon support can be derived from customary systems as well.[63] Similarly, what is a God-given right within one system of convention might not be considered so within another. This is the case when Samburu consider it immoral to deny a person access to pasture, whereas a landowner would consider it trespass if people were to graze on his land without permission.[64]

Much research has been done on the complexities of land and the meanings and values it holds. In this study, I have been inspired by works of Li,[65] where land is represented dualistically and as contradictory because it can be privately held while simultaneously creating vulnerability for the owner; Pratt[66] and Berry,[67] with their explorations of colonial authority, legal pluralism, political strife and different types of 'past' to explain the invention of Africa's land question; and Shipton,[68] with his representations of land as a symbolic and physical holder of identity through systems of property, mortgage and inheritance, and how legal changes by the state have had implications for rural people in Kenya.

2.4.2 *Ethnicity and Autochthony*

History has seen various examples of what can be produced by an overemphasis on a perception of ethnic identities. However, the intense focus on ethnic

---

61 Peluso, 'Fruit Trees and Family Trees in an Anthropogenic Forest'; Nancy Lee Peluso and Christian Lund, 'New Frontiers of Land Control: Introduction,' *The Journal of Peasant Studies* 38, no. 4 (1 October 2011), pp. 667–81; Ribot, 'Theorizing Access.'

62 E. Schlager and E. Ostrom, 'Property Rights Regimes and Natural Resources: A Conceptual Analysis,' *Land Economics* 68, no. 3 (1992), pp. 249–62.

63 Ribot and Peluso, 'A Theory of Access.'

64 Interview with research participant, Nyahuruhu, 31 March 2016; interview with research participant, south-western Laikipia, 6 March 2015.

65 Li, *Land's End.*

66 Pratt, *Imperial Eyes.*

67 Sara Berry, 'Debating the Land Question in Africa.'

68 Shipton, *Mortgaging the Ancestors.*

categorisation in Kenya was not a strong phenomenon before colonialism. This is something that becomes particularly apparent when exploring the history of social dynamics in Laikipia. As Lynch argues: 'while colonial experiences encouraged Africans to think and act ethnically, they did not leave a legacy of fixed and unchanging ethnic signifiers.'[69] Ethnic identities are often in a constant process of (re)construction and (re)negotiation. Bearing this in mind when exploring ethnic affiliations in Laikipia, it becomes apparent that efforts to claim membership for some and exclusion of 'others' underline the importance of fluidity.[70] Even when membership of a group has been accepted, it does not prevent it from being renegotiated, the person being rejected or excluded, at a later stage. The concept's fluidity makes it a possible tool for power holders to use to create (new) narratives to obtain more political support. This will be exemplified through the exploration of land-buying companies in Chapter 6.

With the sentiment of competition between the ethnic groups, the lands included by the government in settlement schemes in Laikipia were not enough to meet the demand. With the land reform failing to do what it was intended to, land acquisition became a domain in which those inventive enough could find loopholes in the systems. Although the Kikuyu are the majority in Laikipia, their dominant position is contested internally as well as externally. For instance, many other ethnic groups avoided supporting the Kikuyu in conflicts, so as not to strengthen their position further.[71]

Additionally, many Kikuyu smallholders acquired land in exchange for voting for the political Kikuyu elite, who offered little accountability once the vote had been acquired.[72] Therefore, the Kikuyu are not a united group. The majority of them in Laikipia belong to lower classes without networks linking them to those in powerful positions. Ethnic connectivity to people in power is therefore not necessarily an advantage. Instead, the fluidity of the ethnic affiliation can be used in different ways depending on the context. A Kikuyu man might

69 Lynch, 'What's in a Name?,' p. 211.

70 Patrick Chabal, *Africa: The Politics of Suffering and Smiling* (London: Zed Books, 2009); Peter Geschiere and Stephen Jackson, 'Autochthony and the Crisis of Citizenship: Democratization, and the Politics of Belonging,' *African Studies Review* 49, no. 2 (2006), pp. 1–7; Kevin C. Dunn, '"Sons of the Soil" and Contemporary State Making: Autochthony, Uncertainty and Political Violence in Africa,' *Third World Quarterly* 30, no. 1 (1 February 2009), pp. 113–27.

71 Marcel Rutten and Alamin Mazrui, *Out for the Count : The 1997 General Elections and Prospects for Democracy in Kenya* (Kampala: Fountain Pub. Ltd, 2001).

72 Leo, *Land and Class in Kenya*; M.P.K. Sorrenson, *Land Reform in the Kikuyu Country: A Study in Government Policy* (London: Oxford University Press, 1967).

choose to underline his clan affiliation as a Kiambu Kikuyu in certain situations, while pointing to a Kikuyu-Meru intermarriage in his family in another situation.

The fluidity of ethnic identities has gradually grown in importance over the past three decades, not only in Laikipia but in East Africa in general.[73] For minorities, one can strengthen the position of one's group by constructing a movement around a narrative of indigeneity. As such, *autochthony* denotes the practice of politicising an ethnic category – instrumentalising a claim to a resource while simultaneously contesting any claim made by others.[74] In Tanzania, the Maasai have been successful in constructing narratives of indigeneity. This has granted them exemption from legal measures and exclusive rights to certain resources.[75] In Western Kenya, Okiek, Sengwer, Pokot and Endorois ethnic communities and their community leaders have constructed narratives of autochthony, linking their indigeneity discourse to moral and legal claims to territory.[76] Similarly to those of the Maasai in Tanzania, many of these claims have been successful, although the inherent vagueness of who belongs to the group has often lead to violence.[77] With the assistance of widespread media coverage, the success of indigeneity movements has reached Laikipia as well. In the recent wave of uncertainty, Samburu and Pokot base their invasions of ranches and farms on moral claims of indigeneity.[78] This will be elaborated on in Chapters 4 and 5.

Another strategy to strengthen a position is to form alliances across ethnic divides. A precondition for processes of constructing ethnic alliances is a

73 Lynch, 'Negotiating Ethnicity'; Gabrielle Lynch, 'The Politics of Ethnicity,' in *Routledge Handbook of African Politics*, ed. David Anderson, Nicholas Cheeseman and Andrea Scheibler (Abingdon, Oxon: Routledge, 2013).

74 Peter Geschiere, *The Perils of Belonging: Autochthony, Citizenship, and Exclusion in Africa and Europe* (Chicago: The University of Chicago Press, 2009); J. Igoe, 'Becoming Indigenous Peoples: Difference Inequality and the Globalization of East African Identity Politics,' *African Affairs* 105 (2006), pp. 399–430.

75 Dorothy Hodgson, 'Precarious Alliances: The Cultural Politics and Structural Predicaments of the Indigenous Rights Movement in Tanzania,' *American Anthropologist* 104, no. 4 (2002), pp. 1086–97; Dorothy Hodgson, 'Becoming Indigenous in Africa,' *African Studies Review* 52, no. 3 (2009), pp. 1–32; Dorothy Hodgson, *Being Maasai, Becoming Indigenous: Postcolonial Politics in a Neoliberal World* (Bloomington: Indiana University Press, 2011).

76 Gabrielle Lynch, 'Kenya's New Indigenes: Negotiating Local Identities in a Global Context,' *Nations and Nationalism* 17, no. 1 (1 January 2011), pp. 148–67.

77 Gabrielle Lynch, 'The Wars of Who Belongs Where: The Unstable Politics of Autochthony on Kenya's Mt Elgon,' *Ethnopolitics* 10, no. 3–4 (1 November 2011), pp. 391–410.

78 Kenya NTV, 'What is Ailing Laikipia'; interview with research participant, Nyahuruhu, 31 March 2016.

rootedness in shared histories.[79] This has to a certain extent been the case for Maasai relations with Samburu, Dorobo and Yaaku, as they share certain cultural traits.[80] However, Lynch argues that for the Kalenjin construction, the main argument for the alliance is the potential to gain from the alliance and a fear of exclusion without it.[81] This speaks to ethnic affiliation as a strategy and applies to other ethnic constructions in Laikipia as well. The different understandings and usages of ethnic constructions in the history of Laikipia are confronted in Chapters 3, 4 and 5. Here I argue that the 2016–17 election and the 1990s post-election violence and group hostility can partly be explained by re-examining the history of movement, settlement and ethnicity-based competition in Laikipia, as well as how this history has become multifaceted by opposing experiences and beliefs surrounding it.

2.4.3 *Fragmentation and Frontiers*

The structures of legislation put in place to control ethnic opposition and land hunger are fragmented by bureaucratic procedures, with exceptions to rules, opposing laws and lengthy casework. Consequently, in practice, people depend on what happens 'in between' the procedures of the legislated systems.[82] That said, fragmentation is far more entangled in Laikipia's case than what immediately surfaces in the everyday context. While one can find a form of fragmentation in every imaginable setting, the term's relevance in this context is a direct product of the area's multifaceted history, in which the field of power has constantly shifted and complexified – circumstances that go back much further than colonial rule. It was the Laikipiak Maasai who held dominance on the plateau in the years immediately prior to colonisation, whereas the colonial administration and European settlement controlled the area in the run-up to Independence.[83] Since then, dominance has been more muddled, as none

79 Gabrielle Lynch, *I Say to You: Ethnic Politics and the Kalenjin in Kenya* (Chicago: The University of Chicago Press, 2011); Carola Lentz and Paul Nugent (eds), *Ethnicity in Ghana: The Limits of Invention* (New York: Palgrave Macmillan, 2000).

80 Neil Carrier, 'Reviving Yaaku: Identity and Indigeneity in Northern Kenya,' *African Studies* 70, no. 2 (1 August 2011), pp. 246–63; Corinne A. Kratz, '"We've Always Done It like This … except for a Few Details": "Tradition" and "Innovation" in Okiek Ceremonies,' *Comparative Studies in Society and History* 35, no. 1 (1 January 1993), pp. 30–65.

81 Lynch, *I Say to You.*

82 Shipton, *Mortgaging the Ancestors.*

83 Tabitha Kanogo, *Squatters and the Roots of Mau Mau, 1905–63* (London: James Currey, 1987); Sorrenson, *Origins of European Settlement in Kenya*; Paul Lane, 'An Outline of the Later Holocene Archaeology and Precolonial History of the Ewaso Basin, Kenya,' in *Conserving Wildlife in African Landscapes: Kenya's Ewaso Ecosystem*, ed. N. Georgiadis, J. Moss and D. Malleret-King (Washington, DC: Smithsonian Institution Scholarly Press, 2011).

of the governments, the Kikuyu majority or the pastoral groups have been able to take complete control. These types of dominance, or lack thereof, have created a fragmentation of land management, land use and the physical features of the landscape.[84]

According to Galvin, fragmentation of social-ecological systems can be defined as: 'the dissection of natural systems into spatially isolated parts [...] caused primarily by social-economic changes.'[85] Examples of such drivers are changes in tenure systems, in which land under communal ownership is transferred into private holdings; and changes in land use, in which grassland is parcelled into agricultural units with fences. As such, a piece of land on which livestock are grazing becomes pastoral territory, whereas land planted with crops in square fields becomes the territory of a farmer. These territorial practices fragmenting the landscape are visible on aerial photographs. They are examined in Chapter 7.

Fragmentation relates to Laikipia today, therefore, not merely by virtue of the presence of multiple people, but rather as a result of the fact that they perform different practices of dominance in different areas of the plateau and in different spheres, which increases contestation over the social and physical landscape.[86] The boundaries in the physical and social landscape, loosely defined by the borders of the former colonial land plots, now demarcate islands of enclosed territories. Where one plot is controlled and formed by pastoralists, the ranching of a third-generation European settler may control the neighbouring plot, whereas yet another plot might be distinguished by smallholder farming communities of mixed ethnicity.[87] The smallholders may have different reasons for subdividing their limited areas further, such as issues of debt or inheritance.[88]

Fragmentation relates to the concept of frontiers, as frontiers are often marked by an induced fragmentation of state control, exacerbating the effects of fragmented land-use systems and tenure relations.[89] Kopytoff defines the African context as one constituted by frontiers through omnipresent

84 Daniel Branch, *Kenya: Between Hope and Despair, 1963–2011* (New Haven, CT: Yale University Press, 2011); David Throup and Charles Hornsby, *Multi-Party Politics in Kenya: The Kenyatta and Moi States and the Triumph of the System in the 1992 Election* (London: James Currey Publishers, 1998).

85 Kathleen A. Galvin, 'Transitions: Pastoralists Living with Change,' *Annual Review of Anthropology* 38 (2009), pp. 185–98.

86 Kohler, *Land Use in Transition.*

87 Field notes, conversation with research participant, Nyahururu, 2 March 2015.

88 Shipton, *Mortgaging the Ancestors.*

89 Galvin, 'Transitions.'

hinterlands.[90] Frontiers are positioned far enough from urban centres and state governance to be considered fully included in societies and simultaneously within reach for colonisers and adventurers. Frontiers denote sovereign demarcated zones of the state, which are at the same time categorised as inferior, though strategic, territories.[91] According to Hughes, frontiers are constituted by the sense of their in-between positionality.[92] As such, during colonisation, Laikipia was the zone bordered by the unruly Northern Frontier District, which made it into a 'contact zone,' to use Pratt's terminology.[93] 'The frontier is the fence line where conquest has stopped,' as Hughes suggests, although 'the same frontier can both permit and circumscribe conquest.'[94] With a demarcation of the extent, value and ownership of the land, it could more easily be taxed and thus included as state space. The British colonisation of Laikipia was thereby an example of occupation of space through cadastral demarcations – demarcations that have persisted into Independence and present-day Kenya. Even today in Laikipia, where the colonial land demarcations still hold significance, one can speak of a second colonisation through cadastral dominance, so that, 'spirit-blessed soil now constitutes hectares, counted, measured, and contested,' as Hughes suggests.[95]

2.4.4 *Commons and Customary Resources*

The category of customary land tenure is only meaningful in relation to private-property rights. Neither category existed before the latter was invented.[96] Related to customary land tenure is the concept of *commons*. Commons can broadly be defined as shared resources that belong equally to their users.[97] Whereas Hardin considers commons as open-access resources, bound to overuse and depletion with population growth,[98] Ostrom illustrates how common

90 Igor Kopytoff, *The African Frontier: The Reproduction of Traditional African Societies* (Bloomington: Indiana University Press, 1989).

91 Kopytoff, *The African Frontier*.

92 David McDermott Hughes, *From Enslavement to Environmentalism: Politics On a Southern African Frontier* (Seattle: University of Washington Press, 2008).

93 Pratt, *Imperial Eyes*.

94 Hughes, *From Enslavement to Environmentalism*, p. 3.

95 Hughes, *From Enslavement to Environmentalism*.

96 Terence O. Ranger, 'The Invention of Tradition in Colonial Africa,' in *The Invention of Tradition*, ed. Eric Hobsbawm and Terence Ranger (Cambridge: Cambridge University Press, 1983), pp. 211–62; Hughes, *From Enslavement to Environmentalism*.

97 Elinor Ostrom, *Governing the Commons* (Cambridge: Cambridge University Press, 2015).

98 Garrett Hardin, 'The Tragedy of the Commons,' *Journal of Natural Resources Policy Research* 1, no. 3 (8 July 2009), pp. 243–53.

resources often entail complex systems regulating their use, making them into common-pool resources.[99]

Immediately prior to colonization, the Laikipiak Maasai maintained their control over the grazing area in Laikipia using force against other pastoral groups.[100] As such, the pre-colonial lands in Laikipia can be described as open-access resources or common grazing areas, depending on whether one subscribes to Hardin or Ostrom's definition. When the Laikipiak Maasai were defeated the area became open to access by others. Contrastingly, the Crown Land was determined as land with private-property rights held by the white owners; here, there were systems to control the land use in terms of colonial policies on water use, pest control, livestock vaccination, transportation of goods etc.[101] Furthermore, ethnicity and work status determined who was allowed into the area. In this sense, rules and regulations clearly determined who was included and how resources were to be used.[102]

What the term *commons* deals less well with is change. After Independence the homogeneity disappeared, and the system of common use lost legitimacy. With social heterogeneity and fragmentation of land use and control came a new system, namely that of access opportunism, transferring certain areas back to de facto open-access resources, or new commons, defined by their absence of clear systems for regulating resource use.[103] Here individuals and groups navigate the weak state institutions and biased political processes through opportunism or through informal twilight institutions.

2.4.5 *Plural Perspectives on Sustainable Land Management*

Less related to political ecology, although not less relevant as a recurrent theme for this study, are disagreements on what constitutes sustainability in a landscape. Such different perspectives turned conflictual during colonial times. Pastoralists would have large families to increase the household's labour capacity, move their livestock according to where grazing was available rather than where they held formal ownership rights, and burn areas to add nutrition

99 Ostrom, *Governing the Commons.*

100 Lotte Hughes, *Moving the Maasai: A Colonial Misadventure* (Basingstoke: Palgrave Macmillan, 2006).

101 Sorrenson, *Origins of European Settlement in Kenya.*

102 Kanogo, *Squatters and the Roots of Mau Mau.*

103 Michael Bollig and Carolyn Lesorogol, 'The "New Pastoral Commons" of Eastern and Southern Africa.' *International Journal of the Commons* 10, no. 2 (23 September 2016), pp. 665–87.

to the soil in order for fresh grass to grow.[104] Contrastingly, the settlers and the colonial government were informed by a discourse favouring large-scale plantations, with mixed farming and ranching.

Where pastoralist practices constituted seasonal grazing with locally negotiated access and the aim of expanding stock size, the settlers' practices built on quality and control of stock according to the perceived 'carrying capacity' of the area. Their purpose was economic gain through market access. Defined by the ecologists Botkin and Keller, carrying capacity refers to 'the maximum number of individuals of a species that can be sustained by an environment without decreasing the capacity of the environment to sustain that same amount in the future.'[105] Controlled by this discourse, the settlers in Laikipia had difficulty understanding the pastoralists' mobility, family structures and ways of keeping cattle.[106]

The concept of carrying capacity has been a dominant approach to natural resource management since Malthus and later Hardin theorised on population growth and overuse of resources.[107] Malthus considered people to be destructive by nature, and believed structural limits to population growth to be the only sustainable solution to natural resource management.[108] He argued that the carrying capacity of a piece of land would ultimately cause population growth to falter every time the imbalance with food production grew too great.[109] However, much has happened since Malthus and Hardin theorised along these lines, and especially within social science the argument is now considered inadequate to explain processes derived from human–environment interactions.[110] Notably, Boserup had a different approach to the dilemma.[111] She argued that

---

104 Michael Bollig and Michael Schnegg, 'Introduction: Specialisation and Diversification among African Pastoral Societies,' in *Pastoralism in Africa: Past, Present and Future*, ed. Michael Bollig, Michael Schnegg and Hans-Peter Wotzka (New York: Berghahn Books, 2013); John Galaty and Pierre Bonte (eds), *Herders, Warriors and Traders: Pastoralism in Africa* (Boulder, CO: Westview, 1991).

105 Daniel B. Botkin and Edward A. Keller, *Environmental Science: Earth as a Living Planet* (Hoboken, NJ: Wiley, 2003).

106 David Anderson, *Eroding the Commons: The Politics of Ecology in Baringo, Kenya, 1890s–1963* (Oxford: James Currey, 2002).

107 Hardin, 'The Tragedy of the Commons.'

108 Thomas Malthus, *An Essay on the Principle of Population* (London: Printed for J. Johnson, in Paul's Church-Yard, 1798).

109 Malthus, *An Essay on the Principle of Population.*

110 James Fairhead and Melissa Leach, *Misreading the African Landscape: Society and Ecology in a Forest–Savanna Mosaic* (Cambridge: Cambridge University Press, 1996); Richard Peet and Michael Watts, 'Liberating Political Ecology,' in *Liberation Ecologies*, ed. Richard Peet and Michael Watts (Abingdon, Oxon: Routledge, 2004), pp. 3–47.

111 Ester Boserup, *The Conditions of Agricultural Growth: The Economics of Agriculture under Population Pressure* (London and New York: Faber, 1965).

people's inventiveness would be able to break the limits of food production to meet the demands of population growth through improved farming methods and new technological inventions.[112]

Although these types of understanding of natural resource management have been influential, they do not speak to everyone in Laikipia's social-ecological system. To pastoralists, sustainable land management is meaningless if reduced to the carrying capacity of an area, since the practice of mobility is not recognised by the concept. Nevertheless, the colonial strategy for controlling the African populations and their land-use practices was justified by use of the scientific perspectives of carrying capacity[113] – a strategy that may well rest on the notion presented by Donald Moore, Jake Kosek and Anand Pandian that regulation of nature and land is an effective way to exercise authority over a social scene:

> Nature [...] works as a contested arena and an effective means for the exercise of power. From the victimization of inferior races to making of national spaces to the replication of inherited differences, natural bodies form the terrain and instruments of power's expression. [...] Power works on and through nature in several overlapping ways: through violent acts of domination, through the constitution of subjects and truths, and through the maintenance of these identities and differences across time and space.[114]

Elaborations in Chapters 3 and 7 will reveal just how relevant such notions of using the regulation of nature to control and exert power over people are for this study.

2.5 Concluding Remarks

When looking at present-day Laikipia and the undeniable problems of overgrazing and overly subdivided land, one can easily be inclined to conclude that there may be limits to people's abilities and inventiveness after all – especially considering the 2016–17 state of emergency. However, revisiting the situation from multiple angles, interrogating a range of voices, makes it clear that it is

112 Boserup, *The Conditions of Agricultural Growth.*

113 William Beinart and Lotte Hughes, *Environment and Empire. The Oxford History of the British Empire* (Oxford: Oxford University Press, 2007); Berry, 'Debating the Land Question in Africa.'

114 Moore et al., *Race, Nature, and the Politics of Difference*, p. 15.

not that simple. Instead the situation may be explained through the fragmentation of land-use and tenure systems, the failed land reforms or the politicisation of the complex ethnic composition of the people present, their beliefs and their claims to the land. Therefore, in conjunction, these thematic components constitute the golden thread of this study, with elements that are intertwined in all chapters of this book.

CHAPTER 3

Macro Perspectives: A History of Laikipia's Contested Lands

> In the end, your past is not my past and your truth is not my truth and your solution – is not my solution.
>
> ZADIE SMITH[1]

This chapter sets the social geography of Laikipia in its historical context, to show how the current land problems of the district have taken shape and how the connotations of ethnicity have shifted over time. The making of identity in Laikipia has been reflected in the emergence of new boundaries, beginning with the administrative controls on movement and residence during colonial times. Present conflict and competition over land is strongly rooted in different experiences and versions of the past. For that reason, to understand the present social dynamics and the nature and diversity of claims in Laikipia, history is very important.

The first part of the chapter will focus on the critical moments of history from the colonial period to the present, looking at the key events and decisions that defined Laikipia's territory. The second part of the chapter will then zoom in on three case studies exemplifying Laikipia's land conflicts – Lorien, Thome and Ol Moran.

In the first half of the twentieth century, Laikipia's landscape was dominated by a few powerful individuals who had benefited from the authority of colonial rule to command vast areas. For most Africans, mobility was heavily regulated and access to land was fiercely restricted. Strong legal authorities protected the individual rights of European holders of land titles, while Africans were contained within communal areas and denied titles of ownership. By the end of the twentieth century this situation had completely transformed. Older forms of judicial and political control over access to land had broken down and the door to extra-judicial claims had been opened, creating opportunities for communities to challenge the rights of others through a variety of legitimate and illegitimate

1 Zadie Smith, *White Teeth* (New York: Vintage International/Vintage Books, Random House Inc., 2001).

 | DOI:10.1163/9789004435209_004

means. In Laikipia, ethnicity became the principal mechanism through which these land claims were mobilised, entrenching its dynamics in political affiliations and accentuating conflict. This shift is familiar in many other parts of Kenya, but in Laikipia it has been especially potent and dangerous.

3.1 Laikipia in the Nineteenth Century

Colonial ideas about African land use in Laikipia were heavily influenced by the early accounts of the first European travellers to traverse the area during the last quarter of the nineteenth century. These narratives presented a picture of Laikipia as 'an empty land,' underpopulated and underdeveloped, and thus ripe for the benefits of European settlement and investment. The rhetoric of the 'empty lands' justified and legitimised British colonial settlement and its oppressive and unstable land and labour policies. Such ideas were not, of course, unique to Laikipia: all over Africa where Europeans grabbed land, this trope was deployed.[2] As Moore, Kosek and Pandian argue,

> Colonial constructions of a pristine nature entailed the forced removal of local inhabitants from the landscape. This reorganization of landscapes and livelihoods in the tropics, trafficking in both nature and culture, emerged out of the powerful circuits of imperial science, natural history, and regimes of rule[3]

Joseph Thomson[4] was the first to describe the Laikipia plateau when he crossed it as part of his expedition through Maasai land to reach Lake Victoria in 1883:

> The district is called Dondolè, which, I am informed, means 'everybody's (that is to say – no man's) land,' from the incessant quarrels for possession that have taken place between the Masai of Kinangop and the Masai (wa-kwafi) of Lykipia.[5]

---

2 Berry, 'Debating the Land Question in Africa.'

3 Moore et al., *Race, Nature, and the Politics of Difference*, p. 13.

4 As many other Europeans would do after him, Thomson gave name to many of the landscape features he 'discovered' and described, such as Thomson's Falls and the Aberdare Range, even naming the Thomson's Gazelle after himself.

5 Joseph Thomson, *Through Masai Land: A Journey of Exploration among the Snowclad Volcanic Mountains and Strange Tribes of Eastern Equatorial Africa*, Vol. 1 (London: Low, Marston, Searle, & Rivington, 1887), p. 203.

His description of a vast and uninhabited land was a story that would later conveniently be used by the colonial administration to entice settlers and investment for the newly annexed territory.[6]

Other explorers also report descriptions of the grassy plains in Laikipia, though few are as explicit as Thomson in drawing comparison with the landscape of Northern Europe.[7] Powell-Cotton, for example, who travelled across Laikipia in 1904, wrote evocatively of the potential of the area:

> Nearly the whole way across the plains of Laikipia the country was well wooded and appeared to be an ideal district for cattle-grazing, judging from the vast herds of antelope [...] that roamed over it; while the belts of trees and little copses would provide a plentiful supply of timber and firewood.[8]

As descriptions of that particular window in time, these were accurate. However, there were reasons for this seeming emptiness of the plateau that were not apparent for any of the travel writers passing through. Laikipia has a deep history of human presence,[9] and its apparent emptiness can be partly explained by the Maasai Iloikop wars of the mid-nineteenth century, which Thomson accounted to have exterminated thousands in fighting between the sub-clans of the Maasai.[10] Historical research into the dynamics of these internecine struggles, which lasted from the 1840s until 1870, now suggests that

6 Thomson, *Through Masai Land*; Beinart and Hughes, *Environment and Empire*; Hughes, *Moving the Maasai*; Richard Waller, 'The Lords of East Africa: The Maasai in the Mid-Nineteenth Century (c. 1840–1880)' (unpublished PhD diss., University of Cambridge, 1979); J.B. Thomson, *Joseph Thomson, African Explorer: A Bibliography by His Brother* (London: Sampson Low, 1897); Thomas T. Spear and Richard Waller, *Being Maasai: Ethnicity and Identity in East Africa* (London: James Currey, 1993).

7 Captain C.H. Stigand, *To Abyssinia through an Unknown Land* (Philadelphia: J.B. Lippincott Company, 1910); Alfred Arkell Hardwick, *An Ivory Trader in North Kenia; the Record of an Expedition through Kikuyu to Galla-Land in East Equatorial Africa. With an Account of the Rendili and Burkeneji Tribes* (London: Longmans, Green, and Company, 1903); H.J. Mackinder, 'A Journey to the Summit of Mount Kenya, British East Africa,' *The Geographical Journal* 15, no. 5 (1900), pp. 453–76; Arthur H. Neumann, *Elephant Hunting in East Equatorial Africa* (London: Rowland Ward, Limited, 1898).

8 P.H.G. Powell-Cotton, 'A Journey through Northern Uganda,' *The Geographical Journal* 24, no. 1. (July 1904), p. 57.

9 Taylor et al., 'Mid- to Late-Holocene Vegetation Dynamics on the Laikipia Plateau, Kenya,' pp. 837–46; Lane, 'An Outline of the Later Holocene Archaeology and Precolonial History of the Ewaso Basin, Kenya,' *The Holocene* 15, no. 6 (1 September 2005), pp. 11–30; G.Y. Gang, *The Middle and Later Stone Ages in the Mukogodo Hills of Central Kenya* (Oxford: BAR Oxford Ltd, 2001).

10 Thomson, *Through Masai Land*.

these wars did not result in significant population loss but did cause major shifts in the territories occupied by different Maasai sections. This, combined with the seasonal patterns of Maasai pastoralist movement, meant that Thomson did indeed witness vast areas that appeared to be unoccupied.[11] But a more directly contingent cause is likely to have been the years of drought and disease that followed the Iloikop wars, from the 1870s until the 1890s. Known to the Maasai by the pejorative phrase 'emutai' ('the finishing'), this saw the Laikipia area and other parts of the Rift Valley swept first by bovine-pleuro-pneumonia and then by cholera, before the devastating rinderpest decimated the cattle herds in the 1890s.[12] The end of the century then brought two years of the worst drought seen for over 50 years, precisely coinciding with the beginnings of the British colonial conquest of the Maasai lands, including Laikipia.[13] Although lacking this background information, Thomson experienced at first hand how these realities manifested in the landscape:

> On our way we were greatly astonished to observe the dried carcasses of numerous cattle which dotted the entire district. They showed no signs of death by violence, and only some parts had been eaten by hyenas and other carnivora. We came to the conclusion that some disease must be raging in the land.[14]

It is evident that Thomson had only a vague understanding of the history that had shaped the landscape he witnessed as he crossed Laikipia. The weakening of Maasai authority had, in fact, brought opportunities for other pastoral groups – the Tugen[15] and Pokot[16] from the west and the

---

11 Waller, 'The Lords of East Africa'; Bethwell A. Ogot, *Kenya before 1900* (Nairobi: East African Publishing House, 1976); John L. Berntsen, 'The Enemy Is Us: Eponymy in the Historiography of the Maasai,' *History in Africa* 7 (1980), pp. 1–21; John L. Berntsen, 'The Maasai and Their Neighbors: Variables of Interaction,' *African Economic History* 2 (1976), pp. 1–11.

12 Richard Waller, 'Kidongoi's Kin: Prophecy and Power in Maasailand,' in *Revealing Prophets: Prophecy in Eastern African History*, ed. David Anderson and Douglas Hamilton Johnson (London: James Currey Publishers, 1995).

13 Richard Waller, 'The Maasai and the British 1895–1905. The Origins of an Alliance,' *The Journal of African History* 17, no. 4 (1976), pp. 529–53; Gordon Hudson Mungeam, *British Rule in Kenya, 1895–1912: The Establishment of Administration in the East Africa Protectorate* (Oxford: Clarendon, 1966); Sorrenson, *Origins of European Settlement in Kenya*; Katherine Homewood, Patti Kristjanson and P. Trench (eds), *Staying Maasai? Livelihoods, Conservation and Development in East African Rangelands* (New York: Springer-Verlag New York, 2009).

14 Thomson, *Through Masai Land*, p. 206.

15 Anderson, *Eroding the Commons*.

16 Michael Bollig, 'Adaptive Cycles in the Savannah: Pastoral Specialization and Diversification in Northern Kenya,' *Journal of Eastern African Studies* 10, no. 1 (2 January 2016),

Samburu[17] from the north, for example – while Kikuyu agriculturalists were also able to encroach upon former Maasai lands after 1900.[18] None of this complexity, or the transient character of the 'empty lands,' was apparent to Thomson, who merely noted his surprise that 'between Mount Kenya and Baringo there were no inhabitants.'[19]

Thomson's elaborate and evocative landscape descriptions reached hundreds of thousands of people through the publication and popular sales of his travelogue.[20] While Thomson often evoked the characterisations of African's savagery typical of European writing in the late nineteenth century – he described the Maasai as a 'ferocious and blood-thirsty tribe'[21] – his writings had a de-exoticising influence, opening up an interest in Laikipia, and in Kenya more generally, as a place for European settlement. Thomson advocated a European 'civilising mission' and provided the justifications that would support the British 'land grab' in Laikipia after 1900.[22]

3.2 Colonial Rule in Laikipia

The British East African Protectorate was officially annexed by the British in 1895, and from 1902 a policy of European settlement was advanced under the guidance of Sir Charles Eliot.[23] Over the first two decades of British rule in Kenya, an administrative system evolved in which ownership of and access to land was defined by both race and ethnicity. Firstly, the colonial state, through the Crown Lands Act, awarded itself control and regulation of all lands, making all local claims subsidiary.[24] This allowed land to be designated and set aside for specific purposes, for example as forest reserves,[25] or to be awarded to

pp. 21–44; Michael Bollig, *Risk Management in a Hazardous Environment: A Comparative Study of Two Pastoral Societies* (New York: Springer Science & Business Media, 2010).

17 Spencer, *Nomads in Alliance: Symbiosis and Growth Among the Rendille and Samburu of Kenya* (Oxford: Oxford University Press, 1973).

18 Sorrenson, *Origins of European Settlement in Kenya.*

19 Thomson, *Through Maasai Land*, p. 226; Beinart and Hughes, *Environment and Empire.*

20 Beinart and Hughes, *Environment and Empire.*

21 Thomson, *Through Masai Land*; Kantai, 'In the Grip of the Vampire State,' pp. 107–22.

22 Beinart and Hughes, *Environment and Empire.*

23 Mungeam, *British Rule in Kenya, 1895–1912*; Sorrenson, *Origins of European Settlement in Kenya.*

24 Crown Lands Ordinance, No. 12 of 1915, as referenced by Tash P. Ghai, J.P.W.B. McAuslan and Patrick McAuslan, *Public Law and Political Change in Kenya: A Study of the Legal Framework of Government from Colonial Times to the Present* (Nairobi: Oxford University Press, 1970).

25 David Anderson, 'Managing the Forest: The Conservation History of Lembus, Kenya, 1904–63,' in *Conservation in Africa: Peoples, Policies and Practice*, ed. David Anderson and Richard H. Grove (Cambridge: Cambridge University Press, 1989).

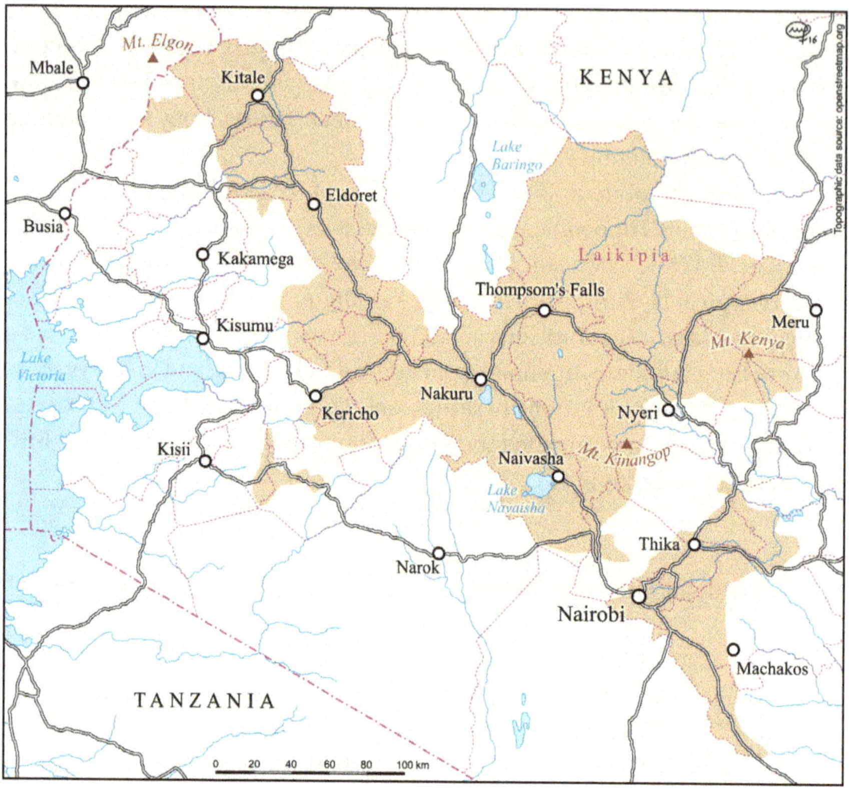

FIGURE 2 The extent of the White Highlands.
© Monika Feinen 2016

the control of certain communities, for example through the creation of ethnically defined 'Native Reserves.'[26] This also allowed 'scheduled land' to be set aside exclusively for the use of European settlers. By defining African rights in terms of communal ownership of land in designated and protected 'reserves,' the creation of a 'European Reserve,' known as the 'White Highlands,' could be justified and legitimised.[27]

In Laikipia, the few remaining Maasai were forced to move to the designated Maasai Reserve in the south-western part of present-day Kenya with the Maasai Agreement in 1911. Yet, although the land in Laikipia was then vacated, settlement by European immigrants did not start until after the Second World

26 Sorrenson, *Origins of European Settlement in Kenya*; Mungeam, *British Rule in Kenya, 1895–1912*.

27 Sorrenson, *Origins of European Settlement in Kenya*; Leo, *Land and Class in Kenya*.

War in the early 1920s.[28] The fact that the plateau was de facto uncolonised for a decade after the last Maasai were gone became defining for the narratives behind the land claims of other ethnic groups, particularly the Samburu, as this decade allowed for their presence in Laikipia to take root and a sense of entitlement of the place to take shape.

Nevertheless, after the end of the Second World War, several waves of European settlement in Laikipia followed, though to begin with only the southern, more fertile part of the plateau was scheduled for settlement. First to arrive were the pioneers, then, following the Anglo-Boer War, came a wave of South African settlers and later arrived veterans from the First and Second World War who had been offered land in the colony in appreciation for their service.

By 1934, the area of alienated high-potential land amounted to 6,543,360 acres across the White Highlands, although only 11% of this land was under cultivation.[29] At this time, most of these areas were held by 2,027 settlers of European origin. Each occupied an average of 1,410 acres.[30] About half of the farms were smaller than 900 acres, down to as little as 20.1 acres – the legal minimum size of a farm – whereas farm sizes extended to more than 40,000 acres in the more arid areas.[31]

In Laikipia, the ecological dynamics defined the designated farm sizes. The southern areas of the plateau had more permanent water sources and relatively stable rainfall, and required relatively limited investment in infrastructure. These factors made it possible to sustain mixed farming of cash crops such as pyrethrum, millet, maize and wheat on small-sized farms. For these reasons, these areas were the first to become settled. In contrast, in the central and northern parts of Laikipia the landscape was more arid and required more infrastructural investment. This land held more potential for large-sized ranches with merino sheep and dairy or beef cattle.[32] Yet, the poor performance of the beef market up until the 1940s made ranching a risky venture to engage in. Hence, settlement on the central rangelands of the plateau grew more slowly than in the southern parts. Moreover, the very northern parts of Laikipia, bordering present-day Samburu County, were not scheduled for settlement before the 1940s. Until then the settlers could access these open ranges via Temporary Occupation Licences.[33]

28 Hughes, *Moving the Maasai.*

29 Elspeth Huxley, *White Man's Country: Lord Delamere and the Making of Kenya* (London: Chatto & Windus, 1968); Sorrenson, *Origins of European Settlement in Kenya*; Leo, *Land and Class in Kenya.*

30 J.F. Lipscomb, *The History of Kenya Agriculture* (Nairobi: University Press of Africa, 1972), p. 59.

31 Lipscomb, *The History of Kenya Agriculture*, p. 81.

32 East African Women's League, 'Golden Jubilee Scrapbook,' Laikipia Branch, 1968.

33 Sorrenson, *Origins of European Settlement in Kenya*; Leo, *Land and Class in Kenya.*

The colonial administration offered easy terms to encourage Europeans to settle in the White Highlands. Land was cheap – at times it could even be offered as a free grant if the buyer in turn agreed to spend a given amount on development of the farm.[34] To bring labour to the new farms, the state set tax rates on African communities, regulated wage levels (to keep them low) and found other ways to encourage workers into the labour market.[35] While European settlers were assisted and given advantages, African rights were curtailed. The African population was contained within ethnic reserves, movement was regulated, access to natural resources was legally restricted, and customary hunting practices were criminalised and rearticulated as poaching and trespass.[36] In effect, this created a plural system in which African rights were socialised through communal principles, while Europeans were privileged with private-property rights.[37]

3.2.1 *The Kenya Land Commission, 1932–34*

Though these changes marginalised and disadvantaged Africans, they did not go uncontested. Over the 60 years of colonial rule numerous petitions, delegations and commissions of enquiry challenged the European settlers' control of the 'lost lands' among the African population in and around Laikipia. On the one hand, the contestations over land rights ethnicised African claim-making, as communities mobilised to protect or extend 'their' rights. On the other hand, they hardened the views of European settlers, who took active steps to strengthen and defend their position against African claims.[38] European farmers in the White Highlands campaigned to increase control of the Laikipia plateau during the colonial period.[39] As these struggles over land emerged, the links between politics and ethnicity became clearer, culminating, from the 1990s, in open violence.[40]

The Kenya Land Commission (KLC), which sat from 1932 and reported in 1934, was the most important statement of this emerging land crisis to be witnessed under colonial rule. The Land Commission was to evaluate claims to land made by the African population and assess them in relation to the needs

34 Sorrenson, *Origins of European Settlement in Kenya*, pp. 70–71.

35 Van Zwanenberg, *The Agricultural History of Kenya to 1939*.

36 Moore et al., *Race, Nature, and the Politics of Difference*, p. 13.

37 Beinart and Hughes, *Environment and Empire*; Sorrenson, *Origins of European Settlement in Kenya*.

38 Sorrenson, *Origins of European Settlement in Kenya*.

39 Gary Wasserman, *Politics of Decolonization: Kenya Europeans and the Land* (Cambridge: Cambridge University Press, 2009), p. 17.

40 John O. Oucho, *Undercurrents of Ethnic Conflicts in Kenya* (Leiden: Brill, 2002).

of the different groups.[41] The European settlers anticipated the Land Commission with concern because of its authority to recommend boundary adjustments to the Crown Land. With redistributions of land between the races, this could potentially threaten the settlers' supremacy in the White Highlands. To the African population, the Land Commission brought hope that past wrongs could be resolved and compensated. However, a change in political power led to a reformulation of the Land Commission's mandate, which instead safeguarded settler interests by focusing on their claims rather than re-evaluating those of the African population.[42] Yet this shift did not relieve the settlers of their concern. They prepared well for the discussions and focused their argumentation on problematising overstocking while challenging the narratives brought forth by the African groups of historical presence in the Crown Lands. Consequently, if the African groups were to safeguard their interests and access to vital resources, it became essential for them to portray an extensive and precise account of their history of settlement and use of the land.[43]

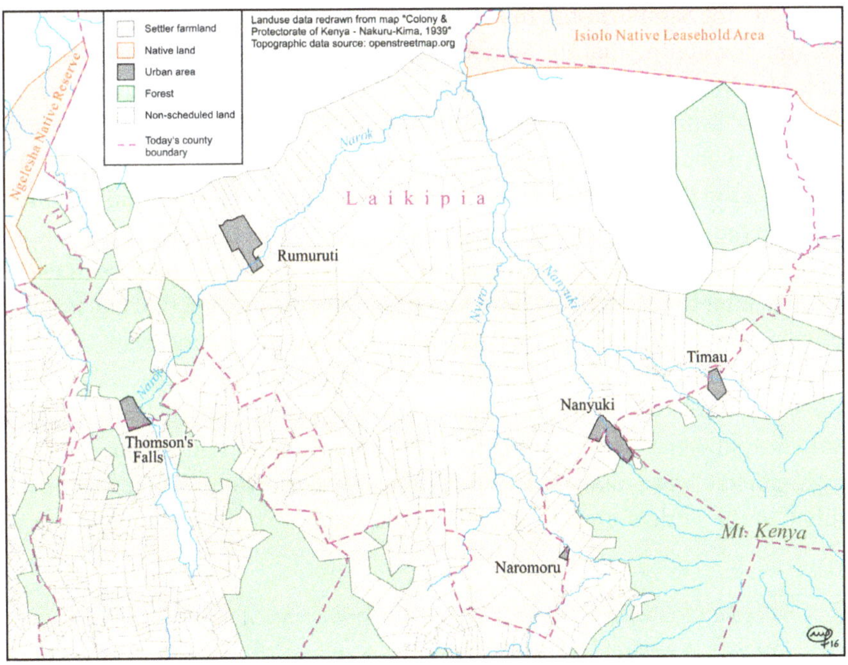

FIGURE 3 Colonial land-use map of Laikipia in 1939.
© Monika Feinen 2016

41 O.F. Watkins, 'The Report of the Kenya Land Commission, September, 1933,' *Journal of the Royal African Society* 33, no. 132 (1934), pp. 207–16.

42 Anderson, *Eroding the Commons*, pp. 126–34.

43 Anderson, *Eroding the Commons*.

3.2.2 *The Land Commission Questions*

The colonially scheduled areas in Laikipia are illustrated in figure 3. This shows how the Laikipia plateau was surrounded by Turkana and Samburu from the north in the early twentieth century. Coincidentally, the Kalenjin from the Rift Valley in the west pushed for grazing access, while the Embu and Meru from the east, and in particular the Kikuyu from the south around Nyeri, pushed to acquire favourable positions on the plateau.[44] The KLC was not focused on Laikipia itself but tackled two specific land questions on Laikipia's frontier. The first concerned claims from the north over the Leroghi plateau; the second related to Kikuyu claims in the south.

The Leroghi plateau towards the north of Laikipia had been inhabited by the Samburu for at least the preceding 20 years. Rare as it was for these plains, this area was well watered.[45] The European settlers made a claim to the area because they wished to secure a stable water source for the northern ranches – a claim that had only become more pressing following years of drought and disease in the early 1930s.[46] The Leroghi plateau was no less important to the stock-owning Samburu, and the elders made a claim to maintain it on historical grounds, stating that the Samburu had used the area as a subgroup of the Laikipiak Maasai before their move but that a quarrel with the Laikipiak had driven the Samburu north into the interior of the Samburu territory prior to the Maasai being forcibly moved to the Southern Reserve. This was claimed to be the reason that the Samburu were not annihilated and forcibly moved along with the remaining Maasai in 1912.[47]

However, the settlers argued that the Samburu could only have been using the area after the Maasai had been moved out in the 1910s and that any form of cooperation in grazing with the Maasai before then was inconceivable.[48] They also made the point that the Samburu's terminology for themselves, *Loibor Kenejie*, referred to 'those who keep goats,' suggesting that the Samburu had not always been a cattle-owning tribe.[49] This was important because the Leroghi plateau was grassland and therefore, the settlers implied, it was better suited to the settlers' grazing cattle than the Samburu's browsing goats.

---

44 Adapted from William Ochieng, *East African Protectorate. A Modern History of Kenya: 1895–1980* (Ibadan: Evans Brothers, 1989).

45 Report of the Kenya Land Commission (KLC), Evidence and memoranda, Vol. II, Rift Valley Province, Part II, Chapter VI (Nairobi: Government Printer, 1934).

46 Rhodes House (RH), Africa.mic.515 reel 25, Laikipia Annual Report, Trafford, 1932; British Institute of East Africa (BIEA), Laikipia Farmers Association (LFA), 'Minutes from Meetings,' 1927.

47 KLC, Evidence and memoranda, Vol. II, Rift Valley Province, Part II, Chapter VI.

48 KLC, Evidence and memoranda, Vol. II, Rift Valley Province, Part II, Chapter VI.

49 KLC, Evidence and memoranda, Vol. II, Rift Valley Province, Part II, Chapter VI, p. 231.

The commissioners, however, considered it unjust to cut off the Samburu from the water source, and the case was concluded to the advantage of the Samburu:

> Whatever claim they may have had dates back before the time of European administration. However logical it might seem to say to the Samburu, 'You did not occupy this land when we came, but you did occupy Marsabit, and therefore you must go back there,' such a course would be impossible, because that area is now occupied by other tribes and no Government would contemplate the continual moving of tribes for such reasons.[50]

This concession made this the only case in the KLC where the commissioners sided with the Africans. Even so, they recommended tightened regulation of the Samburu stock, with stricter rules on branding and forced livestock selling. This was done in order to control movement and pressure on the carrying capacity of the land, based on the Malthusian argument that 'the Europeans would be able to use the land to better advantage than the natives in their present state of development.'[51]

Towards the south from Laikipia, the Kikuyu made claims of expansion to their areas on grounds that the population pressure was becoming critical. In this claim, the KLC placed weight on historical records of the Kikuyu area. The settlers used accounts by travel writers to illustrate that the Kikuyu had not ventured far up into Laikipia for fear of the Maasai. That way, the European settlers were able to circumvent the threat from the Africans' historically backed claims to the White Highlands.

The Kikuyu's main argument was that their areas were becoming congested and the soil quality was deteriorating, making farming practices more risky. These claims, however, did not alarm the director of agriculture, who stated: 'Generally speaking, I see no evidence of the soil being worn out, and I do not think there is any reason to be unduly apprehensive about the future.'[52] This Kikuyu claim was therefore rejected, and their experiences of deteriorating soils were explained by reference to undeveloped farming practices with inadequate use of manure, too much focus on single crops and failure to dig deep enough when they ploughed.[53]

50 KLC, Evidence and memoranda, Vol. II, Rift Valley Province, Part II, Chapter VI, p. 236.
51 KLC, Evidence and memoranda, Vol. II, Rift Valley Province, Part II, Chapter VI, p. 236.
52 KLC, Evidence and memoranda, Vol. II, Rift Valley Province, Part III, Chapter I, p. 354.
53 KLC, Evidence and memoranda, Vol. II, Rift Valley Province, Part III, Chapter I, p. 356.

Additionally, the Kikuyu argued that their areas were overstocked. Senior Chief Koinange argued:

> All the counts that are made of the sheep and stock by the Agricultural Department are purely imaginary, because we keep back the true number which we possess, for fear that we shall be told that we have got too many.[54]

This statement was seconded by Dr Leakey, as well as by the Veterinary Department. Every time the Veterinary Department did inoculations of Kikuyu livestock they found the estimates to be much lower than the actual numbers of stock.[55] Yet once more the KLC did not find enough convincing arguments that there was no room for improvement of Kikuyu farming practices and that there were no possibilities for diversifying their income:

> In civilized countries the soil is not regarded as the only means of livelihood, and [farmers] on an overcrowded farm are willing to allow one of their members to buy the others out and seek alternative employment elsewhere. Such fluidity is unattainable among Kenya natives at [the present] stage, both because of the undeveloped state of industries and because of the habits and the customs of the people. [...] The problem is essentially one of educating people in the better use of their land.[56]

On those grounds, the KLC rejected the Kikuyu claim of expansion into the White Highlands unless the tendencies of congestion became more acute and farming practices did not improve.[57] Nevertheless, it was undeniable that the immigration of Kikuyu into Laikipia increased steadily. The KLC had to recognise this, and it recommended another 153,000 acres to be added to the Kikuyu areas, although this was taken not from settler areas in Laikipia but from forested zones towards the south.[58]

Besides the claim from the north and the claim from the south, the KLC was engaged in a claim relevant to the internal administration of Laikipia, namely

54 KLC, Evidence and memoranda, Vol. II, Rift Valley Province, Part III, Chapter I, p. 356.
55 KLC, Evidence and memoranda, Vol. II, Rift Valley Province, Part III, Chapter I, p. 356.
56 KLC, Evidence and memoranda, Vol. II, Rift Valley Province, Part III, Chapter I, pp. 357–58.
57 KLC, Evidence and memoranda, Vol. II, Rift Valley Province, Part III, Chapter I, p. 358.
58 Rutten, 'Fresh Killings: The Njoro and Laikipia Violence in the 1997 Kenyan Election Aftermath,' in *Out for the Count : The 1997 General Elections and Prospects for Democracy in Kenya*, ed. Marcel Rutten and Alamin Mazrui (Kampala: Fountain Pub. Ltd, 2001).

the categorisation of people referred to as Dorobo. The settlers were interested in categorising them as a homogeneous group within the Maasai ethnic category, so that they could be moved from Laikipia to the Southern Reserve in accordance with the 1911 Maasai Agreement.[59]

The group that appears in the KLC as Dorobo in Laikipia argued that they had been present on the land as hunter-gatherers when the Maasai prevailed in the area, but despite sharing Maa as a language, they claimed to have no affiliation with the Maasai. Leratia Ole Turumet explained:

> Our origin is Dorobo. We used to live on wild game and honey. Then the hunting of animals was forbidden by the Government and we were told that we could not put our honey barrels in the forest and were told to go out of the forest. We had nothing from the Government but there was a gentleman called Bwana Nasori (Mr. Colvile) who caused trouble and told us we should go away from where we were because we were Masai, but we say we are not Masai because we do not marry with the Masai or have anything to do with them.[60]

If the Land Commission acknowledged the hunter-gatherer status, it could mean acknowledging rights of access to the plateau for this group on the grounds that they were the 'original owners' of the land, and therefore they were a risk factor for the European settlers.

According to Spencer, it is problematic to term the Dorobo as an ethnic group because they can be divided into at least two sections: those who can claim to be among the first hunter-gatherers in the Rift Valley area; and those originating from the lower class of other groups.[61] For people in the area today, some define Dorobo as meaning 'one quarter,' explaining that they are a mix of many different people.[62] Others explain that in the Maa language it denotes a person who has no cattle, meaning, to them, a poor person.[63] Ultimately, those claiming Dorobo affiliation in the KLC may have come from many different ethnic groups.

The settlers and the British assumed ethnic categories to be static, whereas to the Dorobo and Maasai they were fluid. A change of affiliation could be used strategically, to fit a claim to a resource. Alternatively, in a process of exclusion

59 KLC, Evidence and memoranda, Vol. II, Rift Valley Province, p. 2000.
60 KLC, Evidence and memoranda, Vol. II, Rift Valley Province, p. 1800.
61 Spencer, *Nomads in Alliance*.
62 Interview with research participant, northern Laikipia, 14 April 2015.
63 Interview with research participant, Rumuruti, 14 July 2015; Spencer, *Nomads in Alliance*.

one could be forced to change affiliation and be termed Dorobo for lack of a better term for one's status as an outlaw.[64] In that sense, it is an umbrella term for a person with no cattle, without specifying their reason for not having cattle.[65]

Ultimately, the recommendations of the KLC did not declare the Dorobo to be the true holders of the areas in Laikipia, nor did they recommend a removal of them from the plateau altogether:

> Many of them have good claims of right to the areas where they now reside, and their removal, although for their own benefit, is also governed very largely by dictates of administrative convenience. Furthermore, they are taxpayers, and as such, should suffer no disturbance without due compensation. We wish to lay particular stress on the necessity for arranging that the Dorobo are fed, until such time as they can make new arrangements.[66]

Thus, the handling of the Dorobo groups became open to the definition and decision by whichever district administration needed to deal with them. Without much livestock, they did not need to move across the plateau to look for grazing and posed no threat to the settler community in terms of spreading livestock diseases.

The most important recommendation transpiring from the KLC was that no further land alienations should be authorised in African frontier areas, limiting further expansion of the White Highlands.[67] The general concessions towards the African population remained minor adjustments to the boundaries, and any possibility for transferring land without settler consent was removed – much to the frustration, especially, of the pastoralists in and around Laikipia, who resented the systematic control.[68]

Following the KLC, there were hardly any confrontations between the Dorobo and the settlers. The Dorobo claim to the land has only been revived more recently as part of the new wave of indigeneity movements.[69] Contrastingly, the Kikuyu's unmet expectations led to the Mau Mau rebellion, and the Samburu continued to rebel against the settlers' presence in the northern

64 Spencer, *Nomads in Alliance*.

65 Enid Guene, *The End of Hunting and Gathering: Identity and Livelihood Transformation among Foraging Communities in Kenya* (PhD diss., Universität zu Köln, forthcoming).

66 KLC, Evidence and memoranda, Vol. II, Rift Valley Province, Part II, Chapter VII, p. 260.

67 Lipscomb, *The History of Kenya Agriculture*, p. 24; Watkins, 'The Report of the Kenya Land Commission, September, 1933,' pp. 207–16.

68 Anderson, *Eroding the Commons*.

69 Carrier, 'Reviving Yaaku,' pp. 246–63.

Laikipia ranches throughout the colonial period.[70] The KLC represented the first coherent protest over land rights by the Africans, and it became a point of reference for the struggles that followed.

Although the conclusions of the KLC favoured settler interests, the political divide between them and the colonial government continued to produce opposition among settler farmers and uncertainty about whether the government would support them should an unmet claim from African groups turn violent.[71] This concern was grounded in a sense of misrepresentation, for instance in relation to government plans for the creation of a stock route between Samburu and Thomson's Falls, and their refusal to divide the Samburu and Laikipia District.[72] Moreover, the settler farmers struggled with the general inefficiency in the provision of institutional infrastructure, for which they blamed the government.[73]

3.2.3 *The African Reaction*

Following the KLC, numerous trespasses by the pastoral groups occurred, along with cattle raids aimed at diminishing the European cattle holdings. The colonial administration attempted to protect European property rights through fines, resettlement and imprisonment of African offenders. Moreover, they increased patrols and pass controls to diminish mobility within the Crown Land area – effectively policing the movement of Africans onto the farms.[74] But none of this had any significant impact in reducing the levels of conflict.[75]

Samburu *morans*, in particular, frequently stole cattle and attacked Kikuyu labourers on the Laikipia farms.[76] Between 1922 and 1936 these *morans* were allegedly responsible for the deaths of 24 labourers and squatters on the white

70 David Throup, *Economic and Social Origins of Mau Mau* (Nairobi: Heinemann, 1988); Fratkin, 'The Samburu Laibon's Sorcery and the Death of Theodore Powys in Colonial Kenya,' pp. 35–54.

71 Wasserman, *Politics of Decolonization*, p. 20; RH, Africa.mic.515 reel 25, Laikipia Annual Report, Nimmo, 1949; RH, Africa.mic.515 reel 25, Laikipia Annual Report, Brown, 1942; Kenya National Archives (KNA), PC/RVP/2/13/21, 'Unalienated Land – Crown Lands South of the Kittermaster Line,' 1934–1939.

72 At the time Samburu and Laikipia functioned as one district.

73 RH, Africa.mic.515 reel 25, Laikipia Annual Report, Nimmo, 1949; RH, Africa.mic.515 reel 25, Laikipia Annual Report, Brown, 1942.

74 BIEA, Laikipia Farmers Association, 'Minutes of meeting,' 19 August 1933; RH, Africa.mic.515 reel 25, Laikipia Annual Report, Trafford, 1932; RH, Africa.mic.517 reel 10, Laikipia Handing Over Report, Simpson to Shirreff, 1947.

75 Anderson, *Eroding the Commons*.

76 Richard Waller, 'Bringing Murder to Court: The Death of Theodore Powys,' *African Studies Association Annual Meetings* (New York, 2007); Fratkin, 'The Samburu Laibon's Sorcery and the Death of Theodore Powys in Colonial Kenya,' pp. 35–54.

farms of Laikipia and north Nyeri.[77] District Commissioner Trafford described the challenges in controlling movement by increasing police presence in the northern boundary area:

> A Police post was provided by the Rumuruti Police Unit and stationed at Suguta Marmar. This post was supposed to work on a sort of railway time table with posts established by Isiolo district. The whole idea was sheer waste of time and money and the Rumuruti post was withdrawn in September.[78]

British efforts to recruit *morans* into the police and military did prove successful, and by 1943 there were 300 Samburu in the British armed forces.[79] Yet, such measures did not halt the local problems in Laikipia. The Samburu–Kikuyu

TABLE 1 Ethnic composition of the population in Laikipia District for the years around the KLC

Ethnic groups	1926		1931		1934	
Kikuyu	4,489	88.5%	8,671	90.4%	7,642	86.0%
Europeans	216	4.2%	262	2.7%	379	4.2%
Dorobo	98	1.9%	500	5.2%	338	3.8%
Maasai	33	0.6%	50	0.5%	136	1.5%
Nandi/Lumbwa	82	1.6%	N/N	N/N	88	1.0%
Turkana/Samburu	N/N	N/N	8	0.08%	48	0.5%
Indians	11	0.2%	23	0.2%	89	1.0%
Kavirondo	103	2.0%	12	0.1%	103	1.1%
Others	39	0.7%	65	0.7%	37	0.4%
Total population	5,071	100%	9,591	100%	8,880	100%

SOURCE: RHODES HOUSE LIBRARY, UNIVERSITY OF OXFORD (RH), AFRICA.MIC.515 REEL 25, LAIKIPIA ANNUAL REPORT, TRAFFORD, 1926; RH, AFRICA.MIC.515 REEL 25, LAIKIPIA AND SAMBURU ANNUAL REPORTS, 1930–1933, 1935–1945; RH, AFRICA.MIC.515 REEL 25, LAIKIPIA ANNUAL REPORT, SHARPE, 1934.

77 Fratkin, 'The Samburu Laibon's Sorcery and the Death of Theodore Powys in Colonial Kenya,' pp. 35–54.

78 RH, Africa.mic.515 reel 25, Laikipia Annual Report, Trafford, 1932, p. 4.

79 RH, Africa.mic.515 reel 25, Laikipia Annual Report, Mckean, 1943; Sorrenson, *Origins of European Settlement in Kenya.*

conflict was in part driven by the growing numbers of Kikuyu coming into Laikipia. In the annual report for 1934 the total population for Laikipia District was reported to be 8,880, out of which 7,642 were registered as Kikuyu and only 379 as Europeans.[80] While these numbers may not take the seasonal presence of pastoral groups into adequate consideration, they do give a sense of the general distribution.

The Kikuyu were present in the southern parts of the area in great numbers already before the British alienated the land, and even in 1945 more than 90% of the estimated ethnic population in Laikipia was Kikuyu.[81] Many acquired access rights in Laikipia due to the increasing population pressure in the Kikuyu areas. To stay there would mean landlessness, as District Commissioner Hennings described in 1945:

> Applications from Kikuyu for permission to start businesses of various sorts at Thomson's Falls and Ol Joro Orok poured in throughout the year [...]. It was apparent that a good many of the applicants were more interested in securing a footing in this desirable neighbourhood than with earning their livelihood by trade.[82]

Most of these Kikuyu immigrants came from the neighbouring district of Nyeri, with which they retained close cultural and family links.[83] They were hired as farm labourers and were approved for residence as squatters within small designated areas of the particular settler's farmland. They worked on the farms and were able to gradually accumulate wealth through keeping livestock, even though not all farmers allowed this for fear that the squatters' livestock would contaminate the settlers' livestock with pests and diseases.[84] The squatters were the de facto users of three quarters of the land in the White Highlands, essentially problematising the 'White Highlands' as a category. In essence, it was always a 'Black Highlands.'[85] Following population estimates,

80 RH, Africa.mic.515 reel 25, Laikipia Annual Report, Sharpe, 1934.

81 RH, Africa.mic.515 reel 25, Laikipia and Samburu Annual Report, Hennings, 1945.

82 RH, Africa.mic.515 reel 25, Laikipia and Samburu Annual Report, Hennings, 1945, p. 9

83 For instance, a tribunal court composed entirely of Kikuyu elders was established in Laikipia to settle Kikuyu legal cases according to Kikuyu law and custom. Such cases related to bride prices, adultery, debt and other social issues (RH, Africa.mic.515 reel 25, Laikipia Annual Report, Nimmo, 1949).

84 BIEA, Laikipia Farmers Association, 'Minutes from Meeting,' 12 September 1933; Kanogo, *Squatters and the Roots of Mau Mau.*

85 John Lonsdale, 'Kenya: Home County and African Frontiers,' in *Settlers and Expatriates: Britons Over the Seas*, ed. Robert Bickers (Oxford and New York: Oxford University Press, 2010).

90% of squatters employed on the settler farms were Kikuyu, and only 8% were Kalenjin.[86]

The fact that Kikuyu were preferred as squatter labourers explains the drastic increase in registered Kikuyu in Laikipia between the years 1926 and 1931. This was a period when the European population became more stable and increased their demands for farm labourers.[87] It also illustrates the hierarchical nature of the European domination in the Highlands.

The relations between the Kikuyu squatters, the European settlers and the colonial administration were not without conflict.[88] Some Europeans held large numbers of squatters on their farms; others sought to restrict and regulate numbers, especially as they developed the farm and began to have less need for resident labour. By the 1930s there was already great pressure to reduce squatter numbers, so as to protect the legal sanctity of the White Highlands, and by the 1940s significant numbers of squatter evictions were well underway in Laikipia.[89] The colonial government ceded authority over squatters to local district councils, and allowed European settlers to decide independently whether to restrict the number of squatters.[90]

3.2.4 *The Emergent Urban Population and Trade*

The Indians gradually took up much of the growing business in the urban area of Thomson's Falls in the 1930s and 1940s.[91] Besides pushing for improvements to the township facilities, they were strictly controlled by the British administration.[92] Similarly, the Somali were present in the district both inside Rumuruti, to engage in market activities, and outside, to graze their cattle. The settlers wanted to minimise contact between their own cattle and those of the Somali in order to avoid disease.[93] The question of whether to allow the Somali to graze therefore divided the white farmers. Those who had less focus on

86 Lipscomb, *The History of Kenya Agriculture*, p. 62.

87 Anderson and Throup, 'The Agrarian Economy of Central Province, Kenya, 1918–1939,' in *The Economies of Africa and Asia in the Inter-War Depression*, ed. Ian Brown (Abingdon, Oxon: Routledge, 2014); Kanogo, *Squatters and the Roots of Mau Mau*.

88 RH, Africa.mic.515 reel 25, Laikipia and Samburu Annual Report, Hennings, 1945; RH, Africa.mic.515 reel 25, Laikipia Annual Report, Perreau, 1947.

89 Kanogo, *Squatters and the Roots of Mau Mau*; Throup, *Economic and Social Origins of Mau Mau*.

90 Van Zwanenberg, *The Agricultural History of Kenya to 1939*; Throup, *Economic and Social Origins of Mau Mau*.

91 *The Home News*, 'From the Diary of a Senior Citizen, with Kigera Theuri: Apartheid in the White Highlands,' 19–24 August 2004, p. 8.

92 RH, Africa.mic.515 reel 25, Laikipia and Samburu Annual Report, Hennings, 1945.

93 BIEA, Laikipia Farmers Association, 'Minutes from Meetings,' 1923.

livestock or who controlled areas large enough to keep their own livestock securely out of reach of the livestock of the squatters benefited from the grazing arrangements. Nevertheless, in 1937 the former settler group pushed for general limitations and the Laikipia Farmers Association determined that 'no occupier shall allow any native or Somali to reside on his farm with stock, unless he is an attested Resident Labourer.'[94]

The demography of the population in Laikipia's towns was becoming increasingly diverse, with the Kikuyu groups now trying to compete with Indians in trade, transportation and construction businesses. District Commissioner Nimmo said of the Kikuyu that 'the African is becoming more and more experienced in trade and should with industry and honesty become an unwelcome rival to the Asians.'[95]

Turkana, on the other hand, were rarely reported to be involved in trade, but were preferred for manual labour such as the construction of roads, fences and so on by the British.[96] The Turkana remained relatively few in number compared with the Samburu up until the 1970s and 1980s.[97] However, the population numbers from the annual reports might be misleading here, as the narratives on the ground tell of a seasonal Turkana presence already in the 1930s, when insecurity in the Lake Turkana region caused people to migrate.[98] District Commissioner Sharpe said of the Turkana, in an annual report from 1936, that they were:

> the most persistent of the labour employed: he penetrates everywhere, needs a job, knows nothing about the work, but tries hard and becomes good at it. His friends come to join him, then his women and then his dependents old and young and a Turkana village has sprung up.[99]

Here District Commissioner Sharpe points to an immigration pattern particular to the Turkana in that one person's employment meant movement of a whole group of people. As a Turkana elder in Thome explained it: 'if one gets [a job], he brings his whole family even if the settler does not like it.'[100]

94 BIEA, Laikipia Farmers Association, 'Minutes from Meetings,' 22 May 1937.

95 RH, Africa.mic.515 reel 25, Laikipia Annual Report, Nimmo, 1949, p. 7.

96 RH, Africa.mic.515 reel 25, Laikipia and Samburu Annual Report, Sharpe and Atkins, 1935; RH, Africa.mic.515 reel 25, Laikipia Annual Report, Nimmo, 1949.

97 See table 2 and figure 6.

98 Interview with research participant, Rumuruti, 21 January 2015; RH, Africa.mic.515 reel 25, Laikipia Annual Report, Trafford, 1932.

99 RH, Africa.mic.515 reel 25, Laikipia Annual Report, Sharpe, 1936, p. 12.

100 Interview with research participant, Thome, 6 March 2015.

3.3 Independence Politics and the Repercussions of the Mau Mau

The political initiatives in the 1960s were marked by the Mau Mau revolt, and the provision of land for the Kikuyu evolved directly out of a fear of reigniting the revolt. But the emergency years were also instrumental in pointing to the internal differences in the settler community.[101] Settlers in Laikipia, as well as their farm labourers, underwent multiple raids and violence perpetrated by gangs operating north of Thomson's Falls, in Ol Arabel and Marmanet.[102] The colonial government used ethnicity as a tool to administer the African population – suspecting all Kikuyu of being supporters and thereby deserving of receiving punishment. In turn, the Mau Mau supporters enforced their recruiting methods.[103] One third-generation rancher explained that:

> not all were Mau Mau. I have a fellow who works here, and he was born in my grandfather's farm 1948. When he was 4 years old, his mother hung herself because Mau Mau were threatening to kill his father who worked for my grandfather and had a small house in the farm. They also went and threatened his wife. It was a very bad time for them. They were called collaborators. There were Kikuyu who also were not Mau Mau but they were forced into being Mau Mau. They really even didn't know what it was all about.[104]

The emergency fragmented the white settler community, who reacted very differently towards the firm initiatives to run down the rebels. Some of the farmers in Laikipia sought to protect their workers when administrators came to collect them for interrogation and screening.[105] The workers would be brought to one of the screening centres, such as the one in Thomson's Falls, which missionaries referred to as 'the cruelty camp.'[106] Interrogations often involved torture if the interrogators were dissatisfied with the answers given,

---

101 Daniel Branch, *Defeating Mau Mau, Creating Kenya* (Cambridge: Cambridge University Press, 2009).

102 The National Archive, Kew (TNA), FCO 141/5830, 'Laikipia District Intelligence Committees – Summary for Period 13th November to 20th November 1955,' 26 November 1955.

103 David Anderson, *Histories of the Hanged: The Dirty War in Kenya and the End of Empire* (New York and London: W.W. Norton, 2005).

104 Interview with research participant, south-western Laikipia, 6 March 2015.

105 Interview with research participant, south-western Laikipia, 6 March 2015.

106 Caroline Elkins, *Imperial Reckoning: The Untold Story of Britain's Gulag in Kenya* (New York: Henry Holt and Company, 2005), p. 63.

and according to Elkins: 'the screening teams whipped, shot, burned, and mutilated'[107] victims.

However, by no means all settler farmers were sympathetic to their workers, and many feared the Mau Mau attacks. They fired their Kikuyu workers, replacing them with Kalenjin and Turkana labourers.[108] It was generally believed by Kenya's white settlers that brutality was the only way to maintain control. Hence, as Anderson notes: 'Happy Valley, as some liked to call the White Highlands, was always a violent place if you were African.'[109]

3.3.1 *Pre-independence Mobility*

When emergency restrictions were lifted, there was a need to bring labourers back into the Highlands.[110] Specifically, the Executive Committee of the Thomson's Falls District Association agreed to a pilot resettlement scheme returning loyal Kikuyu labour to the district's farms in 1955.[111] Not all settlers supported this development. Despite the shortage of good farm labour, many settlers worried how to distinguish the neutral Kikuyu from the mistrustful ones.[112]

Lonsdale describes the Kikuyu immigration in the following way:

> Many squatters returned to their employment before the end of the Emergency; the settlers, as the legend of the squatter Wamugumu told, could not do without them. […] Indeed, their agrarian war resumed as the military one came to an end and Independence loomed.[113]

Apart from the lack of an alternative, a contributing element in the Kikuyu's willingness to go to Laikipia at this time had to do with the politics of land distribution after the Swynnerton Plan, which had allowed Africans to take part in cash-crop production, assisted by credit facilities and farm planning.[114] Resembling a European-style feudal system, the plan aimed to create 'a landed elite and an agricultural labouring class.'[115]

107 Elkins, *Imperial Reckoning*, p. 66.
108 Interview with research participant, Lorien, 26 May 2015.
109 Anderson, *Histories of the Hanged*, p. 78.
110 Branch, *Defeating Mau Mau, Creating Kenya*, p. 128.
111 TNA, FCO 141/5830, 'Laikipia District Intelligence Committee – Summary for Period 25th August to 9th September 1955,' 14 September 1955.
112 TNA, FCO 141/5830, 'Laikipia District Intelligence Committee – Summary for Period 24th August to 10th September 1955,' 30 September 1955.
113 Berman and Lonsdale, *Unhappy Valley: Conflict in Kenya and Africa* (London: James Currey Ltd, 1992), p. 460.
114 Branch, *Defeating Mau Mau, Creating Kenya*.
115 Branch, *Defeating Mau Mau, Creating Kenya*, p. 121.

In Central Province, these steps benefited the elite among those loyal to the colonial government, which supported them in land seizures and expansion of boundaries for land plots. The Kikuyu elite in particular took advantage of this situation, while suspected Mau Mau supporters, still in detention camps, were unable to protest the reallocation of resources.[116] This early land reform underlined the Kikuyu class system by increasing the wealth of the elite rather than supporting the landless loyalists.[117] Consequently, those who left Central Province to seek labour and land outside of the Kikuyu-dominated areas tended to belong to the lower classes in the Kikuyu clans.[118]

The numbers of landless people on the plateau, and the inherent pressure on unemployment rates, were also increased in part by Turkana squatters, and by Nandi and Kipsigis migrating into Laikipia from the surrounding reserves. Some depended on encroachment on settler farms, while others undertook formalised labour agreements with the farmers.[119]

Political mobilisation to (re)gain access to land in Laikipia increased in the mid-1950s, as Nandi and Luo organised unions and meetings in Thomson's Falls.[120] Witnessing political pressure on colonial governments in many of the other African colonies reinforced the movements in Kenya and created awareness about the significance of political organisation. Also in Kenya, reactions materialised when the pressure from African elites manifested itself in constitutional changes allowing African representation in government. These events motivated the more educated Africans to position themselves strategically in order to strengthen a claim for future political positions and land.[121]

3.3.2 *Transition of Power and Land*

In 1960, the British government passed an Order in Council that ended exclusive rights for Europeans to the White Highlands.[122] The colonial government feared an upsurge of conflicts over land along ethnic lines once the resources

116 Leo, *Land and Class in Kenya*.

117 Branch, *Defeating Mau Mau, Creating Kenya*, p. 126.

118 Berman and Lonsdale, *Unhappy Valley*; Leo, *Land and Class in Kenya*.

119 TNA, FCO 141/5830, 'Laikipia District Intelligence Committee – Summary of Period 16th to 29th October 1955,' 2 November 1955; TNA, FCO 141/5832, 'Laikipia District Intelligence Committee – Summary for Week Ending 13 November 1953,' 17 November 1953.

120 TNA, FCO 141/5830, 'Laikipia District Intelligence Committee – Summary of Period 16th to 29th October 1955,' 2 November 1955; TNA, FCO 141/5833, 'Laikipia District Intelligence Committee – Summary for the Period Ending 28th October 1957,' 1 November 1957.

121 TNA, FCO 141/5833, 'Laikipia District Intelligence Committee – Summary for the Period Ending 28th October 1957,' 1 November 1957.

122 Wasserman, *Politics of Decolonization*; Branch, *Kenya: Between Hope and Despair*.

became available.[123] To avoid this, they employed two strategies for the Independence negotiations: (1) a portrayal of the Nandi as invaders on the land, to give Kikuyu priority access to the former Crown Land, and (2), an amalgamation of political competition and violence.[124]

Another point of worry for the colonial administration immediately after Independence was the realisation that colonisation of Kenya, and the ideal of settler-driven agricultural development, had failed. To avoid losing face, they shifted their strategy to attempt to preserve the colonial system in a new layout of Independence policies.[125] By designing the new political realm to be multiracial, they sought to ensure that decolonisation could be formed according to principles of colonial political economy and that the fruits of colonisation could be maintained.[126]

The practices of the European farmers were often glorified despite the hardship prevalent for many of them. However, the farmers' political opposition to the colonial government remained strong. This was relevant for the colonial government in their efforts to find meaningful transfers of land to Africans.[127] For instance, in comments on the Stamp Mission Report,[128] European farmers were described as confident and aggressive in relation to the offers they were given to induce the transfer of land.[129] Only few were assumed to be cooperative and willing to sell unless the prices were right. The Mission recommended that the British government should provide 'no or very little funds' to buy out European farmers.[130]

Also, minister for agriculture Bruce McKenzie accused the settlers in Laikipia of being absentee landlords, not developing their farms to the benefit of Kenya but instead milking the farms when they were present during the European winter to support their lives in Europe during the summer.[131] Indeed, the economic contribution to colonial Kenya made by the mixed farmers had ever only been adequate to feed the farming labour force and the urban populations – and

123 Charles Hornsby, *Kenya: A History since Independence* (London: I.B. Tauris, 2012).

124 Lynch, *I Say to You.*

125 Colin Leys, *Underdevelopment in Kenya: The Political Economy of Neo-Colonialism, 1964–1971* (Berkeley and Los Angeles: University of California Press, 1975).

126 Wasserman, *Politics of Decolonization*, p. 22.

127 Keith Kyle, *The Politics of the Independence of Kenya* (Basingstoke and New York: Palgrave, 1999); Wasserman, *Politics of Decolonization.*

128 The Stamp Mission Report was set up by the British High Commission to clarify transfers of European farms.

129 Leys, *Underdevelopment in Kenya.*

130 TNA, FCO 142/19007, 'H.C. to Bottomley,' File no. 16.

131 TNA, FCO 141/18962, 'Action Planned on Absentee Landlords,' East African Standard, 22 September 1965.

moreover at inflated prices. Because the farmers had been heavily supported during the colonial period through subsidies and market support, the government's desire to leave a legacy would effectively bolster an agricultural sector that was financially unsustainable at its core.[132] The colonial government had long known about this discrepancy but had agreed to protect the interests of the British citizens who had chosen to settle and invest in Kenya, although doing so contradicted the economic goal of setting up East African manufacturers that could produce for a British market.[133]

On the eve of the end of British rule in Kenya the political landscape was fragmented, and neither the settlers nor the Africans stood as united forces. During the Lancaster House talks,[134] it became clear that the land question and the fate of the white farmers were hindrances to a phase of peaceful transition towards an independent Kenya.[135]

The settlers were divided between those who sympathised with the new African elite, and those who sympathised with the right-wing United Party.[136] Many of the farmers in the Highlands belonged to the latter group. If they could not maintain their landholdings, their future in Kenya would be doubtful. In the middle was the somewhat multi-racially founded New Kenya Party, which in effect was the only realistic collaborator on the side of the settlers for reaching an inclusive agreement.[137]

On the side of the Africans, the budding modern politics was reflected in the relationships between the different ethnically based political movements. They could broadly be categorised into three.[138] The first group were the Kikuyu, who constituted the majority; the second group were the Luo; and the third group included all the remaining smaller ethnic groups, such as the Nandi and the Maasai, who were united in their wish to avoid Kikuyu and Luo dominance.[139] However, with the unification of the Kikuyu and Luo, and agreements on the terms of Independence with the remaining group, a somewhat stable solution seemed to be possible.[140]

132 Wasserman, *Politics of Decolonization*, p. 23.

133 Wasserman, *Politics of Decolonization*.

134 The Lancaster House talks were three meetings in 1960, 1962 and 1963 setting up the frameworks and foundation for Kenya's independence and new constitution; see Kyle, *The Politics of the Independence of Kenya*.

135 Wasserman, *Politics of Decolonization*, p. 17.

136 The United Party was formed in 1959 as a response to the establishment of the more liberal Europeans' New Kenya Party.

137 Wasserman, *Politics of Decolonization*; Kyle, *The Politics of the Independence of Kenya*.

138 Kyle, *The Politics of the Independence of Kenya*, p. 44.

139 Kyle, *The Politics of the Independence of Kenya*.

140 Throup and Hornsby, *Multi-Party Politics in Kenya*; Wasserman, *Politics of Decolonization*; Kyle, *The Politics of the Independence of Kenya*.

3.3.3 *Post-independence Politics*

The end of the white exclusive right to the plateau meant opportunities for Africans to gain access and legal rights to land. But the African population in Kenya was never a unified one, and Laikipia became an ignition site for ethnic tensions.[141] The Kalenjin and Maasai partnered in the political party the Kenya African Democratic Union (kadu), opposing the Kikuyu and their then Luo allies in the Kenya African National Union (kanu). The ethnic first-comer narratives stimulated the political movement in kadu, with Turkana and Samburu arguing for pastoralist control of the Rift Valley and the Highlands based on a version of history in which they had been structurally disregarded in resettlement of these areas. Contrastingly, the kanu narratives built on respect for private-property rights.[142] Political involvement thereby brought the claims to land up from localised disputes and into the political sphere, establishing the foundation for coalitions and oppositions.[143] Nevertheless, the unification remained unstable, as both party structures were founded on the expectation of getting a share in power. In addition, both relied on a few powerful individuals and their ethno-regional supporters.[144]

All groups looked towards national politics for leading figures to support their claims to resources, of which Jomo Kenyatta was the strongest figure. Due to a lack of political awareness among the majority of voters, he managed to gain adequate support to stipulate that land redistribution should be conducted in a manner that respected titles as private property. The perspective of kanu, that land should be acquired through private-property right by willing African buyers, spoke to the British government in that it safeguarded their policies and the remaining European settlers.[145]

Kenyatta's *majimbo* rhetoric,[146] promising power to the people, and his preservation of private-property rights were somewhat contradictory as the devolution of power was limited to certain groups and individuals rather than benefiting all Kenyan citizens. Therefore, many groups did not obtain support for the resolution of their grievances, and the land question remained unresolved.

141 Lynch, 'Negotiating Ethnicity,' pp. 49–65.

142 Hornsby, *Kenya: A History since Independence*; Kanyinga, 'The Legacy of the White Highlands: Land Rights, Ethnicity and the Post-2007 Election Violence in Kenya,' *Journal of Contemporary African Studies* 27, no. 3 (July 2009), pp. 325–44.

143 Throup and Hornsby, *Multi-Party Politics in Kenya*; Kanyinga, 'The Legacy of the White Highlands.'

144 Hornsby, *Kenya: A History since Independence*, p. 61.

145 Branch, *Kenya: Between Hope and Despair*, p. 9.

146 *Majimbo* is a Swahili term referring to devolution of political power to a regional level. As Kenya's political landscape is strongly affected by patrimonialism, Kenyans tend to vote along ethnic lines. Therefore, the *majimbo* rhetoric, with its reference to the transfer of power to the regions, has an air of politicisation and even favouritism.

Instead, Independence spurred new opportunities for resource allocation, encouraging political opportunists to get involved. This was an environment which the new political elite could choose to either take part in or lose out on.[147] Kenyatta-supporting politicians took part in the formation of associations and groups to safeguard the interests of their own ethnic voter base.[148] gema (Gikuyu-Embu-Meru Association) and Mutukanio Farmers Company both bought land in western Laikipia in order to subdivide sections of the land plots among members.[149]

3.3.4 *Land Reform and Resettlement Schemes*

In the Independence years, the government and the settlers worried that staying on European land would attract squatters to occupy their farms. Therefore, the government launched a range of land-purchase programmes and resettlement schemes that specifically focused on settling the Kikuyu.[150] However, Kalenjin were also demanding land in Laikipia, although their claims were made on different grounds than those of the Kikuyu. Theirs were historically founded, as they claimed to have been present in the western parts of the plateau before colonisation.[151]

Land reform was a central feature in the decolonisation process, as a balanced redistribution of land had the potential to secure a peaceful political transition.[152] Yet the first settlement schemes were not designed to address landlessness, and they instead ended up reinforcing existing tensions between groups. At this point, the British government was more worried about securing the vision of the White Highlands, preserving the European large-scale agriculture and ranching by only gradually replacing European farmers with African farmers.[153] This preservation of the colonial ideal was paradoxical given the

---

147 Branch, *Kenya: Between Hope and Despair.*

148 Hornsby, *Kenya: A History since Independence.*

149 Thomas Kohler, *West Laikipia: Report on Small-Scale Farming and How It Could Be Assisted in Development* (Berne: Institute of Geography, University of Berne, 1987); Hornsby, *Kenya: A History since Independence.*

150 Kanyinga, 'The Legacy of the White Highlands,' p. 331.

151 Jacqueline Klopp, 'Can Moral Ethnicity Trump Political Tribalism? The Struggle for Land and Nation in Kenya,' *African Studies* 61, no. 2 (1 December 2002), pp. 269–94; Kanyinga, 'The Legacy of the White Highlands,' p. 331.

152 Gary Wasserman, 'Continuity and Counter-Insurgency: The Role of Land Reform in Decolonizing Kenya, 1962–70,' *Canadian Journal of African Studies/Revue Canadienne Des Études Africaines* 7, no. 1 (1 January 1973), p. 133.

153 P. Pestalozzi, 'Historical and Present Day Agricultural Change on Mt. Kenya,' in *Mount Kenya Area: Contributions to Ecology and Socio-economy*, ed. Matthias Winiger (Berne:

already proven economic failure of the Highlands to become an agricultural production bank.

It was the British government's point of view that the demand for land especially from the Kikuyu and Kalenjin represented a security risk, but that it would be possible to remove the risk if their demand were partly met. Therefore, redistribution of land was designed to be limited to certain parts of the Highlands, enabling the remaining European farmers to stay on their land comfortably and undisturbed.[154]

One strategy to hold at bay the pressure from land hunger was to add restrictions on the procedure for including settler farms in the schemes. For instance, the finance to buy settler farms in each scheme was limited, and they had to be constituted of mixed farming in order to be included.[155] In effect, this made only the very southern settler farms in Laikipia eligible for inclusion in the schemes.

To the extent of limiting Africanisation, the strategies of the British government seemed to work. By 1968, up to 75% of the former Crown Lands were still unaffected by the settlement schemes. The plantations, amounting to 1.5 million acres, were safeguarded on grounds that they were important to export and too costly to convert. The ranches, constituting 2.7 million acres of the Highlands, were maintained on grounds that they were unsuitable for subdivision and that they produced much-needed meat for urban populations.[156]

Another paradox in the design behind the settlement schemes was the terms for evaluating their success. It was an illusion that a European farm would necessarily be more productive if transferred to a large-scale African farmer. There were even indications that transfers made into small-scale plots would give greater yields if they were intensively farmed.[157] That said, it was part of the procedure to measure the size of each plot according to ecological factors, as farms in the northern and southern parts of Laikipia could not be evaluated under equal terms. The schemes' limitation to only include mixed-farming land put the European farmers in the northern parts of Laikipia in a compromised position that made it difficult for them to sell their farms and

Geographica Bernesia, 1986); Wasserman, 'Continuity and Counter-Insurgency,' pp. 133–48.

154 Wasserman, 'Continuity and Counter-Insurgency.'

155 Christopher Leo, 'Who Benefited from the Million-Acre Scheme? Towards a Class Analysis of Kenya's Transition to Independence,' *Canadian Journal of African Studies/Revue Canadienne Des Études Africaines* 15, no. 2 (1 January 1981), pp. 201–22.

156 Wasserman, 'Continuity and Counter-Insurgency,' p. 134.

157 Wasserman, *Politics of Decolonization.*

leave the country.[158] Furthermore, the way many of the settlement schemes were designed did not fit the reality of how the smallholders could and would manage their land.

Concurrently, many smallholder farmers relocated, hopeful that acquiring their own land could transform their disenfranchised situations, only to find themselves faced with a long list of regulations requiring them to 'plant, harvest, and tend their stock according to officials' instructions, and limiting their rights to accumulate wealth.'[159] In several of the schemes the smallholders lacked the essential farming skills to be able to make a profit from farming. They consequently became unable to follow the strict plan of repayment for the loans they had taken when they became shareholders.[160] Although many of the new structures around land transfers included training, these initiatives were inadequate, of poor quality or lacking in consideration for small-scale farming procedures. Nevertheless, the inadequacy of training did not change the repayment requirements, and many shareholders were forced to subdivide and sell parts of their farmland in order to meet a deadline for repayment. Consequently, many ended up deeply indebted.[161] An administrator for resettlement schemes in Laikipia notes in the handing-over report to his successor that:

> The [Marmanet] scheme has not had the title map finalized. It is situated in a fertile area. Loan repayment is not as good as expected. […] The [Lariak and Ol Arabel] schemes have had similar problems. Almost all animals given to them on loan by S.F.T. [Settlement Fund Trustees] died of tick borne diseases. […] The co-op society of the two schemes 'Ngarachi' failed to function for a long period causing disorganisation among the farmers. […] I understand that the settlement of this [Marmanet Forest Scheme] was hastily done. Proper demarcation of plots had not been completed hence [there are] numerous boundary disputes.[162]

158 TNA, FCO 141/19572, 'Minutes of Meeting between Dykes and Godley,' 20 August 1975.

159 Berry, 'Debating the Land Question in Africa,' p. 647.

160 Leo, *Land and Class in Kenya*; TNA, FCO 141/18961, 'Repayment of Loans Made by the Settlement Fund Trustees,' File no. 4.

161 Kenya National Archives, Provincial Deposit Nakuru (KNA Nakuru), DSW/1/1. File no. DSO/LKA/13/Vol I/4, 1981; TNA, FCO 141/18961, 'Repayment of Loans Made by the Settlement Fund Trustees,' File no. 4.

162 KNA Nakuru, DSO/LKA/13/H&T/13, 'Brief Handout Notes on Settlement Schemes in Laikipia District,' 18 November 1981.

In other resettlement schemes, such as the Nyandarua Scheme, the shareholders were required to pay with work on common farming areas within the purchased farmland. This design was an example of how the British government's retention of large-scale farming could be materialised as part and parcel of resettlement.[163] However, this collectivist design did not fit well with shareholders who thought little of the common returns and were more preoccupied with investing their time in their own shares of farmland. Ultimately, the common farming areas quickly turned uneconomical and unproductive.[164]

The sudden possibility for Africans to gain rights and access to formerly restricted lands led to the mobilisation of considerable funds, leading people to become innovative in their land-acquisition strategies. Kenyans, and in particular Kikuyu, of lesser wealth, who were unable to gather enough capital on their own, pooled their funds and bought plots of land as groups through established land-buying companies.[165]

Other wealthier figures were restricted by the design of the schemes, targeted as they were at landless Kenyans.[166] Consequently, various high-profile political figures found their way into the schemes with misuse of funds and opaque transactions.[167] Mr Angaine, minister for land and settlement, addressed this issue in Nyahururu on 27 January 1968 after a trip around Laikipia. The *East African Standard* reports:

> Referring to previous schemes, the Minister warned families who had deceived his Ministry and managed to obtain more than two plots in a single settlement scheme.[168]

The most expansive of the schemes was the Million Acre Scheme, funded by the British and German governments. It aimed to provide each African farmer with a net yearly income of between £25 and £70.[169] It was initiated right before Independence in 1961 and was finalised towards the end of the 1970s. In

163 Wasserman, 'Continuity and Counter-Insurgency,' pp. 133–48.

164 KNA Nakuru, DSO/LKA/13/H&T/13, 'Brief Handout Notes on Settlement Schemes in Laikipia District,' 18 November 1981; TNA, FCO 141/18961, 'Repayment of Loans Made by the Settlement Fund Trustees,' File no. 4.

165 TNA, FCO 141/18966, 'Kenya Land Development and Settlement Report on Visit of July 1965 by T.A. Phillips.'

166 Leo, *Land and Class in Kenya.*

167 TNA, FCO 141/18960, 'Brockett to Wootton,' 11 February 1966.

168 TNA, FCO 141/19014, 'Minister's Warning to Settlers,' 27 January 1968.

169 TNA, FCO 141/19007, 'Kenya Land Purchase and Central Development,' 19 November 1965.

Laikipia, the areas included were again the high-density areas in the south of the plateau.[170] The expansive scheme designated one million acres (about 400,000 hectares) of land for Africanisation. Large blocks of land were purchased specifically on the margins of existing African areas. However, for the Million Acre Scheme as opposed to other resettlement schemes, the quality standards for ensuring potential income generation were lowered. This made the scheme costly and locked many smallholders into debt, unable to make the land productive.[171]

Specifically, the land planned for inclusion in the scheme was of poor quality and the amount was not extensive enough to adequately accommodate the landless people. Although the Million Acre Scheme settled 35,000 families, that number is at odds with the annual population growth in Laikipia. In the Mount Kenya region alone, in the 1970s the population grew by 35,000 people. So the land-transfer programmes did little to reduce the pressure on land access. In contrast, the inadequacy of land further increased the pressure on the Kenyan government. Indeed, even though the Million Acre Scheme was promoted as benefiting the landless, its main purpose was to settle as many smallholders as possible so as to remove pressure from the large-scale farms and ranches.[172]

In addition, the scheme's Africanisation design bypassed the landless, as only those able to pay the 10% deposit were able to secure the right to the bigger and better plots of land.[173] This added an ethnic and class-based bias to the scheme by favouring the already wealthy and resourceful Kikuyu.[174] The smaller and poorer plots of land went to those who had formerly been landless or who were of a lower economic class. But they were not necessarily advanced by the schemes. Rather, as with many other resettlement schemes, many of these people also ended up in poverty traps, unable to pay off their debts.[175]

Some European settlers could use the Million Acre Scheme to their advantage in the selling of their land, for instance by forcing exaggerated valuations of their farm plots.[176] Where the land was considered ideal for inclusion in a resettlement scheme but the settlers were unwilling to sell at the market valuation, many were offered a price settled by a second, increased valuation.[177]

170 Leo, *Land and Class in Kenya*.

171 Leo, *Land and Class in Kenya*, pp. 97–101.

172 Leo, *Land and Class in Kenya*, p. 112.

173 C.P.R. Nottidge and J.R. Goldsack, *The Million-Acre Settlement Scheme 1962–1966* (Nairobi: Settlement Department, 1966).

174 Leo, 'Who Benefited from the Million-Acre Scheme?'

175 Leo, *Land and Class in Kenya*; Leys, *Underdevelopment in Kenya*.

176 Reuters, 'Britain Rejects Kenya Loans Idea,' *The Daily Nation*, 29 July 1967.

177 Leys, *Underdevelopment in Kenya*.

The average prices for buying and selling land within the schemes favoured Europeans and others who already owned land and encouraged them to speculate. The land sales were financed by the World Bank's 'Settlement Transfer Funds Scheme,' which made it possible for many of the white settlers to leave the tension-laden plateau with a profit and even to bring this profit out of the country.[178]

Many settlers, especially in the eastern parts, chose to remain in Laikipia. The eastern part of Laikipia had better infrastructure than the west, and Nanyuki, with a more vibrant social life, attracted more settlers than Nyahururu did. Moreover, many of the settlers in the west had immigrated from South Africa following the Boer war. These settlers tended to be more critical towards an African government and were therefore more willing to sell and leave after Independence.[179]

With many Africans unable to acquire land through the public resettlement schemes and multiple settler ranches deemed unsuitable for inclusion in the schemes, alternatives for linking willing buyers and willing sellers started to emerge. Few African buyers had the means to acquire the former ranches single-handedly at their designated sizes. However, by constituting cooperatives or land-buying companies, they could pool adequate funds to buy a ranch. This explains why most of the land in Laikipia was bought collectively rather than individually.

Figure 4 provides an example of the changing land use and land ownership of a land plot in eastern Laikipia, which gives an impression of the transition from land-use homogeneity to land-use fragmentation. In 1960–61 the plot was owned by one European and used as a ranch and large-scale farm. In 1982–83 a land-buying company had subdivided the plot and the land had come under African ownership to be cultivated as small-scale mixed farming.[180]

As the white plots in the map of 1982–83 illustrate, many chose to leave their plot in Laikipia. However, reasons for leaving were manifold. The wealthier shareholders who had acquired inclusion in the schemes had mainly bought for investment purposes and already owned land elsewhere.[181] Others had tried to settle and cultivate but had given up when they realised that their hard

178 Wasserman, *Politics of Decolonization*.

179 Interview with research participant, northern Laikipia, 24 July 2015.

180 Adapted from Bodleian Libraries, University of Oxford. *Erdkunde*, 'Laikipia District Kenya: Map 2. Changing Land Use and Land Ownership: The Example of Ngenia (Upepo),' G. Per 86. Pub. (Bonn: Dümmlers Verlag, 1988).

181 *The Daily Nation*, 'Inquiry Urged into Ownership of Plots,' 16 December 1967.

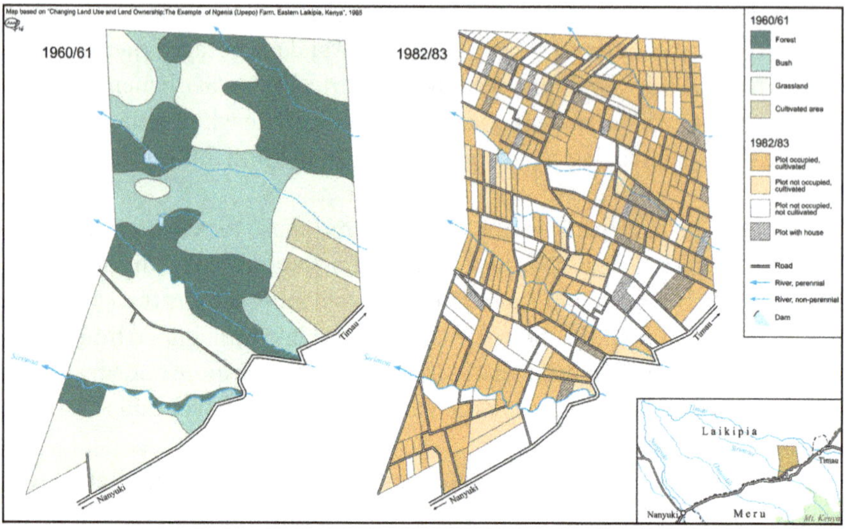

FIGURE 4 Changing land use and land ownership of Ngenia farm in Laikipia East. © Monika Feinen 2016

work was not paying off.[182] Nevertheless, few sold their land again. As a shareholder in Ol Moran explains, 'that is what Kenyatta had advised us.'[183]

3.4 Post-colonial Land: Times of Autochthony

Land distribution continued to dominate the debate in the decades following Independence. As a site for competition between ethnic groups, the highlands held a growing potential to be exploited politically. Land access gained autochthonous connotations, with the narratives of historical presence of one group set against the narratives of others. Many ethnic groups had held a marginal historic presence in Laikipia, which nonetheless could be inflated into autochthonous narratives that came to constitute important components in claims to land.

Across Laikipia, the narratives of autochthony became part of everyday rhetoric through sayings such as '*Laikipia ni yetu*' ('Laikipia is ours').[184] As such,

182 Field notes, Rumuruti, 21 August 2015.
183 Interview with research participant, Ol Moran, 2 July 2015.
184 Field notes, conversation with research participant, Nyahururu, 2 June 2015; interview with deputy county commissioner, Laikipia West Subcounty, Wilfred Kinyua, Rumuruti, 15 July 2015.

the anxiety to take part in the land rush was tied just as much to class, ethnicity and politics as it was to greed. As such, a rhetoric based on autochthonous claims was a means to an end, as Klopp notes:

> Kenya's violent ethnic barons continue to [...] move between being 'ethnic chiefs' in rural areas, speaking the language of 'custom' over land and threatening violence against 'outsiders' to using liberal rhetoric and portraying themselves as protectors of 'private-property rights' to facilitate their own accumulation.[185]

The diversity of people taking part in the Laikipia land rush was extensive enough to become visible in the way the landscapes transformed. Many of the land-buying companies were composed along ethnic lines, shaping a patchy landscape. The Kikuyu would fence and cultivate the land in these small sections, whereas the Kalenjin land would typically look like grazing areas with minor cultivation. Even today, as islands of enclosures, these areas stand in sharp contrast to the remaining ranches and conservancies in the landscape.[186]

3.4.1 *Immigration and Land-use Fragmentation*

The migration into Laikipia came from mainly Kikuyu-dominated areas such as Nakuru, Nyandarua and Nyeri. This is illustrated in figure 5, showing an overview of the gross immigration to Laikipia for the year August 1978 to August 1979.[187] But there was also considerable migration from Meru and Samburu districts. Comparatively, there was little to no immigration from the coastal districts and Western Province.

There is a slight bias in using these figures to estimate the proportion of immigrants from different ethnic communities in Laikipia. A survey in the early 1980s among smallholder immigrants in Laikipia illustrated an inconsistency between the place of birth and the place of previous residence. Where 81% would state their place of birth as Nyeri, Kiambu or another Kikuyu-dominated area, less than half would state the same place as their previous place of residence.[188] So, as many already resided outside their home areas before settling in Laikipia, the process of settling on one's own farming land was often gradual

185 Klopp, 'Can Moral Ethnicity Trump Political Tribalism?,' p. 287.

186 Field notes, Conversation with research participant, Nyahururu, 2 March 2015.

187 Adapted from Bodleian Libraries, University of Oxford. *Erdkunde*, 'International Structure of Gross Migration (in or Out) & Migration Balance of District,' G. Per 86. Ferd. (Bonn: Dümmler Verlag, September 1978).

188 Kohler, *Land Use in Transition.*

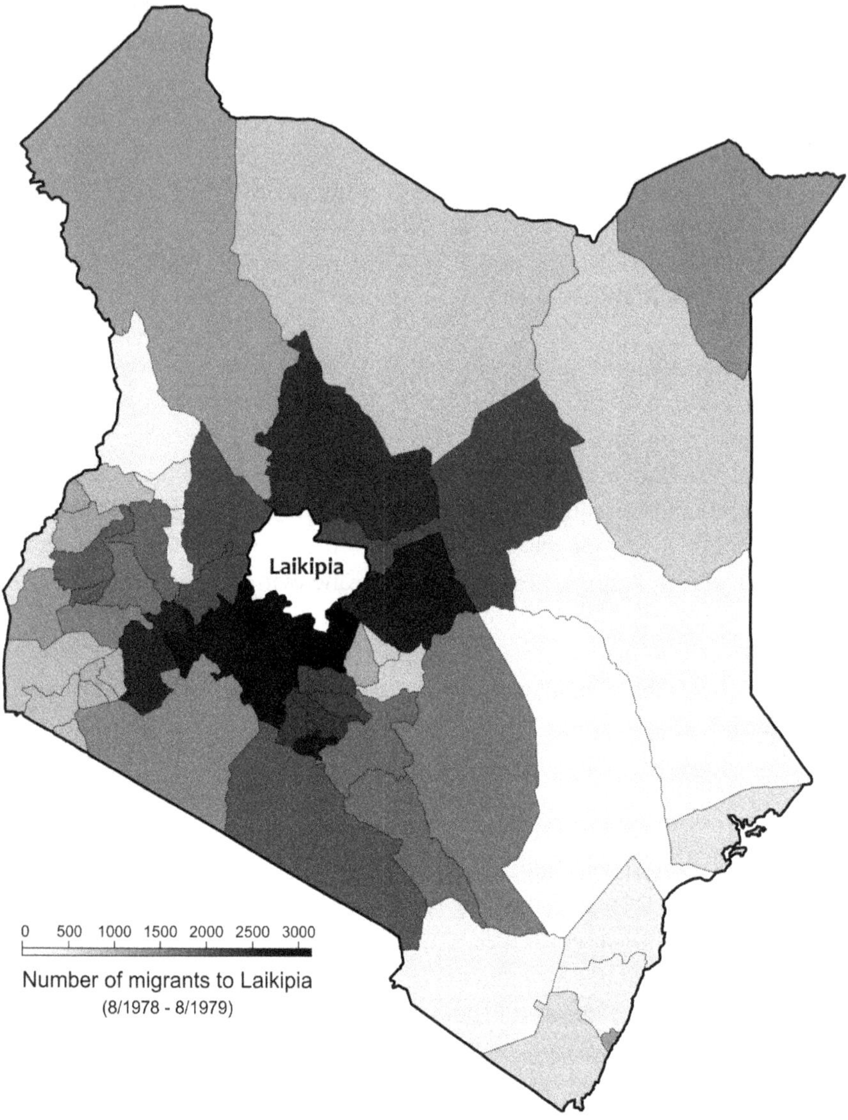

FIGURE 5 Migration to Laikipia in 1978–79.
© Monika Feinen 2016

and lengthy. It may also have increased the pressure on land acquisition and supported the ideology which saw the many Kenyans as 'land hungry.'[189]

189 Yvan Droz and G.L. Sottas, 'Partir Ou Rester ? Partir et Rester: Migrations Des Kikuyu Au Kenya,' *L'Homme* 37, no. 142 (1 April 1997), pp. 69–88; Kohler, *Land Use in Transition*.

The discrepancies between previous residence and place of birth aside, the Kikuyu in Laikipia remained the majority. Table 2 and figure 6 show a similar development of the ethnic population. In just 20 years, from 1969 to 1989, the numbers of Kikuyu residents in Laikipia went from 38,223 to 146,607. As for the increase in the Turkana population, although certain numbers had settled in the district already in the 1930s, another wave of immigrants came after 1974, following drought and insecurity in Turkana District. Additionally, the Moi government was in need of political support in Laikipia, so by assisting the Turkana settlement it secured a new voter base. [191]

TABLE 2 Ethnic composition of population numbers in Laikipia District for the years 1934, 1969, 1979 and 1989[190]

Ethnic groups	1934 (from Table 1)	1969	1979	1989
Kikuyu	7,642	38,223	86,603	146,607
Europeans (Kenyans)	379	431	272	211
Dorobo/Maasai	474	8,440	10,116	11,821
Kalenjin	88	7,406	11,795	15,690
Turkana	24[a]	4,277	9,568	14,396
Samburu	24[a]	701	2317	3996
Others	249	7,028	13,856	26,236
Total population	8,880	66,506	134,524	218,957

a Numbers for the Turkana and Samburu populations are amassed to 48 for the 1934 census.

What is also significant, from these numbers, is the absence of large-scale immigration from Samburu areas. Although it was growing in the 1980s, there

190 Republic of Kenya, *Kenya Population Census 1969*. Volume I. Statistics Division Ministry of Economic Planning and Development (Nairobi: Government Printer, 1970); Republic of Kenya, *Kenya Population Census 1979*. Volume I. Central Bureau of Statistics (Nairobi: Government Printer, 1981); Republic of *Kenya, Kenya Population Census 1989*. Volume I. Central Bureau of Statistics (Nairobi: Government Printer, 1994). All http://www.knbs.or.ke/index.php?option=com_phocadownload&view=category&id=100:population-and-housing-census&Itemid=1176, accessed 16 February 2015.

191 Interview with research participant, Rumuruti, 3 August 2015.

was no vast influx before 1989. This picture was seconded by oral accounts stating that extensive settlement only took place in the early 1990s.[192]

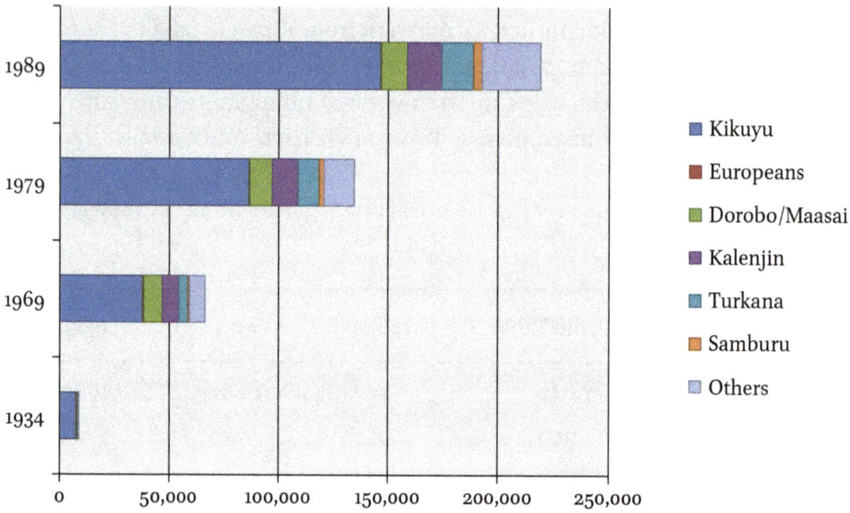

FIGURE 6 Ethnic Composition of population in Laikipia District in quota for the years 1934, 1969, 1979 and 1989

The Kenya National Bureau of Statistics stopped including the ethnic distribution of each county's population after 1989 due to politicisation.[193] In particular, what would have been interesting to see from such census data is the changing distribution of Samburu and Turkana in Laikipia between the 1990s and the present day, wherein they have become numerous enough to challenge the Kikuyu for certain political positions at the subcounty level.[194]

The Kikuyu continued to own most of the land that was under African ownership and assumed power over local government institutions. By 2004 there had been 418 schemes put in place, of which 154 were in Rift Valley Province alone. Out of the 154 schemes, one third were established in Laikipia and Nakuru districts, the largest Kikuyu immigration areas of the former White Highlands.[195]

192 Interview with research participant, Thome, 18 June 2015; interview with research participant, Thome, 26 July 2015; interview with research participant, Nanyuki, 24 August 2015.
193 Interview with KNBS, Nanyuki, 24 August 2015.
194 Interview with DCC Wilfred Kinyua, Rumuruti, 15 July 2015.
195 Kanyinga, 'The Legacy of the White Highlands.'

Looking at figure 7 from 1982,[196] the landscape comprised a remarkable variation in type, from government land, private large-scale horticultural farming, absentee land and ranching, to group farms, land occupations, pastoralism and small-scale farming on subdivided land plots. What is also evident from figure 7 is the substantial representation of land bought by private land-buying companies to be subdivided for small-scale farms.

There is an overrepresentation of private cooperatives in the southern and western parts of Laikipia, along with government settlement schemes. The distribution difference illustrates the relatively low acreage included in public

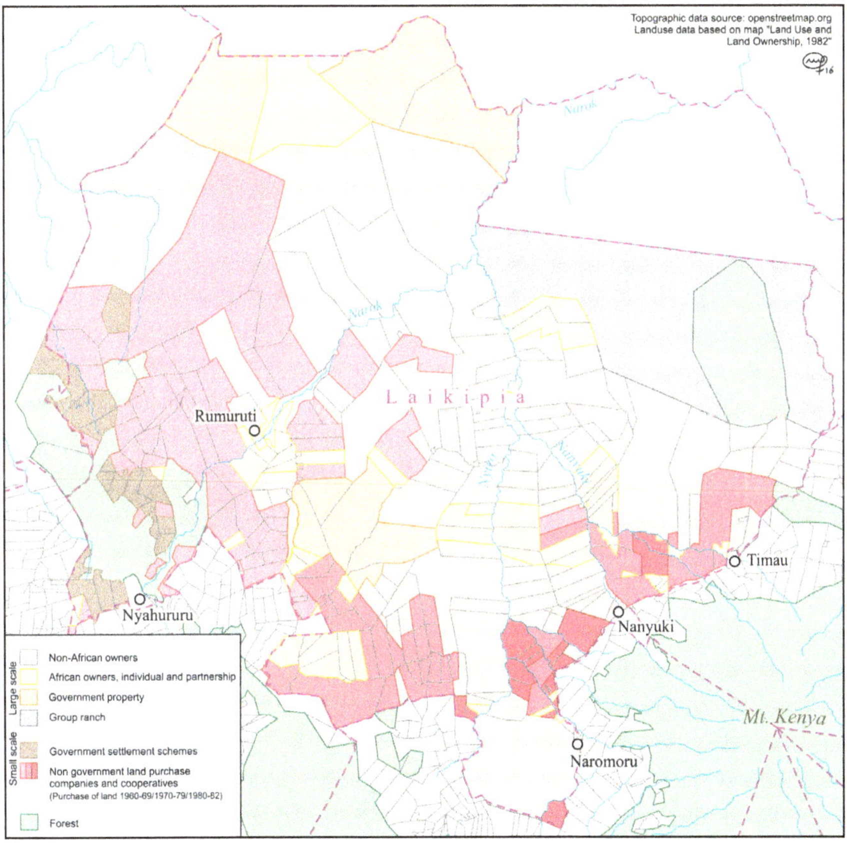

FIGURE 7 Land use in Laikipia in 1982.
© Monika Feinen 2016

196 Adapted from Bodleian Libraries, University of Oxford. *Erdkunde*, 'Laikipia District, Kenya: Map 1. Land Use and Land Ownership, 1982,' G. Per 86. Pub. (Bonn: Dümmlers Verlag, 1988).

land reform compared with the apparent demand for land released through private cooperative land. This also shows people's inventiveness in land acquisition. Two other factors are illustrated in figure 7. Firstly, the land under individual African ownership, comprising more acreage than the government settlement schemes, represents areas held by the Kenyan elite. Secondly, the manifold light brown areas point to the continuous presence of people of European descent. In that respect, the ideal of the British government of preserving parts of the White Highlands as white has endured.

3.4.2 *Violence and Political Instrumentalism*

The frustration at the inadequacy of the settlement schemes was central to local politics from the early 1960s onwards. Over time, the weight of the grievances steadily grew, only to turn violent in the 1990s with the political instrumentalism of the reintroduced multi-party system.[197]

One of President Moi's arguments for holding on to a system of one-party rule was that the nation would succumb to ethnic violence with a reintroduced multi-party system. Looking at the events leading up to the 1990s, and particularly those around the first reintroduced multi-party election in 1992, Moi was arguably right in his prediction.[198] Violent clashes between ethnic groups erupted widely across the country, with the government provoking the clashes for political purposes rather than attempting to control the riots. This type of top-down governance system was characteristic of the Moi era, during which opposition to the government was dealt with ruthlessly. Press freedom was inhibited, academics were oppressed and the only way to become politically successful was to exercise complete loyalty to the president.[199]

The effect was increased animosity between ethnic groups. Specifically for the former White Highlands, clashes occurred between members of Moi's own ethnic group, the Kalenjin, and opposition Kikuyu groups.[200] These uprisings were planned, and the Kalenjin perpetrators had been trained, armed and

197 Anderson and Lochery, 'Violence and Exodus in Kenya's Rift Valley, 2008: Predictable and Preventable?' *Journal of Eastern African Studies* 2, no. 2 (2008), p. 338.

198 Human Rights Watch (HRW), *Divide and Rule: State-Sponsored Ethnic Violence in Kenya* (New York: HRW, 1993), https://www.hrw.org/report/1993/11/01/divide-and-rule-state-sponsored-ethnic-violence-kenya, accessed 11 July 2020; HRW, *Multipartyism Betrayed in Kenya: Continuing Rural Violence and Restrictions on Freedom of Speech and Assembly*, vol. 6, no. 5, (July 1994), https://www.hrw.org/report/1994/07/01/multipartyism-betrayed-kenya/continuing-rural-violence-and-restrictions-freedom, accessed 11 July 2020.

199 Hornsby, *Kenya: A History since Independence*, p. 398.

200 HRW, *Divide and Rule.*

sponsored by government officials.[201] For instance, the *Daily Nation* portrays one of the incidences:

> On February 21, there was a raid by approximately fifty Kalenjins on Kianjogu village in Laikipia District. The attack resulted in several injured and the death of one Kikuyu villager, Kuria Njoroge, as well as the burning of four houses. The victims of the attack reported that their attackers identified themselves as 'tribal executioners who will return soon to finish all of you.'[202]

During the Moi presidency, several initiatives were taken to accommodate autochthony-based narratives. For instance, councils of elders were given a say in the resolution of land conflicts, but as they did not receive salaries they were often open to corruption and became guardians of the wealthy people's land appropriations. In effect, this made local government weak and inefficient.[203] Similarly to many other places on the continent in the 1980s, Kenya's economy was weakening along with popular support for state institutions. Here, the positions of politicians, military officers and civil servants came under threat from rivals, making many prone to weighing personal over national interests and practising the 'politics of the belly.'[204]

The Kalenjin started to mobilise political supporters by building into their narratives how the first government after Independence had favoured the Kikuyu squatters over the Kalenjin. Using historical rhetoric similar to that of the 1960s, they argued for taking back the land in the highlands from the Kikuyu, whom they considered new colonial settlers.[205] Opposers of this rhetoric were subjected to punishment for sympathising with settlers and foreigners.[206] A pattern of mobilisation similar to the 1992 violence, with economic ties to local politicians, surfaced following the 1997 elections as well as in more recent political events, where especially Kikuyu smallholders were victims of Kalenjin violence.[207]

It was not only Kalenjin who were mobilising. The presence of the Samburu in Laikipia had increased since the early 1990s. Incited by a political rhetoric of

201 HRW, *Divide and Rule.*
202 *The Daily Nation*, 'Evicted Group in Plea,' 19 February 1994.
203 Jacqueline Klopp, 'Electoral Despotism in Kenya: Land, Patronage and Resistance in the Multi-Party Context' (PhD diss., McGill University, 2001).
204 Berry, 'Debating the Land Question in Africa,' p. 651.
205 HRW, *Divide and Rule.*
206 Hornsby, *Kenya: A History since Independence.*
207 Kanyinga, 'The Legacy of the White Highlands.'

'claiming back the plateau,' they moved south from Samburu District, especially into the western parts of Laikipia, where they entered seemingly vacant areas.[208] After several devastating droughts and livestock diseases, they gradually moved more permanently into Laikipia.[209] Many of the Samburu who came from Suguta Mar Mar first gathered and settled close to Ol Moran, where many Pokot had also settled after moving south from Lonyiek.[210] For decades, the Pokot had been settled in Lonyiek, and several sources indicate that no Pokot had traversed further onto the plateau than Lonyiek as long as the settlers had been there.[211] However, the Pokot themselves claim to have accessed the plateau seasonally even before colonial times and that they were present together with the Maasai.[212]

Despite a constant level of tension between the Samburu and the Pokot, there have also been examples of collaboration. After President Moi announced his victory in the election and was sworn into office for yet another term, demonstrations, clashes and acts of violence broke out in several parts of the country. In Ol Moran in January 1998, violent confrontations set Samburu and Pokot against Kikuyu farmers, followed by a series of revenge attacks. By the end of January, '19 victims were buried in a mass grave in the Sipili area. The final number of people killed stood at 57, one Turkana, one Pokot and 55 Kikuyu, while 5,000 people had fled their homes.'[213] The Akiwumi report states:

> The raiders were well organized and coordinated. Their attacks were generally under the cover of darkness, and where the attacks were in broad daylight, the raiders would smear their faces with clay to conceal their identities. [...] The attacks were barbaric, callous and calculated to drive out the targeted groups from their farms, to cripple them economically and to psychologically traumatise them.[214]

Also prevalent in the clashes was an absence of action being taken by the police and the Kikuyu-led local government in Rumuruti. The Akiwumi report

208 Interview with research participant, Nyahururu, 21 March 2016.
209 Interview with research participant, Thome, 24 June 2015.
210 Group mapping, Thome, 27 July 2015.
211 Interview with research participant, northern Laikipia, July 24, 2015; interview with research participant, Nanyuki, 16 August 2016.
212 Interview with research participant, Ol Moran, 21 July 2015.
213 Rutten, 'Fresh Killings,' p. 539.
214 Hon. Justice A.M. Akuwumi, *Report of the Judicial Commission Appointed to Inquire into Tribal Clashes in Kenya* (Nairobi: Government Printer, 2001), p. 2, https://digitalcommons.law.seattleu.edu/cgi/viewcontent.cgi?article=1009&context=tjrc-gov, accessed 11 July 2020.

problematises several testimonies given by local officials of having observed suspicious activities while still abstaining from taking action in support of people on the side of the Samburu and the Pokot.[215] Although the Akiwumi report goes further into the politics of land-related conflicts in Laikipia than other investigative commissions, it remains speculative regarding the underlying causes of the hostility and the links to the reintroduced multi-party system.

Yet another relevant product of the history of ethnic tensions in Laikipia is the Mungiki movement. The violent Kikuyu movement, whose founder, Maina Njenga, originated from Sipili in western Laikipia, mobilised in the last part of Moi's reign. Built on Gikuyu traditionalism, Mungiki is considered a revival of the Mau Mau rebellion from the 1950s.[216] Since its founding in the late 1980s, Mungiki has been classified as a new religious movement, a political militia, a social movement, a criminal gang and even an occult sect.[217] It is accused of having been involved in political violence in the elections of 1997, 2002 and 2007. This either took the form of violent intimidation prior to elections or of retaliatory attacks in post-election violence.[218] Moreover, the movement's retaliatory and revenge attacks are suspected to be financed by political actors; their effects include multiple interethnic clashes throughout the 2000s.[219] Mungiki fighters likely also took part in the clashes in Ol Moran in 1998, since it neighbours their Kikuyu-dominated base in Sipili.[220]

There are multiple other examples of clashes and hostility across Laikipia in the 1990s. Many of these had Kikuyu on one side, although clashes can also be attributed to raids either between pastoralist groups or between landowners and pastoralists. Common to most of the tensions was the reinforcing of ties between land, ethnicity and politics. Since then, implications include lengthy casework to determine rightful landowners, and systematic avoidance of land matters by politicians and land commissions up until today. Ultimately, the myriad cases and conflicts illustrate how ethnicity-based fights for resources

215 Akuwumi, *Report of the Judicial Commission Appointed to Inquire into Tribal Clashes in Kenya*.

216 David Anderson, 'Vigilantes, Violence and the Politics of Public Order in Kenya,' *African Affairs* 101, no. 405 (1 October 2002), p. 535.

217 Jacob Rasmussen, 'Outwitting the Professor of Politics? Mungiki Narratives of Political Deception and Their Role in Kenyan Politics,' *Journal of Eastern African Studies* 4, no. 3 (1 November 2010), pp. 435–49.

218 Rasmussen, 'Outwitting the Professor of Politics?,' p. 437.

219 Kanyinga, 'The Legacy of the White Highlands.'

220 Interview with research participant, Ol Moran, 2 July 2015.

and territories have been among the most enduring determinants of how colonial and post-colonial Kenyan history has played out.

3.5 Concluding Remarks

Compared with Thomson's descriptions from 1883, the landscape has transformed from one of social mobility into one characterised by boundaries – boundaries between ethnic groups and classes, comprising a socially diverse map. Other types of boundaries are those between the land plots of former colonial demarcation, as illustrated in figure 7. Each land demarcation has been subdivided into smallholder farming areas, transferred into individual large-scale farms for the Kenyan elite, redesigned as conservancies, or maintained as ranches or large-scale farms under the ownership of European descendants. Consequently, colonisation affected social-ecological relations in three major ways: through displacement; separation through territorial and social categorisation; and the reinstitution of a governance regime determining access, transfer and use of land.[221]

Around the turn of the century, groups adapted their livelihoods to fit ecological conditions, and boundaries were physically negotiated. Despite exchange relations, Laikipia was dominated by a few ethnic groups. In the 1930s, although Kikuyu were the majority, the plateau remained under tight political and administrative control by the minority representing the colonial power and the white farmers. The colonial government insisted on clear-cut geographical, social and legal boundaries, including social categorisation. The land question was formed and solidified partly through the British government's preoccupation with its colonial legacy and the appeasement of the Kikuyu, and partly through the independent Kenyan state's enforcement of class distinctions that favoured the elite. Moreover, waves of violent events in the 1990s illustrate how ethnic categories had become negotiation sites for access to power and resources.[222]

The landscape has transformed into a place where ethnic politics, autochthony-based claims and reconstructions of history determine land distribution and control of resources.[223] It has become a system that holds immobility and control as the ideal – both physically, with fencing, and legally, with

221 Berry, 'Debating the Land Question in Africa,' p. 643.

222 Lotte Hughes, 'Rough Time in Paradise: Claims, Blames and Memory Making Around Some Protected Areas in Kenya,' *Conservation and Society* 5, no. 3 (2007), pp. 307–30.

223 Hughes, 'Rough Time in Paradise.'

administrative regulation.[224] Claims to land are associated with customary laws via narratives of belonging, and statutory law has become subject to ambiguity and interpretation. Strategic presence in the landscape is used to support claims. This is the case for both the pastoralists, who settle on non-occupied land, and the lower-class Kikuyu, organising into groups to enhance their position.

This macro perspective has introduced the dynamics of the social-ecological landscape of Laikipia, with its tension-laden links between land, ethnicity and politics. It illustrates how politics implemented in the 1930s had repercussions for the formation of autochthony-based claims to resources in the 1990s. This macro perspective provides a wider temporal context for how individuals and groups have navigated resources in Laikipia in recent years – connections and correlations that the following chapter explores.

224 Jeremy Lind and John Letai, 'Squeezed From All Sides: Changing Resource Tenure and Pastoralist Innovation on the Laikipia Plateau, Kenya,' in *Pastoralism and Development in Africa: Dynamic Change at the Margins*, ed. Andy Catly, Jeremy Lind and Ian Scoones (Abingdon, Oxon, and New York: Routledge, 2013).

CHAPTER 4

Blaming the Others: Ethnic Identity and Claim-making

> Stories are an important oral manifestation of a local discourse seeking to define and claim 'local' resources. They serve to bolster people's confidence in their own claims.
>
> LOUISE FORTMANN[1]

As laid out in the previous chapter, Laikipia's past bears crucial importance for its present. Thus, many present-day constraints that complicate land use and land redistribution are not new, but rather carry a much longer history of endurance than might first appear to be the case when listening to people's stories. The formation of a claim to resources can often have political connotations, illustrated through narratives that support the presence of an individual or group. Each such individual or group draws on different versions of the past for legitimacy.[2] Therefore, the general history and what actually took place is one thing, as the previous chapter demonstrates. But what different groups believe to have happened is quite another.[3] The political layers of the narratives demonstrate the power and saliency of what created them, and bear reference to similar contexts elsewhere on the continent. In this chapter, I explore the interlinkage between claims and stories in Laikipia, to point to the larger patterns in the use of claims as strategies for acquiring access to land.

I look into the interethnic dynamics in Kenya in the 1930s, as this time period marks an increasing politicisation, during which ethnicity-based claim-making stories first extended into violence. Relevantly, this time mirrors post-colonial Kenya, illustrated in a case study. This allows for an analysis to pinpoint the embedded nature of how each group perceives and voices its place in the world.

1 Fortmann, 'Talking Claims,' p. 1054.

2 Lynch, 'Negotiating Ethnicity,' pp. 49–65.

3 Oucho, *Undercurrents of Ethnic Conflicts in Kenya*.

 | DOI:10.1163/9789004435209_005

To circumvent a de facto ethnicity-based categorisation, I loosely divide groups according to land use and political attitude. I refer to 'the absentees' to describe absentee landlords and absentee livestock owners. Constrained by few limiting factors, they are the resourceful outsiders in the Laikipia landscape, seeking to gain individually. Another group category is 'the smallholders.' Despite being the majority, their lives are bound by uncertainty and depend on decisions made by others. 'The pastoralists' hold strong internal ties but are often opposed to practices and regulations from the outside. 'The conservationists' stand for the protection of biodiversity. Their estates are scattered across the landscape, challenging their necessary collaboration. Finally, 'the ranchers' tend to not get involved with the other groups and would rather fence off their estates to focus on their own lives and ranching businesses.

Each group shapes its version of history to fit a story supporting its claim of presence in Laikipia. At times, these narratives are supported by physical manifestations of the claims, such as raids, illegal grazing, forced settlements and titling of land. I examine this wide variety of storied claims to understand what is at stake for each group and how stories can come to be politicised and incite violence.

4.1 Historical Grievances

First, let me tell you the story of the Powys murder from the 1930s. It reveals a complex narrative related to identity, authority and rights to the land in Laikipia. The wider context of the murder is what makes the case a crucial one for discussing power and resistance to power in Kenya today.[4]

In 1931, Theodore Powys, a white settler managing a sheep ranch in the northern parts of the Laikipia Crown Lands, was found dead.[5] Initially, it was presumed to be an accidental death caused by a lion attack, but suspicion arose when Samburu *morans* were heard singing about killing a white man. From then on, the story takes different shapes depending on where the narrator's allegiance lies. Therefore, what followed were several years of administrative muddles, silencing of witnesses and judicial confusion.[6]

---

4 C.J. Duder and G.L. Simpson, 'Land and Murder in Colonial Kenya: The Leroghi Land Dispute and the Powys "Murder" Case,' *The Journal of Imperial and Commonwealth History* 25, no. 3 (1 September 1997), pp. 440–65.

5 Duder and Simpson, 'Land and Murder in Colonial Kenya.'

6 Fratkin, 'The Samburu Laibon's Sorcery and the Death of Theodore Powys in Colonial Kenya.'

One version of what happened was that the Samburu *laibon*,[7] Ngaldaiya Leaduma, had sent the *morans* on a raid into the Crown Lands in Laikipia with specific directions to find and kill a white man and bring back the head and genitals, for the *laibon* to use in ritual medicine. Upon meeting the horseback-riding Powys, the *morans* had speared him, pulled him from his horse, and brought back his head and genitals to their *laibon*.[8] According to Waller, the *laibon* might not have played such a directing role and might merely have tried to cover up the incident when the *morans* returned with Powys' head – unaware of the kinds of consequences that murdering a white man at that time could have.[9]

The incident followed a period of fierce raids and attacks by Samburu *morans* directed towards settler farms in Laikipia and against their Kikuyu labourers in particular.[10] Fratkin describes the 1930s situation:

> The role of the laibon Leaduma in the Powys murder case reveals a complex interplay between different communities in this time and place. The murder occurred during a time of heightened tension and conflict between the white settler ranching community of Laikipia and the Samburu pastoralists of the Leroki plateau, with each side fearing domination by the other.[11]

The Laikipia Farmers Association and the colonial administration reacted to the attacks by enforcing control of the African population's presence in the Crown Lands through stronger grazing control, disarmament, control of movement and fines on livestock.[12] To them, the issue came down to protection of private property and upholding authority over the native populations. As such, the settler community saw the Samburu as 'a menace to white settlement.'[13]

7 A Samburu witchdoctor.

8 Fratkin, 'The Samburu Laibon's Sorcery and the Death of Theodore Powys in Colonial Kenya.'

9 Waller, 'Bringing Murder to Court: The Death of Theodore Powys.'

10 Fratkin, 'The Samburu Laibon's Sorcery and the Death of Theodore Powys in Colonial Kenya.'

11 Fratkin, 'The Samburu Laibon's Sorcery and the Death of Theodore Powys in Colonial Kenya,' p. 49.

12 BIEA, LFA, 'Minutes from Meetings,' 19 August 1923; RH, Africa.mic.515 reel 25, Laikipia District Annual Report, Trafford, 1932; RH, Africa.mic.517 reel 10, Laikipia Handing Over Report, Simpson to Shirreff, 31 October 1947.

13 *The East African Standard*, 'Squatter System a Menace to White Settlement,' 11 January 1934.

The Samburu used raids and encroachment onto the Crown Land to perform their claim to the land.[14] Their activities signified attempts to scare the white communities, display the integrity of the Samburu and point out the limits to colonial domination. As Fratkin continues:

> the Samburu saw the whites as foreign enemies who threatened to take away their grazing lands and pastoral livelihoods, as they did with Kikuyu lands. Where the Europeans acted to maintain their rule through the power of the colonial state, the Samburu resisted through the physical force of their warriors and the sorcery of their laibon.[15]

During the investigative process, evidence disappeared and witnesses were silenced, and although the Powys murder case was never solved, the British administration eventually managed to get Leaduma deported.[16]

Although the domination of the Kikuyu population led to the 1950s Mau Mau revolt, and these years retrospectively tend to overshadow rebellions among other parts of the African population, the most obvious power struggle in the 1930s was not that between the Kikuyu and the white settlers. Rather, it was that between white settlers in the Crown Lands and encroaching pastoral groups.[17]

The relationship between the Kikuyu labourers and the white settlers tended to be fairly close. Life on a colonial farm was often a tough affair, where poor infrastructure cut one off from commodities. Moreover, the lack of company prompted settlers to find sympathy for those able to relate to the experience of life on the vast plains. Kikuyu labourers often came to hold positions close to the settler families, whether as housekeepers, cooks, farm managers or drivers, and they became integrated parts of the household.[18]

Some white settlers maintained strict control of their labourers, in particular the pastoralists, who were often distanced from the settler families as herders and manual labourers. Regulation of the squatter families included micromanagement of the labourers' activities and surveillance of animals

14 Duder and Simpson, 'Land and Murder in Colonial Kenya.'

15 Fratkin, 'The Samburu Laibon's Sorcery and the Death of Theodore Powys in Colonial Kenya,' p. 49.

16 Waller, 'Bringing Murder to Court'; Fratkin, 'The Samburu Laibon's Sorcery and the Death of Theodore Powys in Colonial Kenya.'

17 Throup, *Economic and Social Origins of Mau Mau*; Fratkin, 'The Samburu Laibon's Sorcery and the Death of Theodore Powys in Colonial Kenya.'

18 Lonsdale, 'Kenya: Home County and African Frontiers.'

kept by the families.[19] Furthermore, the labourers were paid little in terms of wages.[20] However, during the Mau Mau revolt, some of the white settlers attempted to protect their Kikuyu labourers from the colonial administration's harassment.[21]

The strong relations between the Kikuyu labourers and the white settlers made the labourers vulnerable to attacks from Samburu *morans*, even though such attacks would not have the same effect as an attack on a 'white.' However, due to their positions as managers, they were constantly on site and easier to target than the white settlers themselves.[22]

This internal strife among the African populations did not start during colonial times; pre-colonial times too were marked by conflicts between the Laikipiak Maasai and the groups surrounding the Laikipia plateau.[23] However, in the colonial era these tensions were kept in check by strong control of the native population, although the manner in which this control was performed exacerbated the interethnic divides.[24] To better navigate a social landscape that lacked the clear-cut divisions according to class that they knew from Europe, the colonial administrators ended up overemphasising ethnic categories.[25] Some ethnic groups were recognised as 'good natives' and hired as farm labour, while others received the label 'menace to white settlement,' fixing an image of them as destructive and savage by nature.[26]

By controlling how the natural resources were used, one could control populations. Shipton argues that legal measures for administration and regulation of land basically constitute:

---

19 Kanogo, *Squatters and the Roots of Mau Mau.*

20 Labourers were paid as little as 12 Ksh per month, which was low even by 1960s standards: interview with research participant, Thome, 5 May 2015; Kanogo, *Squatters and the Roots of Mau Mau.*

21 Interview with research participant, south-western Laikipia, 6 March 2015.

22 Fratkin, 'The Samburu Laibon's Sorcery and the Death of Theodore Powys in Colonial Kenya'; Waller, 'Bringing Murder to Court: The Death of Theodore Powys.'

23 Michael Bollig, 'Intra- and Interethnic Conflict in Northwest Kenya. A Multicausal Analysis of Conflict Behaviour,' *Anthropos* 88, no. 1/3 (1 January 1993), pp. 176–84; Godfrey Muriuki, *A History of the Kikuyu, 1500–1900* (New York: Oxford University Press, 1974); Ogot, *Kenya before 1900*; Spencer, *Nomads in Alliance*; Spear and Waller, *Being Maasai*; Anderson, *Eroding the Commons.*

24 Spencer, *Nomads in Alliance*; Spear and Waller, *Being Maasai*; Anderson, *Eroding the Commons.*

25 Kyle, *The Politics of the Independence of Kenya*; Oucho, *Undercurrents of Ethnic Conflicts in Kenya.*

26 Shipton, *Mortgaging the Ancestors.*

> devices for simplifying complex realities, and for gaining control over large numbers of people. Where they do this, they also, in one way or another, turn most real people and their situations into misfits.[27]

Illiffe specifies how colonial states produce subjects rather than fully integrated citizens. In creating a new nation, the whole of people's historical experience is brought into the process.[28] Therefore, the impact of colonial social categorisation led acts of domination to be passed on from the colonial context to the post-Independence Kenyan people.[29] To exemplify this, the KLC, as explained in the previous chapter, created the illusion that some groups emerged as winners and some as losers. Ultimately, existing competing grievances and notions of entitlement to certain places were then enforced after Independence, creating tension that in some places manifested into open fights and violence.[30]

The issue of land also fuelled the intensification of conflicts. The dominating view among Africans in pre-colonial and even during colonial times was that land use depended on 'entrustment.' Land held under communal management gave community members access by default. The potential of the land had more to do with creating viable conditions for cattle breeding than with farming outputs, as a person's wealth equalled their cattle numbers rather than the number of acres they owned.[31] Contrastingly, the land-use reforms in the Independence years solidified ownership by emphasising 'entitlement' to land. That way, a manager, owner or land-use planner could focus on production of the land to maximise output. This was a milestone in the transformations of land use, which had extensive consequences for social power dynamics. And so, in present-day claims, with the focus on entitlement, ownership and production rather than entrustment, access and reproduction, it has become the ability to control territory that is at stake rather than the ability to make use of resources.[32]

4.1.1 *Present-day Grievances: Land, Ethnicity and Politics*

So, what is it that led this tension from the 1930s to grow and eventually ignite into violence and division? Land is key. It is a category in which contestation

27 Shipton, *Mortgaging the Ancestors*, p. 29.

28 John Illiffe, *A Modern History of Tanganyika* (Cambridge: Cambridge University Press, 1984), p. 486.

29 Illiffe, *A Modern History of Tanganyika*.

30 Anderson, *Eroding the Commons*.

31 Shipton, *Mortgaging the Ancestors*.

32 Anderson, *Eroding the Commons*; Shipton, *Mortgaging the Ancestors*.

and person-making can take place.[33] Land is a denominator for belonging, a space of resources and a place of value production.[34] The strong connection with identity means that the stakes are high when fights for land are combined with ethnicity.[35] Ethnic groups can be distinguished from other types of group classification that go along lines of race, nation, statehood etc.[36] Lynch argues that ethnic groups hold and perform a type of symbolism related to:

> a sense of in-group connectedness and distinctiveness that is rooted primarily in a notion of cultural peoplehood, whereby individuals of different ages, status and wealth are linked [...] through a conjoining of cultural similarity and perception of common descent.[37]

An ethnically based claim is often linked to autochthony, which Dunn defines as a narrative in which the particular ethnic group constructs its claim to a resource based on being first-comers to it. The elasticity of autochthony discourses makes them attractive as claiming instruments, because they can flatten out other forms of differentiation.[38] Concurrently, ethnic categories and their members represent imagined communities that have to struggle for legitimacy because their inclusion is always up for renegotiation.[39] As such, the demarcation of who is included in an ethnic group is contested and open-ended by its very definition.[40]

Because the distance created towards another group is what feeds it, the potential for creating 'othering' can be unleashed to mobilise one group to turn against another. Opposing claims are thus bound to hierarchies and dominance, and consequently, as Moore, Kosek and Pandian argue: 'geographies of

---

33 Chabal, *Africa: The Politics of Suffering and Smiling*; Geschiere, *The Perils of Belonging*; Carola Lentz, 'Land and the Politics of Belonging in Africa,' in *African Alternatives*, ed. Haan Leo, Ulf Engel and Patrick Chabal (Leiden: Brill, 2007); Christian Lund, 'Property and Citizenship: Conceptually Connecting Land Rights and Belonging in Africa,' *Africa Spectrum* 46, no. 3 (14 March 2012), pp. 71–75.

34 Berry, 'Debating the Land Question in Africa,' pp. 638–68; Juul et al., *Negotiating Property in Africa*.

35 Lentz, 'Land and the Politics of Belonging in Africa'; Elizabeth E. Watson, 'A "Hardening of Lines": Landscape, Religion and Identity in Northern Kenya,' *Journal of Eastern African Studies* 4, no. 2 (2010), pp. 201–20.

36 Moore et al., *Race, Nature, and the Politics of Difference*.

37 Lynch, 'What's in a Name?'

38 Dunn, '"Sons of the Soil" and Contemporary State Making.'

39 Lynch, *I Say to You*.

40 John L. Comaroff and Jean Comaroff, *Ethnicity, Inc.* (Chicago and London: The University of Chicago Press, 2009); Lynch, 'What's in a Name?'

belonging privilege particular subjects' positioning while simultaneously rendering other bodies vulnerable to violence.'[41]

As such, geographies of belonging are highly dynamic. They include when pastoralists were forcibly moved as Laikipia was declared Crown Land; when pastoralists entered smallholder farmland after the resettlement schemes had (re-)Africanised the lands; and when smallholders saw their crops destroyed by wild animals entering from the neighbouring nature conservancies.[42] In these examples, a perceived opposition was spurred into bitterness and resentment and even grown from frustrated rhetoric into political mobilisation to protest the oppressor in the power dynamics.

In certain ways, actions spurred by ethnic othering are similar to motivations for racist practices.[43] Indeed, in Laikipia, racial rhetoric confirming group identity in relation to others overlaps with ethnic othering. Whether among white ranchers positioning themselves towards African groups, or among Kikuyu absentee landowners positioning themselves towards other African groups or the white population, such rhetoric draws on denigration of the other and a simultaneous promotion of one's own.[44] This type of community identity and its salient relationship to positions of power is similar to Anderson's descriptions of an imagined community in which a certain version of history, genealogy or symbolic commonality comes to define a group as one against another.[45]

The inherent flexibility of autochthony arguments is also what makes them effective for political entrepreneurs in their development of political campaigns. By taking advantage of the attraction to homogeneity, people in leadership positions can gather support by building on an 'othering' narrative. Rhetoric such as 'they are greedy,' 'they are arrogant' and 'they live like this or that' legitimises discrimination against the others and lowers their perceived position in the hierarchy. In Laikipia, political leaders have continuously made use of such rhetoric. For instance, former MP of Laikipia North Mathew Lempurkel has defended Samburu encroachment on the private ranches, expressing how the white ranchers have reserved the grass for themselves. He has encouraged revenge attacks by claiming that: 'where the government has

41 Moore et al., *Race, Nature, and the Politics of Difference*, p. 14.

42 Matt W. Hayward and Graham I.H. Kerley, 'Fencing for Conservation: Restriction of Evolutionary Potential or a Riposte to Threatening Processes?,' *Biological Conservation* 142, no. 1 (January 2009), pp. 1–13; Gadd, 'Conservation outside of Parks.'

43 Moore et al., *Race, Nature, and the Politics of Difference*.

44 Field notes, conversation with research participant, Laikipia, 2 August 2015.

45 Anderson, *Imagined Communities: Reflections on the Origin and Spread of Nationalism* (London: Verso, 2006).

failed, [the Samburu] have been forced to introduce their own "jungle" law to survive.'[46] Yet Kikuyu politicians have employed similar rhetoric when gathering support,[47] and the white population too have made use of othering rhetoric to justify their continued presence.[48]

4.2 Meta-Narratives of Claims and Their Repercussions in Lorien

Ethnicity-related claims to land based on one-sided histories can be heard from people in many places across Laikipia – and often, tellers of such stories are met with contradictory claims by their very neighbours. As an example of how such contradicting claims take shape and the consequences they have, Lorien is a case in point. There, such claims have been clashing since the 1980s, turning rhetoric into deep-seated animosity and violence.

Lorien Ranching Company Ltd was formed by a group of Kalenjin in 1968. With a loan from the Agricultural Finance Corporation (AFC) they were able to pay the former ranch owner, Partridge, for the land in 1970.[49] The transaction gave rise to conflict between the Kalenjin group and the later-coming Kikuyu group, both claiming to be the rightful holders of the land in Lorien. However, the conflict did not become violent until 1993. By then, fear had turned into physical reactions, in which Kalenjin youngsters attacked the Kikuyu settled in Lorien, chasing them off the farm on allegations that their presence was illegal.[50] According to a Kikuyu shareholder, 'they did not want to kill. They wanted us to leave. [...] So, the whole village was burnt down.'[51]

After the eviction of the Kikuyu, the conflict continued, although not physically in Lorien. Instead, it has taken place in the numerous and continuous court cases in Nyeri, Nakuru and Eldoret, all evaluating who the rightful shareholders are. The Kalenjin group of 613 members – group A – claim to be the only legitimate group. Of this group, 501 are the Kalenjin members who formed the company, and 112 are former employees of Partridge. The former employees consist of a majority of Kalenjin and very few Turkana and Kikuyu.[52] This group claims to have settled the loan, taken to buy the land, already in the early

46 Kenya NTV, 'What is Ailing Laikipia.'
47 Interview with absentee landlords, Githunguri, 15 September 2015.
48 Interview with research participant, Laikipia, 15 March 2015; interview with research participant, Laikipia, 8 June 2015; interview with research participant, Laikipia, 12 May 2015.
49 Interview with research participant, Nyahururu, 30 May 2015.
50 Interview with research participant, Laikipia, 25 April 2015.
51 Interview with research participant, Lorien, 23 June 2015.
52 Interview with research participant, Nyahururu, 16 March 2016.

1980s. According to them, the other groups, primarily of Kikuyu – groups B and C – are false shareholders, who bought fake shares in the land-buying company. According to the lawyer of the Kalenjin group, Mahida, the Kikuyu group and their company, Rogoro Farmers Ltd, had attempted to cheat their way into Lorien Ranching Company:

> It is well known that Rogoro Farmers Company Limited have failed to obtain a farm and to appease its members they are trying to bulldoze their way into our client's company.[53]

Although all directors and shareholders were undoubtedly interested in acquiring land, there is disagreement about the constitution of the company, in terms of whether it includes group A only, or also groups B and C.[54]

According to the Kikuyu group, they were brought into the company to buy shares specifically for the shareholders to settle the loan when the loaning agreement expired.[55] This statement is supported by minutes of meetings from the 1970s. A meeting between the directors of both companies in 1977 reads: 'Both Companies have agreed to form a company to buy Lorien Farm, and repay loan outstanding.'[56] The Kikuyu group therefore claims that this was when the companies became one. However, after the Kikuyu group had paid for shares the loan turned out to have been settled already, and their money was returned by the bank.[57] As it seems unrealistic for the Kalenjin group to have single-handedly assembled the money, it is likely that an external body interfered. As Lorien was the sole Kalenjin stronghold in Laikipia, there may well have been political interest to ensure continuous Kalenjin control.[58]

Yet even if the loan was paid, this does not change the fact that the Kikuyu group had bought shares to raise the money. However, the Kalenjin group claimed that these shares were illegitimate, that the stamps were fake and that some of the directors in the land-buying company had taken the money for themselves. This is the basis of the claims. Due to the unwillingness of either of the two sides to compromise, the next chapter was played out in courthouses.

---

53 Personal archive of Papias Mathenge (PM), Letter from D.P. Mahida, Jones and Jones Advocates, to Muthoga and Gaturu Advocates, 27 January 1978.

54 Interview with research participant, Lorien, 29 July 2015.

55 Interview with research participant, Ngong, 18 July 2015.

56 PM, minutes of directors' meeting, 16 November 1977.

57 PM, internal letter from the F.M. Rahoe, Branch Manager, AFC Nyahururu to the Chief Legal Officer, AFC Nairobi, 28 November 1981.

58 Interview with research participant, Lorien, 23 June 2015.

The first court case was filed in 1982.[59] It involved the provincial administration and Lorien Ranching Company, which sought to be authorised to subdivide the land for the Kalenjin group. This order, however, was not executed.[60] From 1983 to 1992 a court case[61] ran in Nyeri, determining the Kikuyu group as the legitimate shareholders. Another order of subdivision for the Kalenjin group in 1992, also not executed, culminated in yet another case being ruled upon in Nyeri in 1994.[62] This ruling declared all subdivisions favouring the Kalenjin group to be invalid.[63] Despite this ruling, the Kikuyu were unable to set foot in Lorien. They therefore instituted a civil case to prove their legitimacy as shareholders. However, this time the court ruled that orders from 1983 and 1994 be set aside on the grounds that they were fraudulent orders.[64] Instead, the Kikuyu group was to be barred from entering Lorien. Additionally, the court ruled that:

> The individual titles now in possession of District Land Registrar and District Commissioner Laikipia or his successor be issued forthwith to the plaintiff's bona fide 613 members [group A].[65]

However, another court case,[66] also in 1994, ruled in favour of the Kikuyu group and prohibited land subdivision and the issuance of individual title deeds.

The most recent court case ran between 1998 and 2015 and ruled in favour of the Kalenjin group. Yet several points demonstrated the process to have been biased. Evidence of the loan payment and the share sales to the Kikuyu group was only testified by the Kalenjin group, while the Kikuyu group's version was omitted. Moreover, the violent clashes in 1993, where Kikuyu were attacked and evicted from Lorien, were denied to have taken place; and the court case of 1993–94, ruling in favour of the Kikuyu, was hardly mentioned, despite it being the outcome of this case that resulted in the 1998–2015 case.[67] Additionally, the ruling was made in Eldoret by a Kalenjin judge and only delivered and

---

59 HCCC, Nakuru, No. 19 of 1982, as referenced in HCCC, Nyeri, No. 248 of 1998, p. 32.

60 HCCC, Nyeri, No. 248 of 1998. Ruling, pp. 31–32.

61 HCCC, Nyeri, No. 80 of 1983: Lorien Ranching Company Limited vs Wilson Arap Birgen, John Muritu Karumba, Joseph Murithi Maingu, Kaiga Kamau and Koske Maritim.

62 HCCC, Nyeri, No. 253 of 1994: Lorien Ranching Company Limited vs. Wilson Arap Birgen, John Muritu Karumba, Joseph Murithi Maingu, Kaiga Kamau and Koske Maritim.

63 HCCC, Nyeri, No. 248 of 1998. Ruling, p. 32.

64 HCCC, Nyeri, No. 248 of 1998. Ruling, p. 56.

65 HCCC, Nyeri, No. 248 of 1998. Ruling, p. 56.

66 HCCC, Nyeri, No. 253 of 1994.

67 HCCC, Nyeri, No. 248 of 1998. Ruling, p. 38.

signed by the judge in the High Court in Nyeri, even though the case had been running in Nyeri throughout. And finally, the court ruling ordered the 1983 and 1994 rulings, both of which went in the favour of the Kikuyu group, to be set aside.[68]

The aspects of politicisation, physical acts of territorialisation, and use of courthouses and legal allegations are reminiscent of the Powys murder case. In the Powys case, the judicial process became muddled, with the silencing of witnesses and disappearing evidence. In the Lorien court cases, biased legal procedures, misconduct and evasion of evidence produced an endless string of court cases. In both situations, political interference was likely given their wider political significance – both span well beyond a local disagreement.

Going through the articles written on Lorien in *The Daily Nation* and other newspapers, the political administration is often portrayed as having been actively involved in the case of subdivision. In one article, the Board of Directors of Lorien Ranching Company rejected the subdivision of the farm in 1990, enacted by the provincial administration. They termed the attempt at subdivision 'dictatorial and tribal.'[69] Moreover, both sides of the conflict used the media instrumentally to voice biased versions of events. For instance, an article following the ruling of the latest court case in 2015 portrayed the Kalenjin shareholders with their title deeds.[70] These documents were likely either fake or specifically produced through political channels. The ongoing court cases disputing the number of shareholders would have prevented the surveyor's results from being approved, and without an authorised survey, subdivision cannot get through the Land Board.

Because only one side is settled in Lorien, no current claims between the Kalenjin and Kikuyu are physically acted out on the land today. However, neither group has forgotten the violent clashes in 1993 that led the Kikuyu group to flee the area. Instead, it is the ongoing court cases that illustrate the continuous contestation over the land.[71] Despite the past confrontations depicting a physical manifestation of a land claim, no clashes are visible in everyday interactions any longer. Kalenjin in Lorien have market interactions with the neighbouring areas, Salama and Kinamba – both of which are dominated by Kikuyu and are home to many of those who were forced to flee in 1993.[72]

68 HCCC, Nyeri, No. 248 of 1998.

69 *The Daily Nation*, 'Man Shot Dead,' 22 January 1992, p. 2.

70 *The Star*, 'Laikipia Land Row Ends,' 6 May 2015, https://www.the-star.co.ke/counties/central/2015-05-06-laikipia-land-row-ends/, accessed 11 July 2020.

71 Interview with research participant, Nyahururu, 23 March 2016.

72 Interview with research participant, Salama, 25 April 2015.

The grievances were voiced when the shareholders talked about the court cases – many told me about trying to access their land and getting arrested for trespassing. In such cases, the divisions were supported by a rhetoric of ethnic stereotyping.[73] What both sides agree on is that the directors were responsible for creating the problem, whether it was by selling shares illegally for personal gain, as the Kalenjin side claims,[74] or by taking the Kikuyu shareholders' money while solidifying the Kalenjin presence, as the Kikuyu side claims.[75] On the Kikuyu side, it is explained that suspicion only arose in the 1980s. Many rationalised this change with reference to the shift in government and the increased tribal antagonism that surfaced during Moi's presidency.[76]

'James' is one of the Kikuyu shareholders who fled Lorien in 1993. His story started with the following notion:

> When I came to Lorien, the Chief of police [...] and the [Kalenjin] started harassing us by torching down our houses. They used to come at night but when we came out, they would run away.[77]

James and the other Kikuyu in Lorien dealt with this state of affairs for months, until the provincial administration declared that the Kikuyu group had acquired land legally and could continue to stay in Lorien awaiting allocation.[78] According to James, this was what triggered the Kalenjin group's reaction. In February 1993, a group of Kalenjin armed themselves with machetes, arrows and clubs and attacked Kikuyu houses in Lorien:

> I remember it was around 6pm. Suddenly, there was some shouting and screaming from the outside. [...] I walked out [of my house] and saw people running in the opposite direction. [...] I left everything and at a distance, I saw [the Kalenjin] burn down my house. At that moment, I

73 Interview with research participant, Ngong, 18 July 2015; interview with research participant, Lorien, 29 July 2015.
74 Interview with research participant, Lorien, 29 July 2015.
75 Interview with research participant, Ngong, 18 July 2015.
76 Interview with research participant, Nyahururu, 12 May, 2015; interview with research participant, Lorien, 23 June 2015.
77 Interview with research participant, Salama, 25 April 2015.
78 Order by the provincial administration, 1989, as referred to in HCCC, Nyeri, No. 248 of 1998.

> had my small daughter with me and started walking away. [...] I saw one naked man following us – an attacker. He had his arrow set ready to shoot. I had no weapon, not even a machete. He asked me, 'What are you people doing here? Do you know you don't own land here?' I asked him: 'And who tells you that you own land here?' [...] As we were involved in the argument, a big group of ten attackers came. God gave me power and I ran off! They threw weapons but darkness and the bushes saved me.[79]

On the following day, James was taken to Nyahururu District Hospital. Many others were there with serious injuries from the eviction. Some had been hit by arrows; others had deep machete cuts. Today, James lives a few hundred metres from the border with Lorien but has never been able to go back to his house there.[80]

'Peter' is one of the Kalenjin settled in Lorien. His story starts at a different time, in a different place. He explained how he arrived as part of a group of Kalenjin in 1952 during the Mau Mau revolt.[81] In this southern part of Laikipia, the white population had fired many Kikuyu labourers out of fear of the Mau Mau.[82] The white farmers therefore needed new labourers, and Peter's parents started to work on a farm along with the rest of the group.

> In 1970, after Independence, people got the chance to buy the land left by the white settlers. [...] Many Kalenjin were left landless, so the elders mobilised people to strategise on how to get land. The elders walked into different farms talking to the [Kalenjin] there. They wanted to unite them since they were left in the middle where companies from elsewhere came and bought land to bring their own shareholders. The elders saw that [Lorien] was sufficient land for the Kalenjin. So, they collected money from the Kalenjin to buy this land. Many farms had already been bought and we did not have enough money. So, we had to get a loan.[83]

As Kalenjin, they saw themselves as 'the deserving poor,' with an almost God-given right to acquire land.[84] Lorien Ranching Company was founded and the

79 Interview with research participant, Salama, 25 April 2015.
80 Interview with research participant, Salama, 25 April 2015.
81 Interview with research participant, Lorien, 26 May 2015.
82 Interview with research participant, Lorien, 26 May 2015.
83 Interview with research participant, Lorien, 26 May 2015.
84 Klopp, 'Can Moral Ethnicity Trump Political Tribalism? The Struggle for Land and Nation in Kenya,' pp. 269–94.

elders mobilised people from other farms, as well as Kalenjin who had not yet moved out of Uasin Gishu and Kapsabet. It was when the shares in the land had been sold that the other group emerged, as Peter explains:

> When [the fake director] came here, he started his illegal office and began selling shares in Lorien. He was not a director, nor a shareholder! He was using that name to collect money even though we had our own office and directors here inside Lorien. [The fake director] was based in Nyahururu. That was the genesis of land conflict here. [...] First, we only had 47 Kikuyu squatters, but that number continued to increase. The land was not subdivided yet, so, it was easy for people to come and settle.[85]

Peter explained that the fake directors kept stating that there was available land in Lorien. The 47 households soon turned into 60.[86]

> When we visited those people, we found unoccupied houses. They would tell us that the owners were there but had gone to Marura to do farming. They used that as an excuse. We realised that those houses were built for incoming members.[87]

The day that James chose to focus on in his account also appears in Peter's story. However, his account takes the position that most Kalenjin in Lorien were unknowing about the uprising to evict the Kikuyu shareholders:

> On that day, I was coming back from herding and visited a neighbouring elder. We saw light in the far distance. The wife claimed that it was the farmers who were burning fields in Marura to clear it for farming. At night I could hear vehicles moving around in the area. That was very unusual. In the morning, we heard that there were attacks. [...] We also heard that some [Kalenjin] elders had hidden some people who were being evicted and had showed them the way to Salama. So, some [people] in Lorien were not aware of it and were very innocent.[88]

The two accounts of the settling and eviction in Lorien bear witness to a complicated course of events. Both stress certain parts of the story and disregard

85 Interview with research participant, Lorien, 26 May 2015.
86 Interview with research participant, Lorien, 26 May 2015.
87 Interview with research participant, Lorien, 26 May 2015.
88 Interview with research participant, Lorien, 26 May 2015.

others. On the Kikuyu side, the day of the eviction is stressed as a point of atrocities committed against them,[89] whereas the Kalenjin stress the dubious settlement as incitement for the tension.[90] Both stories employ an othering rhetoric about the opposing group. The Kikuyu describe themselves as courageous, intelligent and honest, while portraying the Kalenjin as fearful, aggressive and primitive.[91] In contrast, the Kalenjin group refer to themselves as peaceful people, who go by the rules and keep to themselves, while depicting the Kikuyu as people who cheat and strategise to win.[92]

4.3 Discursive Claims to Land

As explained in the introduction, there are currently five types of groups claiming land in Laikipia. The first group is the pastoralists without private-property rights. The second group is the smallholder farmers, agro-pastoralists and other smaller-scale actors. The third group is the absentees, constituting absentee livestock owners who keep livestock in Laikipia without holding land, and absentee landlords who own land but have not settled there. These three groups can be portrayed as opportunists in the landscape, manoeuvring their way to gain at the costs of others – albeit that this is far from how they see themselves. The fourth group is the ranchers. Although they have tenure security, they are confronted by immense pressure from encroachment. The fifth group, the conservationists, also have to struggle with this pressure. However, in contrast to the ranchers, they build their claim around a moral rhetoric of being the protectors of wildlife and biodiversity. Rather than being opportunistic in negotiating their way onto said land, the ranchers and the conservatives are protectionist with regard to what is already under their control, at least formally.

In the following sections these five types of actors and their claims to the land in Laikipia are examined. Although few actors fit solely into one category, the categorisation illustrates the dominant tendencies. In reality an actor would be positioned in between small-scale and large-scale land use, and in

89 Interview with research participant, Nyahururu, 12 May 2015; interview with research participant, Lorien, 23 June 2015; interview with research participant, Salama, 25 April 2015; interview with research participant, Salama, 30 May 2015.

90 Interview with research participant, Lorien, 29 July 2015; interview with research participant, Lorien, 26 May 2015; interview with research participant, Lorien, 30 January 2015.

91 Interview with research participant, Ngong, 18 July 2015; interview with research participant, Nyahururu, 12 May 2015.

92 Interview with research participant, Lorien, 29 July 2015; interview with research participant, Lorien, 26 May 2015; interview with research participant, Lorien, 30 January 2015.

between defining rights according to private-property principles and according to general ethics of what is right and fair. Moreover, there are both similarities and differences in motivations and mindsets. Although there are overlaps, the categories are to a large extent based on livelihoods and ontological perspectives, rather than the simplifying notions of ethnic categorisation.

4.3.1 *The Pastoralists*

The first group making claims to land is the pastoralists, constituting Samburu in most places and Pokot towards the north-east of Laikipia. They typically do not have title deeds for the land they occupy. To these groups, having a title deed is meaningless. Instead their claim is made on the basis of autochthony. They associate themselves with the Maasai, in order to legitimise their claim to 'take back the land.' A Samburu elder settled in Sugoroi near Thome illustrates the autochthony rhetoric in the statement:

> We don't really care about the title deed. That is just a paper! Our forefathers had no title deeds. We are using history. History has it that Laikipia was for the Maasai. […] They [the Maasai and Samburu] are one and the same people. There is no difference. […] A lot of names here are also Maasai names. 'Suguroi' is a Samburu name for herbs that grow here.[93]

In this argument, the elder first gives history legitimacy over private-property rights, then constructs his Samburu identity as one that is closely connected to that of the Maasai. The Maasai is the only ethnic group holding written proof of their pre-colonial presence in Laikipia, in the form of the Maasai Agreement declaring their displacement. So by associating with the Maasai, the Samburu can draw on their legitimacy as people who have been robbed of their land. The elder's nephew supported his uncle, stating that the Samburu could not be considered trespassers on the land, since Laikipia was already theirs. He explained how the stories of elders speak of a time long ago, before the coming of the white man, where the Samburu, the Purku Maasai and the Laikipiak Maasai were the owners of Laikipia, their presence stretching between the Aberdare Range in the south to Samburu in the north. In these stories, the Laikipiak Maasai lived at the north-eastern parts near Dol Dol, the Purku Maasai lived near Aberdare in the south and the Samburu lived in what is today called Rumuruti.[94]

93 Interview with research participant, Sugoroi, 12 June 2015.
94 Interview with research participant, Laikipia, 15 July 2015.

Yet the Maasai Agreement was made between Maasai and the colonial administration and did not include the Samburu – despite them being present in the northern frontier of the plateau throughout colonial times, as the Powys murder case shows.[95] Without formal documentation of having been moved, the Samburu's claim to belong has to build on oral narratives alone.

Also, the proximity of the Maa language spoken by both Samburu and Maasai is used in this argument as a way of situating the Samburu claim to the naming of landscape features and areas. However, this connectedness does not seem to be felt to the same extent by the Maasai. Their name for the Samburu is *Loikop*, meaning butterfly. It refers to the Samburu being fragile, rather than beautiful, underlining the difference between the two groups.[96] The Maa chairman for Laikipia, a Maasai, further underlines that:

> When the Laikipiak left, a few Samburu got an opportunity to come in seasonally before the Maasai came and evicted everyone [...]. The Samburu had no specific place; they [...] have never been here permanently. The ones you see came not long ago. They don't have any land here. [...] They were passers-by until the Europeans took control of the place.[97]

The Maa chairman positions the Samburu historically alongside other pastoralist groups surrounding the plateau rather than confirming the alleged bond between the Maasai and the Samburu.

History can vary depending on what an individual seeks to find. In that sense, one can construct a narrative in such a way as to selectively include details that support the claim to belong, while omitting details that contradict it. This is what the Samburu elder does here:

> my father got initiated in Laikipia. It was a very long time ago. [...] I was told that by his age-mates, who were also circumcised in Laikipia. This is their land. [...] They were chased out of Laikipia by the Europeans. [...] That is what is also making them conflict with the white ranchers. They stole the land from us.[98]

95 Fratkin, 'The Samburu Laibon's Sorcery and the Death of Theodore Powys in Colonial Kenya.'

96 Interview with research participant, Rumuruti, 14 July 2015; interview with research participant, northern Laikipia, 14 April 2015.

97 Interview with research participant, Rumuruti, 14 July 2015.

98 Interview with research participant, Sugoroi, 12 June 2015.

I found this justification for Samburu presence in Laikipia to be typical of the Samburu sentiment – and the Pokot use a similar narrative.[99] What this elder chose not to tell is that most rituals performed by the Samburu in Laikipia are still performed in Samburu County, except for circumcision ceremonies, which are performed in Laikipia for reasons of convenience. There is little connectivity to landmarks in Laikipia, meaning that their cultural connectivity to place is still associated with Samburu County, and Mount Nyiro in particular, where all initiation ceremonies take place.[100]

However, constructing a close link to the Maasai is not beneficial unless the Maasai are successful in reclaiming the land in Laikipia. In 2004, such a campaign did take form, based on the idea that all leases to colonial land were given for 99 years right after the Maasai Agreement. And since 99 years had passed since the first of two rounds of Maasai evictions, these leases were thought to have expired. Samburu, Kikuyu and others supported the Maasai in their land invasions in case the Maasai proved successful in their political campaign. The protesters gathered in groups, armed with guns, and cut the fences to the larger white landholdings.[101]

The owner of Lolldaiga Hills Ranch experienced these land invasions first hand. He explains that:

> It was an idea in people's minds. [...] There was [in 2004] an idea that something might take place because of this 99-years idea. In fact, I have a feeling that the move that was imposed on the Maasai in 1911 was more regrettable than the earlier Treaty. [...] It was the Maasai but certainly many pastoralist groups took part in these invasions including the Samburu. [...] Perhaps the idea was that pastoralists would reoccupy Laikipia.[102]

The wish to reoccupy Laikipia transformed from a point of historic injustice for the Maasai into a wide-reaching movement attracting opportunistic souls from many ethnic groups in want of land.

Taking into account that the Maasai had been waiting 100 years to reach an opportunity to receive justice, the demonstrations could have been expected to be larger in scale. Indeed, the warnings given prior to the events indicated

99 Interview with research participant, Nyahururu, March 21 2015; interview with research participant, Ol Moran, 21 July 2015.

100 Group mapping, Thome, 27 July 2015; conversation with research participant, Thome, 27 July 2016.

101 Kantai, 'In the Grip of the Vampire State,' pp. 107–22.

102 Interview with research participant, eastern Laikipia, 24 July 2015.

such a threat. In the local Nyahururu-based newspaper, *The Home News*, from 2004, Maasai elders issued warnings of their intended reclamations:

> The Laikipiak and the Maasai in Kenya are demanding restitution for historical injustices and losses committed by the colonial and successive regimes over the last one hundred years. Take note that not only shall we seek legal redress locally and at the international court of justice, but also we are ready to use any available avenue to right the wrongs however long it will take. [...] The one million acres in the hands of few individuals in Laikipia have pushed us to the limit of survival with rampant poverty, being squatters in our own soils [...] and now, enough is enough.[103]

However, the campaign was built on misinformation. The agreement between the colonial administration and the Maasai was not specified in time, but the leases given to the European settlers would typically be of a length of 99 years in the early days of settlement, whereas for the later-established settlers the length of the lease could be up to 999 years.[104] The pastoralist narrative of 'taking back the land' had therefore been fitted to a narrative that the agreement made with the Maasai would expire when the early leases of the European settlers expired.[105] Additionally, European settlement only started after the Second World War, so even if a correlation could be drawn, the timing was wrong and 99 years had not yet passed.

Although other groups joined forces with the Maasai and supported the claim, the response from other parts of the African population in Laikipia was far from supportive. Many smallholders who had bought shares of land in Laikipia saw the Maasai campaign as a threat and feared a new ethnic uprising similar to that of the 1990s post-election violence.[106] The editor of *The Home News* covered the events of the campaign during 2004.[107] He states:

> [T]here is a clique of individuals out to cause a political sensation over very sensitive issues. This team has tried to use their advantage, a historical loophole, without minding the consequences of such an irresponsible move. [...] Those agitating for their land must not remind us about differences that appear to have a tribal bearing. This is because in the Laikipia

103 *The Home News*, 'Maasai Land Claim,' 29 July–4 August 2004, pp. 1–2 and 10.

104 Hughes, *Moving the Maasai*; interview with research participant, central Laikipia, 12 May 2015.

105 Interview with research participant, eastern Laikipia, 24 July 2015.

106 Interview with research participant, Nyahururu, 18 March 2016.

107 *The Home News*, 'The Maasai in War Cry,' 29 July–4 August 2004, pp. 2 and 10.

> Puzzle, some communities are being presented as the aggrieved parties, while others come out as the villains. This scenario can only explode into a serious spontaneous tribal uprising. We are tired of this.[108]

The Maasai claim had the potential to affect the smallholders, and many Kikuyu in particular, who had bought shares in these former colonial ranches. If successful, the campaign could therefore have turned large numbers of smallholders into internally displaced people (IDPs).[109]

Ultimately, the campaign received little external support and recognition, and did not result in a second Africanisation wave in Laikipia.[110] Instead, it left the Maasai and Samburu communities more frustrated. What began as a hope of regaining access to land ended up deepening their sense of being dominated or even ignored by a political establishment which seemingly served the ruling class rather than pastoralists.[111] Unlike the campaign, this resentment has not disappeared.

Few 'white'-managed ranches have been converted into smallholder land since the early 1990s when Samburu started to settle in Laikipia. Yet, looking at these lush lands with restricted entry continues to frustrate them. Former MP for Laikipia North Mathew Lempurkel was elected based on the conviction that he would evict the white landholders and return the plateau to the Samburu people.[112] However, with more scandals creating headlines than actual results, many Samburu people lost faith in him. Up until 2016, all Lempurkel had created was false promises, attracting even more pastoralists to the plateau, which in turn increased security measures to control encroachment on the white estates.[113] Yet these enforcements expanded pastoralist protest measures, and starting from March 2016, Samburu and Pokot groups attacked conservancies and ranches at an even greater intensity and scale than before.

Again the purpose was to take back their land by referring to historical injustices. Autochthonous argumentation is fluid and easily adaptable. This also makes autochthony suitable for people seeking political support, such as

108 *The Home News*, 'Commentary: A Wrong Way to Approach Land Issues,' 9–15 September 2004, p. 8.

109 *The Home News*, 'Commentary: A Wrong Way to Approach Land Issues.'

110 Interview with research participant, eastern Laikipia, 24 July 2015; Kantai, 'In the Grip of the Vampire State,' pp. 107–22.

111 Kantai, 'In the Grip of the Vampire State,' pp. 107–22.

112 Kenya NTV, 'What is Ailing Laikipia'; interview with research participant, Nyahururu, 21 March 2016.

113 Interview with research participant, Nyahururu, 21 March 2016.

Lempurkel. However, it is up against the dominating discourse of private-property rights and therefore falls short of formal legitimacy.

Moreover, the pastoralists' narrative is vulnerable to historical scrutiny, because the claim to present-day resources refers to one brief period in history in the 1910s when no one else barred them from accessing Laikipia – seasonal presence would hardly be enough to substantiate a claim. Going further back in history, someone else can make a similar claim to the same land. That said, the pastoralist mindset, if such a thing exists, appears to carry activist notions that run on a moral economy. To them, the fencing of and the exclusion of people from grazing is simply immoral.[114]

As an alternative strategy for appropriating resources, pastoralists have attempted to invoke legal support for their claim of presence by use of the Limitation of Actions Act, according to which 12 years of settlement can give one constitutional rights of access.[115] However, after the constitutional change in 2010,[116] courts could no longer rule according to the Limitation of Actions Act.[117] Thus, even though pastoralists continue to verbalise such rights, this strategy no longer carries legitimacy.

4.3.2 *The Smallholders*

The second group of actors is the smallholders. Their claim to land in Laikipia is that usually constituted by agro-pastoralists, farmers and other petty actors who have bought into the private-property discourse and paid for land – although many continue to build their lives around tenure insecurity due to lengthy casework and politicised land deals. Insecurity in Laikipia hit the smallholders hardest. Unlike the other groups, they have small social networks to depend on and are limited by external actors and factors determining the ways in which they live their lives.

---

114 Interview with research participant, Sugoroi, 12 June 2015; interview with research participant, Sugoroi, 12 June 2015; interview with research participant, Ol Moran, 21 July 2015.

115 The Limitation of Actions Act states that: 'where a person claims to have become entitled by adverse possession to land [...] he may apply to the High Court for an order that he be registered as the proprietor of the land or lease in place of the person then registered as proprietor of the land' (The National Council for Law Reporting with the Authority of the Attorney General, *The Limitation of Actions Act*, Chapter 22, Section 38, 2010).

116 The National Council for Law Reporting with the Authority of the Attorney General, *The Constitution of Kenya*, 2010.

117 The Land and Environment Court in Malindi ruled in 2011 that: 'the court no longer has jurisdiction to dispose the true and or registered owner of the land in order to give the property to a trespasser' (Environment and Land Court, Malindi, Land Case no. 108 of 2011, Kahindi Ngala Mwagandi vs Mtana Lewa).

That said, the smallholder group is diverse. It includes Turkana, many of whom have ties in Laikipia going back to the 1930s.[118] Others left Turkana County around 1974 due to attacks from the Ngoroko gang.[119] Many had lost everything they had and walked the 200 km from Lodwar to Suguta, across Baragoi in the Samburu region, where some chose to stay and others boarded vehicles to reach Laikipia in search of work on colonial farms.[120]

As a labourer on a ranch, one was paid and provided for with flour and milk, and there was no need to reacquire livestock. One respondent recalls, from his father's employment with Carr Hartley in Thome, how:

> the only bad thing was that you weren't as free because the land was under him. Otherwise, life was better with the salary and the food ration every Saturday. Life wasn't as difficult as now. […] He got a lot of milk, which he could even use to make ghee and sell. So he had other sources of income.[121]

Following the emigration of colonial settlers, many Turkana fell into poverty. Today, large parts of the Turkana population in Laikipia have started to farm and diversify their income – much like the Kikuyu do.[122] Few keep livestock, because it puts a household at risk of raids. Instead, they get employment in construction work, burn charcoal, farm cash crops for markets or invest in property to collect rent from housing.[123]

Another group among the smallholders are Kikuyu. Many have acquired land from the former colonial ranches through either settlement schemes or land-buying companies.[124] Many have a few acres of land – sometimes as little as one quarter of an acre. Most of the smallholders have some farming and market interaction selling food crops. Many also have other smaller incomes, as skilled masons, smiths, drivers or carpenters, and some are teachers, preachers, or managers of guesthouses and gas stations.[125]

---

118 Interview with research participant, Rumuruti, 21 January 2015.

119 Interview with research participant, Thome, 6 March 2015.

120 Interview with research participant, Thome, 5 May 2015; interview with research participant, Thome, 6 March 2015.

121 Interview with research participant, Thome, 6 March 2015.

122 Interview with research participant, Rumuruti, 21 January 2015; interview with research participant, Thome, 6 March 2015.

123 Interview with research participant, Thome, 6 March 2015.

124 Interview with research participant, Nanyuki, 16 August 2016; interview with research participant, Rumuruti, 21 January 2015.

125 Interview with research participant, Thome, 6 March 2015; interview with research participant, Thome, 13 May 2015; interview with research participant, Thome, 13 May 2015;

With different ethnic affiliations, the smallholders are not entirely homogeneous despite their similar livelihoods. This affects their sense of allegiance and limits their strength as a group. For instance, insecurities in Rumuruti in November 2016 arose in the swamp area, Marura, next to Thome, allegedly pitting the Turkana community against the Samburu community as they retaliated for raiding attacks.[126] However, despite the Kikuyu being subject to raids too, they did not support their Turkana neighbours in the riots.

In most smallholder areas in Laikipia, Turkana and Kalenjin are the minority. They need to collaborate with Kikuyu in order to maintain stability. But often such collaborations are poor.[127] In Lorien, the Kalenjin constitute a considerable proportion and there are no pastoralists to challenge their use of the resources. Instead, the grievance is directed towards the outside Kikuyu populations.[128] As explained in the case study above, the Kalenjin vied to gain access to land on equal terms with Kikuyu at Independence, illustrating an element of ethnic competition over land in Laikipia – a competition that has only grown stronger over the years. Being greatly outnumbered by Kikuyu, they are essentially left fighting over this single ranch in Lorien. This spurs a sense of animosity that extends into Kikuyu–Kalenjin relations across Laikipia.

There are also smaller groups of Somali, Borana, Meru, Kamba and Luhya among the smallholders.[129] Common to all is their inability to protect their small farms from encroaching pastoralists, marauding wildlife and environmental imbalances. Without title deeds they cannot take up loans from the bank to invest in security and develop their farms.[130] Although there is a pronounced imbalance between the smallholder farms of a few acres and those of their white neighbours on the large estates, the smallholders are easier targets for illegal grazing due to their poor security investments. As one Turkana smallholder explains:

---

interview with research participant, Marura, 17 June 2015; interview with research participant, Rumuruti, 3 August 2015.

126 The situation escalated, leading 450 families to flee the area after seven people from both sides were killed (see Joseph Muraya, 'Hundreds Flee Their Homes in Latest Wave of Violence between Samburu and Turkanas,' *Capital News*, 9 November 2016, https://www.capitalfm.co.ke/news/2016/11/hundreds-flee-their-homes-in-latest-wave-of-violence-between-samburu-and-turkanas, accessed 29 September 2017).

127 Interview with research participant, Thome, 27 May, 2015; interview with research participant, Thome, 27 May 2015.

128 Interview with research participant, Lorien, 26 May 2015.

129 Interview with research participant, Thome, 21 February 2015.

130 Interview with research participant, chief's office in Thome, 20 February 2015.

> what brings problems is the small size of the area. Some have a feeling that others own big pieces of land while they themselves are concentrated at one place. For instance, the pastoralists graze in the vacant fields till grass is exhausted there. After that they come to graze in the interior where people are settled. So, the farmers and the pastoralist constantly conflict. […] This ought to have been the first place to get title deeds. We have several mission centres where most people want to develop. But they can't fully develop since they have no title deeds.[131]

Although the smallholders are frustrated about their situation, few have any substantial links to people in power, do not feel politically represented and are unable to congregate into political movements to protest. Many politicians have problematised the stalled processes of land distribution, but their addressing of these issues tend to end in lip service.[132] Instead the smallholders remain caught in a limbo between lack of protection by the state on one side, and the encroachments by pastoralists and wildlife on the other. All their energy is used to fend for themselves, protecting what they can of what they feel they have a right to control.

They refer to private-property rights to support their claims, although they do not necessarily expect support from state institutions such as the police and the local government. They have come to learn that their lives matter less than those of wealthy people in urban centres.[133] Although the rhetoric behind their claims is similar to the ranchers' in that both make use of issues of private-property rights and the absence of support from state institutions, these two groups are far from alike. In fact, this may be the only common ground between the two.[134]

As mixed-ethnicity groups, their sense of togetherness is something they have learned – a capacity that has evolved out of necessity. Even after being neighbours for decades, their interethnic relations are bound up with mistrust, restraint and uncertainty. This makes collaboration a risky necessity, more than an active choice. They are weakened by their inability to plan long-term, because they live at the mercy of those with power. This can lead them to make

131 Interview with research participant, Thome, 5 May 2015.

132 Interview with research participant, Marura, 9 March 2015; interview with research participant, Thome, 6 March 2015; interview with research participant, Rumuruti, 3 August 2015.

133 Interview with research participant, Thome, 13 May 2015.

134 Interview with research participant, Ol Moran, 21 July 2015; interview with research participant, Nyahururu, 18 March 2016.

short-term decisions that may give an immediate profit but increase risk in the long term. For instance, many subdivided farms have had public utility installations dismantled by the resident smallholders themselves in order to sell spare parts in exchange for quick money – a choice that leaves them more destitute in the long term.[135]

4.3.3 *The Ranchers*

Another group claiming the right to be present on the land in Laikipia is the ranchers. Although many sit on large landholdings, are of European descent and are of financial means, this is far from the case for everyone in this group. The ranchers also include wealthy Kikuyu politicians, as well as poor whites, unable to enforce security measures to retain viable farming activities.

The priority for the ranchers is not the wildlife on their land. Rather, it is the ability to take care of their property and livestock without interference.[136] Their common challenge is the pastoralists' encroachment to access grazing. Often, the ranchers have fenced their land and invested in security personnel. However, many have to spend much time fixing fences, retaining pastoralists' confiscated cattle and driving to the police station to file charges, all of which can compromise their farming or ranching activities.[137]

The ranch owner explained his frustration in trying to manage a farm of which Samburu pastoralists are the neighbours:

> You've got all these Samburu with a lot of livestock and they get into the river and make it muddy. So, I fence and leave a strip some metres from the river. We put cattle into the strip for grazing, and after the grass is finished, we move away. Some people [Samburu] come after you leave and get their cattle into that strip. So, if you don't catch them and stop them, then they will just be there, all the time, in front of you, in broad daylight.[138]

On a neighbouring ranch, the manager had similar experiences: 'We discovered that leasing [grazing] to 3,000 [cows] is probably leasing to 8,000 plus the sheep and goats. […] That's more than the carrying capacity!'[139] Although this realisation adds to the challenge of management, he believed that it would be

135 Interview with research participant, Rumuruti, 3 August 2015.
136 Interview with research participant, Laikipia, 6 March 2015; interview with research participant, Laikipia, 8 June 2015.
137 Interview with research participant, Laikipia, 8 June 2015.
138 Interview with research participant, Laikipia, 6 March 2015.
139 Interview with research participant, Laikipia, 8 June 2015.

impossible to keep them out completely, since the farm is bigger than others in the area and it is incredibly time-consuming to constantly repair the fence.[140]

Most of the ranchers agree on a firm approach, although degrees of firmness vary: some go into dialogue and allow for arrangements of grazing, and some do not. However, despite attempts to collaborate, all ranchers are frustrated with their surrounding community. One of them termed the trespassers as non-conformers, arguing that they only cooperate if it is beneficial to them:

> I use the term 'capitalists' because they have left where they were because they were no longer allowed access to resources. They come here because they can access resources for free and genuinely for free. [...] They don't pay for the cost of managing the grass![141]

One ranch owner was equally frustrated, explaining that it is difficult for him to leave his farm for long. Without his constant presence and policing of his property the pastoralists would encroach, he said:

> When you get busy doing other things, they will be there. When we catch them, we take them to the police and make sure they are prosecuted. If they do it again, you catch them. So, it is an ongoing thing. You must not allow them to do it. And the other thing is all the vegetation they will come across, they will clear for firewood. So, there is no peace, you have to be here all the time. [...] If they could get away with [crossing the fence], they will. They do on other people's property, cut their fence. If you have a good fence, they won't. The Samburu especially are notorious for that. [...] They have come here in large numbers, and there is a particular 'bad' politician [...] that incites them all the time. [...] This is all politics. There is a lot of that going on. It gives them courage.[142]

Another ranch owner, whose family has been in Kenya since colonial times, also has opinions about the African groups around his ranch:

> Mostly, Kikuyu areas are fine. Kikuyu are very good at respecting boundaries. [...] The landlords [at my former farm] were the main problem. [...] They wanted money. They always wanted money. [...] Kalenjins are

140 Interview with research participant, Laikipia, 8 June 2015.
141 Interview with research participant, Laikipia, 8 June 2015.
142 Interview with research participant, Laikipia, 6 March 2015.

> always short of money. So, by the end of the year you have already paid half of next year.[143]

Without disregarding the ranchers' experience and frustrations, this rhetoric is reminiscent of that of colonial Kenya, with its ranking of groups according to ethnicity.[144] The rhetoric of the pastoralists as 'a menace to white settlement' and the Kikuyu as more trustworthy is a way to navigate the social landscape using labelled categories.[145]

Moreover, the ranchers' rhetoric is in line with Locke's principles of protection of private property as a 'natural right,' based on the argument that labour on land protected by private-property rights was an improvement on nature as common land. Locke argued that the prime concern of any government should be to protect its citizens' private property.[146] One of the ranchers described his understanding of private property as an untouchable entity: 'private land is private land and if I decide to go onto someone's private land and do what I want and no one stops me, even the government, then something is wrong.'[147]

The ranchers' relationship with the government is complicated. In certain situations, such as dealing with illegal grazing, the police and judicial system need to be involved. As one rancher explains:

> you don't always want to fight. I will continue to provoke and alienate those who want to fight because I have come to the conclusion that if they want to fight the best people to deal with it [...] are the administration. And if they [the Samburu] keep doing it, they are marked as inciters and troublemakers. [Then we can say] 'it is always this family that is involved, look, we have got 1, 2, 3, 4, 5 court cases against them, or incidents in the police books,' and that will in time enable the sorting and we will be able to do away with them.[148]

However, in other situations, the ranchers would rather remain uninvolved with the state and tend to their own matters. A rancher explained how he attempted to have as little to do with the state as possible and in turn did not

143 Interview with research participant, Laikipia, 12 May 2015.
144 Oucho, *Undercurrents of Ethnic Conflicts in Kenya*.
145 Lonsdale, 'Kenya: Home County and African Frontiers.'
146 John Locke, *Two Treatises of Government*, ed. P. Laslett (Cambridge: Cambridge University Press, [1690] 1991).
147 Interview with research participant, Laikipia, 6 March 2015.
148 Interview with research participant, Laikipia, 8 June 2015.

expect the state to help him. He believed that allowing wildlife to prosper on a farm would become one's ruin, because scaling down security for the sake of the wildlife would 'make you weak' towards encroachment.[149] Another rancher agreed with this perspective: 'You know, to Samburu, if they see grass like that [in a conservancy], they can't resist.'[150] One rancher rejected inclusion in rancher associations, such as Laikipia Wildlife Forum, arguing that organising the white community into a semi-political entity could incite the government to evict the whole white community – as in Zimbabwe. He saw the government as a sleeping lion that could wake up at any minute and that it would only take a mention in one of President Kenyatta's speeches for people to revolt and start entering the ranches.[151]

From the outside, the ranchers and conservationists seem similar. Having a shared past as foreigners can be a uniting factor. However, the bases for their lifestyles are very different and they tend not to agree on the politics of the land. For instance, upon one rancher being asked whether he would like to include more conservancy practice on his ranch, he exclaimed:

> I don't want to! I mean, we are not chasing animals out, we look after them the best we can. But we don't make any money out of them. It is not a priority. And for the future of the country, we can't have areas that could be producing foodstuff just set aside for wildlife. The population needs to eat; the population needs to get employment. Those are the things for us.[152]

Other ranchers agree on this perspective on sustainable land management. One used Ol Pajeta Conservancy to illustrate his point:

> The bills in the farm [Ol Pajeta Conservancy] are paid by donations from people. It is not sustainable. That is a big organisation, they have a big fence around it, and so I don't think they have issues with illegal grazing. But don't think people like it! I tell them in 2040 or 2050, half of Ol Pajeta will be under farming. There will be big tractors there because the world needs food. You can't just have 90,000 acres of land just for a few tourists here and there. Half of the farm is good soil. On one side, there is a person who has leased 3,000 acres and he is farming wheat successfully. [...] He

149 Interview with research participant, Laikipia, 6 March 2015.
150 Interview with research participant, Laikipia, 12 May 2015.
151 Interview with research participant, Laikipia, 6 March 2015.
152 Interview with research participant, Laikipia, 12 May 2015.

> makes more money and pays taxes to the government than the whole of that 90,000 acres at Ol Pajeta.[153]

Ranchers and smallholders seem to agree that what characterises good land is its potential for farming. To both parties, good land is productive land, and wildlife is not as important as food production.[154]

In general, the ranchers establish themselves in islands of enclosures where they strive for non-involvement with their surroundings. The control they claim is over their own private property, and they pay little attention to what belongs to others. Likewise, they are not controlled by others and only get involved with state institutions to the degree that they must. In other words, they strive for autonomy in their livelihoods.

4.3.4 *The Conservationists*

The fourth group making claim to land and presence in Laikipia is the conservationists. Similarly to the ranchers, most of them immigrated to Kenya during colonial times or immediately after. Unlike the ranchers, they are often engaged in limited agricultural and ranching activities and only maintain them to financially support their effort to protect wildlife and biodiversity. Their conservancies consist of former ranches converted into zones for wildlife. They rely on income from tourism or international donors rather than on agricultural production, and therefore the ranchers and conservationists disagree on the definition of what valuable land consists of. According to Hughes, it was by identifying with nature and nature-based tourism that 'whites found a reason for being in Africa. They gained footing on a moral foundation stronger and more lasting than the state and the nation together.'[155] This ideology, although referring to conservationists in South Africa, also applies to Laikipia's conservationists and their way of perceiving their place in the world. As a group, they share an active opposition to the outside world – by blaming the 'system,' they reinforce their group identity and sense of purpose.

Like the ranchers, the conservationists are challenged by the pastoralist encroachments. However, they tend to have to deal with greater pressure from these intruders than the ranchers due to the dilemma of fencing. With a fence the encroachers are easier to keep out, but the movement of the wildlife is

153 Interview with research participant, Laikipia, 6 March 2015.

154 Interview with research participant, Thome, 13 May 2015; interview with research participant, Laikipia, 12 May 2015; interview with research participant, Laikipia, 6 March 2015.

155 David McDermott Hughes, 'Third Nature: Making Space and Time in the Great Limpopo Conservation Area,' *Cultural Anthropology* 20, no. 2 (1 May 2005), p. 161.

restricted. Without a fence the wildlife move more freely, but the ability to control the pastoralist encroachers is reduced. Whereas the ranchers would choose the option of fencing, the conservationists tend not to because the wildlife takes priority. This view is held even when the wildlife crosses the conservancy boundaries and marauds in the neighbouring smallholders' land. The executive director of one of the conservancies demonstrates this viewpoint, saying:

> Elephants are migratory animals and the people are living on the elephants' land. [...] We do not feel responsible for damages and injuries outside our fences. We are paying taxes to the Kenyan state. If the KWS [Kenya Wildlife Service] is not compensating the local people for damages, that is not the problem of the conservancy.[156]

This statement almost confirms the claim by the smallholders that the conservationists care more about the life and wellbeing of wildlife than those of the smallholders subject to attacks and ruined harvests on account of the wildlife.

In 1985, the Laikipia Wildlife Forum registered 1,648 elephants in Laikipia; in 2016, the number had increased to 3,321.[157] Moreover, elephants have also learned where it is safe to stay and where it is not. A conservancy manager explained the challenge of protecting something that is a burden to biodiversity: 'The land where the elephants are free to roam has drastically decreased. So, they cannot roam where they used to, and so, end up over-staying and destroying you.'[158]

The way the conservationists argue for protection of biodiversity is in line with Hughes' description of 'third nature':

> Third nature refers [...] to the potential of landforms in a given area to support specific types of wildlife communities. [...] It is not past, present, or future, but conditional; not a tense, but a mood of speech. When they write or speak, cautious conservationists use 'should,' 'would,' and other markers of this mood. Just as often, however, conservationists misuse the indicative mood. They impute current existence to a desired future and conjure a material form for third nature.[159]

---

156 Interview with research participant, Laikipia, 9 September 2016.

157 A.K. Kes Hillman Smith, Gordon O. Ojwang and Victor N. Mose, *Systematic Aerial Sample Survey of Laikipia County*, preliminary report (Nanyuki, Kenya: Impala Research Centre and Laikipia Wildlife Forum, April 2016).

158 Interview with research participant, Laikipia, 14 April 2015.

159 Hughes, 'Third Nature,' p. 158.

One can look at the Laikipia conservationists' attitudes to the future of land use in Kenya to exemplify this position. A common viewpoint among them is that the future use of rural areas in Kenya *should* be planned on the state level. With urban migration, rural land *should* be made available for large-scale farming of food crops and ranching, as well as areas being set aside exclusively for wildlife rather than sustaining smallholders and pastoralists.[160] According to one conservancy manager:

> There is no future in pastoralism; they need to change their culture and have alternatives in livelihood activities. [...] If we were to give the pastoralists, 90,000 acres of our lands to graze, what would happen to that land? After a few months or years, they would have destroyed it, just like their own land. [...] They [the Pokot] need to de-stock their cattle – they are destroying the land. Seventy per cent of the north of Kenya is already completely dry. There is soil erosion and nothing growing there anymore. Sheep and goats are the worst; they are eating all the small plants. [...] Pastoralism is not doing anything for the national economy. [...] The elders of the Pokot are not cooperative. When we are trying to cooperate with them, they burn down our grassland. They are heavily armed with AK-47s – every family has a weapon.[161]

Another conservancy owner was less categorical towards the pastoralists, although he also supported the position of the state structures of land-use schemes and engaged with the way his own position as a large-scale landowner was represented:

> the Samburu just pour in with thousands of cattle. It is a very good political strategy. You know Lempurkel has been recorded saying: 'if you vote me in, I will drive all the Europeans out – they can go back to where they came from. The grass is yours.' This is really why the problem has arisen. I was just telling these chaps [Samburu] today [...] that we have actually been in Laikipia for 100 years! And Lempurkel has probably not even been here for 30 years – he is not native to Laikipia at all. So, when he tells us to go back to where we came from, this *is* actually where we came from.[162]

160 Interview with research participant, Laikipia, 12 May 2015; interview with research participant, Laikipia, 9 September 2016.
161 Interview with research participant, Laikipia, 9 September 2016.
162 Interview with research participant, Laikipia, 24 July 2015.

According to some of the conservationists, the future solution to the encroachment is stronger regulation of livestock by the government – for instance through a set quota per acre enforced by the state.[163] Reminiscent of Malthus' principle of carrying capacity and Hardin's 'tragedy of the commons,' the presumption is that such a solution would limit those who owned more livestock than their own land could sustain.[164]

Others employed the idea of sustainable land use to argue more pragmatically for government-authorised zoning. A conservancy manager explained:

> So, for instance for a 35,000-acre plot; it's a lot of land, and people say 'wow, and it's owned by one man!' And in Kenya now, a lot of people disagree with that but if you look at what's sustainable land use then some people will start to understand why it has to be kept in one unit. It can be owned by a thousand people, but it should never be cut up into smaller units. It's not sustainable. Then it causes environmental degradation.[165]

Unlike some of the other conservationists, this manager did not argue that Africans are destructive by nature.[166] Rather, he argued against subdivided land use. Zoning of land is an option that has been mentioned in election campaigns as a way of dividing the land according to its highest potential to be productive. In that sense, you would have zones for tea and sugarcane, zones for ranching and wildlife, and zones for pastoralism.[167]

This worldview is supported by a belief in the state as the guardian of long-term environmental decisions. Yet the executive director of one of the conservancies argued that it is the responsibility of the state to protect the private property of the conservancies rather than the rights of the encroachers: 'the Pokot and other communities can exploit the formal laws and informal corruption better than we can. After all, [the Conservancy] is a legal entity and the Pokot [activities] are not!'[168] He asked rhetorically: 'why is there private property, national parks and national forests in Kenya, if it is not being protected by the police and local politicians?'[169]

The conservationists are a strong group bound together by their common struggle to protect wildlife and biodiversity. Following Hughes, they

163 Interview with research participant, Laikipia, 9 September 2016.
164 Hardin, 'The Tragedy of the Commons'; Malthus, *An Essay on the Principle of Population.*
165 Interview with research participant, Laikipia, 14 April 2015.
166 Hardin, 'The Tragedy of the Commons'; Malthus, *An Essay on the Principle of Population.*
167 Interview with research participant, Laikipia, 14 April 2015.
168 Interview with research participant, Laikipia, 9 September 2016.
169 Interview with research participant, Laikipia, 9 September 2016.

see themselves as the moral upholders of order in shared opposition to the outside world – often to their immediate pastoralist or smallholder neighbours.[170] The conservationists are dependent on support from government authorities such as KWS and the police to be able to handle the pressure on their land from outside actors, and they even advocate for stronger state involvement. Despite their struggles with encroachment, they have been successful in occupying the moral high ground in general international debates, gathering widespread sympathy across the globe for their fights and efforts. This can be illustrated in the way they managed to occupy the international media's portrayal of Laikipia's 2016–17 land invasions with headlines such as *The Guardian*'s 'Armed Herders Invade Laikipia's Most Important Wildlife Conservancy.'[171]

4.3.5 *The Absentees*

Unlike the four other groups, the absentees are not physically present in Laikipia, and their claim to the resources is less of a claim than a passive position that looks to gain without making a claim.[172] Nevertheless, their position has been a determinant for many others. The ranchers', the smallholders' and the conservationists' insecure situations can partly be explained by the fact that the absentee landlords have not settled on the land they own. Had they done so, there would not have been any seemingly vacant land to attract pastoralists to settle on.[173] Moreover, without the absentee livestock owners, the general pressure for the pastoralists to acquire grazing would be eased, benefiting all groups present in Laikipia.

I use the term *absentees* to refer to absentee landlords as well as absentee livestock owners to stress the element of investment that applies to both. Individuals in this category have few internal group unifications. The individuals are driven by personal gain in competitive environments. They are not subject to control by others, nor do they wish to control others. Yet their practices can have serious consequences for others.

---

170 Hughes, *From Enslavement to Environmentalism.*

171 Adam Cruise and Bibi van der Zee, 'Armed Herders Invade Laikipia's Most Important Wildlife Conservancy,' *The Guardian*, 2 February 2017, https://www.theguardian.com/environment/2017/feb/02/armed-herders-elephant-kenya-wildlife-laikipia, accessed 12 January 2020.

172 Interview with absentee landlord, anonymous, Githunguri, 15 September 2015.

173 Interview with research participant, Nyahururu, 21 March 2016; interview with research participant, central Laikipia, May 12 2015; interview with research participant, central Laikipia, 8 June 2015.

When land-buying companies were buying colonial ranches, many oversold shares in the land. In some cases, settling was not allowed before the land sale processes were finalised. These processes often stalled, functioning as a loophole for company directors to sell more shares and gain financially from the high demand for land. This was a problem for those shareholders who were smallholders and needed to settle. But, a large proportion of shareholders had bought shares with no intention to settle. This made the negotiating power of the settled shareholders weak, and in many cases they have not managed to put enough pressure on company directors to provide them with title deeds even after 20 years.[174]

The shareholders with no intention to settle were often wealthy Kikuyu from Central Province. As absentee landlords, they defend their investments by saying that anyone could have bought land when the companies were founded and that they should not be condemned for seizing an opportunity to invest.[175] As an absentee landlord in Githunguri argued:

> There are those that will prosper more than others. That is what happens when it comes to land. When most Kikuyu were buying land, those there [the non-Kikuyu] did not buy. They never realised that land would eventually be subdivided and become scarce. The Kikuyu had seen the future. They needed to get enough land for their families. One acre of land today isn't enough. […] Most Kikuyu here [in Central Province] own land elsewhere. They reached out to other places for new land. That is a form of investment.[176]

The absentees consider themselves successful for recognising an opportunity to invest. One of them used the term *Mugikuyu*, referring to Kikuyu investors as more intelligent than others.[177] This rhetoric has a racial element, resembling that of the ranchers reproducing colonial categories. The absentees described how their own community had been enlightened into seeing the true value of land. One absentee explained:

> Basically, Kikuyu made land to be part of their life, so it is as essential as life is. You must have somewhere to settle. […] Land matters are not a joke. […] I think the other communities do not really know the value of

174 Interview with research participant, Rumuruti, 3 August 2015.
175 Interview with absentee landlords, Githunguri, 15 September 2015.
176 Interview with absentee landlord, Githunguri, 15 September 2015.
177 Interview with absentee landlord, Githunguri, 15 September 2015.

> land. [...] Some people even say title deeds are just mere papers. [...] The Kikuyu were able to open their eyes earlier and [have] a culture of investment.[178]

While Kikuyu present in Laikipia tended to be more positive towards the mixed ethnic composition,[179] the absentees were more reluctant to acknowledge the usefulness of such complexities, and used stereotyping to support their arguments:

> Since the land was bought by the Kikuyu, it is the Kikuyu who should be settled there. [...] It is not good to live [mixed with other communities]. The cultural conflict will not make people progress. So, people should have a place where they are only one community that understand one another, hence progression. [...] When I was [in Thome in Laikipia], no Samburu was farming. Today, a few of them have learnt from the Kikuyu and have started farming. [...] We could not copy anything from them since most of their behaviour is not good. [...] We transformed the Turkana. [...] It is for them to copy us since we advanced.[180]

To the absentees, the opposition to mixed communities and the denigration of them justified their position as better resource users.

However, there are some absentees who have started to use their land. With the focus on gaining a return on their investment, they have been reluctant to use their land for small-scale agriculture in the way the smallholders do. Instead, some have sought out their fellow absentees to buy the neighbouring shares to their land. Thereby, they accumulate enough land to make it worthwhile to farm on a larger scale using a hired manager.[181] This option for making land productive is increasingly taken on the absentee land in Ol Moran, where large fields of maize are becoming more predominant in the landscape.[182] However, this practice necessitates sufficient financial means. It is necessary to invest in security measures, fence the land and equip the manager with

178 Interview with vice chairman of Thome Farmers Company, Githunguri, 15 September 2015; interview with research participant, Rumuruti, 3 August 2015.

179 Interview with research participant, Ol Moran, 21 July 2015; interview with research participant, Rumuruti, 3 August 2015.

180 Interview with vice chairman of Thome Farmers Company, Githunguri, 15 September 2015; interview with absentee landlord, Githunguri, 15 September 2015.

181 Interview with research participant, Ol Moran, 21 July 2015.

182 Interview with research participant, Ol Moran, 17 March 2016.

machinery such as a tractor. For that reason, this option is only relevant to absentees with a secure income from elsewhere.[183]

This strategy corresponds with the argument for zoning, because it goes against the subdivision of the land while providing food for urban market sales, reflecting what several of the ranchers and conservationists considered sustainable land use for the future.[184]

The existence of the other type of absentees, the absentee livestock owners, has also had an effect on the social-ecological system in Laikipia. According to the newspaper *The Star*, 'it is widely believed that most of the cattle driven into Laikipia belong to politicians and cattle barons, who hide their wealth in livestock and employ their relatives to herd them.'[185] Some of the conservationists even claimed that up to one third of the illegally grazing cattle were owned by local politicians or by the police.[186] One of them stated: 'cattle are used for money laundry, because one does not have to pay taxes for them. [...] So many politicians invest in cattle and later sell the meat. The money is washed after that.'[187] This opinion was also voiced by local scholars and many of the smallholders in relation to the 2016–17 pastoralist invasions. 'It is a myth that this is about poor pastoralists who just need grass due to drought,' one Laikipian stated. 'The truth is that the majority of the cattle are owned by MPs, administration officials, top cops and other rich barons who hide their money in cattle to evade taxes.'[188]

Many young Samburu are expected to prosper in spite of the limited access to resources, which makes the herding of an absentee's livestock a welcome task that offers an extra income.[189] However, the presence of the additional livestock on the already depleted grazing areas has increased pressure on all in need of grazing. The pressure to become innovative in measures to acquire resources has pulled some pastoralists into the criminal activity of stealing livestock – often through the highly skilled and organised ventures of cattle-rustling syndicates.[190]

183 Field notes, visit to manager at absentee landholding, Ol Moran, 20 April 2015.
184 Interview with research participant, Laikipia, 14 April 2015; field notes, visit to manager at absentee landholding, Ol Moran, 20 April 2015.
185 *The Star*, 'Land Invasion Wrecks Laikipia.'
186 Interview with research participant, Laikipia, 14 April 2015.
187 Interview with research participant, Laikipia, 9 September 2016.
188 *The Star*, 'Laikipia Clashes Persist as MPs, Cops, Barons Blamed.'
189 Interview with research participant, Nyahururu, 21 March 2016.
190 *The Daily Nation*, 'Politicians, Businessmen behind Cattle Raids: Intelligence Report,' 21 January 2017, http://www.nation.co.ke/news/Politicians--businessmen-fuelling-cattle-raids/1056-3781620-txq5s5z/index.html, accessed 30 January 2017; interview with reformed syndicate member, Salama, 21 December 2016.

The existence of the absentees has encouraged conservationists and ranchers to become more protectionist regarding their property by increasing investments in fencing, enforcement of livestock retention and filing lawsuits against the intruders.[191] However, these measures often only motivate the encroaching pastoralists to become even more innovative in their measures to acquire access.[192]

As a form of independent entrepreneurs, the absentees are free agents. They do not see how they can be held responsible for other people's misfortunes in securing a livelihood on the plateau. They do also not consider themselves as being unfair to anyone or as doing anything illegal because they are simply seizing an opportunity. As opportunists, they attribute the blame for this instead to personal failure or lack of competitive skills. However, as free agents, they risk losing income from their land speculations if prices change, and similarly, they can lose income from illegal grazing if they are caught trespassing. In this sense, as independent agents their lacking cooperation as a group also makes them vulnerable.[193]

4.3.6 *Group Mobility*

The use of categorisation to navigate social and cultural diversity can help to provide an understanding of the complex social-ecological landscape in Laikipia. However, the categorisation does not negate overlap, mobility and change between the groups.

Before Independence, both conservationists and ranchers were engaged in agricultural activities, safeguarded by a colonial government. Independence brought a political change, to which the ranchers and conservationists reacted differently. Whereas the ranchers sought to isolate themselves from the changes to protect what was inside their legal boundaries, the conservationists took on more expansive approaches in their newfound position as custodians of biodiversity – whether inside or outside the legal boundaries of their land. Some of the ranchers support this stance as well; however, they would only invest in the conservationists' cause of protecting biodiversity if it were to benefit their own businesses.

The Kikuyu are overrepresented among the smallholders as well as among the absentees. They used to have closer bonds based on their shared ethnic affiliations. However, variation in the capacity to navigate the new political

191 Interview with research participant, Laikipia, 8 June 2015.

192 Interview with research participant, Nyahururu, 21 March 2016; interview with research participant, Sugoroi, 29 May 2015.

193 Interview with research participant, Laikipia, 21 March 2016.

landscape introduced in the Independence years enhanced existing divisions. In attempts to battle landlessness, some acquired strong political positions while others assumed debt. Not limited by internal group authorities, the absentees were motivated by these new opportunities to pursue their own interests, while the smallholders made similar attempts but ended up as subordinates in the social-ecological system due to their limited financial resources.

4.4 When Claims of Entitlement Are Acted Out

The extent to which the different types of claims are displayed in everyday rhetoric and public debates underlines the power of the discourses inherent in claiming narratives in Laikipia. As has been alluded to in the descriptions of the five groups, as well as in the case of land conflict in Lorien and the historic case of the Powys murder, narratives substantiating a claim to land in Laikipia are not confined only to rhetoric but have extensively manifested in actions. Actions materialise to strengthen a claim to resources not already under the claimant's control or as a way of protecting resources from others. Examples of claims that are acted out include fence-making by ranchers and smallholders; the passive celebration of, or active killing of, wild animals by smallholders and pastoralists; cattle raiding by pastoralists or young men from mixed ethnic groups;[194] and occupational settlements on land that is legally owned by others. All can be actions of protest or manifestations of claims to the resources, although they take different shapes.

4.4.1 *Encroachment and Raiding*

Physical attacks can be seen as demonstrations of power and as protests against the holder of resources. Example of this are the intensified Samburu settlements on absentee land and the subsequent illegal grazing on ranchers' land.[195]

These acted-out claims can be supported by an autochthonous narrative[196] or stand alone as acts of rebellion conveying political statements.[197] In circumstances where it is not possible to voice a claim, such as in the example of the Samburu's murder of Powys in the 1930s, the acts of rebellion alone can be

194 Marie Gravesen and Eric Kioko, 'Cooperation in the midst of Violence: Cattle Raids and Land Deals in Laikipia and Narok,' *Africa* 89, no. 3 (August 2019), pp. 562–85.

195 Interview with research participant, Nyahururu, 21 March 2016.

196 Kenya NTV, 'What is Ailing Laikipia'; interview with research participant, Nyahururu, 21 March 2016.

197 Interview with research participant, Nyahururu, 21 March 2016.

enough to challenge the holders of the resources. The Powys case illustrates that the physical manifestation of claims is not a new phenomenon.[198] That said, the pressure on resources has increased since the 1930s, and so have the frequency, intensity and complexity of the physical manifestations of claims.

Yet there is more to encroachment than mere protest. One older conservancy owner explains:

> in the past, there has always been stock theft. It was mostly the Dorobo and they are very good stock thieves, and also Samburu. And that was quite fun, in tracking stolen stock. They regarded it as a sport and so did we. You wouldn't have a month go by without an incident.[199]

This quote illustrates the systematic dynamics between raiders and trackers of stolen animals, in which both can be considered simultaneously victims and perpetrators. However, more significantly, the respondent points to a continuing high prevalence of encroachment even during colonial times. This alludes to a reality in which protest is linked to the necessity of accessing resources. Laikipia was always, and continues to be, a challenging place to be – despite the glorifying descriptions used in campaigns to attract settlers. Pastoralists, colonial settlers and post-colonial land-users alike have all dealt with the same ecological limitations, many of which relate to the fact that Laikipia has never been a well-watered place.

For instance, the struggle behind the context of the Powys murder and the Samburu's fight to protect access to the Leroghi plateau during the KLC in the 1930s relates to a struggle to protect access not only to land alone but also to water. Leroghi is one of few well-watered places in the northern parts of the plateau. This lack was part of what kept these northern lands from being scheduled for European settlement far into the 1940s. The Samburu needed access to water, including in Leroghi, to maintain their grazing movements, which also necessitated encroachment onto the northern ranches, such as that of Powys. Concurrently, the lack of water is at the heart of many other challenges faced by the land-users. These aspects will be dealt with in more detail in Chapter 7.

So, whereas raiding activities are often seen as isolated events with a perpetrator claiming livestock and a victim being subjected to the claim, this is not

198 Fratkin, 'The Samburu Laibon's Sorcery and the Death of Theodore Powys in Colonial Kenya.'

199 Interview with research participant, northern Laikipia, 24 July 2015.

necessarily all there is to it.[200] Instead they encompass deep-seated patterns and are grounded in fundamental resource challenges that over time have come to illustrate larger movements of protest.

4.4.2 *Killing of Wildlife*

To many of the smallholders and pastoralists, the elephant is a menace that has less right to be present in Laikipia than the communities. Often, the elephant is considered owned by the *wazungu*, the white people, reducing it to a property rather than an equal actor in the landscape. A common opinion among Laikipians was that conservancies are 'a rich man's playground.'[201] This opinion was voiced by smallholders, who either found their crops continually destroyed by elephants or had difficulty finding grazing for their livestock on the lands next to conservancies.

Occasionally, these frustrations would be acted out. The security manager at one of the ranches explained how KWS internal intelligence reports had described incidents where the Pokot:

> shoot the elephant because [the owner of the conservancy] has no cattle in the farm. [The owner] gets the money from tourism, so they want to destroy that. [...] They go and shoot but don't take the elephant's tusk. Then, they say that if they do that, the tourists will not come to that conservancy, then they will take their animals inside to graze because there are no cattle inside, but tourism.[202]

Although I did not see these reports myself, the described actions coincide with explanations given by pastoralists and smallholders neighbouring the conservancy.[203] By killing the elephant, the pastoralists wish to harm the owner's business and inhibit the tourists from coming to see the wildlife. They are not poachers but wish to make a statement of protest regarding the way the resources are being used. They felt unable to voice their opinion due to the

200 David Anderson, 'Stock Theft and Moral Economy in Colonial Kenya,' *Africa* 56 (1986), pp. 399–416; Fratkin, 'The Samburu Laibon's Sorcery and the Death of Theodore Powys in Colonial Kenya.'

201 Interview with research participant, Laikipia, 12 May 2015.

202 Interview with research participant, Laikipia, 12 May 2015.

203 Interview with research participant, Ol Moran, 21 July 2015; interview with research participant, Nyahururu, 21 March 2016.

imbalanced power relations. Yet they kept watching grass being 'wasted' on wildlife, while their own farming investments were at risk of marauding.[204]

Practices of acting out a claim by means of targeted livestock raids, forced grazing and killing of wildlife on tourist sites in conservancy areas are all actions that culminated in the recent invasions of ranches and conservancies in Laikipia, where especially Samburu *morans* but also Pokot youth rose against the large ranches and conservancies.[205] Here the invading pastoralists shot wildlife to protest against their exclusion from the grazing resources and from political representation.[206] Indeed, a memo to the cabinet secretary for the interior, Joseph Nkaissery, signed by eight political leaders in Laikipia read: 'It is obvious that the happenings in Laikipia are […] a result of expansionism, with the main aim being forceful eviction of ranchers in private and group ranches.'[207] Therefore, the wave of invasions illustrates the potency of the tension in Laikipia, and how little it would take for frustrations and everyday narratives of claim-making to ignite and materialise into violence.

Besides the killing of wildlife and encroachment, another way to act out a claim is fencing. This is mostly done by smallholders and ranchers with title deeds and share certificates. Besides materialising the claim to the territory, fencing is a tool to control intrusion and counter claims from the outside. As resources become increasingly scarce, the measure of establishing new fences and enforcing old ones has become increasingly prevalent.[208]

4.5 Concluding Remarks

The representations of the actors, their justifications for using resources and the historical narratives of grievance illustrate claims of belonging and entitlement to resources. The fact that certain claims have been allowed to gain weight illustrates that the titling of land has become institutionalised as a

204 Interview with research participant, Thome, 24 June 2015; interview with research participant, Thome, 18 June 2015; interview with research participant, Maa chairman for Laikipia West, Rumuruti, 14 July 2015; interview with research participant, Marura, 9 March 2015, interview with research participant, Marura, 6 May 2015.

205 Kenya NTV, 'What is Ailing Laikipia'; interview with research participant, Nyahururu, 21 March 2016.

206 *The Star*, 'Land Invasion Wrecks Laikipia'; interview with research participant, Nyahururu, 21 March 2016.

207 *The Star*, 'Land Invasion Wrecks Laikipia.'

208 Interview with research participant, Laikipia, 6 March 2015; interview with research participant, Laikipia, 12 May 2015; interview with research participant, Laikipia, 9 September 2016.

legitimised tool to exclude others. One does not need proof of a historical presence to make a claim of private property, because the title deed undermines the validity of any other claim, given its legal authority. Therefore, as the vice chairman of Thome Farmers Company explains it, 'the title deed is a weapon of displacement – if you have it, you can confidently settle and fence, hence displacing those who do not own land there.'[209] Without it you must manoeuvre the landscapes without legal backing – constantly risking removal. Such risks of landlessness may even make 30 years of court cases worthwhile.

Without political representation, some feel forced to independently act out their claim to either protect or acquire resources they consider theirs. Whether issues arise between competing shareholders in a land-buying company, between encroachers and ranchers, or between smallholders killing an elephant and conservationists supporting the elephants' roaming, all represent claims to resources. All attempt to move or retain the power balance determining who holds access to the resources.

209 Interview with research participant, Githunguri, 15 September 2015.

CHAPTER 5

Enclosing the Land: From Common Land to Freehold Farmland and Back

> Fences and other property lines constitute the second crucial concept of territorial mentality. In order to be exclusive, zones of ownership must mark the landscape in a way that signals the geographical terminus of one claim and the beginning of another – no overlap allowed.
>
> DAVID MCDERMOTT HUGHES[1]

∵

Laikipia is a frontier full of ambiguity and contradiction – divided and connected by fences. It is a space where abundance exists alongside starvation, and where there is opportunity, yet also risk. At times, it seems the Kikuyu smallholders have more in common with the pastoralist encroachers than with their better-off kin further south. The lives of both tend to be bound by insecurity, whereas those that are better off have invested in land and made use of large networks and political connections.[2] This makes class and wealth another aspect of ethnic land politics.[3] The particular way this is played out distinguishes Laikipia from adjoining areas, almost as if Laikipia in itself is an enclosure: an island within the nation-state of Kenya.

This chapter investigates the materiality of the land claims and what has led them to intensify. Several cases are illustrative of political strategies and power struggles that materialise in the attempt to gain control over land in Laikipia. In this chapter, I highlight the story of the settler family Dykes from the 1970s. According to Fortmann, telling a story serves at least three purposes for the storyteller: 'to create meaning and validate action, to mobilize action, and to define alternatives.'[4] The Dykes story is indicative of the different ways of making claims to the resources. Furthermore, the story illustrates the influence of ethnicised politics in the post-Independence years, and of how the division of land resources drew lines far into the political system.

1 Hughes, *From Enslavement to Environmentalism*, p. 9.
2 Kohler, *Land Use in Transition*.
3 Leo, *Land and Class in Kenya*.
4 Fortmann, 'Talking Claims,' p. 1054.

 | DOI:10.1163/9789004435209_006

I also use this case to ponder the transitioning of the landholding systems. Before colonisation, the land in Laikipia could be characterised as a common-property regime, with collective access defining the use of the resources.[5] During colonialism, the landholding system transitioned into a private-property regime, with ownership and exclusion as the defining characteristics. In present-day Laikipia, parts of the private-property landholdings have now transitioned back to common-property landholding systems.[6] This is the case when pastoralists settle and use resources in the private absentee lands, as well as accessing the ranches and conservancies. Whereas the transition from common land to private-property land has been studied many times before, the transfer from private land to common land has not been extensively documented.[7]

Finally, I relate the context to two types of practice for claiming space: the naming of places as symbolic enclosure and the fencing of space as physical enclosure, both of which function as tools to divide the landscape into separate entities that relate to the holder of each partiality.[8] This process envisions what Lefebvre describes as the transition from mental space to real space.[9]

5.1 The Construction of Enclosure in Laikipia: The Story of the Dykes

Among the files of the Foreign and Commonwealth Office released to the public at the National Archives in Kew, I came across a file, compiled by the British High Commission, with letters of correspondence and minutes of meetings in relation to a settler family in Laikipia in the years around Independence.[10] Later, in Laikipia, I was again confronted with the story when ranch owners referred to the Dykes family.[11]

5 Ostrom, *Governing the Commons.*

6 John Galaty, 'Reasserting the Commons: Pastoral Contestations of Private and State Lands in East Africa,' *International Journal of the Commons* 10, no. 2 (30 September 2016), pp. 709–27.

7 Bollig and Lesorogol, 'The "New Pastoral Commons" of Eastern and Southern Africa.'

8 Lauren A. Evans and William M. Adams, 'Fencing Elephants: The Hidden Politics of Wildlife Fencing in Laikipia, Kenya,' *Land Use Policy* 51 (February 2016), pp. 215–28; Lawrence D. Berg and Robin A. Kearns, 'Naming as Norming: "Race," Gender, and the Identity Politics of Naming Places in Aotearoa/New Zealand,' *Environment and Planning D: Society and Space* 14, no. 1 (1 February 1996), pp. 99–122.

9 Henri Lefebvre, *The Production of Space*, translated by Donald Nicholson-Smith (Oxford and Cambridge, MA: Wiley-Blackwell, 1991).

10 TNA, FCO 141/19572, 'Kenya Land Transfer Programme – John Alison Dykes, Marmar Ranching and Trading Ltd, Laikipia,' 1975 – 1976.

11 Interview with research participant, south-western Laikipia, 6 March 2015; interview with research participant, central Laikipia, 12 May 2015.

The Dykes story is relevant because the Independence years were a time of transition with regard to the holding and use of land. This was when outsiders challenged old systems of landholding, leading to a paradigm shift in land relations. This means that the story is essentially about place-making through enclosures, and how such processes were consistently challenged.

Mr Andrew Dykes was a prominent settler in Laikipia up through the 1940s and 1950s. Following the Soldier Settlement in 1919 Andrew Dykes took up his first farm, Melwa Ranch Ltd, in 1921. In 1950, when the scheduled areas had been expanded towards the north of Laikipia, he took up his second ranch, Marmar Ranch Ltd, situated directly bordering the Samburu area.[12]

Two of Andrew Dykes' sons, John and Andrew, managed the northern ranch for their father. This was not an easy task. Bordering the Northern Frontier District and Suguta Marmar in Samburu, the ranch held water and grazing grounds that were used by Samburu pastoralists. They were no less eager or dependent on the resources just because the land was now formally held as a ranch. Both the father and the sons were advocates for their right to carry guns to protect their land. The Samburu's claim to the area was now reduced to physical protest through bush fires and illegal grazing. For years the brothers and the Samburu fought back and forth – the brothers with attempts to enforce security and the enclosing of the ranch, and the Samburu with persistent protests through encroachment – until one day in 1975, when Andrew was caught in one of the bush fires and died of his injuries.[13]

The Northern Frontiers District in present-day Samburu County continues to denote an area outside the state. Indeed, even today, people commonly speak of 'travelling to Kenya' when going south from Samburu County, and likewise, people travelling north from Laikipia talk of 'leaving Kenya.'[14] People in these northern parts find themselves on the edge of the state, with little political representation and lacking service delivery and institutional infrastructure.[15] With a weak state presence in land matters and manifold types of access opportunism, Laikipia can be determined as a frontier.

12 TNA, FCO 141/19572, 'Dykes to Wigan,' 26 December 1975.

13 TNA, FCO 141/19572, 'Godley to Avery,' 12 June 1975; TNA, FCO 141/19572, 'Dykes to Wigan,' 26 December 1975.

14 Field notes, Maralal, 25 October 2014.

15 Field notes, Maralal, 25 October 2014.

Following Kopytoff[16] and Hughes,[17] the term *frontier* is to be understood not as a static label but as a fluid category that changes over time depending on the degree of state presence and control. An interchanging precariousness means that there are links between times where the state has practised inaction and times when the violence has erupted in Laikipia.[18] Recent examples of this are the 2004 and 2011 land invasions by Maasai on Laikipia ranches to claim back the land they had been evicted from 100 years earlier, as well as the 2016–17 wave of land invasions by Pokot and Samburu onto conservancies and ranches.[19] The incidences in 2004 followed a campaign in Nairobi, which politicians refused to take notice of.[20] The same can be said of the land invasions in 2016–17.[21] Other examples of political unwillingness to react to land issues in Laikipia include the political positions taken when the land question has been discussed in land commissions.[22] Only the KLC in the 1930s was able to touch the area, although it reached into a hornet's nest of opposing claims and narratives of belonging.[23] In practice, rather than reconciling tensions, it contributed to a deepening of the grievances in the following decades, when the scheduled areas for foreign settlement were expanded into the very areas that the commission had recommended should stay under the use of the Samburu. Here, Marmar Ranch is a case in point.[24]

As explained in Chapter 3, the British and colonial governments wished to isolate the Northern Frontiers District – even after Independence.[25] By enclosing Laikipia and demarcating it as a scheduled area for foreign settlement, one could exclude people from the north and rob them of any voice with which they could protest. Shipton explains how such enclosures, dispossessions and

---

16 Kopytoff, *The African Frontier.*

17 Hughes, *From Enslavement to Environmentalism.*

18 See Chapter 2 for considerations around the terms *frontier* and *fragmentation.*

19 Rutten, 'Fresh Killings.'

20 Kantai, 'In the Grip of the Vampire State'; Thomson, *Through Masai Land.*

21 *The Star*, 'Pokot Gunmen Invade Laikipia Conservancy, Kill Wild Animals'; *The Star*, 'Land Invasion Wrecks Laikipia.'

22 Anderson, *Eroding the Commons*; Kenya Human Rights Commission (KHRC), *Recurrent Ethnic Violence and Claims of Communities Arming Ahead of the 2012 General Elections* (Nairobi: KHRC, 2011); Akuwumi, *Report of the Judicial Commission Appointed to Inquire into Tribal Clashes in Kenya.*

23 See Chapter 3.

24 KLC, Evidence and memoranda, Vol. II, Rift Valley Province (Nairobi: Government Printer, 1934); Anderson, *Eroding the Commons: The Politics of Ecology in Baringo, Kenya, 1890s–1963.*

25 Interview with research participant, Laikipia University, Nyahururu, 28 January 2015.

displacements constituted the 'main force behind the formation of a British Proletariat.'[26]

Laikipia became a frontier space because of its position next to the excluded north.[27] Lefebvre speaks of the hyper-complexity of space, in the sense that all spaces are defined by their connection to other spaces. Such relations are dynamic, and frontiers are in effect neither linear nor closed entities, but exist in complex infinite temporalities, where they open and close interchangeably.

As such, the lands in Laikipia have been opened and closed to different groups and individuals at different points in time.[28] For instance, before colonial times, enclosure could be defined through changing physical control rather than fixed demarcations.[29] Different ethnic groups constantly challenged the access to the land and consequently moved interchangeably between being excluded and included. During colonial times, the British colonial administration formally defined to whom the space was open and closed, which was also informally challenged by the excluded.[30] The preference for hiring Kikuyu labourers on the farms made the space formally open to Kikuyu.[31] Correspondingly, the space was closed to pastoralists unless they too had obtained labourer status.[32] Thus the area functioned as a socially enclosed space.[33] It had few fenced borders at the time, although invisible boundaries were defined through private-property formalities, including surveying, mapping and valuing.

Additionally, the environment for settlers and Africans changed greatly between early and late colonisation. Early on, the European settlers were challenged by poor infrastructure and long periods of drought and disease.[34] Besides impacting living conditions and farming prospects, these factors hampered the settlers' ability to control intruders. Around Independence, pressure on the farms in Laikipia grew with population increases and the continued scheduling of native land for white settlement, as the Dykes story illustrates. However, with better infrastructure and more experience in dealing with the social-ecological landscape in Laikipia, the settlers grew more

26 Shipton, *Mortgaging the Ancestors*, p. 28.
27 Public lecture with Michael Watts, Copenhagen University, 10 September 2015.
28 Hughes, *Moving the Maasai*; Kanogo, *Squatters and the Roots of Mau Mau*.
29 Thomson, *Through Masai Land*.
30 Fratkin, 'The Samburu Laibon's Sorcery and the Death of Theodore Powys in Colonial Kenya.'
31 Kanogo, *Squatters and the Roots of Mau Mau*.
32 Interview with research participant, south-western Laikipia, 6 March 2015.
33 Interview with research participant, northern Laikipia, 14 April 2015.
34 Wasserman, *Politics of Decolonization*.

efficient.[35] More of the farms were fenced, and the farmers continuously invested in security personnel and improvements to their farming practices.[36]

The transition from common-land usage to enclosures of land as private property became especially clear after individual freehold tenure was introduced.[37] It was a somewhat logical development, given that the British colonial administration had introduced private-property rights with the introduction of Crown Land. Yet it materialised further when the settlers started to establish fences to protect their claimed land.[38] As such, distinctions gradually grew between land that could be privatised and land beyond the reach of European ideals of land management, namely the Native Reserves.

Contrastingly, the dominant discourse today is that everything can be bought.[39] An argument of belonging to a piece of land is more determined by a person's wealth (and political connections) than by their connectivity to the land, regardless of its personal or historical relevance.[40] So, whereas traditional landholding systems were founded on access and use, colonial entry redefined landholding as dependent on ownership and exclusion, as described in Chapter 4.[41] This type of landholding system was reproduced after Independence, when existing divisions and oppositions were enhanced on the basis of ethnicity, clan and class.[42]

Only a few days after Andrew Jr's death, the brother, John first contacted the High Commission to voice his interest in selling the farms to return to Scotland. But the family's ranches could not be included in the subsidised resettlement schemes. The government valuers held that as both farms were working ranches and not mixed farms, inclusion in the schemes was not possible.[43] *Another obstacle was*

---

35 East African Women's League, 'Golden Jubilee Scrapbook.'

36 Interview with research participant, south-western Laikipia, 6 March 2015; East African Women's League, 'Golden Jubilee Scrapbook.'

37 Shipton, *Mortgaging the Ancestors*.

38 M.J. Sheridan, 'Introduction: The Ecology of Fencing,' *Africa* 78 (2008), pp. 153–156; interview with research participant, Laikipia, 14 April 2015.

39 Field notes, Nyahururu, 30 April 2015.

40 Lynch, 'The Wars of Who Belongs Where'; Kanyinga, 'The Legacy of the White Highlands.'

41 Anderson, *Eroding the Commons*; Shipton, *Mortgaging the Ancestors*.

42 Leo, *Land and Class in Kenya*; Wasserman, 'Continuity and Counter-Insurgency'; Wasserman, *Politics of Decolonization*; Karuti Kanyinga, 'The Land Question in Kenya: Struggles, Accumulation and Changing Politics' (PhD diss., Roskilde University, 1998).

43 TNA, FCO 141/19572, 'Godley to Department of Lands,' 26 August 1975.

that John officially had Kenyan citizenship, complicating assistance from the High Commission. However, both his parents and his wife held UK citizenship.[44]

Rumour then started to spread among Africans that the Dykes wished to sell outside the government settlement schemes. However, while there was considerable interest from buyers in purchasing Melwa, all possible buyers would buy the farm in Kenyan pounds. This would mean that the family would be restricted from bringing that money out of the country.[45]

In August 1976, another incident on Marmar Ranch once more changed the family's situation. It transpired that John Dykes had accidentally run into a trespassing Samburu with his car.[46] *John was charged with murder and jailed in Nakuru Remand Prison pending a legal case.*

Mr Godley at the High Commission personally sympathised with the family, but was tied to the political terms of how the British tax money could be spent in the plans for Africanisation. In a report of a meeting with Mr Dykes, Godley stated: 'such as I sympathized personally and despite what most of the farmers in this country seemed to think, the programme that I was administering was one of aid for African farmers and I could not, whatever the circumstances, take on a farm that was not suitable for settlement.'[47]

Being a European settler in the White Highlands was not always as blissful and untroubled as some of the settler biographies describe.[48] The living conditions were often harsh, and cases of bankruptcy or fatalities were far from rare.[49] Around and following the Independence years, many of the settlers were, like the Dykes, interested in selling their land and returning to Europe.[50] Fourteen families had already decided to leave in 1961, and many more followed in the proceeding years.[51]

---

44 TNA, FCO 141/19572, 'Godley to The British High Commission,' 29 October 1975.

45 TNA, FCO 141/19572, 'Godley, Minutes of Meeting with Dykes,' 29 August 1975.

46 Interview with research participant, south-western Laikipia, 26 April 2015.

47 TNA, FCO 141/19572, 'Minutes of Meeting, Dykes and Godley,' 29 August 1975.

48 Elspeth Huxley, *The Flame Trees of Thika: Memories of an African Childhood*, Edition Unstated edition (New York: Penguin Classics, 2000); Elspeth Huxley, *The Mottled Lizard*, English Language edition (Harmondsworth and New York: Penguin Books, 1982); Sara Wheeler, *Too Close to the Sun: The Audacious Life and Times of Denys Finch Hatton*, reprint edition (New York: Random House Trade Paperbacks, 2009); Kuki Gallmann, *I Dreamed of Africa* (London: Penguin Books, 1992); Karen Blixen, *Out of Africa*, new edition (London: Penguin Classics, 2001).

49 Van Zwanenberg, *The Agricultural History of Kenya to 1939*.

50 KNA, DC/LKA/1/10, DAR, 1960, pp. 18–19.

51 KNA, DC/LKA/1/10, DAR, 1960, pp. 26–27.

Up until 1965 one could export the proceeds of a sale of land; however, once Exchange Control was introduced the seller needed approval from government to do so, which it was not possible to obtain if the farm had been sold in Kenyan currency. Foreign currency, such as the British pound, was only used if the farm was part of the British-funded resettlement schemes.[52] Many of the less well-off settlers had invested all of their capital in their farms in the highlands, so their only option to keep a private pension upon return to Europe was to get their farms declared suitable for inclusion in a resettlement scheme. But the schemes only accepted mixed-farming plots and not ranches, because the land had to be suitable for small-scale farming.[53] One older ranch owner explains the farmers' difficulty:

> all these [farms in the North] could not qualify for the British land-buying scheme. In fact, [one rancher] even got a tractor and ploughed this sort of land and said, 'this is agricultural land, come buy my farm.' But that didn't work.[54]

When many of the farmers to the north of the district did not qualify directly, they applied to the High Commission to get accepted on the basis of a compassionate case.[55] Contrastingly, the more wealthy settlers to the south of the district, whose farms fit the profile for the resettlement schemes, would often be threatened to join the schemes if they were reluctant to sell.[56]

Many did in fact fulfil the demands for compassionate cases, but the Dykes were too late to be included in either the first or the second round of compassionate case funds. From the side of the British government, there was a continuing concern about the British farmers but there were also strong opinions that the funds for the transfer of land were meant to benefit Kenyans rather

---

52 Leys, *Underdevelopment in Kenya*.

53 TNA, FCO 141/19011, 'Wetham to Shaw, The Compassionate Farm Purchase scheme,' 20 June 1966.

54 Interview research participant, northern Laikipia, 24 July 2015.

55 Compassionate cases could be granted on the basis of old age, bad health, limited income from outside the farm, inability to maintain the farm or security issues relating to the location of the farm close to areas of heavy African settlement (TNA, FCO 141/19000, 'Correspondence with Owners of Farms, Smallholdings and Residential Properties,' January 1964 – December 1965; TNA, FCO 141/19004, 'Stanley to British High Commission,' 3 April 1965; TNA, FCO 142/19007, 'Record of Meeting held at the Ministry of Overseas Development,' 15 November 1965; Kanyinga, 'The Land Question in Kenya').

56 Interview with research participant, Laikipia, 6 March 2015; interview with research participant, Thome, 6 March 2015; interview with research participant, Thome, 5 May 2015.

than Europeans, as they had been approved in Parliament as development assistance for Kenyans.[57]

However, it was not entirely irrelevant what type of Kenyan could benefit. As part of post-Independence agricultural policy the British government retained an interest in structuring and managing land according to formal consolidation and holdings in Kenya, and used its influence to create firm conditionalities for how aid funds could be spent.[58] For instance, in the Kenya Parliamentary Sessional Paper no. 10 of 1965, it is declared that:

> the need to develop and invest requires credit and a credit economy rests heavily on a system of land titles and registration. The ownership of land must, therefore, be made more definite and explicit.[59]

In such a way, the re-Africanisation of the White Highlands was designed to favour smallholder farmers from the middle class rather than Kenyans who either lived according to traditional landholding systems or had limited funds to invest.[60]

John's case in Nakuru was showing signs of interference. The judges first dismissed the case, only to change their minds and commit him for trial. The lawyer, Georgiadis, thought it to be part of a conspiracy among parties interested in the farms.

The attorney general was faced with legal impediments to keeping John in detention. They considered forcibly revoking his Kenyan citizenship and sending him to the UK, or making him renounce it himself and leave the country voluntarily. Both options could put the Kenyan state into a 'ticklish'[61] *position, as it would be problematic to let him leave Kenya before having been tried for an offence committed while still a Kenyan citizen.*[62]

Meanwhile, John's wife was approached by the aspiring politician G.G. Kariuki, who had promised her she would be able to bring proceedings from the sales out of the country via his political position as assistant minister for lands and settlement. Mr Avery from the High Commission indicated in correspondence that:

57 TNA, FCO 141/19011, 'Shaw to the British High Commission,' 14 February 1966.

58 Leo, 'Who Benefited from the Million-Acre Scheme?'

59 Kenya Parliamentary Sessional Papers no. 10, 1965, as referenced in Shipton, *Mortgaging the Ancestors*, p. 9.

60 Leo, *Land and Class in Kenya*; Kyle, *The Politics of the Independence of Kenya*.

61 TNA, FCO 141/19572, 'Avery to Godley,' 12 November 1975.

62 TNA, FCO 141/19572, 'Godley to The British High Commission,' 29 October 1975.

> *it appears certain that Mr. G.G. Kariuki,* [...] *is after it* [Melwa Ltd] *for settlement purposes. The reason for his interest seems to be political, and perhaps tribal would be the better word, i.e. Nyeri Kikuyu trying to keep up with Kiambu Kikuyu and others, e.g. Kalenjin, in the ranch purchase race.* [...] *It seems likely that ranchers will be faced with increasing pressure for sale to influential Kenyans as the months go by.*[63]

There were now five parties interested in acquiring Melwa farm. The governor of the Central Bank, Duncan Ndegwa, directed one party, while G.G. Kariuki headed another. The Dykes feared for the family's safety as G.G. took on threatening rhetoric, stating that 'unless the sale of Melwa went through to his people he would ensure that Mr. Dykes [*John*] *faced a murder charge.'*[64]

Two key factors are significant in this part of the Dykes story. Firstly, fights for land were prevalent both between ethnic groups, as with the Kikuyu and Kalenjin, and internally within the Kikuyu, as with the Kiambu Kikuyu and the Nyeri Kikuyu. Secondly, political involvement in the land race included high-ranking political figures.

The desire of the new political elite to gain access to land was part of a strategy on their part to become perceived as well-wishers for the Kenyan people unable to access land on their own. By selling land on to them or establishing collaboratives, the politicians bought support that enabled them to take advantage of the political power void left by the British exit.[65] Indeed, there were several examples of influential Kenyans using their political influence to acquire ranches in Laikipia, by reassuring the settlers that their proceeds could be safely taken with them out of the country. Both Vice President Moi and Mwai Kibaki are specifically mentioned in several archival files and interviews.[66]

The Dykes' negotiation process for selling their land illustrates the extent and scale of political involvement not only in the process for Africanising the lands but in the strategic ethnic competition in the transfers – an element that is also apparent in the case studies from Thome and from Lorien in chapter 4.[67] The tension created by this competition was instrumental in producing today's landscape of enclosures, in which the continuity of opposing claims necessitates an inflation of physical boundaries and turns tension into violence.

63 TNA, FCO 141/19572, 'Avery to Godley,' 12 November 1975.

64 TNA, FCO 141/19572, 'Avery, Minutes of meeting with Dykes,' 18 November 1975.

65 Kanyinga, 'The Land Question in Kenya.'

66 TNA, FCO 141/19572, 'Avery to Godley,' 12 November 1975; interview with research participant, south-western Laikipia, 26 April 2015.

67 Anderson, *Eroding the Commons*; Shipton, *Mortgaging the Ancestors*.

When the Dykes learned that the High Commission had held on to their classification of Melwa as a ranch, they got in contact with an MP in the UK to appeal for a solution from the Foreign and Commonwealth Office in London. They explained how they were caught in an administrative loophole that put pressure on all ranchers in Laikipia. 'The Laikipia Ranchers are caught between two fires,' they explained in the letter:

> *They are being pressed on the one hand to sell to a number of wealthy Africans, many of whom hold Government posts. Their apparently insatiable appetite for land can no longer be filled elsewhere. […] In their hands lies the influence that permits the export of funds from Kenya. The temptation to sell to them is strong – as strong as it is wrong for Kenya. On the other hand pressure is mounting from the North. The pastoral tribes have had no share in re-settlement. […] Grass is scarce and they are pushing down onto the northern ranches, grazing illegally by day and night. The authorities are doing little to stop this practice. Their young men are traditionally encouraged to steal their neighbours' cattle […] and their stealing is not only getting worse, it is accompanied by more and more personal violence. The incident which led to [John Dykes'] arrest is a symptom of a dangerous situation. […] The feeling among the ranchers is of some despair. They have been excluded from access to re-settlement funds. They have watched their arable counterparts sell, take their money and leave to find a new life elsewhere. They have become a small and isolated community.*[68]

This appeal was to no avail and in March 1975, the Dykes informed Godley that they had now offered Melwa to Muhotetu Ltd, a Kikuyu cooperative. They had accepted an offer in local currency for Marmar on the condition that they would be able to repatriate all the proceeds from Melwa. Indeed, in February 1978 President Kenyatta personally signed the letter of exemption from the Transfer Act. Thus, the Kikuyu group, Muhotetu Ltd, secured their land and the Dykes family secured the transfer of their economic output.[69] *The elderly parents could now leave Kenya with funds for their retirement. John was released on the agreement that he would leave Kenya, and he moved to the UK with his family.*[70]

The Dykes letter explains the difficult situation that many Laikipia white farmers were in, suggesting that without the law on Exchange Control, many more

---

68 TNA, FCO 141/19572, 'Dykes to Wigan,' 26 December 1975.

69 TNA, FCO 141/19572, 'Exemption from Land Control Act,' 24 February 1978.

70 Interview with research participant, south-western Laikipia, 26 April 2015.

would have prioritised a lawful buyer rather than the opportunistic new political elite.[71] One can only ponder whether this might have been significant enough to produce a different outcome in Laikipia's land redistribution process. At least, there would have been fewer ways for political elites to influence the land transactions.[72]

What is also interesting is that much of the description of the white community in the 1970s continues to be applicable today. With continuous challenges from physical encroachment and public opinion, the pressure on the white community to sell their land and leave the country endures.[73] It is also still the case that the pastoralist areas are less included in development initiatives than the rest of the country, and that authorities continue to be reluctant to take necessary action.

After Independence, the policies of both the new Kenyan government and the British government effectively intensified the demand for land with their procedures for re-Africanising the highlands. The restrictions of the formal schemes meant that the remaining settler islands in the enclosed Laikipia landscape became open to informal land grabbing according to a first-come-first-served principle whenever a settler decided to leave. The intense fight for these land units made it necessary for the acquirers to enforce boundaries to hold on to the land. The lack of formal structure in these processes consequently bolted ethnic competition and insecurity to the new landscape. This competition to acquire land in the 1960s and 1970s show how the tension in Laikipia today regarding land matters merely reflects a continuation of a post-Independence situation, where land control determined a person's political power.[74]

The Dykes account is relevant to understanding the present-day landscape of enclosures in Laikipia because a social space is determined by the conditionality of its materiality, including how its resources are used and controlled.[75] The social space in pre-colonial Laikipia was defined by its use as a

71 Kanyinga, 'The Legacy of the White Highlands'; interview with research participant, 6 March 2015.

72 Kanyinga, 'The Legacy of the White Highlands.'

73 *The Star*, 'Laikipia Invasions Are Political, Governor Hopeful Says after Kifuku Ranch Raid'; *The Star*, 'Laikipia Farm Invasions Continue'; *The Star*, 'Laikipia Clashes Persist as MPs, Cops, Barons Blamed.'

74 Branch, *Kenya: Between Hope and Despair*; Anderson and Lochery, 'Violence and Exodus in Kenya's Rift Valley, 2008'; Klopp, 'Can Moral Ethnicity Trump Political Tribalism?'

75 Peluso, 'Coercing Conservation: The Politics of State Resource Control,' *Global Environmental Change* 3 (1993), pp. 199–217; Stuart Elden, 'Land, Terrain, Territory,' *Progress in Human Geography; London* 34, no. 6 (December 2010), pp. 799–817; Vandergeest, 'Mapping Nature.'

territory with common resources for pastoral grazing, whereas in colonial times it was a territory with resources for the use of settlers under private-property regimes. In post-colonial times, Laikipia's materiality became defined by whatever approach people took to marking their claimed territory and resources. For instance, when pastoralists settled on the absentee lands, the private lands reverted to a common-resource regime.[76] As such, the prevailing tension arising from opposing claims is reflected in the fragmentation of the use and holding of the land seen today. As a result, the Laikipia frontier turned into a battleground between physical strength and newly claimed property rights.[77] As different as they were, the systems for claiming resources became, and continue to be, defined by their durability.

5.2 Towards Land Enclosures in Ol Moran and Thome

It is not always the case that claiming land through practices of enclosure is linked to ethnicised politics and exclusion, yet in Kenya it is. This can be visualised by looking at patrimonial relations between politicians and possible voters. Here the concept of political enclosures applies when certain ethnic groups are prioritised in institutional service delivery while others are excluded.[78] The significance of social and ethnic diversity in Laikipia means that such divergences are further intensified here.

Space is territorialised through the symbolic use of place naming and the physical use of fencing. Every time physical pressure to cross a boundary grows, the fence is reinforced with electrification and trenches, only for this enforcement to feed back into the larger situation and result in encroachers' efforts becoming more inventive and effective. Opportunistic land access and navigation between legal systems have become the predominant responses to the increasing enclosure of common land in Laikipia. All of these dynamics are present in the two case studies.

5.2.1 *Symbolic Enclosures in Thome*

With multiple ethnic groups and clans present, aspects of the territorialisation of space and the production of enclosures are especially present in Thome. As

76 Galaty, 'Reasserting the Commons.'
77 Galaty, 'Reasserting the Commons.'
78 Jacqueline Klopp, '"Ethnic Clashes" and Winning Elections: The Case of Kenya's Electoral Despotism,' *Canadian Journal of African Studies/Revue Canadienne Des Études Africaines* 35, no. 3 (2001), pp. 473–517; Oucho, *Undercurrents of Ethnic Conflicts in Kenya.*

a colonial ranch, its name was Rumuruti Ranch. It was Kikuyu clan fights that lead to the renaming of the place as 'Thome,' denoting ownership by or presence of Kikuyu from Kiambu, whereas other place names within Thome bear witness to the presence of Kikuyu from Nyeri.[79] For instance, the southernmost part of Thome Centre is called North Tetu, along with the primary school in Thome, which bears the name North Tetu Primary School.[80] This links the space to Tetu near Nyeri, which symbolically defines the space as a territory held by the Kikuyu clan from Nyeri.

As figure 8 shows, there are 13 villages inside Thome, connoting different histories of holdership. Share Kumi,[81] Share Nne[82] and Share Ishirini[83] are populated exclusively by Turkana. They still hold their numeral names referring to the share number used in the balloting division of the shares by the

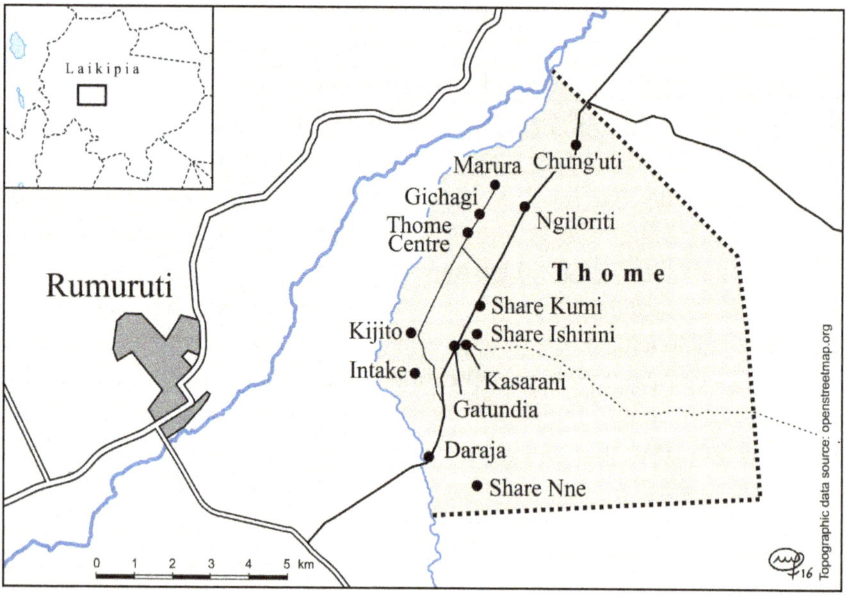

FIGURE 8 Place names in Thome.
© Monika Feinen 2016

79 Interview with research participant, Nyahururu, 21 March 2016; field notes, conversation with research participant, Nyahururu, 2 March 2015.
80 Field notes, Thome, 16 May 2015.
81 Kiswahili for 'share number ten.'
82 Kiswahili for 'share number four.'
83 Kiswahili for 'share number twenty.'

land-buying company.[84] These numbers signify that the Catholic Mission in Rumuruti assisted in buying shares specifically to settle former Turkana ranch labourers who had become landless.[85] The areas have maintained their names as acts of gratitude to the Catholic Church by the settled Turkana.

The most valuable plots of land in Thome are those adjacent to the river, in the Ewaso Narok swamp. Marura,[86] Gichagi,[87] Thome Centre, Kijito[88] and Intake[89] are the most populous areas, with intense irrigation for crops. Kikuyu dominate all these areas except for Gichagi. The Kalenjin population is present in Thome Centre, along with Somali, Kikuyu, Meru, Turkana, Kisii and Samburu. They do not engage as much in farming activities near the river.[90] Instead, the Kalenjin stay in the southern corner of Thome in the settlements Share Nne[91] and Daraja.[92]

When Samburu started to settle in Thome, they reclaimed the land by giving parts of it new names to denote the space as their territory.[93] For instance, grazing areas close to Marura are referred to as Lorora,[94] and the village Ngiloriti,[95] exclusively settled by Samburu, has been given the name to denote Samburu territory, even though few of the settled Samburu have bought the land they are settled on.[96] Formally, absentee landowners own this land, and the renaming of it supports their claim by indicating a repatriation of the soil.

In addition to settlements in Thome, the Samburu control the area Sugoroi, east of Thome. Like other Samburu areas, there are no physical enclosures besides the fact that this land is used exclusively for grazing, which is also visible

84 Interview with research participant, Thome, 6 March 2015; interview with research participant, Thome, 5 May 2015.

85 Interview with research participant, Thome, 5 May 2015; interview with research participant, Rumuruti, 21 January 2015.

86 The name *Marura* is used by both Kikuyu and Samburu to refer to the type of grass there, but the place also has sister areas or towns in several places across Kenya, both in Laikipia East and close to Mombassa.

87 Kikuyu for 'village' or 'rural area.'

88 Refers to a place in Kiambu.

89 Denotes a position on the river with a dam.

90 Interview with research participant, Nyahururu, 21 March 2016; field notes, conversation with research participant, Nyahururu, 2 March 2015.

91 Kiswahili for 'share number five.'

92 Kiswahili for 'bridge.'

93 Interview with research participant, Nyahururu, 21 March 2016; field notes, conversation with research participant, Nyahururu, 2 March 2015.

94 Refers to a clan *manyatta* in Samburu and is a name often given to new settlements.

95 A Samburu name.

96 Interview with research participant, Nyahururu, 21 March 2016; field notes, conversation with research participant, Nyahururu, 2 March 2015.

in the features of the landscape, featuring neither trees nor bushes but only grass.[97] Nobody else in the area lives exclusively off livestock, and therefore this is enough to mark it as Samburu territory. Hence, the land-use practice employed can suggest an enclosure and support the more symbolic claim to the territory that lies in the name. In this case, a fence is not necessary to mark the enclosure.

A Samburu resident in Thome explained that many Samburu came in 1992 because they had heard that the white farmers were moving and that the land was being given to Kikuyu. They also wanted a share. Although he claimed to have bought the land his house sat on, it could not sustain his livestock. He was dependent on grazing on the nearby large-scale farm owned by a descendant of a white settler.[98] It was run down as a result of the pressure on the resources following intense encroachment and unauthorised grazing. The owner no longer kept his own cattle, there were no agricultural activities, and there were few security staff defending the unfenced boundaries to claim grazing fees and rent from those leasing agricultural land.[99] Only his name still signified the enclosure.

5.2.2 *Physically Enacted Enclosures in Ol Moran*

Ol Moran town and its vicinity is a place of contradiction and division.[100] The road from Sipili town to Ol Moran defines the boundary between the areas claimed by the two land-buying companies. Compared with Thome, there is less pressure on the settled land. This is partly so because the land-buying companies no longer exist and most of those wishing to acquire a title deed have done so. With the largest proportion of shareholders being absentee landowners, there are few to claim the land that is now settled by Pokot and Samburu.[101] This is different in the southern part around Sipili town. Here, there is clearly fenced farmland and very few absentee areas.[102] With the better-quality soil at this southern end, this area is dominated by Kikuyu shareholders.

In the northern part of the former ranch, around Ol Moran town, the ethnicity of shareholders is more mixed. The fenced shares are parcelled out and, except in the town centre, people do not live right next to each other. These

97 Field notes, Sugoroi, 29 May 2015.
98 Interview with research participant, Marura, 6 May 2015.
99 Interview with research participant, Marura, 6 May 2015; interview with research participant, Nyahururu, 21 March 2016.
100 Field notes, Ol Moran, 21 July 2015.
101 Interview with research participant, Ol Moran, 21 July 2015.
102 Field notes, Ol Moran, 21 July 2015.

lands are dominated by pastoralist land-management regimes, with smallholder plots as fenced enclosures here and there.[103] That said, a few of the Pokot have bought the land plots they are settled on, where the women build fences around their farmed fields.[104]

Although Ol Moran has less tension between shareholders, this does not mean that there is less tension here generally. On the contrary, Ol Moran has much ethnic-territorial tension. This means that conflict can easily be ignited if someone makes a claim to the area based on ethnicity or land use.[105] Besides the scattered fenced enclosures, the landscape holds invisible boundaries, disrespect for which can lead to conflict. The tension regularly spills over into physical violence, ignited for instance by cattle raids. Depending on the nature of the conflict, the tension forces different alliances. For instance, in the post-election violence in 1992 and 1997, Samburu and Pokot joined forces against the Kikuyu farming community, claiming that the place was meant to be an area for pastoralists, judging by its Maa name, Ol Moran.[106] The fights resulted in many hundreds of Kikuyu deaths.[107] However, in both 2006–07 and 2013 there were extensive conflicts between the Pokot and the Samburu, as both groups made a claim to the land.[108] The pastoralists' territorial claims erupted into a war-like situation in the early 2000s, and again in 2010. These were conflicts that had the aim not only of evicting but rather of exterminating the other.[109]

These conflicts have in common that they are about ethnic territorialisation. One Pokot elder explained: 'The Samburu came here wanting to take over this land to graze so that they would push the Pokot to the other side. But the Pokot refused.'[110] When peace was finally settled, the Pokot and Samburu divided the area between them into two territories divided by the road to Maralal.[111] Pokot are therefore settled north-east of Ol Moran town, whereas the Samburu are settled in areas such as Survey and Maundu Meri to the east and

103 Field notes, Ol Moran, 21 July 2015.
104 Interview with research participant, north of Ol Moran town, 21 July 2015.
105 *The Home News*, 'Ethnic Clashes,' 16–31 August 2001, pp. 1–2; *The Home News*, 'The Samburu–Pokot War,' 1–7 September 2006.
106 Literally means many different colours mixed together (*Lmarani*), but as a place it refers to the ownership of a young warrior.
107 Rutten, 'Fresh Killings.'
108 *The Home News*, 'The Samburu–Pokot War'; interview with research participant, Nyahururu, 21 March 2016.
109 Interview with research participant, Nyahururu, 15 April 2015.
110 Interview with research participant, Ol Moran, 21 July 2015.
111 Interview with research participant, Nyahururu, 21 March 2016.

south. Although this is a boundary that has not been aligned to a map, it is agreed upon and respected from both sides.[112]

Whenever a Samburu enters Pokot territory, people become suspicious that the straying Samburu is scouting for raiding possibilities and hence he must be escorted around until he finds his proclaimed missing goat.[113] However, there are situations in which the Samburu and the Pokot *morans* interact. One is when they graze inside the enclosure of Laikipia Nature Conservancy, where maximising grazing benefits demands coordination between the *morans*.[114] Ol Moran town is neutral ground and therefore the safest for the mixed-farming communities, who are all settled in the vicinity.[115]

The Laikipia Nature Conservancy illustrates the contrasts in the landscape of enclosures in this area. With a size of almost 100,000 acres and few functioning fences, it would require a small army of security personnel to keep encroachers out. The conservancy does not have such resources, yet the management refuses to enter into grazing agreements with the neighbouring pastoral communities.[116] Instead, the conservancy is fighting a battle it cannot win, and the more strongly it fights, the more determined the strategies employed by the pastoralist herders, as recently exemplified in the 2016–17 wave of invasions.[117]

All types of conflict are present in people's minds as a risk that must be constantly manoeuvred around.[118] Whereas the risk of raids tends to be a seasonal affair, the tension between the settled Kikuyu and the Pokot and Samburu seems to be increasing in intensity, as more and more wealthy Kikuyu are buying up absentee land to start intense large-scale farming around Ol Moran town, which then pushes the settled pastoralist groups further north. This has led to protest attacks and killings of Kikuyu by Pokot and Samburu perpetrators. Notably, there were incidences of stabbings and a beheading in February 2015.[119]

112 Interview with research participant, Nyahururu, 21 March 2016.

113 Interview with research participant, Ol Moran, 21 July 2015.

114 Interview with research participant, Ol Moran, 2 August 2015; interview with research participant, Nyahururu, 21 March 2016.

115 Field notes, Ol Moran, 21 July 2015.

116 Interview with research participant, 9 September 2016.

117 *The Star*, 'Land Invasion Wrecks Laikipia'; *The Star*, 'Pokot Gunmen Invade Laikipia Conservancy, Kill Wild Animals.'

118 Field notes, Nyahururu, 2 August 2015.

119 Interview with research participant, Nyahururu, 15 April 2015.

5.3 Present-day Enclosures in Laikipia

Although strong associations between ethnicity and land are present in most of Kenya, Laikipia is especially interesting because the social and ethnic mix intensifies the relationship between ethnicity and land in a way that visibly divides the landscape according to use and holding. Fragmentation of space creates islands of places. As islands of fenced enclosures, the 'white ranches' lie scattered across the landscape in between smallholder farms and pastoral plains.[120] Since Independence the number of non-African landowners has gradually reduced from more than 600, to less than 300 in 1980[121] and merely 150 in 1999.[122] Samburu pastoralists opportunistically or for lack of alternatives force themselves through the weak fences to access grazing.[123] Whether with barbed wire, stone walls or medieval-style trenches, fences around the private-property lands constantly grow to match the pressure put on them from outside.[124] The smallholders in between these islands have inadequate funds to fence their claimed pieces of land, leaving them especially vulnerable to encroachment.

This fragmentation of space has consequences for how the frontier is integrated as a combined, governed state space.[125] To examine a fragmented frontier, Watts proposes looking at types of capitalism, in terms of what is at stake. Because we are at the edge of the state, the state itself with its institutional operations is merely one of multiple stakeholders, as described in Chapter 4.[126] With multiple alternatives to state practices, individuals become independent and opportunistic – especially those who do not feel protected or represented by the state.[127]

According to Lefebvre, a space is coincidentally a production of thought and action as well as a means of production, control, dominance and power.[128] He argues that a territory is difficult to contain and govern, especially for a state that is not extensively present. Yet the same goes for any other player unless they are constantly present and have the means to defend their position.

---

120 Interview with research participant, central Laikipia, 8 June 2015.
121 Kohler, *Land Use in Transition.*
122 Projection of ethnic distribution, in Rutten, 'Fresh Killings.'
123 Interview with research participant, Ol Moran, 22 March 2015.
124 Interview with research participant, south-western Laikipia, 6 March 2015.
125 Joireman, *Where There Is No Government*; Kopytoff, *The African Frontier.*
126 Public lecture with Michael Watts, Copenhagen University, 10 September 2015.
127 Lund, 'Twilight Institutions.'
128 Lefebvre, *The Production of Space*, p. 26.

This makes the space penetrable for political entrepreneurs and opportunistic actions. The pastoralist groups exemplify this through three decades of settlement on absentee land; and so do the smallholders, in their settling and development of land for which they may still lack a title deed. Opportunists or not, it is necessary for everyone to enforce their claims. This can be done in different ways.

5.3.1 *Practices of Enclosing Space: The Naming of Places*

The practice of naming a place carries power, reflecting both the name-giver and the original bearer of the name, whether a person, a place, an object or an event. In discussing land claims in the Cherangany Hills, Lynch reflects that:

> The names we give to people, places, events and things are more than mere labels. They help to 'structure and nuance the way we imagine and understand the world'; with accepted names embedded in 'a larger politics of storytelling.' As a result, names, and the ability to name, are inherently political due to the power relations involved and the discourses and actions they facilitate and hinder.[129]

Thereby, the practice of naming is an empowering factor as part of a narrative supporting a claim. It can justify the enclosing of space and determine who is excluded from using it. The very practice of naming can function as an instrument of control, because the reference to the name-giver is value-laden. For a person, the name denotes ancestry, heritage, ethnic affiliation, and perhaps class and wealth.[130] Many places in Australia carry a name given by James Cook to denote colonial ownership. Joseph Thomson did the same when travelling through Kenya and Laikipia, as his own way of claiming the landscape, giving his name to the Thomson's gazelle, Thomson's Falls and the peak Point Thomson on Mount Kenya.[131]

The naming of a place justifies its holding. For the Maori in New Zealand the name-giver of a place would be the natural owner and the person authorised to permit settlement.[132] For many Native Americans the naming and renaming

129 Lynch, 'What's in a Name?,' quoting, firstly, Julie Peteet, 'Words as Interventions: Naming in the Palestine–Israel Conflict,' *Third World Quarterly* 26, no. 1 (2005), p. 153; and, secondly, Michael Schroeder, 'Bandits and Blanket Thieves, Communists and Terrorists: The Politics of Naming Sandinistas in Nicaragua, 1927–36 and 1979–80,' *Third World Quarterly* 26, no. 1 (2005), p. 67.

130 Lynch, 'What's in a Name?'

131 Thomson, *Through Masai Land.*

132 Berg and Kearns, 'Naming as Norming.'

of clan members has been a status denominator, in that a name should be earned. Yet it has also been a practice used to undermine – for instance, when a malt liquor or a strip club is named after the Lakota leader Crazy Horse, or when the Native American name of a place is changed, such as when the area Shawmut had its name changed to Boston.[133]

Naming can be a method of domination because it establishes a hierarchy in relation to the politics of identity in a society. Therefore, the practice of naming is an important part of norming.[134] As Berg and Kearns note: 'names are part of both a symbolic and a material order that provides normality and legitimacy to those who dominate the politics of (place) representation.'[135] This means that whoever decides to refer to Boston rather than Shawmut, or Nyahururu rather than Thomson's Falls, adds legitimacy and support to the power of the new name-giver.

In Kenya prior to colonialism, the names of places were not written down. Therefore, a place could have different names for different people. The dominant name would be that used by those controlling the particular place at the particular time. As one ranch owner explains: 'Even in the times my family has been here, the names of hills have changed. [...] Unless it is written down, they change very quickly. [...] You can find in as little as three years, some names have been replaced.'[136] With a shift in power relations, the name of a place would also change.

However, the early white explorers changed that practice of naming when they wrote down the names.[137] In fact, the naming and mapping of landscapes was a widely used practice, a graphic tool that supported the British colonisation of space. In that way, the space was transformed from an 'oral space' into a 'written space,' shifting authority away from those who gave the names to those who wrote them down.

In Kenya, the naming of places became a tool with which to control both a physical and a social space when groups were fighting one another. This coincides with Berg and Kearns' conception, in their statement that the politics of naming 'is both a politics of space (deciding who names and controls space) and a spatialised politics (whereby the spatial defines who has legitimacy to speak).'[138] As a means to control, this practice is illustrated by the colonial

133 Winona LaDuke, *Recovering the Sacred: The Power of Naming and Claiming* (Boston, MA: South End Press, 2005).
134 Lynch, 'What's in a Name?'
135 Berg and Kearns, 'Naming as Norming.'
136 Interview with research participant, eastern Laikipia, 24 July 2015.
137 Beinart and Hughes, *Environment and Empire*.
138 Berg and Kearns, 'Naming as Norming.'

administration's efforts to name and map space.[139] With the mapping of the landscape, the names of places entered a less flexible state, which was defined by chance in the sense that the place would formally be given the name that was used by the person asked by the travel writer or mapper. The fact that the names were now written down added legitimacy to them, and contributed to securing the name-givers and map-makers in their position as holders of the place.[140]

One might consider it luck for the Maa-speaking Maasai and Samburu that they were the ones who met the British explorers asking for names. This enabled them to base their present-day claim to the lands in Laikipia on the fact that the written-down names are Maa. This point is also raised by the ranch owner: '[at the onset of colonialism] the British asked people who were there. The [naming of places] deals with a window industry and probably if somebody had asked 100 years before they could have had different names.'[141]

However, the use of resources in a place does not necessarily ensure ownership; likewise, ownership does not necessarily grant one usury rights. If not denoting ownership, the naming of places can support a claim to use even without private-property rights, due to the denotation of a symbolic enclosure.

In the Independence years, the (re)naming of places gained more importance, and Maa speakers integrated the travel writers' use of Maa names.[142] This is the case for Suguroi and Ewaso Narok, denoting Samburu or Maasai presence.[143] More proactively, Samburu people would rename a place when they arrived somewhere to settle. For instance, the Samburu settling in Thome in the 1990s renamed the settlement 'Lorora' to reclaim what they believed was theirs, thereby marking their territory as a symbolic enclosure.[144] They would deliberately use the Maa name of the place rather than whatever name it might have been given during colonial times.[145]

Similarly, when land-buying companies bought a piece of land, that place often received a new name.[146] The ethnic competition to control land in Laikipia

---

139 Beinart and Hughes, *Environment and Empire*; Lynch, 'What's in a Name?'

140 Berg and Kearns, 'Naming as Norming.'

141 Interview with research participant, eastern Laikipia, 24 July 2015. By 'window industry' I understood him to refer to a situation which the rebels could only take advantage of for a short time – while the window was open.

142 Kantai, 'In the Grip of the Vampire State'; Hughes, *Moving the Maasai*.

143 Interview with research participant, Nyahururu, 21 March 2016.

144 Field notes, email correspondence with research participant, 14 December 2016.

145 Lynch, 'What's in a Name?'

146 Kohler, *Land Use in Transition*.

through land-buying companies was a fight that the Kikuyu won. For instance, settlements such as Sipili and Gatundia are Gikiyu names.[147] The names given to the land-buying companies themselves also denote the Kikuyu dominance. Some examples are Mwiremia ('the defiants'), Mutirithia ('slow and steady development'), Ethi ('somebody who is looking hard for something'), Mwireri ('helping oneself') and Kihato ('the broom of the village,' referring to the control of people during the Mau Mau emergency);[148] all refer to a Kikuyu narrative of being responsible and self-reliant in the search for land despite being oppressed by colonial dominance. This may seem innocent, but the practice of naming was evidently used to claim ownership of the landscape, connecting a symbolic ethnic narrative to the place.

When different groups claim the same place, the practice of naming can lead to dispute. For instance, when mixed settlements intensified in Marmanet in south-western Laikipia, the place gained several names. Now, Maa speakers refer to it as 'Ol Jabet' whereas Gikuyu speakers call it 'Jebi' – each building a narrative around their claim legitimised by the name-giving.[149] This is also the explanation for the different origins of the town name Rumuruti that I came across upon my first visit to the region.

In the Dykes account, the competition between the Kiambu and the Nyeri Kikuyu to acquire land in Laikipia is illustrated in the names Thome and Kieni, which refer back to Kiambu County.[150]

The effect of the practice of naming of symbolically enclosing a space for some while excluding others is also visible in relation to IDP camps. An IDP camp near Nyahururu has been named Shalom[151] to denote the residents' reaction to being excluded. Their peace-denoting name affirms their wish to start afresh.[152] Shalom's 3,000 IDPs claim to have created a 'new country.' Everything inside is new: roads, hospitals, schools, markets and perhaps even their community identity.[153] In this way, the place is visibly different from neighbouring places, and the internal resources and imagined community denote an enclosure to the outside. Other IDP camps have been named according to the place from which the residents were evicted.

Some places in Laikipia are named after influential people who have noticeably impacted the residents. For instance, some places are named after the

147 See table 2 and figure 6.
148 Kohler, *Land Use in Transition*, p. 44.
149 Field notes, email correspondence with research participant, 14 December 2016.
150 Field notes, Thome, 16 May 2015.
151 Referring to peace.
152 Field notes, email correspondence with research participant, 14 December 2016.
153 Field notes, email correspondence with research participant, 14 December 2016.

white settlers, such as Kalampton, south of Lorien, because the settler of that name left the land for his former workers.[154] Similarly, a former ranch near Sipili was bought by former president Moi. Right before the 2002 general election, Moi gave the land to a group of Turkana, supposedly to buy their vote. The Turkana, in turn, called the place Kaichakuni, meaning 'fallen from heaven,' to denote Moi's generosity and emphasise their political support.[155]

Despite the symbolic power of naming, the 2010 constitution rejects squatter rights to land. Therefore, simply naming a place is not enough to provide one with legitimate holder rights.[156] Rather, and especially in Laikipia, an enforcement of a land claim is needed in order to keep out protesters. This need to enforce has led to the combining of symbolic enclosure and physical enclosure. The practice of fencing is ideal as a physical enclosure, and it is widely practised by ranchers and smallholders alike, although with varying success.[157]

5.3.2 *Physical Enclosures: Fencing*

Another method for enhancing a claim is through the construction of physical boundaries. As physical and symbolic markers, fences embody political standpoints legitimised by private-property rights. Similarly to the act of writing down place names, the establishment of a fence adds a sense of fixity to a boundary. Evans and Adams describe how fences in Laikipia function as: 'a spatial projection of power that transforms not only the relations between nature and society but also social relations within a landscape in which people negotiate the meanings of land, resources and property.'[158] Fences serve the dual purpose of enclosing resources from which wealth is extracted and of barring impostors from entering. They can take physical form as barriers, such as hedges, wires or walls, but they can also take a less rigid form, which nevertheless has the same functionality,[159] such as guard dogs, barriers of smells from territorial animals, loud noises or smoke.[160]

---

154 Field notes, Lorien, 30 January 2015.

155 Field notes, email correspondence with research participant, 14 December 2016.

156 The National Council for Law Reporting with the Authority of the Attorney General. *The Constitution of Kenya*, 2010.

157 Gadd, 'Conservation outside of Parks'; Evans and Adams, 'Fencing Elephants: The Hidden Politics of Wildlife Fencing in Laikipia, Kenya.'

158 Evans and Adams, 'Fencing Elephants,' p. 216.

159 M. Spierenburg and H. Wels, '"Securing Space": Mapping and Fencing in Transfrontier Conservation in Southern Africa,' *Space and Culture* 9 (2006), pp. 294–312; Evans and Adams, 'Fencing Elephants.'

160 Hayward and Kerley, 'Fencing for Conservation.'

While the idea of protecting resources from intruders is not a new phenomenon in Kenya, the use of the physical fence gained weight in the mid-twentieth century.[161] At their inception, the fences did not need to be completely impassable, as one ranch manager explains:

> for the first ranches in these areas there were no herdsmen and there weren't electrified fences. There just weren't elephants to break the fences. Every now and then a lion would come through but it would very quickly be shot.[162]

While this was the reality in the early days of colonisation, the Dykes story illustrates how this changed over time. Because Marmar Ranch lacked a fence, it became impossible to secure the invisible boundaries against intruders through patrolling alone.[163]

Prior to the 1970s, the risk that wild animals would threaten livestock and destroy fences was also much lower. However, then as now, intruders were present to either steal livestock or illegally graze their livestock on the ranches.[164] Especially in the northern parts of the plateau, where the Dykes' northern ranch was located, settlers struggled to keep the pastoralists out of their properties.[165] Judging from the reports and minutes of the Laikipia Farmers Association, this was a considerable problem. In a 1933 general meeting, the ranchers Mr Colville and Mr Armstrong wished to:

> draw the attention of Government to the serious position arising from the continuous trespass and breach of quarantine in this District by Natives from the Northern Frontier Province. Repeated complaints to the Native administration have been worse than useless. We are determined to put a stop to this lawlessness and indiscipline.[166]

161 Interview with conservancy manager, northern Laikipia, 14 April 2015; interview with research participant, south-western Laikipia, 6 March 2015.

162 Interview with conservancy manager, northern Laikipia, 14 April 2015.

163 TNA, FCO 141/19572, 'Godley to Avery,' 12 June 1975.

164 Fratkin, 'The Samburu Laibon's Sorcery and the Death of Theodore Powys in Colonial Kenya'; interview with research participant, central Laikipia, 8 June 2015.

165 Interview with conservancy manager, northern Laikipia, 14 April 2015; Fratkin, 'The Samburu Laibon's Sorcery and the Death of Theodore Powys in Colonial Kenya.'

166 BIEA, LFA, 'Minutes of Meeting,' 19 August 1933.

At the same meeting, Mr Dykes and Mr Collinson proposed to remove the Samburu 'by force, if necessary.'[167] As Independence approached, the pressure from the raiders intensified and many settlers started to enforce security around their land.[168] They did so by creating physical enclosures. With a simultaneous gradual Africanisation, the landscape grew increasingly contrasting, with varying environmental conditions on either side of fences.[169]

Conceptually, a fence can denote several things in relation to enclosure. It surrounds a place of desire or dread – whichever is opposed to what the other side represents.[170] A fence can relate to a place of memory, or to mobility. It functions as a preventative measure against further movement, whether in terms of entrance or escape.[171] Therefore, a fence can also denote disagreement. It relates to the extraction and use of resources for certain individuals while excluding others, and it can denote a protest or a manifestation of power. As Evans and Adams phrase it: 'protected area boundaries are often fenced to exclude local people, redefining human movement onto protected land as trespassing; the collection of fuel wood, cattle fodder or food as theft; hunting for meat as poaching; and making a home as encroachment.'[172] The term *fence* is derived from the term *defence*, signifying protection, security or resistance.[173] It refers to the fence as a barrier, an enclosure or a defender of something considered valuable. Moreover, a fence can function as a landmark and thus as a navigation device – following a fence can guide one in a certain direction.[174]

According to the executive director of one conservancy, 'the community and the conservancy have to work together to ensure that there is a good fence in place, because after all a good fence is in the interest of both.'[175] He assumes that fences symbolise agreements in themselves, and that the lack of a physical boundary creates disorder. Indeed, the American poet Robert Frost, in his poem 'Mending Wall' from 1916, uses the common saying 'good fences make

167 BIEA, LFA, 'Minutes of Meeting,' 19 August 1933.

168 Interview with research participant, south-western Laikipia, 6 March 2015.

169 See Figures 12, 14 and 16.

170 Spierenburg and Wels, '"Securing Space"'; Evans and Adams, 'Fencing Elephants.'

171 Evans and Adams, 'Fencing Elephants'; Hayward and Kerley, 'Fencing for Conservation'; Margaret F. Kinnaird and Timothy G. O'Brien, 'Effects of Private-Land Use, Livestock Management, and Human Tolerance on Diversity, Distribution, and Abundance of Large African Mammals,' *Conservation Biology* 26, no. 6 (2012), pp. 1026–39.

172 Evans and Adams, 'Fencing Elephants.'

173 *Merriam-Webster*, 'Definition of Fence,' available from https://www.merriam-webster.com/dictionary/fence, accessed 19 August 2017.

174 Tim Cresswell, *Fence* (London: Penned in the Margins, 2015).

175 Interview with research participant, 9 September 2016.

good neighbours,'[176] denoting that the building of a fence between two properties is a product of agreement between the two sides. However, the speaker in the poem seems to disagree with the saying, indicating that it is primitive reasoning to assume that it is the building of a fence that provides good neighbour relations. The construction of a fence might also signify an inability of the two sides to reach an agreement, making it necessary to establish a physical boundary between them.[177]

Frost's poem also points to the agency in the construction of a fence, as well as the agency in the destruction of it.[178] A fence can be constructed by one person and torn down by another. The act of building and the act of tearing down can also in some sense represent a game, in which both sides accept the premise of the pendulum. One ranch manager explained how Samburu dug up stones and built boundaries on his roads on the ranch. This did not upset him. Instead, he collected the stones:

> My guys are asking, 'What do we do?' I tell them, 'You just go there with the tractor; they have done us a favour; they have dug a pool of rocks. You just go and collect and bring them to where we need them [for fencing].' If they dig them up again we just do it [again] and eventually, they will get bored.[179]

The fact that the status quo is disrupted by this endless process of demolishing and construction becomes a feature that holds it all together. As Gramsci once said: 'destruction is difficult; indeed, it is as difficult as creation.'[180]

Nevertheless, a boundary without a fence does not necessarily lead to disorder. Without a fence, other elements in the landscape can denote the boundary.[181] A line of trees or a water source can be just as effective to indicate a boundary – so long as both sides of the boundary agree to it.[182] For instance, the agreement between Pokot and Samburu after their 2006–07 fights in Ol Moran relied on an agreed division of the landscape. This illustrates that orally

176 Robert Frost, *North of Boston* (London: David Nutt, 1916).
177 Hayward and Kerley, 'Fencing for Conservation.'
178 Frost, *North of Boston.*
179 Interview with research participant, 8 June 2015.
180 Proverb by Antonio Gramsci, paraphrased by Shipton, *Mortgaging the Ancestors*, p. 230.
181 Hughes, *Moving the Maasai*; Thomson, *Through Masai Land.*
182 D. Newman, 'The Lines That Continue to Separate Us: Borders in Our "Borderless" World,' *Progress in Human Geography* 30, no. 2 (2006), pp. 143–61; J. Häkli, 'Re-Bordering Spaces,' in *The Sage Handbook of Political Geography*, ed. K.R. Cox, M. Low and J. Robinson (Los Angeles: SAGE, 2008); Evans and Adams, 'Fencing Elephants.'

agreed-upon boundaries can be considered just as legitimate as boundaries produced by a surveyor and marked by a fence.[183]

According to Jones, the practice of boundary-making involves four stages:[184] first, the allocation of the territory; then the theoretical delimitation or mapping; followed by the physical boundary-marking and -making; and finally, the administration of the physical boundary.[185] Yet even though the line on a map appears clearly and unanimously defined, it is usually the product of a complex or even contested negotiation between involved parties. And the fact that the boundary is imprinted on a map does not necessarily free it from contestation.[186] As such, the simplified reproduction of landscapes on maps can be misleading given its silence regarding the process behind their production – with the possible dominance inflicted in the process.

Communication and enforcement are also often considered key points in the process of turning space into property.[187] Yet, in practice, these activities are neither necessarily separate nor a linear process. For instance, Samburu *morans* in Laikipia use their encroachment to communicate a protest towards a property holder and enforce their claim to the land.[188] The smallholders and pastoralists settled in Thome have two neighbouring ranches, a larger and a smaller one, with good resources for grazing. To the north-east is the larger ranch, with its 38,000 acres of grass and bushland. The manager keeps 500 cattle himself and leases grazing for 3,000 Samburu cattle,[189] but the management is difficult and thousands more are on the ranch to graze illegally. Due to its large size, it is challenging for the manager to construct a proper fence around the ranch. The price for both construction and maintenance would be too high.[190] Additionally, he advocates not limiting the ability of the wildlife to roam freely. Therefore, an enforced fence with stone walls and trenches would not be the solution for this ranch – at least not all the way around it. Comparably, up until the 2016–17 state of emergency, the smaller ranch to the other side of Thome had 6,000 strongly fenced acres. This fence was strong enough to

183 Interview with research participant, Nyahururu, 21 March 2016; interview with research participant, northern Laikipia, 24 July 2015.

184 S.B. Jones, *Boundary-Making: A Handbook for Statesmen, Treaty Editors and Boundary Commissions* (Washington, DC: Carnegie Endowment for International Peace, 1945).

185 Jones, *Boundary-Making*.

186 Newman, 'The Lines That Continue to Separate Us'; Häkli, 'Re-Bordering Spaces'; Evans and Adams, 'Fencing Elephants.'

187 Vandergeest, 'Mapping Nature.'

188 Fratkin, 'The Samburu Laibon's Sorcery and the Death of Theodore Powys in Colonial Kenya'; *The Star*, 'Is Rebellion the Next Phase of Laikipia Violence?'

189 Interview with research participant, central Laikipia, 8 June 2015.

190 Interview with research participant, central Laikipia, 8 June 2015.

keep out possible encroachers while protecting the ranch's own Borana cattle. This practice of complete enclosure also meant the exclusion of wildlife. In contrast to the manager of the larger ranch, this ranch owner happily accepted this in order to avoid trouble.[191]

Many of the smallholders in Thome are understanding of the difficulty of keeping the Samburu out of the ranches, as they themselves deal with the same problems. To them, the solution to the fencing dilemma is clear: the clearer and stronger the enclosure, the better. As one Turkana farmer stated:

> The style [of the smaller ranch] is better. It is difficult for the animal or pastoralists to get in or out there. […] The wild animals destroy crops here. This is a farming area. People would like wild animals enclosed like it happens in Ol Pajeta, where complaints of human–wildlife conflict are not reported. In this place it is different, so the best [approach] is enclosing the wild animals.[192]

To pastoralists in Laikipia, a fence remains a symbol of enclosure in that it can be disrespected if demolished. The practice of breaking it is in itself a symbolic action that contests the claim marked by the fence. However, if the fence is physically impassable, it comes to denote an actual limit to resources rather than a symbol of exclusion.[193] Yet, depending on how such an exclusion was put in place, it could invite respect.

When the late owner of the smaller ranch was still alive, the fence enforcement was successful. What he had managed to build was not merely an electric fence but a two-metre-high electric fence with a one-metre-high stone wall supporting it. The lower wire was in the ground, the second and third were covered with stones, and the fourth and the fifth were above the stones. If a wire was cut, an alarm notified the security manager, who was able to arrive at the scene before anyone would be able to create a large enough hole to let in any animals to reach the grass and water. As far as the eye could see there were posts, stones, posts, stones. Inside the fence it was lush, and the cattle were well nourished. Outside the fence it was bare, and the cattle were dusty and thin.[194] According to the late owner, to get rid of trespassing, ranchers ought to build a proper fence and show that they prioritise livestock over wild animals:

191 Interview with research participant, south-western Laikipia, 6 March 2015.
192 Interview with research participant, Thome, 5 May 2015.
193 Interview with research participant, south-western Laikipia, 6 March 2015.
194 Field notes, conversation with research participant, south-western Laikipia, 26 April 2015.

> From the outside you need to look like you are busy. You better have a boundary fence […]. You better have a lot of cows and if you have good land, start growing crops, start planting trees. Develop the farm because if it is well developed […] people will leave you alone and will go and bother those who are lazy and are not doing anything.[195]

This also illustrates the aspect of fencing that people on the other side of the fence have an opinion about how one's land is managed, which can either lead to respect for the boundary or justify intrusion. Many pastoralists consider good land management to depend on whether one offers grass to wild animals or cares for livestock first.[196] A Samburu herder looking at a conservancy through a fence would envy the owner his grass, and disrespect him for giving it to wild animals rather than cattle.[197] To them, this would be a mismanaged place and they would consider their own cattle to have more right to the grass than the wild animals grazing on it. Such conditions would legitimise trespass. The moral perceptions are little different for many Kikuyu smallholders, as one states:

> [The owner at a large conservancy] has allowed [elephants] to come and destroy our crops. So, if we come to know some livestock are eating wildlife pastures, we will wait to hear that some elephants are dying due to lack of pastures. We will be happy since they […] cannot disturb us. […] At the end of the day, we don't get any benefit from the wildlife.[198]

Many of the ranch owners are understanding of the smallholders' opinion that it is problematic for a rancher to limit the number of cattle and instead allow wildlife to consume the grass while disallowing neighbours from securing grazing agreements. One ranch owner stated:

> In Sipili they all complain that [the conservancy's] animals are eating their crops. And then the Pokots: 'Oh, we need grass because [the conservancy owner] doesn't have any cattle and she's got grass.' So, if you have your own cattle, at least they can't say you don't have anything. […] But if you set aside an area as a conservancy where there is purely wildlife and

195 Interview with research participant, south-western Laikipia, 6 March 2015.
196 Interview with research participant, Nyahururu, 21 March 2016.
197 Interview with research participant, Ol Moran, 2 August 2015.
198 Interview with research participant, Ol Moran, 21 July 2015; interview with research participant, Nyahururu, 21 March 2016.

> there is no cattle around, nobody will [respect you]. They think it is like a rich man's playground. You are wasting good land.[199]

The land-management practice at conservancies can come across as provocative and biased. As such, a conservancy manager will find little sympathy if they vie for respect for private property when it comes to the grazing of pastoralist livestock, while coincidentally supporting the morals of wildlife protection when it comes to the free roaming of wildlife on conservancy land as well as neighbouring smallholder land. In such cases, pastoralists as well as smallholders consider the owner to be asking for trouble and inviting people to trespass.[200]

5.4 Concluding Remarks

Taking a bird's-eye view of the social constructions of the governance of space, one understands Polanyi's notion that the economisation and institutionalisation of land must be one of humankind's more peculiar inventions.[201] The history of transition in Laikipia's systems of landholding has been one of transformation from common-property land, through a period dominated by freehold property, into the current fragmented state of landholding systems. Although the area continues to be formally dominated by private-property regimes, the Dykes story illustrates how this regime was already being challenged in the Independence years. The islands of enclosures that make up grids in the landscape today have come about because of the manifold types of claim and the multitude ways to enforce them. As such, naming and fencing function as tools to create enclosures that enforce a claim, regardless of whether one holds private-property rights or not. Meanwhile, the renaming of places, illegal grazing, deconstruction of fences and killing of wildlife can function as protests against an enclosed claim.

199 Interview with research participant, Laikipia, 12 May 2015.
200 Interview with research participant, Ol Moran, 21 July 2015; interview with research participant, Nyahururu, 21 March 2016.
201 Karl Polanyi, *The Great Transformation: The Political and Economic Origins of Our Time*, second edition (Boston, MA: Beacon Press, 2001).

CHAPTER 6

Ambiguous Institutions: Twilight Actions of Land-buying Companies

> [I]t is difficult to ascribe exercised authority to the 'state' as a coherent institution. Rather, public authority becomes the amalgamated result of a variety of local institutions' exercise of power and external institutions' imposition of it, joined together with the idea of a state.
>
> CHRISTIAN LUND[1]

In 2016, an anti-corruption commission started to investigate a number of land-buying companies in Laikipia which, they stated, had swindled innocent people out of their lands.[2] It was not the first time that government institutions and the media had focused their attention on land-buying companies. In 2015, President Kenyatta announced that he wanted all land-buying companies closed:

> Those who started these land-buying companies had good intentions but due to greed, lives have been lost as residents continue to lose millions of their hard earned cash. […] We want all the directors of land-buying companies to be identified and their contacts provided to ensure in future that if issues arise, they can be traced and held accountable for their actions.[3]

The widespread tension created by land-buying companies in Laikipia is strongly linked to the social ecology of land (re)distribution since Independence,

---

1 Christian Lund, 'Access to Property and Citizenship: Marginalization in a Context of Legal Pluralism,' in *Legal Pluralism and Development: Scholars and Practitioners in Dialogue*, ed. Brian Z. Tamanaha, Caroline Mary Sage and Michael J.V. Woolcock (Cambridge: Cambridge University Press, 2012), p. 199.

2 *The Star*, 'EACC Probes Four Laikipia Land Buying Companies,' 27 August 2016.

3 Boniface Gikandi and Lydiah Nyawira, 'President Uhuru Kenyatta Issues Kihiu Mwiri Titles, Says No More Land-Buying Companies,' *The Standard*, 17 September 2015.

 DOI:10.1163/9789004435209_007

and specifically to the way in which land under former white control became Africanised.

In the Independence years, it was typically prospecting politicians from the new political elite who founded the land-buying companies. They bought the former colonial ranches and farms as complete entities and subdivided them once enough shareholders had been recruited. Because of land being in high demand among the population, shareholders were easy to recruit and each politician could target the supply of land specifically to potential voters. That way, the land-buying companies became instruments for securing the political positions of their founders by exchanges of votes for land. Moreover, this instrumentalism fed into a politicisation of the land transfers, because each politician recruited individuals from the particular ethnic groups from which they needed political support.[4] From the perspective of the land claimants, there were numerous bureaucratic processes to go through before they could achieve formal ownership of the land purchased from the land-buying company. Many often only realised the extent of these challenges once the founding politician had been elected to initiate his political career. As such, the completion of the transfers into the hands of the shareholders could take decades. It is for this reason that the land-buying companies remain an important factor contributing to the land-use fragmentation, ambiguity of ownership and ubiquity of disputes in Laikipia.

The land-buying companies have become points of interest in developing an understanding of historical and present-day dynamics in Laikipia, as well as in Kenya more broadly. Kanyinga has studied the social dynamics relating to land transfers in other parts of the White Highlands, namely in Trans Nzoia and Uasin Gisho.[5] Furthermore, Wasserman, Hornsby, Branch and others have dealt with public land redistribution in the years following independence and the implications of this for Kenya's political landscape.[6] However, little research has dealt with the social-ecological dynamics on the Laikipia plateau, including links to land distribution and land-buying companies.[7]

4 Branch, *Kenya: Between Hope and Despair*.

5 Kanyinga, 'The Land Question in Kenya.'

6 Leo, *Land and Class in Kenya*; Kyle, *The Politics of the Independence of Kenya*; Wasserman, *Politics of Decolonization*; Hornsby, *Kenya: A History since Independence*; Leys, *Underdevelopment in Kenya*; Branch, *Kenya: Between Hope and Despair*.

7 Marie Gravesen, 'Twilight Institutions: Land-Buying Companies and Their Long-Term Implications in Laikipia, Kenya,' in *Land, Investment and Politics: Reconfiguring Africa's Pastoral Drylands*, ed. Jeremy Lind, Doris Okenwa and Ian Scoones (Woodbridge, Suffolk: James Currey, 2020).

This chapter approaches the land-buying companies as shadow institutions, representing entities that are untouchable for the state and its citizens. It starts with an ethnographic account of a meeting between shareholders and directors in a land-buying company. It continues with a conceptual overview of institutional pluralism in Laikipia, and then proceeds to investigate the historical context around the rise of the companies. The issues are exemplified in a case study of a land-buying company. Subsequently, the chapter examines the repercussions of the land-buying companies' existence. These include the construct of the absentee landlord, the ambiguity of being settled without having a title deed and the appearance of vernacular land markets.

6.1 All Things Come to Those Who Wait – or Do They?

On 16 May 2015, a meeting was convened between the shareholders and the directors of Thome Farmers Company.[8] The deputy county commissioner (DCC) for Laikipia West Subcounty, Wilfred Kinyua, had called for the meeting in response to pressure from the shareholders. It was only the third meeting that had been held between the directors and the shareholders since the company was formed and the company office established in Githunguri in 1974.[9] When I visited Thome in the weeks prior to the meeting, some of the shareholders had been joking about how the concept of annual general meetings is a beautiful idea but this company seemed to be exempt from having them every year. They also told me that the directors had been reluctant to hold the meeting in Thome, as they feared the shareholders.[10]

When we arrived at North Tetu Primary School in Thome, where the meeting would be held, the police had arrived and a tent had been erected awaiting the arrival of the DCC and the directors. Shortly afterwards, the DCC and his entourage arrived. A few members of the county administration accompanied him, among whom was the area chief and the DCIO (divisional criminal investigation officer) of the area. The shareholders were present in considerable numbers. They were seated in groups according to ethnicity in front of the tent. There was a group of Kikuyu women, a group of Turkana women, and a group of Turkana elders and youth. Looking around, I found that there was no sign of the Samburu community. When I asked the Turkana men why that was,

8 Field notes, Thome, 16 May 2015.

9 Interview with research participant, Thome, 13 May 2015.

10 Field notes, conversation with research participant, Rumuruti, 16 May 2015.

the response was quick: 'Hao watu hawana mashamba hapa' ('Those people don't own land here'). They explained that the Kikuyu were open-minded and accommodative, and the Turkana felt they could easily reason with them. On the other hand, the Samburu were very ignorant, they said. One Turkana man exclaimed in frustration: 'Hawa watu ata ukijaribu kuwaelezea kitu wanajifanya wanjinga' ('If you try to explain something to these people, they pretend not to understand'). He said that they came and forced themselves on people's land and farms, pretending not to know that somebody owned them. A well-respected Turkana man in his late 40s, 'Jacob,' said that were it not for the presence of the Kikuyu in Thome, the Turkana would be fighting with the Samburu, to which the other men nodded in agreement. Jacob continued, saying that the Kikuyu were not confrontational like the Turkana, and another man knowingly added: 'Sisi ni watu wa hasira' ('We are an easily angered community').[11]

When the directors arrived, their cars brought them past the crowd and they headed straight for the seats in the tent, without stopping to greet the shareholders, and the meeting began. As the chair, the DCC outlined the agenda for the meeting: (1) the payment for title deeds. The farmers wanted to know why they had to pay another sum for the same title deeds. They had already paid 2,400 Kenyan shillings (Ksh) when they bought the shares, and now the directors were demanding another Ksh 14,000 per share. (2) The credibility of the survey done on the land. Over the years there had been two surveyors commissioned to measure the acreage of Thome and prepare it for subdivision, both of which surveys had been deemed invalid by shareholders as well as directors. The shareholders wanted to know whether they would have to pay for yet another survey. (3) The size of the land in question. The members knew that the land-buying company's land amounts to 37,676 acres,[12] with 53,138 shares bought. Given that each share is one acre, the shareholders wanted to know whether this increase in shareholding would lead to a reduction of the individual's share size.

After the announcement of the agenda, the DCC moved on to introduce the chairman of the company. He was an elderly man with grey hair, wearing a black suit and shiny shoes. When the DCC had calmed people down, the chairman started to speak:

> Thank you very much. [...] So, let us all try, starting with me as the chairman, to speak the truth. ... I am from Githunguri. I have been the chairman

11 Field notes, Thome, 16 May 2015.

12 Thome itself is 17,000 acres; however, in addition, Thome Farmers Company comprises the areas of Sugoroi and Lombara – areas that also neighbour Ngorare Ranch and Thome.

> for some time. In short, the history of Thome: in our place we had the politician, Arthur Magugu. He saw it was good to buy land [from the ranchers] for our members. He did like Njenga Karume and other politicians of the time [and founded a land-buying company]. [...] We had a plan of how people would buy shares [after the company was founded], but people continued buying shares and it reached a point when anybody could buy shares.[13]

It seemed the chairman attributed the cause of the current situation, with more shares than the land could sustain, to the shareholders' continued purchasing of shares, while taking no responsibility for the directors' choice to continue selling them.[14] The chairman's talk initially calmed the shareholders, but as he became more defensive they grew uneasy and started to talk. The chairman seemed uncomfortable with the situation and occasionally glanced towards the acacia tree 20 metres to the left of the tent, under which the police turnout watched lazily. The audience started talking among themselves. 'The Directors should know when there was no more land to be sold,' a few shareholders shouted. But the chairman continued to speak:

> The first surveyor came, Mr Kangere. He subdivided the land [...]. All that was under Mr Magugu. When it came a point when individuals had to be shown their respective land, that was done. However, when he was concluding, it was realised that the surveyor was not registered! I don't know how it happened. [...] So, we brought in a new surveyor, Kamwere. When he came, he duplicated what Kangere did. He asked for Ksh 2,000 from [each of] the members. But, we realised he was not doing a good job either. So we terminated that. We had to look for someone to guide us. The new surveyor said that we needed to know the total acreage of Thome. Secondly, the total shares. And thirdly, total members. He realised that with so many shares and so many members we had a big task ahead. I know you are intelligent people. The surveyor we have is also our advisor; he told us how to get title deeds. So, Mr Commissioner, allow me to invite our surveyor to explain how the Ksh 14,000 figure was arrived at.[15]

---

13 Chairman of Thome Farmers Company, field notes from shareholders' meeting, Thome, 16 May 2015.

14 Field notes, Thome, 16 May 2015.

15 Chairman of Thome Farmers Company, field notes from shareholders' meeting, Thome, 16 May 2015.

After some noise and yelling from the crowd, the DCC managed to invite the surveyor to speak. The surveyor was considerably younger than the chairman – a clerk well on his way to establishing his career.[16] The surveyor started to talk:

> I have been asked to talk about surveying. In 2005, I was given this work. [...] In 2006, we went to Thome. [...] The first thing to do as a surveyor, you must identify the size of the land to subdivide, the total number of people and where to place the public utilities. That is what we call the Land Planning Act, which outlines the size of land to be left out for public utilities; schools, hospitals and all that. [...] So from the register, the total number of shares was 53,138. [The total acreage of Thome] sums to 37,676 acres. When you divide that by the number of shares, you get that every share will get 0.71 [acres].[17]

Some of the shareholders now started booing. One man aggressively yelled: 'Shut up! Are we buying the land again? You want to buy an airplane?' The surveyor sat still. The sweat started to show on his forehead, and he nervously held on to his piece of paper without lifting his gaze up towards the crowd. Trying to ignore the murmurs, he continued to read from his paper:

> If you were to give every member one share it means that some will be locked out of the farm. If we were to give members 0.71 we must subdivide the land again. I now want to address the issue of payment. Our charges according to our calculations: for one share one will pay Ksh 13,905.[18]

This figure prompted the whole crowd to stand up and shout, raising their fists in the air. The surveyor was forced to stop talking and the DCC intervened, telling people to calm down. The surveyor looked tired. It was easy to imagine that he regretted agreeing to announce these unpopular statements when the chairman had asked him to, likely wishing to avoid the situation himself, knowing what a fuss it would result in. But the surveyor continued amid the shouts: 'The money we are charging involves three things: one, drawing a plan and taking it to relevant authorities for approval: they will charge. Second, surveying and getting new plot numbers. Third, to process title deeds. If you pay this

16 Field notes, Thome, 16 May 2015.
17 Surveyor of Thome Farmers Company, field notes from shareholders' meeting, Thome, 16 May 2015.
18 Surveyor of Thome Farmers Company, field notes from shareholders' meeting, Thome, 16 May 2015.

money, we will bring you the title deeds.'[19] He proceeded to go through the particulars of the expenses, after which the DCC thanked him for covering all three points on the agenda.

The shareholders now realised it was their turn to speak, and many stood up to compete for the floor. The DCC tried to facilitate, and gave precedence to a man in the crowd close to the tent. The latter calmly asked: 'All those who have paid that money, when will you show them their land? I have paid everything: Ksh 16,500.' This question was met with a nod from the DCC, and, surprisingly, he asked the surveyor to reply immediately. This procedure was not followed for questions from anyone else among the crowd. 'We are going to show you that either in July or August,' the surveyor calmly replied. People in the crowd now started to talk inaudibly among themselves, debating who the man posing the question was. They were mistrustful of all communication coming from the company and decided that the person must be colluding with the directors. They now started shouting questions one after another: 'Who appointed those surveyors who made mistakes here? How do we know whether they will do the same again?,' one man shouted. 'Why has the office never met with the shareholders to tell them that Kangere was not a registered surveyor?,' another man asked accusingly. He continued, 'Kosa si kosa, kosa ni kurudia kosa' ('A mistake is only a mistake if repeated'). People clapped and shouted in agreement.[20]

One of the Kikuyu residents was given the floor:

> We have not been called for this meeting to be taken round and round. I am saying that because people asked for money for surveying, Ksh 1,175, almost 20 years ago! We have paid that money [...]. We have not been told the interest gained by that money. We also know that some [Samburu] man has been leasing out land for grazing from the directors. He does that on behalf of his community. We have not been told where that money goes.[21]

This statement was met by applause from the crowd, and the resident went on:

> We have not also been told where the money they got after selling the animals and the vehicles in the farm went. We had so many cattle here.

19 Surveyor of Thome Farmers Company, field notes from shareholders' meeting, Thome, 16 May 2015.

20 Field notes, Thome, 16 May 2015.

21 Shareholder in Thome Farmers Company, field notes from shareholders' meeting, Thome, 16 May 2015.

> We fear that the directors might bring conflicts here. Mr Chairman has no land in Thome. It would be a big blunder to ask a person to look after one's cows, who has no cows himself![22]

His sarcasm led people to laugh, and a few pointed towards the tent. 'You see, now that the land has gained value, that is when they want to tell us they must reduce it. We are the shareholders; we have made its value increase. I assure you that it will never happen! We have nowhere else to go!' People shouted and clapped.[23] An elderly Kikuyu man exclaimed in Gikuyu: 'Tutingitikira!" ('We cannot accept!'). Another older Kikuyu took the floor: 'Honestly speaking, we cannot pay for title deeds the same amount as in Kikuyuland! Even Kibaki himself said the charges for a title deed in Laikipia should not exceed Ksh 500!' The crowd applauded. 'Why now bring us new figures?,' he continued furiously. He was now shaking with anger and spoke uncontrolledly, and the DCC put a hand on his shoulder to calm him down until he sat down again.

Now a woman was given the floor: 'Why is it that my land has two share certificates while I am not the one who sold to that other person! I bought 11 acres, and when I went to Githunguri, I found a different share certificate and owner! Where did that come from?'[24] The turn to speak was immediately passed on to another old Kikuyu man:

> This issue has taken us long! From 1974 we wanted title deeds! I was born here. [...] I know everything here. The surveyor, Kangere, was brought here by Arthur Magugu, the former minister for health. I am highly convinced that Mr Magugu was a very wise man. He could not have just picked an amateur from the streets to come and survey such a farm. So, when we were buying shares, we were told one share is five acres. When Kangere came here and subdivided the land, people were shown their land from 1980. [...] So, people started settling on their land. In 1991 the directors told us that those who had paid for the title deeds were 670 members. When we started asking for the title deeds, they kept quiet. In 2007, they told us that if you wanted your title you had to pay Ksh 14,425. Is that not true, members?[25]

22 Shareholder in Thome Farmers Company, field notes from shareholders' meeting, Thome, 16 May 2015.

23 Field notes, Thome, 16 May 2015.

24 Field notes, Thome, 16 May 2015.

25 Shareholder in Thome Farmers Company, field notes from shareholders' meeting, Thome, 16 May 2015.

The crowd of shareholders confirmed with applause. I was surprised to find that the shareholders did not seem to question the founder of the company, the politician Magugu. He had died long ago, but perhaps that fact would have even made it easier to put the blame on him. Nevertheless, the anger was instead focused on the directors. The man continued:

> We cannot agree to that. That is our stand! You have never called us for a meeting to brief us. [...] We don't want a tug of war anymore. Let it end today! We cannot carry other peoples' crosses; those that missed land elsewhere. [...] We have heard people are killing one another elsewhere because of land; we don't want that to happen here! We have seen some strangers coming here. We want transparency; strangers can't come here and harass us. I thank you people of Thome for keeping peace. I know you would have attacked them but you have chosen to handle it through a legal process.[26]

Another old Kikuyu man stood up to speak. The man next to me told me that he used to be the driver for Carr Hartley, the former owner: 'I was born here; our directors stole our cattle here. I am surprised that they are still stealing from us to date.' The crowd cheered and clapped their hands for him. He continued:

> They want to take the little we have. As a member, I want to categorically state that there is no inch of our land that will be cut off! We have lived here for a long time. We have become elders. [...] What will we give to all these children that we have had? We will continue living where we are settled till God comes for us![27]

When the old man sat down again, the DCC turned to the chairman and invited him to reply to some of the statements. As he stood up to speak, some of the people shouted him down. 'Let me tell you,' he began. 'I only sold this land for 20,000 – and 15,000 only in some cases. If I ever sold to you and you want your money, come to me and kneel and I will return you money.'[28] People shouted him down. The chairman, however, continued speaking, and it was difficult to

26 Shareholder in Thome Farmers Company, field notes from shareholders' meeting, Thome, 16 May 2015.

27 Shareholder in Thome Farmers Company, field notes from shareholders' meeting, Thome, 16 May 2015.

28 Chairman of Thome Farmers Company, field notes from shareholders' meeting, Thome, 16 May 2015.

catch what he was saying. People continued heckling more and more and gathered closer to the tent. The police had now stirred and moved closer. It was crowded and noisy. The people's disrespectful responses clearly annoyed the elderly chairman. The Turkana elder, Jacob, started to move around the crowd to calm down the shareholders.[29]

The DCC now stood up and asked the members to provide possible solutions to the issue since there were no title deeds yet. The crowd met this suggestion with more shouting and angry outbursts: 'We have said we want title deeds! Period!'[30] one man shouted. Another one bellowed:

> The government is here to protect us and our property. [...] The government should help us to know the authenticity of the surveys that were done. Also, these newcomers are settling on our land since we don't have title deeds. So, let us get the title deeds as soon as possible![31]

Another person stood up and shouted: 'We only have certificates, how do we tell a genuine certificate. Maybe they are all fake! We don't want the office, we want our title deeds!'[32]

The DCC had to find a way to end the meeting. 'I can see people are very angry.' He started acknowledging the shareholders' frustrations. People began to settle down, and let him continue: 'We as the security team have decided this; you give us five people. [...] We are going to put them in touch with the directors. [...] If we fail to agree, I am going to tell them what action to take. [...] I now want the five people.'[33] The crowd started to discuss this between themselves. Every ethnic community struggled to ensure that one of their own would be on the committee. Names were shouted, and one by one the crowd started to agree and the names were written down. The DCC called for order and announced the final list. It included the names of two Kikuyu men, one Turkana man, one Kalenjin woman and one Somali man. The DCC also included Father Makau from the Catholic Mission in Rumuruti on the list as a sixth person: 'just in case you need the word of God.'

29 Field notes, Thome, 16 May 2015.

30 Shareholder in Thome Farmers Company, field notes from shareholders' meeting, Thome, 16 May 2015.

31 Shareholder in Thome Farmers Company, field notes from shareholders' meeting, Thome, 16 May 2015.

32 Shareholder in Thome Farmers Company, field notes from shareholders' meeting, Thome, 16 May 2015.

33 Deputy county commissioner of Laikipia County, field notes from shareholders' meeting, Thome, 16 May 2015.

With this decision, the DCC called the meeting to an end. There was a sense of contentment among the members, despite the fact that no resolution had been reached. With the assurance given by the DCC, the members seemed to accept that no more could be done today and started to disperse from the meeting ground.[34]

More than a year after this meeting, the committee had managed to meet a few times, although no resolution had yet been reached.[35]

6.2 The History of Land-buying Companies and Land Hunger

As explained in chapter 3, the Independence years opened up the possibility of the settlement of former colonial subjects on former Crown Lands.[36] The Africans who had been settled in the neighbouring areas to the White Highlands were especially eager to access these lands. However, despite the abolishing of the racial and ethnicity-based legal foundation for the White Highlands, the redistribution of land continued to be unequal.[37]

Although the political forces in the outgoing colonial government acknowledged the urgency among Africans to acquire land, the extent of the pressure was underestimated in the British government subsidised resettlement schemes.[38] Moreover, land reform and the British-funded resettlement schemes failed to benefit the broader population over the wealthy, which encouraged the landless to look for patrons to support them.[39] The new Kenyan political elite anticipated that the state's land reform would be insufficient and saw an opportunity to gain from private initiatives. While the disenfranchised were dependent on a patron or cooperative, the Agricultural Finance Corporation (AFC)[40] supported 'those with salaries and people of political influence [to become] the main beneficiaries of large land holdings,' following Kanyinga.[41] Thus, by founding land-buying companies, the new political elite could

34 Field notes, shareholders' meeting, Thome, 16 May 2015.

35 Field notes, email correspondence with research participant, Laikipia, 14 December 2016.

36 Branch, *Kenya: Between Hope and Despair*.

37 Kohler, *Land Use in Transition*; Leo, *Land and Class in Kenya*; Leys, *Underdevelopment in Kenya*.

38 P. Pestalozzi, 'Historical and Present Day Agricultural Change on Mt. Kenya'; Wasserman, 'Continuity and Counter-Insurgency.'

39 Wasserman, *Politics of Decolonization*; Sorrenson, *Land Reform in the Kikuyu Country*; Leo, *Land and Class in Kenya*.

40 The AFC is a government-funded institution providing development finance.

41 Kanyinga, 'The Legacy of the White Highlands,' p. 332.

become the patrons that the landless were looking for while simultaneously securing a voter base.[42]

In Laikipia, the new economic and political elite were able to purchase the former colonial ranches.[43] Most of the transfers were supported by AFC loans, which gave the government an important role as a creditor in these private land transfers. Its importance is underlined by the figures spent on this support:

> Between 1970 and 1978, the Agricultural Finance Corporation (AFC) originally set up to provide credits for small scale farming, had spent an impressive 216 Million Ksh for land purchase loans, which represented 38% of its total disbursements within this period.[44]

In spite of the power of the creditor position, the authorities proved incapable (or unwilling) of sanctioning the land-buying companies for their poor leadership and ensuring the fair treatment of shareholders.[45]

As exemplified in the Dykes story in chapter 5, another discrepancy in the land reform was the limited amount of white land in the schemes. To preserve a colonial imprint through the continuation of large-scale European-managed land in Kenya, the Africanisation of the lands needed to be held back.[46] Exchange Control[47] was introduced in 1965, limiting opportunities for landholders, such as the Dykes, to sell their land legally outside of the resettlement schemes.[48] As the resettlement schemes accepted mixed-farming plots only, few white settlers qualified for inclusion. This design added pressure to the settlers in the south of Laikipia to sell their land even if they had not envisaged doing so, whereas the settlers towards the north were given no aid to sell their

42 Leo, *Land and Class in Kenya*; Kanyinga, 'The Land Question in Kenya.'

43 Kohler, *Land Use in Transition*.

44 Kohler, *Land Use in Transition*, p. 32.

45 Kohler, *Land Use in Transition*, p. 51.

46 Leys, *Underdevelopment in Kenya*; Leo, *Land and Class in Kenya*; TNA, FCO 141/19572, 'Kenya Land Transfer Programme – John Alison Dykes, Marmar Ranching and Trading Ltd, Laikipia,' 1975–1976; Wasserman, *Politics of Decolonization*; Kyle, *The Politics of the Independence of Kenya*; Leo, *Land and Class in Kenya*.

47 Exchange Control required the seller of land to be approved by government in order to be allowed to export the proceeds of land sales if sold in Kenyan currency. Contrastingly, foreign currency, such as the British pound, could be freely exported. However, the British pound was only used for transfers through the resettlement schemes. Consequently, only settlers included in the schemes could legally leave the country with their capital.

48 Leys, *Underdevelopment in Kenya*.

land, even if they were interested in leaving the country, and make land available for African settlement.[49]

The prospective political elite, such as G.G. Kariuki in the Dykes story, took advantage of the situation, since a person with political connections could provide the government approval for the transaction and allow the export of the profits from the sale.[50] After the prospective politicians had acquired the landholdings from the white settlers, the land could be sold on to potential voters.[51] The public discourse on the lack of land and sense of land hunger made people incredibly willing to buy shares – many were even willing to contribute financially without having seen the land itself.

Yet the willingness to trust their patrons meant that many shareholders were surprised to find that rather than a share of fertile land, they had effectively bought a pile of rocks. Unlike the resettlement schemes, where the ecological conditions had to be evaluated for their suitability for small-scale farming, land-buying companies acquired whatever type of land became available.[52] And due to their interest in maximising the number of voters, shareholders would not be compensated through larger shares. With extensive ecological variation across Laikipia, the prospects for an investment depended greatly on the location of a shareholder's share.

A former director of Mutokanio Farmers Company described how the process of share distribution was meant to be random by use of balloting, although the outcome, for some, was determined beforehand:

> Balloting was done and people picked plot numbers. [...] Anyway, to be honest, since we were the directors, we had picked our plot number of preferred plots in advance. [...] We were leaders. When you are able, you must make out something good for yourself. By then they used to pay us peanuts as directors. So, I had to pick the best; I won't lie. I told the guy who was indicating the plot numbers not to drop my plot numbers in the box. Even before balloting, I had a complete house there. I got six acres.[53]

---

49 Leo, 'Who Benefited from the Million-Acre Scheme?'; Wasserman, *Politics of Decolonization*; interview with Shareholder in Thome Farmers Company, field notes from shareholders' meeting, Thome, 16 May 2015; interview with research participant, northern Laikipia, 24 July 2015.

50 Kohler, *Land Use in Transition*, p. 40.

51 Kanyinga, 'The Legacy of the White Highlands,' p. 332.

52 Kanyinga, 'The Land Question in Kenya'; Leo, 'Who Benefited from the Million-Acre Scheme?'; Kanyinga, 'The Legacy of the White Highlands.'

53 Interview with research participant, Ol Moran town, 2 July 2015.

Consequently, in Laikipia's drier areas many shareholders ended up on land with low economic potential, effectively locking them into poverty traps.[54]

Moreover, many of the opportunistic politicians became tempted to sell to more people than the particular area of land could accommodate.[55] In Central Province, members of registered land-buying companies had contributed Ksh 475 million by the early 1980s, and land-buying companies running in Laikipia District had amassed an amount between Ksh 170 and 240 million between 1962 and 1980.[56] Although it was often an advantage to have a politician among the company's founding fathers, the politicians themselves made great financial profits.

Founding a land-buying company became a widespread phenomenon among prospective politicians – a means to an end as a political short-cut.[57] In 1981, the chairs among 20 selected land-buying companies included three ministers, two leading political administrators, one leading party official and one member of parliament.[58] And even after the shareholders had waited for decades to get their title deeds, the politician would often still retain their moral image as the provider of land, while the company directors would be blamed for the prolonged proceedings.[59]

Underlining the paradoxes of the Africanisation processes, the land-buying companies became sites for ethnic competition, for instance when members were composed of Kikuyu and Kalenjin as in the Lorien Ranching Company. Both groups had been resourceful in terms of getting political links, which reinforced the connection between politics and ethnicity.[60] While the resettlement schemes were officially meant to satisfy claims to land, in practice they reinforced the hostility of interethnic relations by prioritising economic stability over addressing landlessness. Instead, politicians used the cases of land disputes to consolidate their supporter base, making the highlands into sites of political strife.[61]

---

54 Interview with research participant, Laikipia University campus, Nyahururu, 28 January 2015.

55 Kanyinga, 'The Legacy of the White Highlands.'

56 Kohler, *Land Use in Transition.*

57 Kanyinga, 'The Legacy of the White Highlands.'

58 Kohler, *Land Use in Transition.*

59 Interview with research participant, Nanyuki, 16 August 2016; Kanyinga, 'The Legacy of the White Highlands.'

60 Kanyinga, 'The Legacy of the White Highlands.'

61 Leo, 'Who Benefited from the Million-Acre Scheme?'; Kanyinga, 'The Land Question in Kenya'; Kanyinga, 'The Legacy of the White Highlands'; Faith Nyamai, 'Court Postpones Ruling in Moi Land Case,' *The Daily Nation*, 20 January 2015; interview with research participant, Laikipia, 30 January 2017.

Aside from gathering political support, the slow processing of title deeds enabled directors to continue to sell shares beyond the number of smallholders the land could sustain. It is only when all shares are sold that a surveyor can be commissioned to enforce the subdivisions, and therefore directors would deliberately maintain that more shares were available for sale.[62] Often this process could extend for decades, with directors arguing that it is now their job to tackle the repercussions of their predecessors' poor judgements.[63] They have little reason to finalise to process and close down the company as they can collect rent from the unsettled land during this time.[64]

6.3 Institutional Pluralism and Land

As has been argued in previous chapters, Laikipia is located on the frontier where the presence of some state institutions can seem fragmented. Although service provision is much better functioning in Laikipia compared with the neighbouring Isiolo or Samburu counties, state authorities are particularly reluctant to interfere in Laikipia when it comes to land issues. One reason for this is the multifaceted ownership structures and biased lists of people involved in land conflicts.[65] A politician might need votes from one particular ethnic group, and might thus be reluctant to impose sanctions on that group in land disputes with others. This increases divisions and hostility between communities.[66] Frontiers are often defined by this in-between positionality in relation to the state, where control and services are fragmented.[67] This creates omnipresent hinterlands where people are interchangeably excluded in and included

62 Interview with research participant, Rumuruti, 21 January 2015; field notes, visit to county commissioner's office, Nanyuki, 2 June 2015.

63 Interview with research participant, Ol Moran, 2 July 2015; interview with absentee landlords, Githunguri, 15 September 2015; interview with the paramount chief for Laikipia County, Nanyuki, 10 March 2015; interview with research participant, Nanyuki, 16 August 2016.

64 Interview with research participant, Rumuruti, 21 January 2015; interview with research participant, Ol Moran, 2 July 2015; interview with research participant, Thome, 21 August 2015.

65 John Mburu et al., *The Abandoned Lands of Laikipia: Land Use Options Study* (Rumuruti, Kenya: Laikipia Wildlife Forum, The Nature Conservancy and Zeitz Foundation, January 2013); Kantai, 'In the Grip of the Vampire State'; Evans and Adams, 'Fencing Elephants.'

66 For instance in Lorien (see Sam Kiplagat, 'Even in Old Age Land Tussle Splits Group,' *The Daily Nation*, 12 January 2010; *The Daily Nation*, 'Sale of Farm Shares Banned,' 15 July 1980; *The Daily Nation*, 'Land Buyers Warned,' 8 December 1980; *The Daily Nation*, 'Bogus Land Buyers Warned,' 1 July 1980).

67 Hughes, *From Enslavement to Environmentalism*.

from the state through the ever-changing conditionalities of their livelihoods.[68] Such voids created by state absence can be filled by other forms of authority, which leads to institutional and legal pluralism, as Berry suggests.[69] For instance, in lieu of guaranteed statutory land rights, vernacular land markets have been seen to replace state authority in some localities of Laikipia, whereas in other places police support is effective and institutional infrastructure is in operation.

These companies are founded on elite structures and impose authority upon smallholders. Due to their links to powerful politicians, they exist in between what can be clearly termed private or public domains. Falk Moore explains the dichotomy between expectations of the state's legal practice and the reality of the social contexts it is meant to control, and how, if the gap is too large between the two, a vacuum can be generated that enables social engineering to take place.[70] Lund defines these new practices as 'twilight institutions' that take on state-like functions. They prescribe procedures and hierarchies that form around a new local power centre, where they substitute for malfunctioning or absent formal procedures.[71] As parastatal twilight institutions, the land-buying companies are not state institutions but nevertheless lawfully wield authority over land.[72]

Some land-buying companies are still in existence today, even though they were only ever intended as means for their members to obtain land. As in Thome, shareholders may continue to live on land that is not legally theirs even though they already paid for it decades earlier, as the lands have not yet been surveyed, subdivided and titled. Without a title deed, they cannot acquire bank loans to invest in developing their lands.[73] Furthermore, state institutions abstain from getting involved, as they do not wish to interfere with a private company. Therefore, most shareholders are at the mercy of company directors to push for subdivision and titling.

6.4 The Case of Thome Farmers Company

Land purchased by land-buying companies in Laikipia is the source of multiple complex types of present-day conflict over land. This was evident to me in

68 Kopytoff, *The African Frontier*.
69 Berry, 'Debating the Land Question in Africa.'
70 Moore, 'Law and Social Change,' p. 719.
71 Lund, 'Access to Property and Citizenship,' p. 200.
72 Lund, 'Twilight Institutions'; Gravesen, 'Twilight Institutions.'
73 Interviews with residents in Thome, Lorien and Ol Moran, 2015.

several cases in Laikipia. Even though none of the studied case areas bear wider importance in themselves, it is how incidences have unfolded in each of them that makes them relevant and representative of the complex and multi-layered aspects of present-day land issues in Laikipia. All cases studied included ethnic competition, political involvement, over-recruitment of shareholders, long procedures for subdivision and asymmetrical land distribution. These aspects were also present in Thome, even though the conflicts here were indirect. As revealed in the ethnographic detail of the meeting in Thome above, the shareholders were located in Thome, while the company offices lay in Githunguri in Central Province. This was where the founding politician needed his votes. The heart of the conflict in Thome is the shareholders' struggle to acquire individual title deeds for their shares from the directors in the company.[74]

In 1976, Arthur Magugu bought land to found Thome Farmers Company from the rancher Carr Hartley. Hartley owned a company that captured and sold wild animals. As the land could not be categorised as mixed farming, his ranch was not eligible for inclusion in a resettlement scheme, so his only option to exit the country with the sales income from his land was through approval of a compassionate case. Being neither poor nor elderly, such approval would not have been granted. The alternative was to sell privately to a resourceful Kenyan with political ties so that he could export the proceeds of the sale. As a known member of the 'Kiambu mafia,'[75] Arthur Magugu did have political connections, and he was likely under pressure himself to find cooperative land in order to compete with his political contestants.[76] It is unknown whether Magugu put pressure on Hartley to sell, as was the case for other ranchers, or whether his offer was simply too generous for Hartley to decline.[77] One of the factors that might have been relevant for Hartley in agreeing to sell was the hunting ban introduced in Kenya in 1973, complicating the part of his business that was based on trading wild animals.[78]

74 Field notes, Thome, 16 May 2015.

75 In the Independence years and on through the 1980s, an axis of powerful Kikuyu politicians referred to as the 'Kiambu Mafia' were known to exercise their influence on government policies.

76 *The Daily Nation*, 'Magugu Mastered Art of Political Survival,' 16 September 2013, http://www.nation.co.ke/news/politics/Magugu-mastered-art-of-political-survival-/1064-1509146-n6c636z/index.html, accessed 19 April 2017.

77 TNA, FCO 141/19572, 'Kenya Land Transfer Programme – John Alison Dykes, Marmar Ranching and Trading Ltd, Laikipia,' 1975–1976.

78 *The Daily Nation*, 'Hunting Ban Fails to End Bloodbath,' 26 August 2013, https://www.nation.co.ke/kenya/life-and-style/dn2/hunting-ban-fails-to-end-bloodbath-887982,

Magugu was interested in constructing a voter base in Githunguri in time for the 1979 election. With no more land available in Central Province, he had to look for land outside of his constituency area. However, if shareholders settled after obtaining shares, they would move out of his constituency and no longer be a valuable political vote for him. Magugu therefore planned to create absentee landlords by targeting individuals in Githunguri who held land there already. Additionally, rather than positioning the company office on the purchased land in Laikipia, he placed it in Githunguri and extended the process for transferring the land into private titles to deliberately prevent people from settling. That way, he could generate sales to large numbers of shareholders in his constituency and bank them as voting liquidity.[79]

Unlike Thome Farmers Company, the companies Laikipia West Farmers Company and Mutokanio Farmers Company had five Laikipia offices, all with a mandate to sell shares.[80] And in contrast to Magugu, the politician founders of these companies, Kihika Kimani and G.G. Kariuki, were interested in getting people to settle fast.[81] They both ran for seats in Laikipia and therefore needed to settle possible voters in Laikipia. Both therefore opened company offices in areas around Laikipia dominated by Kikuyu and assured buyers that farmland was available for immediate settlement. They promised shareholders that the lands would be subdivided fast, but these promises did not stop them from over-recruiting. Unlike in Thome, where most shareholders are absentees by choice with their primary landholdings in Central Province, the majority of shareholders in Laikipia West Farmers Company and Mutokanio Farmers Company became motivated to buy their shares because of landlessness and therefore needed to settle immediately.[82] Both of these areas are located on the fringes of Pokot and Samburu territories, and therefore the large majority of cases of absentee lands here are attributed to the security situation rather than absentees who did not intend to settle.[83]

However, as in these companies, there were also shareholders in Thome Farmers Company who had no other landholdings. A share was set at one acre at a cost of Ksh 500. However, the company sold an excessive number of shares,

accessed July 9, 2020; field notes, conversation with research participant, Kifuku Ranch, 26 April 2015.

79 Interview with research participant, Rumuruti, 21 January 2015.

80 Interview with research participant, Ol Moran, 2 July 2015.

81 TNA, FCO 141/19572, 'Kenya Land Transfer Programme – John Alison Dykes, Marmar Ranching and Trading Ltd, Laikipia,' 1975–1976.

82 Interview with research participant, Ol Moran, 2 July 2015; interview with research participant, Ol Moran, 21 July 2015.

83 Rutten, 'Fresh Killings.'

and today there is an inconsistency between Thome's total size of 37,676 acres, and its total number of shareholders of 53,138.[84] Nevertheless, shareholders continued to hold Magugu in high regard as their patron. This would show in utterances such as: 'Hon. Magugu did everything for us and we just came in to buy shares. He was the one sourcing land for people.'[85] Thanks to his well-founded support in Githunguri, Arthur Magugu was able to take over the constituency from former vice president Karanja in the elections of 1979 and 1983, forcing Karanja to shift his constituency to Mathare in Nairobi.[86] Magugu became minister of health in 1979 and minister of finance in 1983, and was held in high regard as a politician throughout his life. He died in 2012.[87]

In contrast, for the shareholders settled in Thome, the reality did not meet their expectations. Nonetheless, they continue to be hopeful that they can get tenure security, increased agricultural productivity and income from their land as soon as they get their title deeds. But the reality is that while the title deeds could offer this security for some shareholders, it would increase insecurity for others because of the imbalance between the number of one-acre shares on the land and the number of shareholders. Therefore, the directors have time and again sought to convince the shareholders of the necessity to reduce the size of their shares. The proposition from the directors during the meeting described above was that everyone would get only 0.71 acres rather than the acre per share that they paid for. This is a problem for those shareholders who are already settled and who, unlike the absentee landlords in Central Province, have no other land.[88]

The fact that the issue of title deeds has not been resolved even after 40 years suggests that fraud was involved in the company's establishment. This assumption is supported by several instances in which general enquiries into the land-buying companies in Laikipia have been avoided by land commissions. The same avoidance has become apparent whenever the question of the situation in Thome has entered into parliamentary discussions. For instance, questions about the prolonged casework for title deeds in Thome Farmers Company were posed to Mr Wako, from the attorney general's office, during the National Assembly on 9 October 2002. Mr Wako evaded the questions by referring to other government offices and the police, as well as problematising

84 Approximately 3.7 British pounds.

85 Interview with vice chairman of Thome Farmers Company, Githunguri, 15 September 2015.

86 *The Daily Nation*, 'Magugu Mastered Art of Political Survival.'

87 *The Daily Nation*, 'Magugu Mastered Art of Political Survival.'

88 Field notes, directors' meeting with the shareholders, Thome, 16 May 2015.

the phrasing of the question.[89] A similar avoidance of getting involved is performed by the Laikipia county government. Although it has attempted to facilitate the process, the excuse given to avoid getting too involved is that Thome Farmers Company is a private company and therefore the government cannot interfere.[90]

With an imbalance in the acreage of Thome and the number of shareholders, the transfer of share certificates into title deeds is bound to leave some members landless unless everyone accepts the reduction of their share size.[91] Yet the likelihood of such an acceptance is low, if not non-existent. The shareholders do not see how it can be their fault that the directors sold more shares than the land could support.[92]

6.5 The Power Dynamics of Land-buying Companies

In other parts of the country, President Kenyatta has several times appeared in local meetings to physically hand out title deeds.[93] As much as such demonstrations of opposition to land-buying companies may push for the processing of title deeds and for the companies to be closed, it also creates hope for shareholders in other land-buying companies who also lack their title deeds. Such optimism may provide some with the willpower to hold on another few years, in the anticipation that state authorities will intervene.[94] People holding other positions in government offices can also easily use such performances to gather political support. Similarly to politicians exchanging votes for land in the Independence years, a politician today can be sure of gaining political support if they create the anticipation of people being freed from the grievances inflicted by land-buying companies.[95]

89 Kenya National Assembly, *Official Record* (Hansard, 2002), pp. 2422–23, https://books.google.co.ke/books?id=6Y9CmdV7yu8C&pg=PT10&dq=Thome+farmers+company+magugu&hl=en&sa=X&ved=0CBsQ6AEwAGoVChMI4LeZ5t-IyQIViPEUCh39gQ25#v=onepage&q=Thome%20farmers%20company%20magugu&f=false, accessed 11 November 2015.

90 Interview with Thome elders, Thome, 13 February 2015.

91 Ngugi wa Mbugua, 'Building Castles on Shaky Ground,' *The Daily Nation*, 2 August 1991.

92 Interview with research participant, Thome, 5 May 2015; interview with research participant, Thome, 6 March 2015; interview with research participant, Thome, 13 May 2015.

93 Lucas Barasa and Kennedy Kimanthi, 'President to Hand Out 200,000 Title Deeds,' *The Daily Nation*, 27 February 2015; Ouma Wanzala, '800,000 Deeds Ready for Issue,' *The Daily Nation*, 12 February 2015.

94 Interview with Thome elders, Thome, 25 January 2015.

95 Nicholas Ndirangu, '10,000 Titles Ready,' *The Daily Nation*, 9 March 1992.

However, as illustrated in the case study above, the physical distance between shareholders and directors and the lack of engagement by the directors in relation-building with the shareholders has constrained the creation of familiarity and trust.[96] Initially, many of the relations in the companies formed according to a patron–client model. For instance, Magugu was considered the patron who provided land for the shareholders, who in turn provided him with political support. Many researchers agree that the lack of fairness in the distribution of and access to resources damages cooperation. Likewise, a lack of trust can be detrimental.[97] As such, decades of unfulfilled promises have degraded the ingrained trust in the companies' patron–client relations and shareholders have learned to be suspicious of whatever is conveyed by the directors, which has effectively led the land-buying companies to become unable to function.[98] Yet with regard to the founder Magugu, the settled shareholders uphold an image of him as the patron who gave them land, notwithstanding that he is likely responsible for many of their present-day problems.

Within Thome Farmers Company, the shareholders are fundamentally dissimilar in terms of wealth and class. As the land has limited agricultural potential, the people who still decided to settle in these areas were those with limited alternatives to settle elsewhere. Contrastingly, many of the absentee shareholders bought the land as an investment and did not depend on its productivity. The relationships among the settled shareholders are also unequal, as Chapter 4 underlines. Even though they developed bonds with one another, being neighbours for up to 40 years, their trust for each other carries an element of necessity. They acknowledge their strength as a group, while maintaining strong opposition to intermarriages.[99] Their limited trust for each other is also evident in the way they group together according to ethnic affiliation

96 Niklas Luhmann, 'Trust and Power,' *Studies in Soviet Thought* 23, no. 3 (1982), pp. 266–70.

97 Michael Bollig and Diego A. Menestrey Schwieger, 'Fragmentation, Cooperation and Power: Institutional Dynamics in Natural Resource Governance in North-Western Namibia,' *Human Ecology* 42, no. 2 (1 April 2014), pp. 167–81; Abigail Barr, 'Trust and Expected Trustworthiness: Experimental Evidence from Zimbabwean Villages,' *The Economic Journal* 113, no. 489 (1 July 2003), pp. 614–30; Patrick D. Smith and Maureen H. McDonough, 'Beyond Public Participation: Fairness in Natural Resource Decision Making,' *Society & Natural Resources* 14, no. 3 (1 March 2001), pp. 239–49.

98 Interview with research participant, Thome, 27 May 2015; interview with research participant, Marura, 17 June 2015; interview with research participant, Thome, 13 May 2015; interview with research participant, Thome, 3 August 2015.

99 Interview with research participant, Thome, 6 March 2015; interview with research participant, Thome, 28 May 2015; interview with research participant, Thome, 9 March 2015; interview with research participant, Thome, 13 May 2015.

during meetings, and in their settlement patterns, where for instance Kikuyu and Kalenjin settle in separate clusters.

6.6 Repercussions of Private Land Redistribution

Changing the focus to the contemporary implications of the land-buying companies' operations illustrates their wider significance for the everyday lives of Laikipians. At Independence, the manifold types of land grievance constituted the basis for Kenya's land question.[100] The fact that some received benefits while others did not shaped the social dynamics at the local level. Two repercussions of the private land redistribution have been particularly important.

6.6.1 *Absentee Landlords*

The divergent power relations led some to invest in land-buying companies although they were already settled.[101] However, some absentee landlords did settle, only to be forced to relocate again. These people became absentee landlords in the hope that conditions would make it possible to settle again at a later state.[102] Many of these decisions to move out without selling shares of land were made in the 1980s and 1990s during President Moi's rule.[103] In places where Kalenjin were numerous there was political involvement that affected the land transactions. For instance, in Lorien favouritism could be demonstrated through inaction in response to occurrences of violence against Kikuyu, who in turn chose to leave Lorien and become absentees.[104] An absentee Kikuyu farmer explained how the police met cases of harassment with defensiveness and a reluctance to act:

> The administration did not want to recover stolen animals and the police were sarcastic. [...] I remember one day I came to report to the OCS [Officer Commanding Police Station] that one of my cows had been stolen. He told me to draw the diagram of my cow on the ground. That was ridiculous! That's when I realised they were together. [...] The government

100 Leo, *Land and Class in Kenya*; Klopp, 'Can Moral Ethnicity Trump Political Tribalism?'
101 Mburu et al., *The Abandoned Lands of Laikipia*.
102 Interview with research participant, Rumuruti, 21 August 2015; interview with absentee landlords, Githunguri, 15 September 2015.
103 Kanyinga, 'The Legacy of the White Highlands'; Branch, *Kenya: Between Hope and Despair*.
104 Interview with research participant, Nyahururu, 18 March 2016.

> should not say such things. From how they responded to our complaints, we realised they were working together. They did not do it openly. [Instead] they would just complicate the processes.[105]

After this incident, he chose to leave his land in Thome and settle in the more homogeneous Kikuyu area, Sipili, instead.[106] During the Moi years, harassment and inadequate political representation caused many Kikuyu farmers to become absentee landlords and relocate to more socially homogeneous areas.[107]

Besides most often being Kikuyu, there are generally three types of absentee landlords, out of which a person's class and wealth are the most defining factors. The wealthy absentees acquired shares in land-buying companies without any intention of settling but as investments to later be sold or passed down through inheritance.[108] Members of this group tend to be settled in Central Province and might only go to their Laikipia land every ten years.[109] The second group would have been interested in settling upon investing in the land in the 1970s. However, not having been outside of Central Province before, they were surprised to see the aridity of the land they had bought in Laikipia. In a survey among smallholders in eastern Laikipia in 1982, between 43% and 63% of respondents indicated that they had not known the location of their land when they had bought it.[110] Most of these smallholders only settled briefly, if at all, before deciding to relocate to areas with better farming conditions.

The last group of absentee landlords fully intended to settle when they acquired land. Many in this group were already among the poorer Kikuyu, who had settled in Laikipia after having been outpaced by wealthier Kikuyu in land acquisitions in Central Province. As opposed to the second group, this group were aware that conditions would be challenging, but with little other choice they decided to settle anyway.[111] However, they eventually relocated due to the hardship encountered as a result of ecological conditions and political opposition. Yet even upon deciding to move, few wanted to sell their land. This sentiment followed the frequent political declarations at rallies, encouraging shareholders 'not to sell their farms unless absolutely necessary.'[112] According to the

105 Interview with research participant, Rumuruti, 21 August 2015.
106 Interview with research participant, Rumuruti, 21 August 2015.
107 Field notes, Nyahururu, 21 August 2015.
108 Interview with absentee landlords, Githunguri, 15 September 2015.
109 Interview with absentee landlords, Githunguri, 15 September 2015.
110 Kohler, *Land Use in Transition*.
111 Interview with research participant, Rumuruti, 21 August 2015.
112 *The Daily Nation*, 'Gema Boss Calls for Hard Work at Big Land Ballot,' 30 August 1976.

political purposes of ethnic territorialisation, the selling of unused land was never an option.[113]

Absenteeism bears heavy consequences for an area of shareholders, negative as well as positive.[114] In the 1980s, unoccupied lands were used for the collection of firewood and grazing.[115] However, more recently the availability of seemingly vacant absentee land has attracted pastoralist squatters, who have brought with them an excess amount of livestock. The shareholders themselves have reduced their livestock due to the increased risk of being raided. As such, absenteeism has not brought extra resource access for those who stay.[116] Instead, the added resources are causing increased tension and even violent confrontations, in which the police are hesitant to get involved because it is, strictly speaking, not yet the shareholders' private property.[117]

6.6.2 *Absent Title Deeds and Vernacular Land Markets*

Another implication of the land-buying companies' expansion is in the way that local-level response mechanisms have further contributed to institutional pluralism. The absent title deed is a phenomenon that has evolved since the Independence years, although not exclusively due to the land-buying companies. Those without land elsewhere have no choice but to develop and farm their land, despite their legal rights being compromised. Many scholars have reflected on the precariousness of the relationship between resource access and property rights. Several have exemplified how one may hold property rights without having access to the resources on the property. And correspondingly, others may be able to access resources without holding the property rights for the land.[118] Yet the paradox of the shareholders' situation in Laikipia presents something different again. Here, despite having bought the land, people have not been able to invest in it.[119] Following Shipton, tenure security and title deeds hold significant implications for people's lives. They can affect 'decisions

113 Interview with research participant, Rumuruti, 21 August 2015.

114 Mburu et al., *The Abandoned Lands of Laikipia*.

115 Kohler, *Land Use in Transition*, p. 46.

116 Interview with research participant, Thome, 6 March 2015; interview with research participant, Thome police post, 17 June 2015; interview with research participant, Ol Moran, 22 March 2016.

117 Gravesen, 'Twilight Institutions'; interview with research participant, Ol Moran, 2 August 2015; interview with research participant, Sugoroi, 12 June 2015.

118 Lund, 'Access to Property and Citizenship'; Christian Lund, *Local Politics and the Dynamics of Property in Africa* (Cambridge: Cambridge University Press, 2008); Ribot and Peluso, 'A Theory of Access'; Li, *Land's End*.

119 Interview with research participant, Nanyuki, 16 August 2016.

to fertilize, to enclose, to subdivide, to buy or sell, to migrate.'[120] Without tenure security, the settled shareholders are barred from either investing in or selling their land.

Another aspect of not quite having property rights is how one transfers such not-yet-rights to others. With a share certificate only, the land-buying company still legally controls the management of the land. Therefore, to transfer land legally one has to register the transfer at the land-buying company offices rather than in state institutions such as the local Land Boards.[121] However, this system does not fit the reality of how small-scale farming areas function in present-day Laikipia.[122] For a small-scale farmer in Thome, it is an insurmountable expense to go to the company's office in Githunguri in Central Province simply to ask for a piece of paper to be stamped.[123] People are often unable to trust government offices and land-buying companies, as experiences with both have led people to expect costs for bribes and time spent on travelling.

Instead, the transactions are now carried out locally via vernacular land markets.[124] Systems are required in order to be able to follow generational transitions or changing livelihood conditions. Therefore, the legal shareholder or title-holder and the person using the land are not necessarily the same person.[125] In this respect, ways of handling land registration in Laikipia are little different from in western Kenya: people develop land markets with procedures for land transfers with local witnesses and thumbprints or signatures on documents.[126] As opposed to town clerks and land-buying company administrators, the local authorities in vernacular land markets are trusted by all involved in the transactions.[127] This way, people become semi-autonomous, as the combination of the complicated procedures of land-buying companies and state absence changes authority in land matters such that it becomes appropriable by

120 Shipton, *Mortgaging the Ancestors*, p. 234.

121 Interview with deputy county commissioner, Rumuruti, 15 July 2015; field notes, visit to county commissioner's office, Nanyuki, 2 June 2015.

122 Berry, 'Debating the Land Question in Africa.'

123 Interview with research participant, Thome, 13 May 2015; interview with research participant, Thome, 5 May 2015; interview with research participant, Thome, 27 May 2015.

124 Admos Chimhowu and Phil Woodhouse, 'Customary vs Private Property Rights? Dynamics and Trajectories of Vernacular Land Markets in Sub-Saharan Africa,' *Journal of Agrarian Change* 6, no. 3 (1 July 2006): 346–71.

125 Shipton, *Mortgaging the Ancestors.*

126 Interviews with research participants, Thome, Lorien and Ol Moran, February–August 2015.

127 Interview with Thome elders, Thome, 25 January 2015; Shipton, *Mortgaging the Ancestors*, p. 234.

informal institutions designed not by authoritarian, or even predatory, set-ups but rather by community initiatives on the basis of bottom-up principles.[128]

In this way, the impracticality of the distance between Thome and the company office in Githunguri prompts a further complication of the patron–client relations between the directors and shareholders, making it even more difficult to resolve disagreements.[129]

6.7 Concluding Remarks

As a determinant for one's access to resources, trust can shape how people's opportunistic manoeuvres are formed, especially when the protection of legal rights, service provision and law enforcement by the authorities are absent or flawed.[130] In Laikipia's frontier context, opportunism in accessing land has changed from being triggered by political interests, as in the 1970s. Instead, in present-day Laikipia, actors navigate access opportunistically out of necessity.[131] Smallholder farmers cannot wait for the title deeds to be handed to them before settling, since their limited finances necessitate that they see an immediate return on their investment in buying land.[132] To politicians, securing votes through land acquisitions is a necessity – without political opportunism, politicians would not last long in Kenyan politics.[133] For land-buying company directors, extending processes of individual title deed conversions, and ultimately the closing of companies, permits a continuation of income through the selling of shares and renting of unsettled land.[134]

Yet there are certain implications to these opportunistic actions. For the shareholders, although settlement provides a foundation for a farming livelihood, settling without tenure security means limited support and limited protection of the land they consider theirs.[135] To the directors, extending the life of the company enables them to maximise profits, although doing so can

128 Chimhowu and Woodhouse, 'Customary vs Private Property Rights?'; Lund, 'Access to Property and Citizenship'; Moore, 'Law and Social Change.'

129 Group interview with absentee landlords, Githunguri, September 15, 2015; interview with research participant, Thome, 27 May 2015.

130 Bart Nooteboom, 'Trust, Opportunism and Governance: A Process and Control Model,' *Organization Studies* 17, no. 6 (1 November 1996), pp. 985–1010.

131 Field notes, conversation with research participant, 2 August 2015.

132 Interview with research participant, Thome, 5 May 2015.

133 Interview with research participant, Nanyuki, 16 August 2016.

134 Interview with research participant, Ol Moran, 2 July 2015.

135 Interview with research participant, Thome, 13 May 2015.

potentially attract protest, media attention and political interference. The settled shareholders are left to rely only on support from each other.[136]

In present-day Laikipia, the founding of land-buying companies by politicians as a means to secure votes no longer takes place. It is therefore political vote-seeking rhetoric when politicians such as President Kenyatta proclaim that new land-buying companies are banned. Establishing these types of land-buying companies no longer represents the same glamorous opportunity that it once did. Moreover, Laikipia no longer has available land appropriate for prospective companies.[137] That said, the effects of land-buying companies' existence are undeniable. Those companies that are still active stand to illustrate the complications endured by shareholders since their establishment in the Independence years.[138] The future for these shareholders depends on whether or not formal authorities will continue to abstain from interfering.

136 Interview with research participant, Thome, 21 January 2015; interview with research participant, Thome, 27 May 2015; interview with research participant, Thome, 17 June 2015.

137 Interview with research participant, Nyahururu, 18 March 2016.

138 Interview with research participant, Laikipia University campus, Nyahururu, 28 January 2015.

CHAPTER 7

Africanisation or Invasion: Laikipia's Land-use Change

> Across the hill of Enghelesha, Colobus farm was being chopped up into small shambas where wildlife had no place. The forest of cedars and podo, the old black acacias, had been cut and made into charcoal. [...] Maize was planted everywhere. Tin roofs dotted the ploughed fields where buffalo and antelope had been abundant.
>
> KUKI GALLMANN[1]

This chapter explores the transitions in land use that have taken place across Laikipia over the past 120 years. During this time, the landscape has transformed from one characterised by common grazing regimes, through the exclusivity of large-scale private farms and ranches, to smallholder farmlands next to what still remains of the large landholdings. If asked to explain this development in Laikipia, present-day actors would give very different answers. Some would define the current landscape as invaded by intruders who know little about how to manage the land sustainably, while others would deem the land-use transitions to reflect a fair transition towards an Africanisation of the landscape.

The chapter is inspired by works by other scholars on the environmental history of African landscapes. Looking at long-term transitions in landscapes, the dynamic aspects become apparent. These landscapes are never constant, but rather are fundamentally anthropogenic and local.[2] As such, the landscape in Laikipia is the product of human thought and action. Other scholars illustrate how a misplaced perception of a social-ecological system can have widespread implications for how it is transformed.[3] In particular, this chapter

1 Gallmann, *I Dreamed of Africa*, p. 146.

2 McCann, *Green Land, Brown Land, Black Land: An Environmental History of Africa, 1800–1990*, first edition (Portsmouth, NH: Heinemann, 1999).

3 Mary Tiffen, Michael Mortimore and Francis Gichuki, *More People, Less Erosion: Environmental Recovery in Kenya*, first edition (Chichester, NY: Wiley, 1994).

 | DOI:10.1163/9789004435209_008

illustrates the power of perceptions in Laikipia's changing landscape – how perceptions are political and can become directive of the particular land-use practice that is given authority and becomes dominant.

There have been other studies of long-term land-use change in the Laikipia landscape.[4] This work sheds light on the long-term scale of the anthropogenic landscape of the region. This study contributes by including the lived experience of the multiplicity of inhabitants over the past 100 years.

Few studies have focused on the smallholder farmers of Laikipia and the land-use transitions from ranch land to smallholder farmland.[5] In addition to this, the present study covers a wider historical range and includes perspectives on the smallholder lands before their transition into such usage.

Bearing in mind the different perspectives and perceptions on historical transition, the chapter consults an alternative data source to situate the oral data within a different framework. This source is a diachronic study that takes as its point of departure the visual representations of the landscape. Aerial photography from 1969 and 1977 depicts colonial land use, while satellite imagery from 2016 depicts present-day land use (see figure 9). Set against oral representations of change, as well as the historical perceptions of the social-ecological systems, this comparison demonstrates just how politicised oral representations can be.

To frame the differences in land-use representations, I look at four points in Laikipia's history and the inhabitants' perspectives on the state of affairs at the particular time. One such point in time is around the turn of the century, when explorers kept journals of what they encountered while traversing the landscapes. Another time frame is the 1930s, in the years around the activities of the Kenya Land Commission. The sources for these points in time portray the opinions of the colonial administration and the European farmers. The third point in time portrays the perspectives on land use that characterised the end of the colonial era in the 1960s. This was a time of transition. The settlers had, to a certain extent, adapted to the changing dynamics on the Laikipia plains. Yet their understanding of the place continued to be opinionated, despite being presented as scientific. Because the plateau was so heavily settled there are

---

4 Lane, *Landscape and Environmental Change in Semi-Arid Regions of East and Southern Africa*; Lane, 'An Outline of the Later Holocene Archaeology and Precolonial History of the Ewaso Basin,' pp. 11–30.

5 Kohler is one of few (see Kohler, *Land Use in Transition*; Kohler, 'Landbesitz Und Landnutzung Im Umbruch: Das Beispiel Des Laikipia Distrikts Nordwestlich Des Mt. Kenya (Land Use in Transition: The Example of Laikipia District, Northwest of Mt. Kenya),' pp. 37–49.

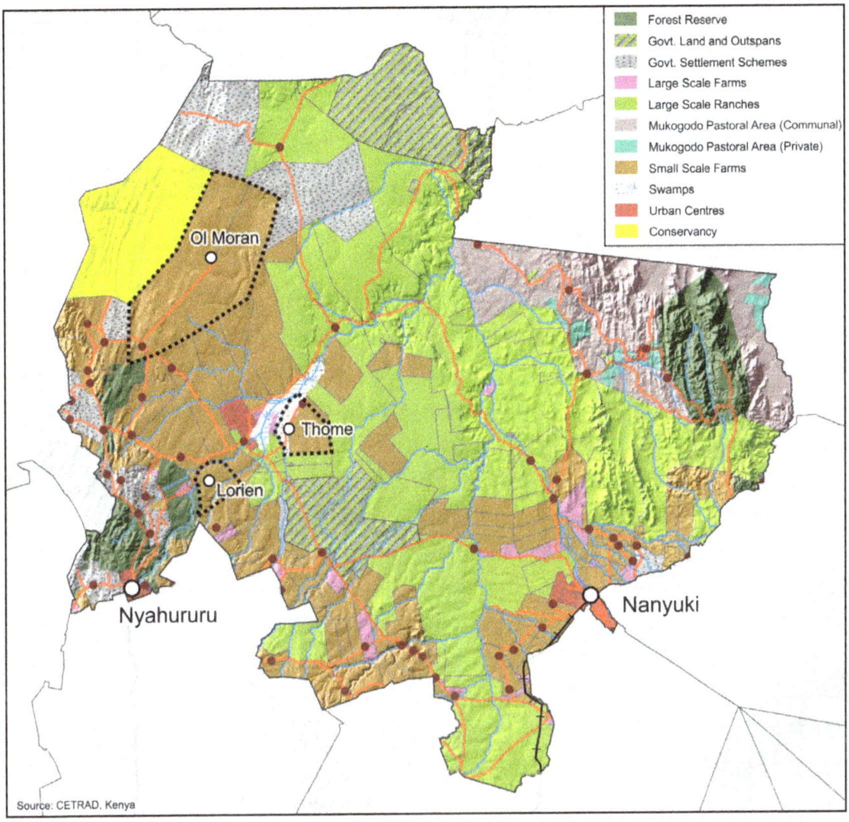

FIGURE 9 Land use in Laikipia in 2015.
© CETRAD 2015

rich sources in the form of settler novels in which such accounts come across.[6] Finally, from the 1980s, 1990s and 2000s, memoirs, baseline studies, government reports and other scholarly works present perspectives on Laikipia land-use matters.

There are certain challenges involved in using oral and written accounts of landscape and land use. Set against one another, the presentation of different types of account portrays the degree of politicisation involved. However, it also

6 Gallmann, *I Dreamed of Africa*; Huxley, *The Mottled Lizard*; Huxley, *The Flame Trees of Thika*; Juliet Barnes, *The Ghosts of Happy Valley: Searching for the Lost World of Africa's Infamous Aristocrats*, reprint edition (London: Aurum Press Ltd, 2014); Blixen, *Out of Africa*; Paul Spicer, *The Temptress: The Scandalous Life of Alice de Janze and the Mysterious Death of Lord Erroll*, first edition (New York: St Martin's Griffin, 2011).

makes it possible to encounter commonalities in inhabitants' challenges in Laikipia, where different actors are confronted with the same environmental conditions, although they tackle them in different ways.

7.1 Diachronic Perspectives on Land-use Change in Three Case Study Areas

The analysis in this section is based on aerial photographs, from 1969 in the case of Ol Moran and from 1977 in the cases of Lorien and Thome. These historical photographs have been analysed and reproduced in historical land-use maps. Similar land-use maps have been constructed on the basis of 2015 satellite imagery, and the two timescales can therefore be compared empirically.

The first resettlement programmes in Laikipia were implemented in 1967 and 1968, while the majority were only implemented in 1978. However, the transition was gradual, and the majority of people only settled in the 1980s. So, even though land was sold by the European owners as early as 1964, the aerial photographic material from 1969 and 1977 depicts land use as it was visualised during the period of colonial land management and presents the landscape as one worked and formed by large-scale land management. Contrastingly, the imagery from 2015 from the Google Earth satellites depicts the fragmented land-use systems that have come to be the reality of the plateau today.

7.1.1 *Lorien*

This land, which has been subject to conflict between a Kikuyu group and a Kalenjin group since the 1980s (see Chapter 4), is a green terrain marked by some bushland and cleared land. It is fertile with dark clay soil; farming is therefore the major economic activity.[7] The area in Lorien has shifted from being a working ranch and large-scale farm (as seen in figure 10) to being a smallholder area for the settled Kalenjin majority (as seen in figure 11).

Even though this area is relatively well watered, the smallholder farmers are not doing particularly well. The farms are small, and few are fully utilised. Comparatively, in the Kikuyu-dominated Salama, bordering Lorien to the south, smallholders farm in a more structured manner, employing wage labour or hiring machinery to maximise farming yields.[8] They strategise to produce for the market rather than merely to cover their subsistence needs, and they diversify their income not only in terms of farming a wide variety of different

7 Field notes, Lorien, 30 January 2015.

8 Interview with research participant, Salama, 1 and 2 March 2015.

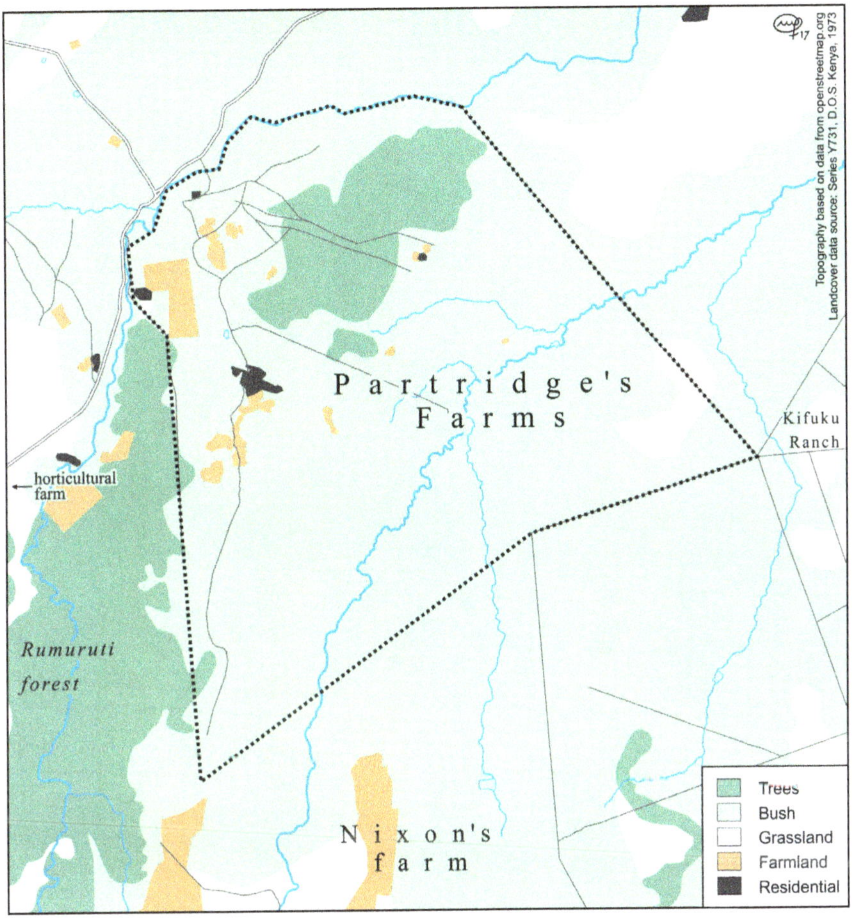

FIGURE 10 Land use in Lorien in 1977.
© Monika Feinen 2016

crops, keeping animals and growing fruit trees, but also in terms of supporting family members to pursue wage labour, urban jobs and education.[9] Contrastingly, people in Lorien live in closely constructed homesteads, the majority comprising mud-plastered and grass-thatched houses. There is little market interaction, and many farm on a subsistence level only. The area has one primary school, Simotwo Primary School. Salama, on the other hand, is an extensive plain land with a flourishing trade centre, a police post, a dispensary, a primary school and a secondary school. As figure 11 shows, the farms in Lorien

9 Interview with research participant, Salama, 1 and 2 March 2015.

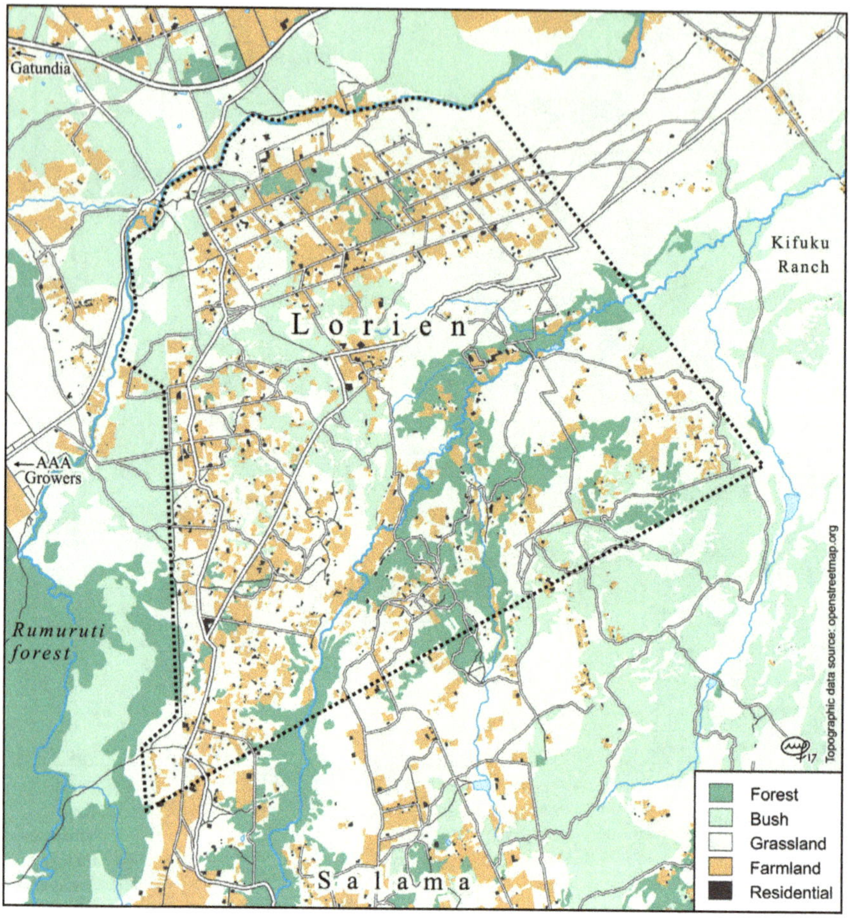

FIGURE 11 Land use in Lorien in 2015.
© Monika Feinen 2016

are smaller than those in Salama while the homesteads are more numerous and dispersed.[10]

One easily gets the impression that this community is somewhat excluded from the surrounding Kikuyu-dominated areas, although based on their animosity towards the Kikuyu community they may have a wish to enclose themselves on their land in Lorien and retain trustful relations within their own community.[11] With little interaction and without deep ties to the surrounding

10 Field notes, conversation with research participant, Lorien, 30 January 2015.

11 Field notes, Lorien, 30 May 2015; Beat Sottas, 'Aspects of a Peasant Mode of Production: Exchange and the Extent of Sufficiency among Smallholders in West Laikipia, Kenya,' *Journal of Asian and African Studies* 27, no. 3 (1 July 1992), pp. 271–95.

communities, the smallholders in Lorien are even more vulnerable to the radical shifts in weather events and unpredictable rainfall. The scant resources accumulated on the farm and the few strong ties to people outside Lorien make it difficult to invest in long-term strategies such as education.[12]

In terms of the land cover, there has also been quite a drastic change. In 1977, the area was dominated by bushland with a forested portion of land inside the farm as well as in the bordering Rumuruti Forest (see figure 10). In 2015, much of the forest and bushland has changed into grassland (see figure 11). The reason for this is that charcoal burning has provided an important subsidy to the farming practices of the smallholders in Lorien. This is often what people do if they have nothing else, which is no different in the case of Lorien.[13] In regard to the area's changing land cover from bush- to grassland, this transition also applies to the neighbouring Kifuku Ranch as well as the ranch to the north, even though these areas are not settled by smallholders. One consequence of encroaching on the forest area for charcoal is that the forest cover gradually disappears and the wildlife dwelling inside the forest needs to exit the forest area. Wild animals are consequently more inclined to maraud the farmlands and become a nuisance to the smallholders.[14] Although Rumuruti Forest has generally shrunk, the vegetation bordering the streams has in certain places been allowed to grow into thicker bush and forest areas, as can be seen when comparing figures 10 and 11. This may also have driven human–wildlife conflict when wildlife started to roam between these areas.

Another change is in the structure of settlement. In figure 10, depicting the area in 1977, the farmhouse is clearly marked next to large cultivated fields. The smaller settlements scattered across the estate would have been home to the squatter labourers, who were given their own small areas as their *shambas*.[15] They were not allowed to keep livestock, though many of them still did so in secret. In 2015, the smallholders had settled across the whole farmland and again the colonial installations and amenities have been removed and sold. In contrast to the situation in Ol Moran, Thome and neighbouring Salama, the old farmhouse has not shaped the new settlement centre in Lorien – in fact there is no centre for the settlements in Lorien.[16]

In addition, it can also be seen in figure 10 that the cultivated share of the colonial farm is very small compared with the size of the farm itself. As

12 Interview with research participant, Lorien, 30 January 2015; interview with research participant, Nyahururu, 30 May 2015.

13 Interview with research participant, south-western Laikipia, 6 March 2015; interview with research participant, northern Laikipia, 24 July 2015.

14 Gadd, 'Conservation outside of Parks.'

15 Kiswahili for a small farm or farmed field.

16 Field notes, conversation with research participant, Nyahururu, 2 March 2015.

previously discussed, this reflects the inadequate productivity of the colonial farms and ranches in Laikipia relative to the farming capacity estimated for the area.

7.1.2 *Ol Moran*

In Ol Moran, the area has gone from being worked as a cattle ranch (as seen in figure 12) to being subdivided for the purpose of smallholder farming (as seen in figure 13). As such, figures 12 and 13 illustrate what has already been discussed in previous chapters based on oral evidence. The area has been politically divided into two wards: Sipili in the south is part of Laikipia North constituency, and Ol Moran in the north is part of Laikipia West constituency. The area was also divided into an eastern and western part by the two Kikuyu

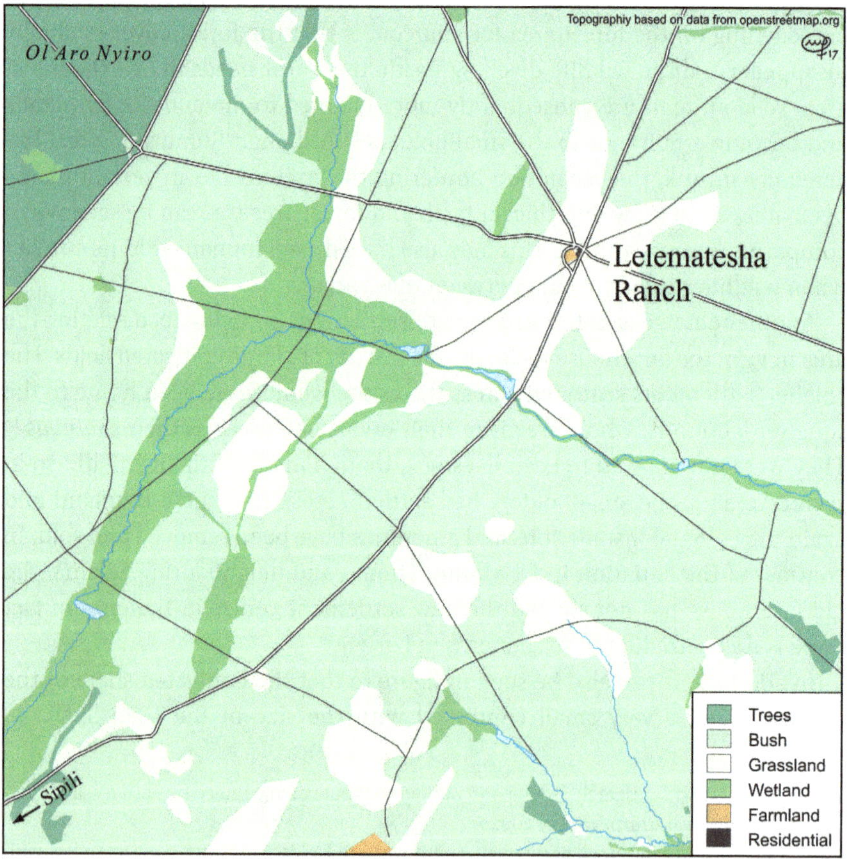

FIGURE 12 Land use in Ol Moran in 1969.
© Monika Feinen 2016

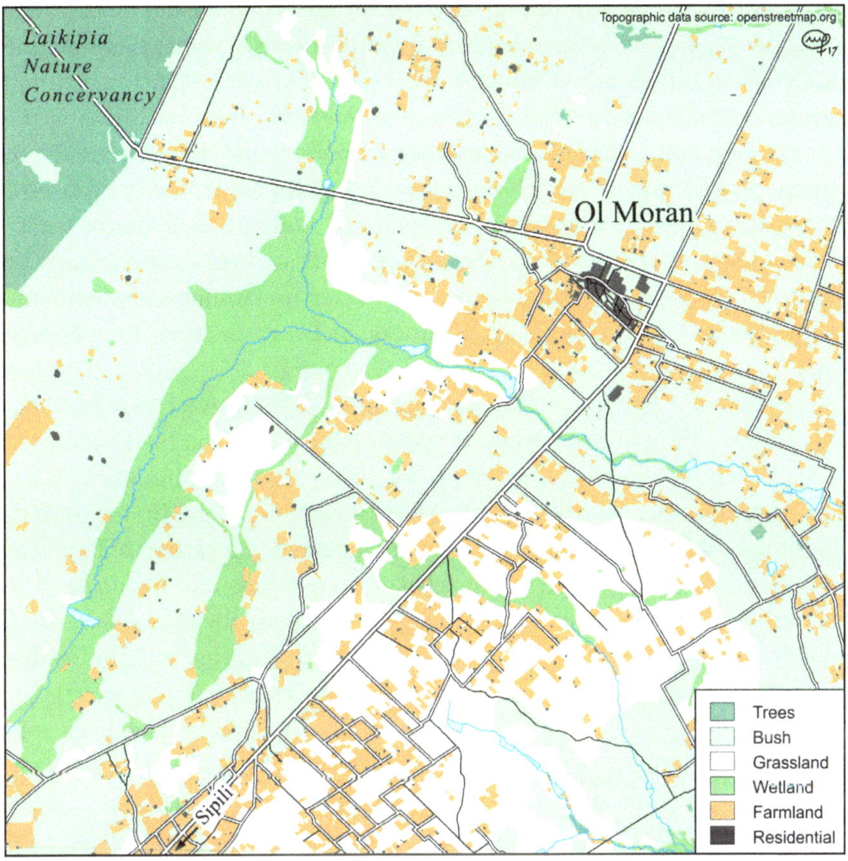

FIGURE 13 Land use in Ol Moran in 2015.
© Monika Feinen 2016

politicians, who each founded a land-buying company. Mutukanio Farmers Ltd is on the western side of the Ol Moran–Sipili road and Laikipia West Farmers Ltd is on the eastern side.

In terms of settlement structures, there are differences both between north and south and between east and west. Towards the south of Ol Moran town lies the Kikuyu town of Sipili.[17] This town is also part of the same land-buying company as Ol Moran, although it is quite different in its constitution. Most of the subdivisions of land here are settled or utilised. Sipili is a farming and business town that is expanding financially, due to intensive agriculture. The land is

17 Sipili is situated further south than the area shown in figures 13 and 14. In figure 7, the difference in land cover between the south and the north of the area is better visualized.

relatively productive and there are few landholdings that are not already fully in use. Most people here have acquired their title deeds, whereas this is not the case in the north towards Ol Moran town.[18] The Kikuyu dominate this area and have done so since the land-buying company sold its shares there. Towards the north the amount of farmed land lessens, except for in the vicinity of Ol Moran town, where security is better.[19] Beyond Ol Moran the settlements and farmed areas change, which is visible in the rounded homestead demarcations of farmland and residential areas. These settlements are held predominantly by Pokot families, in which many women have taken up farming, although some of the smaller circles may depict paddocks for livestock rather than farmed land.

There are also settlement differences between east and west, as seen on figure 13. Most of the settled farmlands appear to be located on the eastern side of the Ol Moran–Sipili road, which makes them part of the Mutukanio Farmers Company rather than the Laikipia West Farmers Company. On the western side of the road, there are also more of the rounded demarcations of farmland and residential areas, depicting the Pokot homesteads and paddocks. The proximity to Laikipia Nature Conservancy may increase the risk of marauding wildlife, while for the Pokot the position may be strategic in terms of the distance to the grazing areas inside the unfenced conservancy (see figure 13).

One tendency is that increasingly more land is being consolidated into slightly bigger farms, when an absentee landlord buys the adjoining shares to his own land in order to make his investment productive. In Ol Moran, it is not particularly difficult to find someone willing to sell because much of the land is practically useless without investment at high costs. Therefore, it is the wealthier absentees who go into consolidating.[20] The investment in machinery and large-scale cash-crop production rather than subsidence farming is a strategy that is better suited to the social-ecological conditions because of the reduced vulnerability to crop failure and security threats.[21] As an Ol Moral pastor explains:

> [The absentee land is] getting less since the area is developing. As you have seen, we now have electricity, network [signal], the roads are tarmacked and the area is passable. Generally, in Kenya, land is becoming scare. So, from other areas of Kenya, we can see some people coming to

18 Field notes, conversation with research participants, Sipili, 2 August 2015.

19 Interview with research participant, Ol Moran Trading Centre, 17 March 2016; interview with research participant, Ol Moran Trading Centre, 17 March 2016; interview with research participant, Ol Moran, 22 March 2016.

20 Field notes, visit to manager at absentee landholding, Ol Moran, 20 April 2015.

21 Interview with research participant, Ol Moran, 21 July 2015.

> prospect for land, and slowly by slowly people are occupying the vacant land here. Those who are not settling are cultivating. When you cultivate that land, you claim it and nobody can interfere.[22]

This means that the interest in land investment has pushed buyers to invest in land in these barer areas. Even in colonial times, Ol Moran was a bare area and even the ranch owner did not use the place as a permanent residence.[23] A combination of land aridity, uncertainties for farmers and their farming practices, and issues of security accounts for the relatively limited settlements in this northern area. As previously mentioned, there was a tendency among shareholders to claim what they could of the instruments and technical installations left behind by the colonial settler. In this regard, Ol Moran is no exception.[24] There is little of the colonial house, garden and amenities visible on figure 12, and the area has fewer trees and more scattered bushland. As one smallholder recollects: 'People started clearing land for farming and gradually it became bare land. [...] Some people burnt charcoal to get money. And some [did it] to clear land for settlement and chase away the wild animals.'[25]

Besides a visible landscape change, the two figures reflect the change in land-use practice away from being exclusively used for grazing by ranch cattle and towards increasingly being cleared and turned into worked farmland. Here, the land cover has shifted markedly from a predominance of bushland to grassland, and there has been an expansion of the wetland areas around the farmlands.

Additionally, the size of the shares demarcated has not been designed to vary according to the agro-climatic conditions.[26] As mentioned previously, Laikipia was never well watered and access to water continues to be a problem. Boreholes, rains and natural water sources are particularly scarce in this arid region of Laikipia, which explains the relatively low degree of shareholder settlement.[27]

7.1.3 *Thome*

Under Carr Hartley's ownership before 1977, the area in Thome was run as a cattle ranch with a major income from the sale of wildlife (as seen in figure 14). In 2015, smallholders had settled the area and the position of the old farmhouse

---

22 Interview with research participant, Ol Moran, 21 July 2015.

23 Interview with research participant, Ol Moran Trading Centre, 17 March 2016.

24 Interview with research participant, Ol Moran Trading Centre, 17 March 2016.

25 Interview with research participant, Ol Moran Trading Centre, 17 March 2016.

26 Interview with research participant, Ol Moran, 2 July 2015.

27 Interview with research participant, Ol Moran, 21 July 2015; interview with research participant, Ol Moran, 2 August 2015.

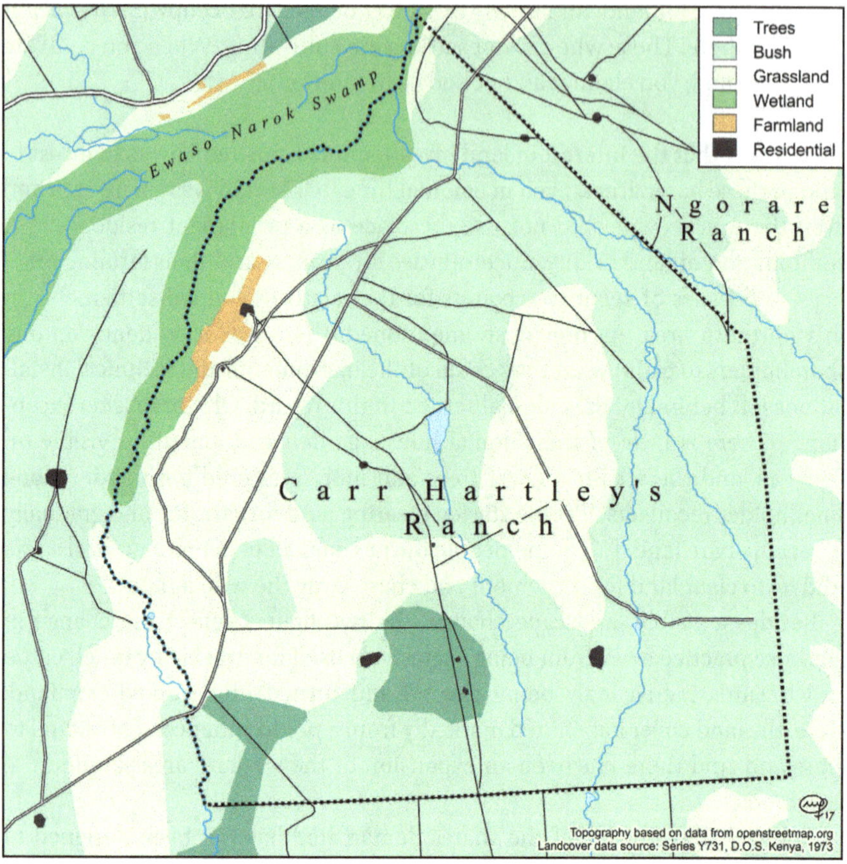

FIGURE 14 Land use in Thome in 1977.
© Monika Feinen 2016

had been turned into Thome's centre, with small shops, a primary school and the chief's office (as seen in figure 15). The settlements and farmlands are concentrated along the water source of the Ewaso Narok swamp and adjoining streams. As explained in Chapter 5, the settlements of people from various communities tend to cluster according to ethnic groups, notwithstanding that ties with the other communities with similar life situations have become stronger over time.[28] These clusters of residential houses are also visible in figure 15. In figure 14, depicting the landscape in 1977, there are small and scattered residential demarcations. Similarly, in Lorien these demarcate the labourers'

28 Interview with research participant, Thome, 21 February 2015; group discussion, elders in Thome, 21 January 2015.

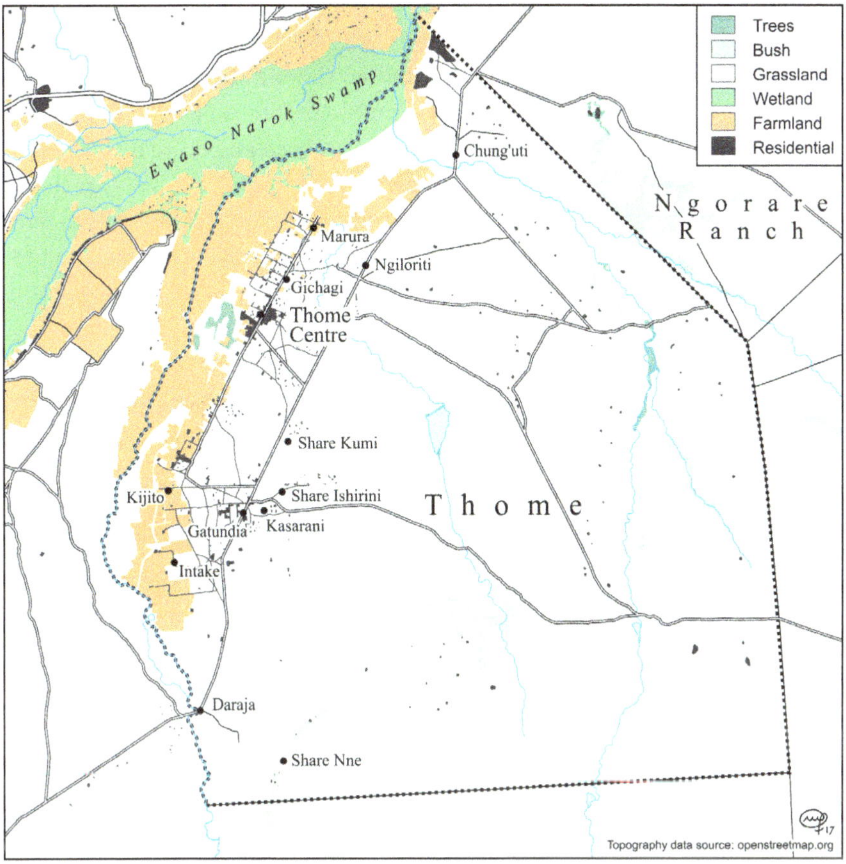

FIGURE 15 Land use in Thome in 2015.
© Monika Feinen 2016

settlements. However, in contrast to the squatter labourers in Lorien, none of the labourers in Thome practised farming. They were instead subsidised with maize flour and milk on a weekly basis as part of their salary.[29]

In terms of land cover, the whole area in Thome and the adjoining areas have changed away from being constituted mainly of bushland with some denser forested areas. In 2015, most of the land cover can be defined as scattered bush and grassland, although, as figure 15 illustrates and oral sources confirm, for the majority of the area that is not adjoining the swamp, grass is never plentiful.[30] A 1987 report on small-scale farming described Thome as 'one of

29 Interview with research participant, Thome, 6 March 2015.
30 Interview with research participant, Thome, 15 March 2015.

the driest areas of the District.'[31] Already then, there were severe problems with access to water, and a yearly yield was almost solely dependent on the amount of rainfall. Fewer people were settled there then, mostly around the old farmhouse. The report foresaw severe problems if the density of settlement were to increase.[32] Today, with the arrival of Samburu and more intense cultivation and dependence on non-settled areas, the foreseen conflicts are now a reality. The continuous low quality of the soil makes the area difficult to farm without a stable water source, and even then the rocky and sandy soil secures little yield without the use of heavy machinery. Based on figure 15, the majority of land in Thome seems unoccupied. While it is certainly not unutilised, the high number of absentee landlords makes much of the land seem idle to land-seeking pastoralists. The best way for people to obtain a subsistence income is by cultivating in the Marura area in the Ewaso Narok swamp using the colonial furrows for irrigation farming, even though this practice is illegal and farmers rely on legislation not being enforced.[33]

The heavy irrigation measures and the constant influx of new settlers, combined with people's land claims by means of different livelihood practices, increase pressure on the landscape's dwindling vegetation resources. In 2001, a survey estimated that 58% of riverine vegetation around the swamp had been cleared, though this figure could vary from dry season to wet season.[34] According to figure 15 illustrating the conditions in 2015, the figure has not drastically changed since then. The survey also established that 92% of the people cultivating the wetland could sustain themselves. Although the tomato farmers target the markets, only a few of them are able to produce enough to trade it further than Nyahururu.[35] The main challenges to secure farming practice are crop failure caused by flooding, poor knowledge about irrigation farming, and destruction of crops by livestock or wild animals.[36] In the case of the final point, pastoralist livestock are herded on the cropped fields in times of drought, and wild animals include hippos that enter from the wetlands and elephants crossing the elephant fence to the east.[37] The smallholders in general have very

31 Kohler, *West Laikipia*.

32 Kohler, *West Laikipia*.

33 *The Home News*, 'Marura Swamp in Crisis,' 7–13 October 2004, p. 3; *The Home News*, 'Letter to the Editor, Marura Swamp: Game Warden is Wrong,' 14–20 October 2004, p. 9.

34 Thenya, 'Challenges of Conservation of Dryland Shallow Waters, Ewaso Narok Swamp, Laikipia District, Kenya,' *Hydrobiologia* 458, no. 1–3 (1 August 2001), pp. 107–19.

35 Interview with research participant, Marura, 28 May 2015.

36 Thenya, 'Challenges of Conservation of Dryland Shallow Waters.'

37 Interview with research participant, Marura, 28 May 2015; interview with research participant, Marura, 9 March 2015.

low regard for the wildlife and largely see wild animals as a menace and a threat to their farming practice.[38] They gain no profit from conserved and protected wetland, and the area is only of use to them if they can farm the land.[39]

Besides these challenges, the people settled in the wetlands suffer from poor health and frequent occurrences of malaria, typhoid and pneumonia.[40] However, in 2001 most smallholders had a diversified income in which 54% engaged in cultivation, 44% were involved in casual labour, 24% kept livestock, and 16% occasionally burned charcoal and cut trees to sell at the market.[41] If a similar survey were done today, these estimations would presumably have changed with regard to livestock and charcoal. Smallholders now own little or no livestock due to the risk of raids.[42] This is something that has changed increasingly since 2001 when pastoralists' settlement of the area increased. Regarding charcoal, it is no longer a cost-effective practice unless it is the only option for income. The area simply no longer contains suitable trees and bush. People who have been settled for a long time spoke of a thick forest that, at one point, hid 500 elephants.[43] However, even though the land cover has been much denser with bush and, in certain areas, patches of forest, the data from aerial photographs do not support this statement.

7.2 Historical Perceptions of the Landscape

Many of the historical accounts from colonial times are biased towards Western methods of farm management rather than being objective and scientific in the formation of their opinions. With such biases, it can be difficult to explain land-use change empirically. Perceptions of environmental features may differ markedly between individuals and groups depending on their use of the environment in different ways and in different time periods. However, the different accounts of life on the plateau also show how some environmental issues have been of wider concern for land-use practitioners. This section illustrates the multiplicity of perceptions and parallel experiences.

38 Interview with research participant, 5 May 2015; interview with research participant, Marura, 9 March 2015.

39 Field notes, conversation with research participants, Nyahururu, 9 March 2015.

40 Thenya, 'Challenges of Conservation of Dryland Shallow Waters.'

41 Thenya, 'Challenges of Conservation of Dryland Shallow Waters.'

42 Interview with research participant, Thome, 6 March 2015; interview with research participant, Thome, 6 March 2015.

43 Interview with research participant, Thome, 6 March 2015.

7.2.1 *Travel Writers' Perceptions of New Land*

In their depictions of the pre-colonial period in Laikipia, the early travel writers present a special type of representation of the landscape and its use.[44] They describe the places they traversed with a focus on features, vegetation and animals fit for hunting. Additionally, for the few who crossed the Laikipia plains, the representations stand in stark contrast to those of the forested regions south and east of Laikipia. For instance, Mackinder describes the Laikipia plateau on his quest to reach the peaks of Mount Kenya:

> The high plains of Laikipia, which surmount the slope at an elevation of about 7000 feet, were dry. So sudden is the change from Kikuyu to Laikipia, that in the course of a single march of about 9 miles we left a dripping forest and came to a land which was the scene during the next few weeks, not merely of prairie fires, but also of forest fires.[45]

Similarly, between eloquent descriptions of his hunting excursions and instructions on how best to shoot an elephant, the ivory trader Hardwick gives elaborate descriptions of the Laikipia plateau:

> We found ourselves on the edge of the tableland looking down a sharp declivity to the plain beneath, which stretched out in desolate barrenness as far as the eye could reach. It was a dreary khaki-coloured landscape, with peculiarly shaped hills in the extreme background. In the middle distance were belts of dusty looking thorn trees, while here and there mounds of broken lava reared up their ugly masses to add to the general air of desolation. Somewhere ahead of us, about four days' march, was the Waso Nyiro; and beyond that lay the desert again [...]. The country we should have to cross in order to reach the Waso Nyiro was, as far as we knew, waterless, with the exception of one tiny brook, which flowed northward from M'thara, probably emptying itself into the Waso Nyiro. [...] After a couple of hours on the road we saw in the distance a large swamp, which we had not previously noticed, surrounded for a radius of a mile or so by thorn bush, which grew a great deal thicker than on other parts of the plain.[46]

What Harwick describes here are the Laikipia plains in a state of drought, at least to his eyes. As described in previous chapters, the waterless features

44 Pratt, *Imperial Eyes*.

45 Mackinder, 'A Journey to the Summit of Mount Kenya,' p. 463.

46 Hardwick, *An Ivory Trader in North Kenia*, pp. 148–50.

posed a challenge not only to Hardwick's own expedition but to future users of the plains as well, albeit in different ways. The swamp he comes across, as the only wetter area he encountered, may have been the Ewaso Narok swamp, near what would become Rumuruti.

Whereas the waterless features seem to be of a more permanent character, the rinderpest haunting the plateau at the end of the 1800s indicated the state of affairs at that particular point in time. Nevertheless, they were taken as permanent features to argue for the plateau's availability for colonial settlement. As previously exemplified, Thomson unknowingly described the rinderpest that haunted the plateau and affected the social-ecological landscape when he traversed the plains in 1885:

> The people were indeed in a very dangerous mood, as the horrid disease was threatening to cut off all their cattle. Round about the kraals the scene was simply fearful – hundreds of animals dying and in all stages of decomposition. No attempt was made to bury these or drag them away.[47]

The descriptions of the local populations and their ways of engaging with the landscape are often sparse in these accounts. When human-environment descriptions occur, they illustrate the Eurocentric and prejudiced sentiments typical of the time. An example of this is Neumann's descriptions of the Maasai's approach to livestock and wildlife:

> I went after some gazelle, which were close by, at the guides' request, and shot one for them, as they turned up their noses at zebra. But they then said they did not eat game at all, and only wanted the skin. The airs these natives give themselves, in imitation of Masai customs, are ridiculous. They own very little stock [...] but pretend they despise game, though in reality most of them will eat it on the sly.[48]

Disregarding the bigotry of the descriptions, it is clear from these accounts that wildlife as well as pastoralists used the Laikipia plains seasonally for the area's pastures. Captain Stigand appears to be the only one describing Laikipia as a place with farming activities along his route through Rumuruti:

> The next day we marched just over sixteen miles in to Rumuruti, the last station at which we should touch. The Guas Ngiro (or Red River) runs in a broad dip through the level of the plains, and in this dip, close to the

47 Thomson, *Through Masai Land*, p. 206.

48 Neumann, *Elephant Hunting in East Equatorial Africa*, p. 67.

> station on either bank, were planted crops of millet and maize to serve as food for the hands employed here. This was the last cultivation we were to see for many months, and from here enough food-supplies for the men must be carried to last till we reached Abyssinia.[49]

With no mention of the specific type of irrigated cultivation, it is difficult to say whether it was comparable to the present-day irrigation farming that surrounds the swamp. Nevertheless, it is safe to say that this type of farming, making use of the well-watered land on the banks of the swamp, is not an entirely new phenomenon, despite what some environmentalists claim.[50] It is relevant to mention that Stigand's travels took place roughly 10 years later than those of Thomson, Neumann, Hardwick and Mackinder, so the millet and maize farming that he mentions may have been a new phenomenon at the time. Stigand also describes the sighting of extensive herds of goats and sheep towards the north of Laikipia near the Leroghi plateau:

> Next day we marched northward from Margwe for five or six miles, and then struck a broad cattle-road, which led us to a sokota, where thousands of sheep and goats were being watered. The heat haze distorts objects so much on these great plains that at a thousand yards' distance it would often be impossible to distinguish between a flock of sheep and a herd of cattle or game if it were not for the herdsmen. In this case we saw waves of moving animals and every here and there a narrow black object rising to a higher level, so we knew them to be sheep and goats.[51]

This description underlines the northern parts of Laikipia as extensively used for the watering of small stock – a representation that would later be disputed by European farmers advocating for a scheduling of these lands as Crown Land in the 1933 Kenya Land Commission talks (see Chapter 3).[52]

7.2.2 *Rights, Borders and Water: Land-use Practices from the 1930s*

With the colonial settlement came a demarcation of land, classifying areas in ways other than merely according to who occupied it.[53] It was not the case that Africans did not value the idea of land, but rather that they did not value it 'as discrete parcels of bounded hectares,'[54] to quote Hughes. When colonialism

49 Stigand, *To Abyssinia through An Unknown Land*, p. 38.
50 See Thenya, 'Challenges of Conservation of Dryland Shallow Waters.'
51 Stigand, *To Abyssinia through An Unknown Land*, p. 45.
52 See Chapter 3.
53 Berry, 'Debating the Land Question in Africa.'
54 Hughes, *From Enslavement to Environmentalism*, pp. 7–9.

introduced this mentality, it simultaneously introduced a new political economy, in which 'Spirit-blessed soil now constitutes hectares, counted, measured, and contested.'[55] To denote these new categories of land-use systems that were prioritised for particular areas, new terms for native reserves and scheduled areas were developed, with clear indications of fixed boundaries between them.[56] One such demarcated boundary was the Kittermaster line, signifying the boundary between the Crown Lands in Laikipia to the south and the Northern Frontier District in present-day Samburu to the north. As the Dykes story in Chapter 5 indicates, the ranchers and farmers towards the south were interested in acquiring access to the water sources on the Leroghi plateau in the boundary region. According to the former district commissioner in Maralal, Gavaghan:

> the uprooted Europeans with some camp followers regarded Laikipia as only part of the 'promised land' and cast envious eyes on the Leroghi plateau, setting up a border tension which was heightened by clashes over stock theft and attendant spearing of herdsmen. The ranches leased nearer to the border were called the '50 or 30 cents an acre' lands to reflect the increased element of such risk.[57]

From that sentiment, the settler community attempted to formally push the boundary further north through the Land Commission trials. C.H. Adams argues:

> The present occupied parts of Laikipia were surveyed before the war, or early in the war, but alienation did not take place until 1919. [...] If there had been no war, white occupation of Laikipia would have taken place earlier, and I am certain that the occupation of Leroki by Samburu would not have taken place. The question would have been taken up so strongly that it would not have been a feasible preposition to put the Samburu there. When white settlement did arrive it found Samburu occupation an accomplished fact, and the situation has been more complicated as time has passed, owing to the rapid rate of increase in Samburu stock which has resulted from their occupation of Leroki.[58]

55 Hughes, *From Enslavement to Environmentalism*, pp. 7–9.
56 Mungeam, *British Rule in Kenya*; Ghai et al., *Public Law and Political Change in Kenya*.
57 Terence Gavaghan, *Of Lions and Dung Beetles* (Ilfracombe, Devon: Arthur H. Stockwell, 1999), p. 168.
58 KLC, Evidence and memoranda, Vol. II, Rift Valley Province, pp. 1906–07.

Similar to the Leroghi plateau, the boundary area in Churo, between Laikipia and Baringo, was also subject to issues of contestation due to its important water source.[59] Those colonial settlers in favour of retaining the boundary took this view on the basis of reports indicating that restricted access to the grazing area at Churo would be detrimental to the Pokot and their livestock. However, those in favour of scheduling the area questioned these consequences envisioned for the Pokot.[60]

In a landscape of plains, the one controlling the water sources is arguably better equipped to tackle the environmental conditions, and therefore these areas were of particular interest to the European ranchers and farmers. In fact, the settlers' worries about their access to water were already an issue in 1925, when District Commissioner Trafford notes in the district's annual report that:

> Laikipia District is mainly pastoral (i.e. used for ranching). The areas known as Leshau – Ol Arabel – and the Aberdares are agricultural. Dairying is also carried out but on a small scale as yet in the latter named areas. The stock farmers have had a fairly good year by reasons of the plentiful grass due to the heavy rains of 1926. Despite land extensions the more progressive and hence heavier stocked farms have been short of grazing during the last two months. Bush fires and the failure of the November rains being responsible. I fear that, without early substantial rains, cattle and sheep farmers generally will be at their wits' ends for water and grazing by the end of the normal dry season in the month of March. The wheat growers on the Aberdares have hopes of good crops – The unfortunate agriculturalists of Leshau and Ol Arabel have experienced a well nigh complete failure of crops. Rains, although abundant in the first seven months of the year, failed to fall during the 'short rains' season. A couple of extra inches of rain in October and November would have produced magnificent wheat crops.[61]

Other than documenting the water scarcity and the high level of local variability in rainfall on the plateau, to which I will return, the district commissioner reported illegal stock and bush fires, which was also of wider concern throughout the colonial period. It represented the pastoralist land-use practice in which the plains were lit to nurture the growth of fresh grass for the livestock.[62]

59 RH, Africa.mic.515 reel 25, Laikipia Annual Report, Trafford, 1927.
60 KLC, Evidence and memoranda, Vol. II, Rift Valley Province, pp. 1926–27.
61 RH, Africa.mic.515 reel 25, Laikipia Annual Report, Trafford, 1927, p. 1.
62 Lane, *Landscape and Environmental Change in Semi-Arid Regions of East and Southern Africa.*

Rather than reproducing this type of cattle management, the European ranchers preferred systematic shifts in grazing inside paddocks. This practice is in line with private-property rights rather than the commons ideology behind the pastoralists' pasture management.[63]

Common challenges brought the settler community together, as Gavaghan recollects:

> The ranchers combined personal individualism and a collective sense of unity to a high degree. Many nurtured a lurking memory of the unsolved mystery of the spear blooded murder in 1931 of young Theodore Powys, [...] at a time when the settlers' claim to Leroghi plateau was hotly disputed.[64]

This sense of togetherness enforced the ranchers' opinion that the areas bordering the scheduled areas needed to be safeguarded to protect their estates.[65] This perspective was also reflected in the District Committee's ongoing concern that the large landholdings were demarcated so that each estate included adequate land to maintain a buffer zone against pastoralist encroachers and protect against their disease-ridden stock.[66]

The settlers' security concerns were strongly related to their need to secure access to stable water sources. This led them to institute claims to the water sources on the boundaries of the scheduled area. However, as documented in Chapter 3, the commission evaluated Leroghi as a place of great importance to the Samburu people and the subsistence of their livestock, notwithstanding that the Maasai had kept them from having a permanent presence on the Leroghi plateau in the past.[67] A register of people and stock in Leroghi from 1928 sets the total figure of the population there at 6,574, while estimating a total number of livestock of 114,947 (cattle, camels, sheep and goats).[68] The commission evaluated the carrying capacity of the area by connecting these estimated numbers of livestock with the size of the area considered sustainable for grazing:

---

63 Interview with research participant, south-western Laikipia, 6 March 2015; interview with research participant, central Laikipia, 12 May 2015.

64 Gavaghan, *Of Lions and Dung Beetles*, p. 194.

65 BIEA, LFA, 'Minutes of meeting,' 19 August 1933.

66 KNA, DC/LKA/1/1, DAR 1929, p. 231; Lane, *Landscape and Environmental Change in Semi-Arid Regions of East and Southern Africa.*

67 TNA, CAB 24/248, 'The Kenya Land Commission Report,' 1934, p. 229.

68 TNA, CAB 24/248, 'The Kenya Land Commission Report,' 1934, p. 236.

> The area available for grazing is limited to about 200,000 acres, which is approximately four acres a beast. It cannot, therefore, be said to be understocked. [...] Although there may be a good growth of grass after rain for a short period, the nature of the soil will not support it for any length of time and it soon withers and dies.[69]

The question of the carrying capacity of the northern Laikipia region was of strong concern to the commission, as they declared: 'we agree with the view that the Samburu would be better off, and that their country would benefit if large numbers of their uneconomic beasts were disposed of.'[70] Yet the colonial administration continued to struggle with efforts to control and reduce the numbers of Samburu livestock throughout the colonial period.[71]

In spite of the general agreement that the carrying capacity was overburdened by the amount of pastoralist livestock, the commission evaluated in favour of the Samburu people's claim to the area:

> On Economic grounds, we agree generally that Europeans would be able to use the land to better advantage than the natives in their present state of development, but Leroki is somewhat remote for mixed farming, and if surveyed for sheep farms [as] seems to be contemplated, the area would in the early days of settlement suffice only for 20 farms at the most. Under native occupation it can and does support some 6,000 Africans with their flocks and herds, and the Samburu do sell considerable numbers of sheep.[72]

Therefore, the commission considered itself unable to recommend the removal of the Samburu from the Leroghi plateau.[73] Consequently, the Kittermaster line remained as the formally set boundary between pastoral land and settler land, even though in reality pastoralist movements across the boundaries continued – as is also evident from chapters 3, 4 and 5. Various enforcements, including a 'Defence Force' south of the Kittermaster Line, were put in place. Yet none proved effective enough to control encroachment.[74]

---

69 TNA, CAB 24/248, 'The Kenya Land Commission Report,' 1934, p. 237.

70 TNA, CAB 24/248, 'The Kenya Land Commission Report,' 1934, p. 239.

71 Lane, *Landscape and Environmental Change in Semi-Arid Regions of East and Southern Africa.*

72 TNA, CAB 24/248, 'The Kenya Land Commission Report,' 1934, p. 236.

73 TNA, CAB 24/248, 'The Kenya Land Commission Report,' 1934, p. 240.

74 East African Women's League, 'Golden Jubilee Scrapbook,' p. 41.

Access to water continued to be problematic for the settlers, in terms of both lacking permanent water sources and rains, which time and again led to grass fires running wild over most of the plateau. For instance, in 1938, District Commissioner Emley reported:

> As a result of the failure of the grass rains at the end of last year and the brevity of the March rains grass fires in Laikipia became so numerous and the situation so serious that the question of compulsory fire-breaks, compensation and inadequate penalties became the all-important political problem of the district.[75]

Towards the end of that year, the Swedish Boring Company was commissioned to make five boreholes across the settler area to tackle the problem of water access. This made 'thousands of acres of grazing come into use,'[76] as District Commissioner Emley notes, reducing soil erosion in areas that were heavily used for tracking cattle.

The above historical perceptions and representations of the social-ecological landscape of Laikipia illustrate the attitude of the European settlers. Farming practices were held in higher regard than pastoralism. As Van Zwanenberg notes: 'a form of estate farming was the background for the British industrial revolution and the first incoming settlers were British landowners whose only experience was of estate farming.'[77] The principle of valuing land-use practices according to large-scale farming and ranching created a focus on carrying capacity and economic output, with which the two land-use systems of pastoralism and small-scale farming are hardly comparable. Furthermore, the European farmers had already scheduled the areas on the Laikipia plateau to make it homogeneous to the extent that conflicting land-use systems were limited to the margins of the plateau in the boundary areas. However, the settler farms suffered from a permanent lack of water, labour, finances and technical knowledge. Additionally, the homogeneity of the land-use systems meant that less than half of the land alienated as Crown Land was productively used as farmland in 1939.[78]

Berry and Throup clarify these concerns about carrying capacity, in that it was in the 1930s that colonial administrators started to realise the signs of erosion, overgrazing and deforestation in the utilised areas. As a response, they

75 RH, Africa.mic.515 reel 25, Laikipia Annual Report, Emley, 1938, pp. 3–4.

76 RH, Africa.mic.515 reel 25, Laikipia Annual Report, Emley, 1938, pp. 4–5.

77 Van Zwanenberg, *The Agricultural History of Kenya to 1939*, p. 8.

78 Van Zwanenberg, *The Agricultural History of Kenya to 1939*.

started to problematise the Africans' land-management practices, exemplified by the rhetoric used in the Land Commission evaluations.[79] The indications of environmental degradation were assumed to signify that primitive land-management practices were not equipped to handle the pressures of an expanding commercial economy. The colonial administrators assumed that, 'if left to cope with modernity on their own, African farmers and herders might well destroy the environmental heritage that constituted the wealth of the empire,'[80] as Berry argues. This viewpoint supported their efforts to control stock numbers through forced sales, grazing management and so on based on perceptions of carrying capacity.[81]

7.2.3 *The Peak and Transition of European Settlement in the 1960s*

This period points to further issues with the contrasting land-use systems. European ranchers and farmers problematised the pastoralists' presence, arguing that they were uncontrollable and lacked formal attachment to the land; that they challenged the boundary areas of the European settlements; and that the ranching cattle risked contracting infectious diseases from the pastoralist livestock. Moreover, this period was haunted by the coming Independence, causing many settlers to leave the place altogether.

In the 1960s, the settlers were more experienced in the Laikipia environment, having lived through the various forms of development that had shaped the highlands. As previously mentioned, many of the settlers had been inexperienced with regard to farming practices that suited the agro-climatic conditions of Laikipia, and consequently 'trial and error, sometimes very costly, was the order of the day,'[82] as the East African Women's League (EAWL) in Laikipia noted in its report in 1968.

However, one thing the settlers were experts in was arranging social gatherings through which they could discuss the various types of challenges a life in the highlands involved. As the EAWL stated:

> Wherever the independent, pioneering type is found, there will also be found Associations, Committees, Boards and the like, as these people like to run their own affairs, rather than sit back and let a bureaucratic government do everything for them.[83]

79 Throup, *Economic and Social Origins of Mau Mau*; Berry, 'Debating the Land Question in Africa.'

80 Berry, 'Debating the Land Question in Africa,' p. 646.

81 Berry, 'Debating the Land Question in Africa.'

82 East African Women's League, 'Golden Jubilee Scrapbook,' p. 12.

83 East African Women's League, 'Golden Jubilee Scrapbook,' p. 41.

The settlers were proud to state that 'in 1920 Thomson's Falls was a waterfall in a forest – no inhabitants of any sorts,'[84] whereas 'the years after 1945 saw tremendous changes with the influx of hundreds of new farmers and businessmen.'[85] By 1960, the district had a sports club, a railway line from Gilgil, a creamery, a cinema, a country club, a dramatic club, three new churches, a boarding school, a hotel, well-stocked shops, two butcheries and a post office with telephone exchange. Thomson's Falls 'boasted an industrial area for wheat, maize, oil and petrol stores: there was the usual timber yard, several garages, besides three streets full of well-stocked shops, one of which had a coffee balcony.'[86] And at the time of Independence, 'there were 206 names on the Voter's Roll, representing about 130 European-owned farms, of an average acreage of between 1,000 to 2,000 acres, producing tens of thousands of bags of grain, thousands of gallons of cream and whole milk and tons of pyrethrum.'[87] Yet, despite these efforts, the area continued to underperform against the initial ideal of developing the White Highlands as a food bank.[88]

After the Second World War the dairy industry had started to prosper and many farmers experimented with various types of breeding of sheep and cattle. Although the climate and frequent pests made it challenging, the mixed-farming areas also attempted to improve certain types of maize, wheat, barley, rye and oats to better fit the environment. One of the most successful of the cash crops produced in the highlands was pyrethrum. It flourished above 7,000 feet – an elevation that was also suitable for apples, plums and peaches, while avocado, pears, pawpaw and certain varieties of banana and oranges also did well.

Despite their greater experience with farming and ranching practices in the highlands, water scarcity continued to be a problem for the settlers. The EAWL explains:

> Ever since the 1920s water supplies have needed a great deal of thought and the farmers have created dams wherever possible and sunk boreholes at vast expense, as the water table in the district is very low [...]. A curious phenomenon has been that with the cultivation of the arable land the existing springs have become stronger – the rains ran off the hard-baked earth but sank into the ploughed land. [...] Land originally considered useless can now be used for ranching cattle and sheep.[89]

84 East African Women's League, 'Golden Jubilee Scrapbook,' p. 17.
85 East African Women's League, 'Golden Jubilee Scrapbook,' p. 19.
86 East African Women's League, 'Golden Jubilee Scrapbook,' p. 17.
87 East African Women's League, 'Golden Jubilee Scrapbook,' p. 27.
88 Van Zwanenberg, *The Agricultural History of Kenya to 1939*.
89 East African Women's League, 'Golden Jubilee Scrapbook,' p. 7.

The developments are romanticised here. The challenges caused by the large fluctuations in rainfall could not be entirely solved through an increase in the number of boreholes and the farming investments in areas of arable land. Rather, looking at rainfall data, it is clear that the period of the end of the 1950s and the 1960s included several years of good rain as well as an absence of extensive periods of drought. Therefore, the farmers' prosperity is more likely attributable to the reliability of seasonal rains.[90]

In contrast, the 1920s and 1930s had been demanding, with extended periods of drought and locusts, which explains efforts to secure control over the Leroghi water sources. During that time, the Great Depression caused the prices to plummet on all farming products, and many abandoned their farms.[91] The 1940s and 1950s provided better conditions for the settler farming practices, so these were years of expansion. Despite the Land Commission's decision to safeguard the Leroghi plateau for Samburu access, the scheduled areas continued to expand into the northern areas. For instance, the ranches Mugie and Marmar furthest to the north in Laikipia were scheduled for settlers on 99-year leases as late as 1955 and 1952 respectively.[92] This continued expansion of areas under colonial control reflects the colonial perspective that Africans' claims to the land were undermined by their failure to establish physical boundaries. Instead, land used for foraging or low-input farming was seen as an open frontier of 'unclaimed' no-man's land. The ploughs of the European settlers demolished age-old traces of connectedness to the soil and grasslands.[93]

Gavaghan, who was not entirely on the best of terms with many of the Laikipia ranchers, described from his time as governor in Maralal how the land management of the Laikipia ranchers functioned:

> On the way to Rumuruti, […] I passed the 50,000 acre border ranch, which had been given as a twenty first birthday present to, unsurprisingly cocky, John Dykes by his father, Andrew […]. Behind the roadside cedar post and barbed wire fencing of well controlled paddocks were orderly herds of beautifully presented dehorned steers. They were run in groups of fifty or more, differentiated by each six months of age and by colour; a pleasure

90 Berger, *Rainfall and Agroclimatology of the Laikipia Plateau, Kenya*.

91 David Anderson, 'Depression, Dust Bowl, Demography, and Drought: The Colonial State and Soil Conservation in East Africa during the 1930s,' *African Affairs* 83 (1984), pp. 321–43; Lane, *Landscape and Environmental Change in Semi-Arid Regions of East and Southern Africa*.

92 TNA, FCO 141/19600, 'Letter of Allotment of Agricultural Land,' 24 March 1956; TNA, FCO 141/19572, 'Dykes to Wigan,' 26 December 1975.

93 Hughes, *From Enslavement to Environmentalism*, p. 9.

> to behold. Their slaughter value was quite disproportionate to the wages of their mainly Samburu herdsmen, who were themselves at risk of attack by their fellows.[94]

Despite the difference between this practice of keeping cattle and that of the pastoralists, it could not be undertaken without pastoralists among the labour force. In addition, the settlers relied on the Borana cattle from the Northern Frontier District for breeding because these pastoralist cattle were well adapted to the environment. Crossbreeding them with their own imported varieties therefore potentially provided good returns.[95] This made the relationship between the pastoralists and the settlers a dubious one. Likewise, for the Samburu, despite their laying claim to valuable resources, the presence of the European ranchers provided labour income for some and presented fruitful raiding conditions for others.[96]

Unsurprisingly, the discourses emanating from the 1930s discussions of environmental stressors as a product of the pastoralists' unbalanced land management in terms of carrying capacity had led to large-scale control and an administration that micromanaged its citizens.[97] This type of micromanagement was a nuisance to many of the settlers, most of whom valued autonomy in their ways of running a farm.[98]

Besides the high regard for their own farming practices, the settlers took pride in the landscape in their dry highlands to a romanticising extent, notwithstanding that these were the same landscapes with extensive variations in climatic conditions that extended times of drought and continued to cause hardship on a regular basis.[99] Descriptions of the Laikipia plains such as the following by Erroll Whittall are not uncommon:

> For much of the year these grazing lands are scorched by the sun and the high north-easterly gales from off the frontier, and they turn to an even brown, scarred only by the trees which follow the winding, dry riverbeds [...]. When the rains at last break, the dry, grey pasture turns to green in a few days, starred with bulbous flowers and of a hue not seen in the higher

94 Gavaghan, *Of Lions and Dung Beetles*, p. 194.

95 East African Women's League, 'Golden Jubilee Scrapbook,' p. 38.

96 Interview with research participant, northern Laikipia, 24 July 2015; East African Women's League, 'Golden Jubilee Scrapbook,' p. 31.

97 East African Women's League, 'Golden Jubilee Scrapbook,' p. 8.

98 See Chapter 4.

99 Interview with research participant, Laikipia, 6 March 2015; interview with research participant, Laikipia, 24 July 2015.

> sourveld [...]. This is the weft and weave of life for those who love the plains.[100]

The large-scale landholders seemed more fascinated than ever by the appearance of the settler landscape in Laikipia. The varied vegetation constituted a conducive habitat for wildlife with favourable conditions for hunting on and between the large-scale farms and ranches, while barring intruders from the grazing areas. Combined with clear boundaries, fenced or at least mapped land had authorised the settlers' control of the landscape in much the same way as in southern Africa.[101] And with control of the landscape came control of the people – a form of control that some scholars consider enslavement via cadastral politics: 'discourses of enslavement give way to those of enclosure, boundaries and maps. Then arises an enduring cultural pattern – a form of "cadastral politics,"' to use Hughes' words.[102]

For this reason, many settlers mourned the land-use changes in the post-Independence years, to which the chapter's opening statement by Gallmann also stands witness. The settlers' high regard for their own practices continued to preserve a higher purpose – of demonstrating the acts of civil living to the African people. As the EAWL describes 'the proud tribe of settlers':

> These hardy, individualistic people carved the wilderness to serve themselves and the inhabitants of the fast-growing urban areas, as well as for the export market. They suffered from locusts, which ate everything, and a profusion of game which wrecked their fences and killed their stock: from pests which attacked their livestock and crops [...]. They demonstrated to the indigenous people how best to use the land they lived in but suffered continuously from the lack of imagination and ignorance of machines and chemicals.[103]

Despite the underperformance of the district's farming output, the practices of the European farmers continued to be praised as the optimal type of land management for the dry highlands. Consequently, their perspectives on the

100 Errol Whittall, 'Dimbilil: The Story of an African Farm,' first edition London: Arthur Baker, 1956, in Elspeth Huxley, *Nine Faces Of Kenya* (Random House ebooks, 2011), p. 190.

101 Interview with research participant, south-western Laikipia, 6 March 2015; interview with research participant, eastern Laikipia, 24 July 2015.

102 Hughes, *From Enslavement to Environmentalism*, p. 11.

103 East African Women's League, 'Golden Jubilee Scrapbook,' p. 30.

future of an Independent Kenya tended to be pessimistic, with worries about population pressure and unsustainable farming practices.[104]

Overall, 1960 was a peak time for the settler community in terms of their presence in the district. Weather conditions had been relatively generous for at least a few years, although internal variation continued to lead to all-encompassing failure of seasonal yields. Ultimately, the settlers did not solve the problem of how to manage an area with large variation in agro-climatic conditions, and merely introducing new technology and methods of farming did not circumvent the unreliable cycle of rainfall. Over the whole period of colonial occupation, the environmental conditions varied to such an extent that what would turn out to be a good year for a sheep farmer might turn out devastatingly for the neighbouring wheat farmer, only for a reversed result to be experienced in the following year.[105]

The 1960s was also a time at which many started to look for alternatives, as the prospects for the future created low morale. A fair share of the settlers did not wish to stay in an independent Kenya, as explained in previous chapters.[106] It was especially the Afrikaaner settlers in Ol Arabel, Leshau and Ol Kalou that were motivated to leave, and 14 farmers left already in 1961.[107] Those who stayed shaped their livelihoods according to the change they saw; many barred themselves behind fences, while others took on the role of custodians of the environment and converted their ranches into conservation areas. This development ultimately shaped the landscape into the present-day islands of enclosures.

7.3 Present-day Land-use Dynamics of an Africanised Landscape

The 1970s was a period of transition in which many of the large-scale farms and ranches were converted into subdivided small-scale holdings. In addition to the political influence described in the previous chapter, the land-use transformation was shaped by agro-climatic and social-environmental conditions. This section builds on the perspectives of the smallholders as the new land-management practitioners in Laikipia.

104 Whittall, 'Dimbilil: The Story of an African Farm,' p. 200.

105 Lane, *Landscape and Environmental Change in Semi-Arid Regions of East and Southern Africa.*

106 KNA, DC/LKA/1/10, DAR, 1960, pp. 18–19.

107 KNA, DC/LKA/1/10, DAR, 1960, pp. 26–27.

Many of the smallholders met the same climatic challenges that the Europeans had struggled with, although their options for handling them were different.[108] Evaluations of small-scale farming in Laikipia County in the 1980s indicate that the environmental challenges were not adequately considered in the resettlement schemes. The colonial government had deemed the area suitable for large-scale farming and ranching rather than small-scale farming. If small-scale farming were to have been viable, it would have been necessary to include a range of supportive measures in the land-transfer phase.[109]

Once again, water availability was the main limiting factor. Due to the unpredictable rainfall on the plains, the government settlement schemes were established in areas either adjoining forest reserves, as with the 'Marmanet Forest Extension Scheme,' or directly in areas demarcated as forest reserves, as in the 'Haraka Scheme' in the south-east.[110] Other government schemes, such as the 'Shirika Scheme,' were implemented towards the east of Nanyuki.[111]

Despite being wetter than the rest of the plateau, in Marmanet the transition to small-scale farming remained challenging. The hilly terrain was eroding, whereas the other areas towards the east had suitable farming terrain but insufficient rainfall.[112] In addition, the political pressure to settle as many as possible undermined concerns about the sustainability of livelihoods. Therefore, the plot sizes were not expanded past two acres per share.[113] Despite the challenges, these conditions remained good compared with those of the private land transfers in land-buying companies. Here, even the consideration of suitability for small-scale farming was completely absent. Moreover, the size of the shares in the land-buying companies was not increased despite the soil being more arid than in the wetter areas in the government settlement scheme.[114]

Most of the areas left for private transfers had inadequate water supply, whether from rainfall or from a stable water source. Therefore, shareholders in land-buying companies tended to be considerably worse off than people in the government settlement schemes. Following some evaluations, if estimated

108 Kohler, *Land Use in Transition.*

109 Kohler, 'Landbesitz Und Landnutzung Im Umbruch: Das Beispiel Des Laikipia Distrikts Nordwestlich Des Mt. Kenya'; Kohler, *Land Use in Transition.*

110 KNA Nakuru, DSO/LKA/13/H&T/13, 'Brief Handout Notes on Settlement Schemes in Laikipia District,' 18 November 1981; KNA Nakuru, DSW/1/1. File no. DSO/LKA/13/Vol I/4, 'Notes on Settlement Schemes,' 1981.

111 Field notes, meeting with research participant, the Land's Office, Nanyuki, 2 June 2015.

112 KNA Nakuru, DSW/1/1. File no. DSO (I)/LKA/13/Vol I/7, 'Hand Over/Take Over Laikipia Settlement Schemes, N.E. Mugita to S.M. Kaburu,' 25 May 1981; KNA Nakuru, DSW/1/1. File no. DSO/LKA/13/Vol I/4, 'Notes on Settlement Schemes,' 1981.

113 Kohler, *Land Use in Transition.*

114 Interview with research participant, Ol Moran, 2 July 2015.

solely on the grounds of agro-environmental potential, the size of each share should have been set between 20 and 40 acres rather than between one and five acres.[115] This would have increased the smallholders' possibility of meeting their subsistence needs in these arid and semi-arid areas. However, larger shares would also necessitate a larger labour force on the farms – something that was already a challenge for many of the small landholders.[116] Surveys from 1997 and 2009 indicate that, on the average plot sizes of 4.5–5 acres, only 10% of smallholders used more than 3.7 acres for cultivation, while more than a third used less than 2.5 acres.[117]

Even for the colonial demarcation of the land, the differences between the types in the south and those in the north were taken into consideration. One conservancy manager explains:

> As you come out of Nyahururu and Nanyuki they have smaller units. And as you go north and it's more arid, then the units become larger, because the agriculture is different. So that's how it came to these 2,000 acres, 5,000 acres [in the south of the district] up to these 40,000-acre units [towards the north]. […] Otherwise it could only be used for livestock. Whereas down there they knew it could be cultivated.[118]

For the transfers and subdivision after Independence, this same consideration of the viability of farming practice was not taken adequately into account. The effects of the land transfer on general land use in Laikipia were striking. The amount of substandard housing increased. In areas where small-scale farming took root the appearance of the rural landscape transformed from having large areas used for ranching to a predominance of small mixed-farming units. Moreover, rural decision-making processes went from being dominated by few farmers' associations to fragmented associations with little authority for long-term planning.[119]

Besides these changes in land use, the 1980s also showed signs of an increasing pressure on water and firewood in particular, and problems with wildlife grew as small-scale crop production expanded. Wildlife encroachments on

115 Kohler, *Land Use in Transition*.

116 Kohler, 'Landbesitz Und Landnutzung Im Umbruch: Das Beispiel Des Laikipia Distrikts Nordwestlich Des Mt. Kenya'; Ulrich et al., 'Small-Scale Farming in Semi-Arid Areas: Livelihood Dynamics between 1997 and 2010 in Laikipia, Kenya,' *Journal of Rural Studies* 28, no. 3 (1 July 2012), pp. 241–51.

117 Ulrich et al., 'Small-Scale Farming in Semi-Arid Areas.'

118 Interview with research participant, northern Laikipia, 14 April 2015.

119 Kohler, *Land Use in Transition*, p. 35.

smallholder farms were exacerbated by the increasing fragmentation of small-scale and large-scale landholdings.[120] This was already a challenge in the 1980s, but with steadily increasing population pressure from smallholders as well as from pastoralists without share certificates, these challenges have only grown. Between 1960 and 2009, population numbers in Laikipia County increased from 60,000 to 400,000 residents.[121]

Also, in terms of settlement structure, subdivisions authorised through resettlement schemes stand in contrast to those controlled by land-buying companies. Authorised subdivision had to follow certain demands, whereby settlements had to be organised in clusters around the Trading Centres or next to a watercourse or road.[122] If the colonial farmhouse had been left intact the subdivided plots had to be kept separate and common grazing areas set aside. The approval of a subdivision plan required shareholders to have cleared all debts, and the physical planning of the settlement had to ensure that all individual plots had access to water facilities and public amenities, such as schools and dispensaries.[123]

Yet the way the land was settled and subdivided rarely lived up to these requirements. Similarly to the land-buying company lands, the processes for subdivision was often extended for so long that settlement took place informally.[124] The balloting procedures dividing the shares, combined with the often large proportion of unsettled shareholders, created a chessboard-like settlement pattern. Moreover, many shareholders were unable to pay the full amount for their share in one payment, and instalments for their payments were often overdue due to the uncertainties of their farming practices.[125] What was also similar to the land-buying company lands was that the valuable technical installations left behind by the colonial settlers were often dismantled and sold.[126]

---

120 Gadd, 'Conservation outside of Parks'; Kinnaird and O'Brien, 'Effects of Private-Land Use, Livestock Management, and Human Tolerance.'

121 Kenya National Bureau of Statistics (KNBS). *The 2009 Kenya Population and Housing Census* (Nairobi: Government of Kenya 2009), https://www.knbs.or.ke/2009-kenya-population-and-housing-census-analytical-reports, accessed 29 September 2017.

122 Field notes, meeting with director of the Land's Office, Nanyuki, 2 June 2015.

123 Field notes, meeting with director of the Land's Office, Nanyuki, 2 June 2015.

124 Interview with research participant, Rumuruti, 21 January, 2015; interview with research participant, Nanyuki, 16 August 2016.

125 KNA Nakuru, DSO/LKA/13/H&T/13, 'Brief Handout Notes on Settlement Schemes in Laikipia District,' 18 November 1981; KNA Nakuru, DSW/1/1. File no. DSO/LKA/13/Vol I/4, 'Notes on Settlement Schemes,' 1981.

126 Field notes, conversation with research participant, Thome, 16 March 2015; Felicitas Bachmann, *Smallholders in Laikipia District, Kenya: Land Use Systems and Perceptions of Water*

The shortage of money and labour were among the factors holding back the intensification of cultivation in the 1990s. The mere cost of building a home could in itself exhaust a family's financial resources, leaving little to invest in agricultural inputs and labour demands.[127] Instead, despite having acquired farmland, most families had to rely on labour migration, through which the husband or sons would pursue work in urban centres.[128] Although this added an alternative source of income, it also created costs because of the necessity to maintain two households, as well as taking away labour from the farming work, which ultimately came to rely more on the women. Nevertheless, complete crop failure remained a frequent occurrence.[129]

As another alternative in order to secure their livelihood, many of the Kikuyu farmers relied on remittances from family members and kin. Yet after more than a generation of settlement outside Central Province, connections have for many started to fade. Surveys from the 1990s show that 60% of smallholders in a subdivided area relied on reciprocal exchange with relatives in their place of origin, although the vast majority of the support received would be limited to times of emergency and could not be expected for comprehensive assistance such as the covering of school fees or investment in farming practices.[130] This survey also shows that more than half of the respondents determined their immediate neighbours in the settlement area to be their closest kin, which was also reflected in financial exchange.[131] This aspect was also apparent in my own interviews, where current smallholders of Luyua, Turkana and Kisii ethnicity supported one another on a daily basis as neighbours, while none of them had strong relations with their places of origin any longer.[132]

Conservation and Agroforestry (Nairobi and Berne: Laikipia Research Programme, Universities of Nairobi and Berne, 1995); Kohler, *Land Use in Transition*; Kohler, 'Landbesitz Und Landnutzung Im Umbruch: Das Beispiel Des Laikipia Distrikts Nordwestlich Des Mt. Kenya.'

127 Bachmann, *Smallholders in Laikipia District, Kenya*, p. 11; Sottas and Wiesmann, 'Practices of Assistance among Small-Scale Farmers of Marura: Direction, Extent and Relevance. Laikipia,' Mt Kenya Papers D10, Laikipia Research Programme (Nanyuki and Nairobi: University of Berne, 1993).

128 Sottas, 'Aspects of a Peasant Mode of Production'; Ulrich et al., 'Small-Scale Farming in Semi-Arid Areas.'

129 Kohler, *Land Use in Transition*; Kohler, 'Landbesitz Und Landnutzung Im Umbruch: Das Beispiel Des Laikipia Distrikts Nordwestlich Des Mt. Kenya'; Sottas and Wiesmann, 'Practices of Assistance among Small-Scale Farmers of Marura.'

130 Sottas and Wiesmann, 'Practices of Assistance among Small-Scale Farmers of Marura.'

131 Sottas and Wiesmann, 'Practices of Assistance among Small-Scale Farmers of Marura.'

132 Interview with research participant, Marura, 28 May 2015; interview with research participant, Marura, 9 March 2015; interview with research participant, Thome, 5 May 2015.

Those who continued to maintain relations with their place of origin were generally better off than those who relied on local connections. Among smallholders, it is therefore not the case that those who have lost their exchange relations to their place of origin do better. Rather, those with strong local ties, as well as active exchange relations with their place of origin, tend to hold stronger positions in the local communities.[133] Additionally, looking at economic aspects of wellbeing, it was those with land areas of 10 acres or more who improved their livelihoods between 1997 and 2009, while the rest either did not improve or experienced a decrease in household income.[134] The depth of the relations is also connected to whether the new place is considered a permanent or a temporary home. According to Sottas:

> An ambivalent attitude between a wish (or necessity) to stay and an urgent desire to leave is significant for the five or six difficult years of getting used to the local conditions. [...] Those who lived on the farm for already more than 11 years have or had simply to accept their uncertain situation. Although their farm produce is not significantly better than the newcomer's, they won't leave their new home anymore.[135]

It can therefore be presumed that smallholder presence in a new place will have stabilised after 10 years of residence, and that the likelihood of them becoming absentee landowners will have reduced considerably.[136] This tendency is confirmed for all three case study areas even though a similar survey has not been conducted. Few mentioned any relations with people outside of Laikipia, and if they did it was rarely with reference to exchange and financial support. Instead, both Turkana and Kikuyu mentioned their immediate neighbours as people they would turn to in times of need. However, it should be noted that some families relied on their kin in Central Province for housing if they or their children needed to travel.[137]

Socio-economic challenges aside, the unreliable availability of water continued to be the main challenge for these new land-users. A survey from the early 1980s once again confirms water availability as the main challenge to livelihoods and farming development among these small-scale farmers: 61% of

133 Interview with research participant, Rumuruti, 3 August 2015; interview with research participant, Thome, 17 June 2015; interview with research participant, Lorien, 26 May 2015.

134 Ulrich et al., 'Small-Scale Farming in Semi-Arid Areas.'

135 Sottas, 'Aspects of a Peasant Mode of Production.'

136 Huber and Oponde, *Land Use Change Scenarios for Subdivided Ranches in Laikipia District, Kenya*; Sottas, 'Aspects of a Peasant Mode of Production.'

137 Field notes, conversation with research participant, Thome, 6 March 2015.

respondents ranked water supply as the top priority for their on-farm development, while 86% ranked water distribution as the most important infrastructural development for the community.[138]

When comparing the 1982 analysis of the subdivided Ngenia farm in eastern Laikipia (See figure 4) with the three case study areas in western Laikipia in their 2015 state, what is prominent is that the proportion of areas where smallholder farming has not been implemented is higher in the three case study areas than in Ngenia. This indicates either that the amount of absentee land has increased or that there is a difference between the eastern and western parts of the plateau. As explained in Chapter 6, there are various reasons for abandoning land. However, the discrepancy between the expectations and the reality of the purchased land's conditions was of significant importance. Those who had a chance to see the land before making their investment would not be surprised when realising the state of what they had bought.[139]

The harsh conditions for the smallholder settlers also had an impact on the ecology of the transforming landscape. Wild olive trees, *Mutamaiyo* in Gikuyu, were widespread in Laikipia up until the land transfers of the Independence years.[140] As a hard wood, it was ideal for charcoal, furniture and devices such as *rungus* and walking sticks.[141] Today, the wild olive trees are a rare sight.[142] Generally, one prominent difference between areas under large-scale management and areas that have been subdivided is that most trees have been felled for firewood in the areas that are no longer under large-scale management.[143]

Indeed, from an ecological perspective, Laikipia's dry highlands demanded a change in farming practices both from the ways in which the land had been managed before the land transfers and from the ways in which the new owners were used to practising farming, if they had such experience.[144] However, a survey from 1995 in smallholder areas in eastern Laikipia indicates that most of those unaware of difficult agro-climatic conditions: 'would have bought the land anyway, indicating that they were under great (economic or social)

138 Kohler, *Land Use in Transition*.

139 Interview with research participant, northern Laikipia, 14 April 2015.

140 Interview with research participant, Ol Moran town, 2 July 2015.

141 A *rungu* is a club made from the knot of a tree, sometimes carried by men with links to pastoralist communities as a weapon or as a symbol of status.

142 Field notes, conversation with research participants, Ol Moran, 21 July 2015.

143 Interview with research participant, Laikipia, 6 March 2015; interview with research participant, northern Laikipia, 24 July 2015.

144 Nakuru Archive/DSW/1/1. File no. DSO (I)/LKA/13/Vol I/7, 'Hand Over/Take Over Laikipia Settlement Schemes, N.E. Mugita to S.M. Kaburu,' 25 May 1981; Nakuru Archive/DSW/1/1. File no. DSO/LKA/13/Vol I/4, 'Hand Over/Take Over: Agricultural Extension, Laikipia Settlement Schemes,' 1981; Leo, *Land and Class in Kenya*.

pressure to obtain land.'[145] This mirrors the previously-mentioned politically prompted public movement to satisfy land hunger in the Independence years.[146] For the Kikuyu smallholders it relates to the Kikuyu traditional concept of *utuuro*, referring to a strategy for acquiring land for permanent residency. The value of independent holdings remains significant for Kikuyu migrants.[147] It also relates to the Kikuyu concept of *githaka*, which refers to clan-based expansionism.[148]

Today, the crops produced in the subdivided areas include beans, potatoes, peas, maize and, in areas with the possibility of irrigating, tomatoes. These are dual-purpose crops, meaning that they can be utilised both for household consumption and for sale.[149] Cash crops have thereby substituted wheat, millet and pyrethrum, as well as the large-scale production of milk, beef and wool preferred by the colonial landowners– although beef is still produced by the functioning ranches.[150]

Despite this shift, the present-day smallholding practices do not necessarily reflect the optimal ways of practising farming in the dry highland.[151] For instance, maize is far too unreliable in Laikipia, with a success rate of only 25% – even in the wetter areas of the plateau.[152] Maize is an uncertain crop simply because the variability in rainfall rarely allows it to mature enough to give a decent yield.[153] The highland demands different approaches to farming compared with the high-potential lowlands in Central Province, where water availability is higher, or the drier lowlands in Baringo, where mean temperatures are more stable. In the 1980s, scholars assumed that the insistence on farming

---

145 Bachmann, *Smallholders in Laikipia District, Kenya*, p. 15.

146 Interview with research participant, Lorien, 26 May 2015; interview with research participant, Ol Moran, 17 March 2016; interview with research participant, Rumuruti, 21 August 2015.

147 Kanogo, *Squatters and the Roots of Mau Mau*; Sottas and Wiesmann, 'Practices of Assistance Among Small-Scale Farmers of Marura.'

148 Eric Mutisya Kioko, 'Turning Conflict into Coexistence: Cross-Cutting Ties and Institutions in the Agro-Pastoral Borderlands of Lake Naivasha Basin, Kenya' (PhD diss., Universität zu Köln, 2016).

149 Ulrich et al., 'Small-Scale Farming in Semi-Arid Areas.'

150 Kohler, *Land Use in Transition*.

151 Bachmann, *Smallholders in Laikipia District, Kenya*; Manuel Flury, 'Small-Scale Farming and Changes of Land Use in the Highland of Laikipia, Kenya,' *Mountain Research and Development* 8, no. 4 (1 November 1988), pp. 265–72; Barbara Gerber, *Land Cover and Land Use of Laikipia District, Kenya: Preliminary Map Based on the Interpretation of* LANDSAT *Images* (Berne: Institute of Geography, University of Berne, 1984).

152 Kohler, *Land Use in Transition*.

153 Berger, *Rainfall and Agroclimatology of the Laikipia Plateau, Kenya*.

maize as the stable crop would gradually change when smallholders became more experienced in dry highland farming.[154]

However, 30 years later, maize is still widely used as one of the most important crops, along with potatoes and beans, which are found in almost any smallholder farmer's yearly farming cycle.[155] This could signify a reluctance to adapt to the difference in environment. Yet the smallholders' preference for farming maize may also indicate the importance of sustaining their own consumption. Although sorghum and millet may be more suitable for the agro-climatic conditions of the small-scale farmers' land, these crops are not part of their general diet. Farming them would create a greater dependence on the market, which would increase uncertainty in their livelihood – the smallholders would not have the option of limiting the yield to their own consumption in times of hardship.[156]

What has also persisted and may even have gained in importance is the diversification of income. Many smallholders rely on investment in rental houses or other types of stable income from employment as guards, clerks, teachers or manual labourers. They also rely heavily on market interactions based on their farming produce. Notably, many have experimented with drought-resistant crop varieties of maize, potatoes and beans.[157] Moreover, many small-scale farmers have entirely moved away from keeping livestock as a response to the risk of raids. As a smallholder in Ol Moran explains: '[before,] most people preferred to keep livestock, which is a good thing here. But they were constantly harassed by raiders. They therefore gave up and left the place [and became absentees]. Farming is not very good here: you need to supplement.'[158] In Thome the situation is similar, a Turkana elder explains: 'I have a few cows, but not as many as my father. If I get money, I direct it to another source of income – not in livestock because this livestock brings many bad issues like cattle rustling.'[159] These statements signify that the smallholders are indeed adapting

154 Berger, *Rainfall and Agroclimatology of the Laikipia Plateau, Kenya*; Kohler, *Land Use in Transition*; Gerber, *Land Cover and Land Use of Laikipia District, Kenya*; Bachmann, *Smallholders in Laikipia District, Kenya*.

155 Field notes, conversation with research participants, Thome, 17 June 2015; interview with research participant, Thome, 13 May 2015; interview with research participant, Marura, 9 March 2015; interview with research participant, Lorien, 27 April 2015; interview with research participant, Ol Moran, 21 July 2015.

156 Bachmann, *Smallholders in Laikipia District, Kenya*.

157 Bachmann, *Smallholders in Laikipia District, Kenya*.

158 Interview with research participant, Ol Moran, 2 July 2015.

159 Interview with research participant, Thome, 6 March 2015.

to the social-environmental conditions at hand in their highland livelihoods and are not simply reproducing practices if they are unviable.

The farmers' reduction in livestock numbers as a direct response to the risk of raids was often underlined in interviews. Pastoralists and farmers alike describe Laikipia as a reservoir for livestock that is used by pastoralist communities surrounding the plateau to come to and raid. Some pastoralists even refer to Laikipia as an ATM – a place they can easily go to when they need to withdraw livestock.[160] Pokot from Churo and beyond come to the area around Ol Moran, while Samburu from Wamba, Isiolo and Dol Dol come to areas near Thome. The pastoralists who are settled in these areas are not actively involved in the raids, but the smallholders suspect that they know the raiders and would house them and cover for them, as the Ol Moran pastor recounts:

> The few [Pokot] who have land are very peaceful. But come the night, they work with their groups from far. They just keep off, but they know what is going on. When our animals are stolen, they do not come up to help pursue the animals.[161]

In Lorien and Salama, there have also been problems of outsiders coming into the area to raid. A resident explains: 'People here don't steal from one another. It is people from other places. The security issue here is cattle rustling. There are no armed robberies of any other property, just cattle rustling.'[162] In response, in 2014, the community initiated Nyumba Kumi. The resident above is the elder in charge of the Nyumba Kumi initiative in his village, located on the border between Salama, Lorien and Kifuku Ranch. He explains:

> We have 74 households. In those households, we've got subdivisions of 17 households. Those 17 households are now the Nyumba Kumi. They said that every village should be subdivided into four[...]. So those households have an elder in charge. When a newcomer comes around, he or she must report to the elder.[163]

This method has reduced the likelihood of raiding in the area.[164] However, there has also been a tendency for Kikuyu youngsters from the targeted areas,

160 Interview with research participant, Maralal, 15 October 2014.
161 Interview with research participant, Ol Moran, 21 July 2015.
162 Interview with research participant, Salama, 1 May 2015.
163 Interview with research participant, Salama, 1 May 2015.
164 Kioko, 'Conflict Resolution and Crime Surveillance in Kenya.'

seeing the potential for acquiring quick money, to cooperate with the raiders by offering intelligence about their own kin. Besides offering a share of the profits to these Kikuyu, the new organisation is a way for the raiders to bypass the Nyumba Kumi security enforcements because they are not reliant on spying on possible targets themselves.[165] The pastor in Ol Moran explains:

> The Kikuyu [who cooperate with the raiders]; yes, they don't even need to spy, they know. This is my neighbour, he has three cows, he sleeps at 10, and he doesn't have a gun. That Pokot from Churo doesn't know that. [...] But a crook from the Kikuyu will befriend them and tell them he'll help. So, they brief them on a homestead, like what are the routes to use. When they take the animals from us, they go and share.[166]

The use of Laikipia as a reservoir of resources is not a new phenomenon. Going back before colonial scheduling of the plateau, Laikipia was used for seasonal grazing – a practice that has persisted since the land was transferred into private ownership.[167] Despite efforts to secure ranches and small farms with fences, security personnel and prosecutions, the use of Laikipia as a grazing reservoir has not reduced. The 2016–17 invasions of private land to access water and grazing signify this. In terms of pastoralist grazing on private or vacant land in Laikipia, it is not the act itself that is new but rather the increase in scale.[168]

Developments have been manifold in Laikipia since Kohler undertook his land-use exploration in the 1980s. What has developed little since then, however, is the transfer from large-scale to small-scale land use. Already in the early 1980s this transition had reached a near standstill. It is not that the demand for land has lessened; on the contrary, prices for land in the area has increased dramatically. Rather, no more large-scale landholdings have become available for Africanisation. This can also be seen when comparing figure 9, which shows the land-use categorisation in 2016, with figure 7, depicting the

165 Gravesen and Kioko, 'Cooperation in the midst of Violence.'

166 Interview with research participant, Ol Moran, July 21, 2015.

167 See Chapters 3, 4 and 5.

168 Interview with research participant, 16 August 2016; Muchiri Gitonga, 'Drive Herders back to Samburu, Leaders Demand,' *Daily Nation*, 19 January 2017, available from http://www.ipsos.co.ke/NEWBASE_EXPORTS/CARE International/161214_Daily Nation – Wednesday_19_c37f6.pdf, accessed 29 September 2017; *The Star*, 'The Diary of Seven Months of Attacks on Kifuku Farm in Laikipia'; *The Star*, 'Pokot Gunmen Invade Laikipia Conservancy, Kill Wild Animals'; *The Star*, 'Land Invasion Wrecks Laikipia'; Kenya NTV, 'What is Ailing Laikipia'; Alistair Leithead, 'Are Kenya Ranch Invasions Driven by Drought or Politics?' BBC News, 4 February 2017, available from http://www.bbc.com/news/world-africa-38866389, accessed 29 September 2017.

land-use categorisation in 1982. Those large-scale landowners who wanted to leave their land following Independence did so, and those who are left have little interest in selling.

Yet a transition that has taken place since the 1980s is that many of the larger holdings have been converted from working ranches into conservancies. In some cases this has happened completely, as in the case of Laikipia Nature Conservancy. Others have partly converted, such as with Loldaiga, Suyian and Mugie, where a certain number of cattle are maintained to financially support the focus on conservation. Some have chosen to convert marginally, such as in Ngorare and Ol Maisor, where the focus continues to be on ranching activities, with a certain degree of protection of the wildlife. The increased focus on conservation has introduced wildlife tourism and the construction of lavish tourist lodges. This transition has resulted in the destocking of the areas used for conservation practices.[169]

This conversion is partly a response to the heightened global focus on biodiversity, climate change and environmental protection, and partly a response to the intensification of pressure on resource use in the areas neighbouring the large-scale landholdings, described by Gallmann in the opening quote. This transition in the larger landholdings from ranch land to conservancy land resembles the new enclosures movement in southern Africa, where the abandonment of fences leads to the encroachment of economic tourist activities on smallholder farmlands, benefiting the larger landowners rather than the smallholders.[170] In contrast to the political culture behind the colonial land-grabs, the new enclosures movement aim to combat physical enclosures and boundaries in the name of conservation.[171]

However, interestingly, the destocking in the areas used for conservation has not led to a general decrease of livestock in Laikipia. Rather, as seen in table 3, while the number of cattle altered little from the 127,735 heads in 1985 to the 156,312 heads estimated in 2003, the numbers of sheep and goats increased significantly from 283,459 in 1985 to 473,856 in 2003. A similar growth rate can be traced for the donkey and camel numbers. For 2016 the cattle numbers had risen to 249,510 heads, whereas the small stock had increased to 546,153. The difference in growth rates for small stock as opposed to cattle has been recorded for other pastoral areas of Kenya as well.[172]

169 Lane, *Landscape and Environmental Change in Semi-Arid Regions of East and Southern Africa*.

170 Hughes, *From Enslavement to Environmentalism*, p. 13.

171 Hughes, *From Enslavement to Environmentalism*, p. 13.

172 Mette Løvschal, Dorthe Døjbak Håkonsson and Irene Amoke, 'Are Goats the New Elephants in the Room? Changing Land-Use Strategies in Greater Mara, Kenya.' *Land Use*

TABLE 3 Estimated population numbers of livestock and wildlife in Laikipia County

Species	1985	1991	2001	2003	2012	2016
Cattle	127,735	172,712	105,118	156,312	149,910	249,510
Sheep and goats	283,459	194,707	241,867	473,856	380,312	546,153
Camels	742	*	3,697	*	4,150	6,936
Donkey	525	*	2,496	*	1,454	2,675
Elephant	1,648	1,337	1,844	2,947	3,493	3,321
Zebra, Burchell's	20,217	35,357	27,544	36,372	24,887	29,671
Zebra, Grevy's	597	691	897	948	614	597
Rhino	*	418	*	223	*	341
Buffalo	2,318	3,192	1,684	1,953	2,071	7,296

SOURCE: HILLMAN SMITH ET AL., *SYSTEMATIC AERIAL SAMPLE SURVEY OF LAIKIPIA COUNTY*; LANE, *LANDSCAPE AND ENVIRONMENTAL CHANGE IN SEMI-ARID REGIONS OF EAST AND SOUTHERN AFRICA*.

Livestock are now the most numerous mammals in the county, and their numbers have more than doubled over the 30-year survey period, with the most dramatic increase over the past 13 years. These numbers correlate with oral evidence of large-scale immigration of Samburu people with livestock during this period.[173] [174]

Comparatively, the numbers of wild herbivores in the county have either stagnated, in the case of zebra and rhino, or increased significantly, in the case of elephant and buffalo. These numbers have decreased considerably in the rest of the country.[175]

In some smallholder areas further subdivision has taken place since the 1980s, for instance in areas that were already subdivided and partly settled by smallholders in the 1980s. Many of the already small subdivisions of five acres have been further subdivided down to 2.1 or even 0.5 acres.[176] The further division is done either for inheritance purposes or because underperforming

Policy 80 (1 January 2019): 395–99; Joseph Ogutu et al., 'Extreme Wildlife Declines and Concurrent Increase in Livestock Numbers in Kenya: What Are the Causes?' *PLOS ONE* 11, no. 9 (27 September 2016): pp. 1–46.

173 Field notes, conversation with research participants, Thome, 17 June 2015; interview with KNBS, Nanyuki, 24 August 2015.

174 This cannot be supported by population data, since the Kenya National Bureau of Statistics (KNBS) no longer publishes ethnic distributions for their population censuses.

175 Hillman Smith et al., *Systematic Aerial Sample Survey of Laikipia County*.

176 Sottas, 'Aspects of a Peasant Mode of Production.'

farming activity has led to insolvency. This has been the case for the private transfers on the land-buying company lands, although areas that underwent subdivision through government settlement schemes are not entirely exempt.[177]

The use of the resources in Laikipia by incoming pastoralists is not new, although the intensity has changed. What has changed since the 1980s is that Samburu and Pokot pastoralists have settled on the absentee lands in Laikipia rather than occasionally entering with livestock. For some pastoralists this has started a trend of buying land. However, the number of acres bought rarely corresponds to the amount of land needed to sustain the pastoralist's livestock. Consequently, much of what was categorised as rangeland in 1984 can now be categorised as barren land, with thin, rocky and sandy soil along with little and widely spaced scrub.[178] Of this increase in pastoralist settlements, a Samburu resident explains:

> Long ago, the Samburu people were referred to as seasonal landowners but later they came to defy that, saying that they also need to obtain land rights to the use of the resource. They argued that their land has been given to strangers who neither live there nor have ever made visits to the land alleged to be theirs.[179]

The Samburu resident acknowledges that private-property rights legitimise control of land, while using this to argue for a conversion to the pastoralist land-use regime, saying that buying land can establish the right to control land so that it comes to reflect the way in which land ought to be used, according to him – namely for pastoral grazing.[180]

7.4 Concluding Remarks

The determination to deem Laikipia's land-use transformation either positive or negative is shaped by one's ideal and experience on the plateau. Former settlers view the changes with remorse and sadness.[181] According to them, the

177 Field notes, conversation with research participants, 6 March 2015; Bachmann, *Smallholders in Laikipia District, Kenya*; Sottas and Wiesmann, 'Practices of Assistance among Small-Scale Farmers of Marura.'

178 Gerber, *Land Cover and Land Use of Laikipia District, Kenya*, p. 22.

179 Interview with research participant, Nyahururu, 21 March 2015.

180 Field notes, conversation with research participants, Thome, 26 July 2015.

181 Gallmann, *I Dreamed of Africa*.

area has become gradually degraded and invaded by intruders who form the landscape with little consideration for environmental sustainability, whereas many smallholders consider the transition from large to small landholdings a positive step towards Africanisation of the landscape. Even though the livelihoods of most smallholders are under pressure, few have regretted settling, and those who have are already gone again. Some pastoralists see the transition period as a welcome occasion to move in and use the grazing areas, while others are adapting to the legal measures of private-property rights in order to buy land themselves.[182] Whether one manages land for the purpose of acquiring grazing, for smallholder farming or for large-scale management determines the type of qualities that are nurtured or protected. To smallholders, a wetland is uneconomical unless it can be farmed or otherwise used, whereas the large-scale practitioners tend to worry about the preservation of the biodiversity and wildlife that are dependent on the wetland areas.

Notwithstanding these differences, all land-users over the past 120 years have been challenged by the erratic agro-climatic variations across the plateau.[183] In pre-colonial times, the pastoralists solved the water scarcity through mobility and relied on grazing to varying degrees depending on the time of year.[184] In colonial times, the large-scale landholders attempted to circumvent the variation by demarcating the lands into different sizes depending on whether they were better suited to ranching or to farming.[185] The agro-climatic conditions also led them to experiment with the breeding of livestock to enhance their productivity and adaptability to the environmental conditions of the dry highlands.[186] In post-colonial times, the smallholders tackled the unpredictable water availability by clustering their settlements in areas adjoining wetlands and forests. Here, they took advantage of the high number of land buyers who did not settle, by taking up the absentee lands for common grazing and farming use.[187] However, today the lack of water has also led pastoralists to graze their livestock on private land by force, pushed the smallholders into

182 Field notes, conversation with research participants, Thome, 26 July 2015.

183 Berger, *Rainfall and Agroclimatology of the Laikipia Plateau, Kenya*; Ulrich et al., 'Small-Scale Farming in Semi-Arid Areas.'

184 Lane, *Landscape and Environmental Change in Semi-Arid Regions of East and Southern Africa*; Spear and Waller, *Being Maasai: Ethnicity and Identity in East Africa*; Spencer, *The Samburu: A Study in Geocentracy* (London and New York: Taylor & Francis, 2003); Bollig, 'Adaptive Cycles in the Savannah.'

185 Gary Wasserman, 'European Settlers and Kenya Colony Thoughts on a Conflicted Affair,' *African Studies Review* 17, no. 2 (1 September 1974), pp. 425–34; Berry, 'Debating the Land Question in Africa.'

186 Van Zwanenberg, *The Agricultural History of Kenya to 1939*.

187 Kohler, *Land Use in Transition*.

encounters with wildlife and caused the large-scale farmers to lose entire harvests. Thus, the water scarcity has neither lessened nor worsened, and most likely it will continue to cause havoc for whoever might be tempted to settle and start working the land after seeing the superfluous generosity the place provides following a wet season.

CHAPTER 8

Conclusion

This study set out to explore the social and political factors that led to the 2016–17 state of emergency in Laikipia. In contrast to media representations at the time of the crisis, I have not argued for a simple case of non-conformist land invaders against rightful landowners. Instead, I consider the main explanatory factors to span from the historical developments of land (re)distribution, politicisation of ethnicity and fragmented land-use systems. In contrast to more traditional types of anthropological studies, where the focus is put on a well-defined group of people, this study has taken a regional approach to explore the social-ecological dynamics of five general groups, namely pastoralists, smallholders, conservationists, ranchers and absentee holders. Since no single theoretical approach can adequately explain these dynamics, a line of theoretically anchored thematic concepts has shaped the analysis. These thematic concepts include landholdership and governance; contradicting perspectives on land-use practices; fragmentation of state presence; and the politicisation of ethnicity in relation to land conflicts.[1] Specifically, the study was shaped around three case areas, Lorien, Thome and Ol Moran, each illustrating distinct aspects of the representation of Laikipia as a contested environment.

In this conclusion, following the above-mentioned general themes, I summarise the main findings and explain more generally what makes Laikipia a unique social-ecological landscape. Finally, I sum up the 2016–17 state of emergency as it stood after the 2017 general election and reflect on its broader significance.

8.1 Understanding Laikipia

Comparing Laikipia with other areas surrounding the plateau illustrates their differences despite their relative geographical proximity. For instance, East Pokot to the west is marked by its pastoralist land use – a non-governed area in terms of state presence, institutional infrastructure and general service delivery. Contrastingly, Naivasha to the south, on the road towards Nairobi, is dominated by its flower industry – a well-governed space, where general authority

1 See Chapter 2 for descriptions of the thematic concepts.

 DOI:10.1163/9789004435209_009

and state services, including health care and education, are functioning. In contrast, Laikipia can be represented neither as an area of large-scale agricultural activities nor as one of pastoralism exclusively, even though both land-use systems are practised extensively. On a scale denoting state presence, Laikipia is located in between the two. And this in-between position is one of the most significant factors when defining Laikipia. Even though health care and education are available, the authority of the state in relation to land issues is more biased. In a place where it has been possible – since the early 1990s – for pastoralists to occupy private land without being removed by the police; where state institutions are unable or unwilling to defend the tenure security of shareholders in relation to private land-buying companies; and where ethnic conflicts are politicised to the extent that state interference and conflict resolution becomes compromised, it must be concluded that the effectiveness of the state authority in Laikipia's land matters is ambiguous at best.

8.1.1 *Frontiers, Fragmentation and Colonial Residue*

For Laikipia, the position in a frontier zone between well-governed and non-governed spaces has intensified the extensive fragmentation of land use.[2] This is also different from surrounding areas.

Samburu County, Isiolo County and Baringo County have greater government presence compared with colonial times, when the government was merely present for tax collection. Yet, the current improvement is limited to towns. Moreover, investments made by the Geothermal Development Company (GDC) and the LAPSSET Corridor[3] may impact infrastructural developments and the presence of authorities even in the hinterlands.[4] In the areas closer to Laikipia, there are increasing enclosures of small *shambas*. This can be seen as a growing land-use fragmentation, although on a considerably smaller scale than in Laikipia.[5]

Throughout the chapters of this book, the different aspects of fragmented investments and institutional presence in Laikipia are laid out. Ranches, conservancies and towns are well connected to the state, with the economic, political and institutional functioning this brings. Yet, the three case studies, Lorien, Ol Moran and Thome, are defined by an absence of state services, including provision of security and protection of private-property rights.

2 See Chapters 3 and 6.

3 Large-scale infrastructural project connecting Lamu Port, South Sudan and Ethiopia.

4 Personal communication with colleague Hauke Vehrs, 20 September 2017.

5 Clemens Greiner, Miguel Alvarez and Mathias Becker, 'From Cattle to Corn: Attributes of Emerging Farming Systems of Former Pastoral Nomads in East Pokot, Kenya,' *Society & Natural Resources* 26, no. 12 (1 December 2013), pp. 1478–90.

This lacking representation and inequality intensify tension and conflict.[6] The absence of authorities creates possibilities for acting opportunistically to prosper at the expense of others. Politicians from the new Kenyan elite acquired votes through land-buying companies in the Independence years, without being held responsible for the shareholders' precarious situation once land had been sold and votes collected. Moreover, pastoralists were able to settle on the absentee lands without being moved by authorities for fear that politicians would then lose potential voters.[7] Contrastingly, the smallholders live with underdevelopment and uncertainty. For instance, those in Ol Moran and in Thome live with small areas of minimally productive land.[8]

8.1.2 *Legal Pluralism and Land Rights*

Except for the group ranches in eastern Laikipia and a few government farms and protected areas, all land is privately held in Laikipia (see figures 6 and 9). With multiple types of actors on the land, there are multiple opinions concerning who holds a legitimate right to the land. All such opinions build on different narratives and particular versions of history on the plateau, substantiating a sense of righteousness about the Laikipia lands. Such claims do not always correlate with legally acknowledged land rights but, with state institutions that do not always interfere in land conflicts, such a diversity of claims is allowed to persist.

When land is seemingly vacant or the present users' legitimacy is contested, rumours that Laikipia holds available land start to spread in areas surrounding the plateau. Such impressions lead people to buy disputed land, or to settle in areas with livestock only to find out later that the accessible resources for grazing are limited.[9] The opportunistic navigation by some has enhanced bureaucracy with prolonged administrative processes. Even though people's legal position with regard to land ownership is locked between being an owner and a squatter, people's lives are not at a similar standstill. Rather, such cases often lead to a demand for developing vernacular land markets to authorise individualised transfers of the 'not yet owned' land, which consequently intensifies institutional fragmentation.[10] Another consequence is that the hope and belief in leaders has changed since the Independence years, and patron–client relations are now marked by mistrust. This is illustrated in the relations both

6 See Chapters 5 and 6.
7 See Chapters 3, 4 and 6.
8 See Chapter 4.
9 See Chapters 4 and 6.
10 See Chapter 4 and 6; interview with research participant, Thome, 27 May 2015; Lund, 'Twilight Institutions.'

between smallholders and directors in land-buying companies and between Laikipians and political leaders.[11]

By contrast, most land in Baringo, Samburu and Isiolo counties is common land. However, external involvement in these areas, with the LAPSSET Corridor and GDC project implementation, is pushing processes of privatisation. This has created an increased awareness about private-property rights and the potential to gain from investments. For instance, pastoralists in East Pokot claim compensation when common land is appropriated for large-scale investments, and people in and around Isiolo town invest in land by purchasing former common land in the anticipation that valuation will increase when the state's promised large-scale infrastructural investments come to fruition. Moreover, cases of trespassing and encroachment onto conservancies and ranches in Laikipia have increased awareness about alternative types of landholdership. Nevertheless, this increase in awareness does not necessarily mean an increasing acknowledgement of private-property rights among pastoralist groups in Laikipia or around the plateau.[12]

By contrast, to the south of the Laikipia plateau, most land is private-property land. Yet in an area such as Naivasha, with large-scale horticultural farms, ranches and workers' settlement areas, there are occasional cases where claims are made on the basis of customary land rights. For instance, Maasai made such claims when forced to move out of the area in which the national park, Hell's Gate, was founded. Yet, in contrast to Laikipia, this case depicted an exception to the peaceful way in which land relations in Naivasha are usually managed.[13] Moreover, absentee land is a well-known phenomenon in many areas dominated by private-property land across Kenya. Yet these areas often differ in composition from Laikipia. In areas closer to Nairobi, many acquired land when it was affordable although they themselves are no longer present on the land. Instead they are able to rent out their land to maintain an income. Trans Nzoia and Uasin Gisho are examples of areas where the establishment of land-buying companies has led to a similar politicisation of the resources.[14]

8.1.3 *Ethnicity and the Politicisation of Land Claims*

Another factor leading to opportunistic methods for manoeuvring around legal frameworks is the high demand for everyone to control land. The historic

11 Interview with research participant, Nyahururu, 18 March 2016; see Chapter 3.

12 Personal communication with colleague Hauke Vehrs, 20 September 2017.

13 Gerda Kuiper, *Agro-industrial Labour in Kenya: Cut Flower Farms and Migrant Workers' Settlements* (Cham, Switzerland: Palgrave Macmillan, 2019).

14 Kanyinga, 'The Legacy of the White Highlands.'

discriminatory resource allocation based on ethnicity and race has created a basis for land to be instrumentalised into functioning as a binder for group identity and political mobilisation. The politicisation of land has become a strategic practice employed in order to acquire land resources. For instance, Kalenjin shareholders in Lorien believe they have a more legitimate claim to the land than the Kikuyu, while Samburu and Pokot herders occupy unsettled land supported by autochthony claims and the naming of places.[15] Where naming can support a claim to territorial expansion, so can the practice of fencing. A fence builder can claim a space and define a boundary, which in turn can be challenged by a fence demolisher.[16] The absence of a fence can make the boundary fluid, which functions as territorial expansion. This is the case for the 'new enclosures' of lightly fenced conservancies engaging in tourism activities. Here, the freely roaming wildlife becomes instrumentalised in practices of territorial expansion onto areas beyond the conservancy boundaries.[17] Such practices further enhance mistrust in elites and patrons among the impacted smallholders.[18]

Mistrust relates to the lack of representation. Set in the context of historic unequal resource distribution, such actions can ignite existing grievances and provoke them into violence. This can happen either in active rebellious land invasions and symbolic protest killings of wildlife, or as passive support or celebration of such acts.[19] It is not only the pastoralists who are critical of the continued presence of white Kenyans on land that could potentially be Africanised. Rather, the critical approach to the 'white lands' is widespread among Laikipians.[20]

Categories of ethnicity, autochthony and class relate to the acquisition of resources in other areas surrounding the Laikipia plateau as well, although to different degrees. And in this regard, the homogeneity or heterogeneity of the social context and possible alliances between groups are relevant. Similarly to Laikipia, Naivasha is an ethnically diverse place. In settlements housing the labour migrants, the ethnic composition is especially mixed, whereas the town is homogeneous, with the Kikuyu as the majority. Former Kikuyu labourers on settler farms, who were given land when the settler left, now construct claims

15 Interview with research participant, Lorien, 26 May 2015; interview with research participant, Ol Moran, 21 July 2015; interview with research participant, Thome, 6 May 2015; see Chapters 4 and 5.

16 Interview with research participant, Laikipia, 8 June 2015.

17 Hughes, *From Enslavement to Environmentalism*; see Chapter 7.

18 See Chapters 4 and 7.

19 Interview with research participant, Ol Moran, 21 July 2015; see Chapter 4 and 5.

20 Gadd, 'Conservation outside of Parks.'

to that land, although such claims are not built around autochthony. Interestingly, and in contrast to Laikipia, the property rights of the often white flower farmers are never challenged. This can partly be explained by the fact that the flower farms provide more labour than the ranches in Laikipia, and none of the Naivasha labourers are impacted by wildlife breaking through their boundaries onto the large landholdings.[21]

8.1.4 *The Sustainablity of Land-management Practices*

Another significant factor for Laikipia is the multiple perspectives on what makes a landscape sustainable or valuable. The reply to this question depends on people's land-use practices, and here the smallholders, ranchers, absentee landlords, conservationists and pastoralists have distinct and opposing opinions.[22]

Smallholders in Laikipia tend to be critical of conservationist land-management practices and see little value in a landscape that does not benefit them and their livelihoods.[23] It is necessary to distinguish between the ranchers and conservationists, because a positive attitude towards ranching activities does not necessarily mean an equally positive attitude towards wildlife, and vice versa.[24] Yet, the attitude that Laikipia is under environmental threat is held by ranchers and conservationists alike. Contrastingly, absentee landlords would declare that having many people increases demand for land and housing. This increases sales value and rent levels for tenants.[25] For pastoralists, a valuable landscape is one that supports pastoralism. Many voice concern about whether there will be pastoralism in the future. Some adjust to the changes they experience by diversifying their livelihoods into farming, education and investments in land. Yet, especially for Samburu and Pokot communities outside Laikipia, mobility is often maintained as a fundamental way of life, in the sense that if a landscape changes there is always the option to go somewhere else.[26] Contrastingly, even though pastoralists in Laikipia typically do not own the land they are settled on, there are few alternatives to go elsewhere and thence mobility does not hold the same adaptive power. When the Samburu in Laikipia change their settlement, they move to absentee lands that are de facto open-access areas, although the pressure on the resources makes them

21 Personal communication with colleague Gerda Kuiper, 20 September 2017.

22 Douglas, *In the Active Voice*.

23 See subsection titled 'The Smallholders' in Chapter 4.

24 See subsections titled 'The Ranchers' and 'The Conservationists' in Chapter 4.

25 Personal communication with colleague Gerda Kuiper, 20 September 2017; see Chapters 4 and 6.

26 Personal communication with colleague Hauke Vehrs, 20 September 2017.

dependent on encroachment.[27] Similarly, landowners and shareholders have locked their livelihoods and investments to the land. Few conservationists and ranchers have a realistic option of leaving the country and settling somewhere else, because most of them are Kenyan citizens.[28] The smallholders have the option to migrate as labour, as in other areas of Kenya. Yet with stronger ownership relations to the land they are on, they are less inclined to leave. With court cases and unresolved tenure security issues going on for decades, one wonders whether they would not already have left if they considered doing so a better option.[29] So, for Laikipia, only the absentees have a genuine choice to go elsewhere.

With this contextual information in mind, let us now return to the way the Laikipia emergency was resolved and reflect on what it is indicative of on a grander scale.

8.2 Resolving the State of Emergency in Laikipia, 2016–17

After the general elections on 8 August 2017 had passed, tension started to settle down in Laikipia. However, with the Supreme Court's annulment of the election results, the conclusion of the post-election state of affairs had to wait for the re-run election in October 2017. This meant a continuation of clashes at the level of national politics, and consequently the media lost interest in the land invasions in Laikipia even though they had not yet settled down. To evaluate the long-term effects of the 2016–17 state of emergency in Laikipia, some points of interest are worth noting from the media coverage around the election.

Lempurkel's efforts to get re-elected through incitement to violence continued up until the eleventh hour. Two days prior to the election, he was caught on a recording stating that 'white people [would] go home' if the people in Laikipia voted for the opposition party and re-elected him to his Laikipia North seat[30] – statements that once again led the MP for Laikipia North to be charged with incitement to violence and racial hatred. Coincidentally, Vice President Ruto's manoeuvres to claim the ADC Mutara Ranch were seen by many Laikipians as a political move to position himself favourably for the next election. It

27 See subsection titled 'The Pastoralists' in Chapter 4.
28 See subsections titled 'The Ranchers' and 'The Conservationists' in Chapter 4.
29 See subsection titled 'The Smallholders' in Chapter 4.
30 *The Star*, 'Kenya Election Heats up Conflicts over Ethnicity, Laikipia Land,' 7 August 2017, http://www.the-star.co.ke/news/2017/08/07/kenya-election-heats-up-conflicts-over-ethnicity-laikipia-land_c1612075, accessed 30 August 2017.

seems generally agreed that owning land gives access to power because land can be exchanged for votes and political support.[31] The political strategy of buying votes by giving land to or arming certain ethnic groups is a strategy that has been employed many times before in Kenya.[32] Specific to this wave of invasions, certain media outlets such as *The Star* gradually changed their views on the situation, and began to increasingly consider the invasions of ranches and conservancies as 'political[ly] instigated in an attempt to repossess the rancher's land.'

The demand for this land was already high in the post-Independence years, when many British landowners chose to leave the country.[33] The difference in this emergency was that those willing to leave had already done so, and no more land was available for Africanisation. However, pastoralists as well as many smallholders continued to consider the remaining ranches and conservancies as land that was yet to be Africanised.[34] Any politician able to take responsibility for transferring the rest of the White Highlands to voting Kenyans would ensure political support. Lempurkel recognised this, but his awareness was by no means novel.

Despite his recruitment efforts, many Samburu in Laikipia turned against Lempurkel with their vote, and the national elections in 2017 ultimately led Lempurkel to lose his Orange Democratic Movement seat to his Jubilee opponent, Sara Korere. Two weeks prior to the election, President Kenyatta publicly denounced Lempurkel, encouraging voters to elect Korere.[35] Many of Kenyatta's Kikuyu voters were targeted in clashes, although the media did not cover this as widely as it did the land invasions on the white landholdings. One Kikuyu farmer near Ol Moran declared to *The Star* that 'every time there is an election, there are attacks, but this year is the worst. [...] It seems

31 Lekamario speculated that Rutu's decision to take over ADC Mutara may have been motivated by a wish to position himself in a favourable negotiating position for the 2022 election. Field notes, email correspondence with research participant, Laikipia, 30 January 2017.

32 Branch, *Kenya: Between Hope and Despair*; Leo, *Land and Class in Kenya*; Human Rights Watch (HRW), *Ballots to Bullets: Organized Political Violence and Kenya's Crisis of Governance*. Vol. 20, no. 1(A) (March 2006), https://www.hrw.org/report/2008/03/16/ballots-bullets/organized-political-violence-and-kenyas-crisis-governance, accessed 11 July 2020.

33 Branch, *Kenya: Between Hope and Despair*; Leo, *Land and Class in Kenya*.

34 Interview with absentee landlords, Githunguri, 15 September 2015; interview with research participant, Thome, June 18, 2015; interview with research participant, Thome, 18 July 2015.

35 *The Star*, 'Don't Re-Elect Lempurkel, Uhuru Tells Laikipia Voters,' 29 July 2017, http://www.the-star.co.ke/news/2017/07/29/dont-re-elect-lempurkel-uhuru-tells-laikipia-voters_c1606078, accessed 30 August 2017.

[the pastoralists'] intention is not pasture, but to make people flee,' noting that many of the smallholder farmers were believed to have been specifically targeted in attacks in a plot to prevent them from voting.[36]

However, despite the election result, it cannot be concluded that people in Laikipia have shifted their allegiance to Kenyatta's Jubilee Party. In fact, the ruling party lost the governor's seat to the independent candidate Muriithi. Laikipia and Isiolo counties were the only two in the country that elected independent candidates for the governor's seat. Coincidentally, both areas have been highly implicated in the 2016 and 2017 insecurities.[37] This makes Kenyatta's victory in the Laikipia region highly ambiguous.

According to the chairman of Laikipia Wildlife Forum, the people in Laikipia wanted peace, and this was the driver for the way people voted at the polling stations on 8 August.[38] Two weeks after the August election, the former governors of Nyandarua, Nakuru and Laikipia counties pledged to support their successors and encouraged their supporters to do the same.[39] This position reinstated general peace in the region, following elections that many feared could evolve into post-election violence mirroring the situation in 2007. That said, there continued to be reports of herder invasions on ranches, conservancies and smallholder farms late into the autumn despite the fact that the drought conditions had ended. In September 2017, the estimated damages from the invasions had amounted to Ksh 4 billion and had led hundreds of local jobs to be lost, along with growing numbers of deaths, injuries and incidents of vandalism on property.[40]

More than a year later, it still could not be assumed that things had merely returned to normal. This situation would have been the same even if the election results had been different, because it was never exclusively about the

36 *The Star*, 'Kenya Election Heats up Conflicts over Ethnicity, Laikipia Land.'

37 *The Daily Nation*, '#Frontrow: New Governors Had Better Deliver or Be Ready to Serve,' 22 August 2017, http://www.nation.co.ke/lifestyle/DN2/New-governors-should-deliver/957860-4066692-ppwtsh/index.html, accessed 30 August 2017.

38 *The Star*, 'Residents of Laikipia Are Tired of Violence, Association Says,' 21 August 2017, http://www.the-star.co.ke/news/2017/08/21/residents-of-laikipia-are-tired-of-violence-association-says_c1619801, accessed 30 August 2017.

39 *The Daily Nation*, 'Ex-Governors Pledge to Support Successors,' 22 August 2017, http://www.nation.co.ke/counties/Nakuru-Laikipia-Nyandarua-governors/1107872-4065998-oce3rsz/index.html, accessed 30 August 2017.

40 *The Star*, 'Kenya Election Heats up Conflicts over Ethnicity, Laikipia Land'; *The Star*, 'Residents of Laikipia Are Tired of Violence, Association Says.'

election. The election merely created a power vacuum, permitting deep-rooted grievances to spur into uprising without interference from the authorities.

8.3 Final Thoughts

What is significant about the 2016–17 state of emergency in Laikipia is not that the types of attacks illustrated a new phenomenon. Similar ways of protesting have been employed before. Rather, what is worth noting is the scale on which the attacks took place. They signified a highly contextual rebellion from below, originating among those who have for a long time felt themselves to be without representation in political spheres or in the media.[41] The rebellious land invasions therefore cannot be isolated as merely the result of expansionist political ideologies, even though that was what they became. The sense of misrepresentation or lack of representation was an indisputable fact that grew to unprecedented proportions in Laikipia. Ranchers even started to reflect on similarities with Zimbabwe, where white ranchers had been forced out of the country in the not-so-distant past.[42]

There have been many similar waves in the recent past in Laikipia – to recount a few, the 2007 post-election violence,[43] the campaign for the restitution of Maasai lands in 2004,[44] the 1997 post-election violence in Ol Moran[45] and the 1992 evictions of Kikuyu shareholders from Lorien. During colonial times, the murder of Powys and the continued attacks on colonial ranches such as that of the Dykes also signify acts of rebellion against the dominant holders of land resources.[46] Therefore, notwithstanding that the state of insecurity impacted people widely and seriously, the explorations of the historical, social, political and environmental dynamics of life on the Laikipia plateau illustrate that it remains a wave of uncertainty that will disappear and return at regular intervals, as it has done before over the past 100 years.

With the political situation up in the air and continued waves of insecurity in these mixed landscapes, research on contested lands has proven more

41 This is also argued in Chapters 4 and 5.

42 Statement from Anne Powys in Gettleman, 'Loss of Fertile Land Fuels "Looming Crisis" Across Africa.'

43 Anderson and Lochery, 'Violence and Exodus in Kenya's Rift Valley, 2008.'

44 Kantai, 'In the Grip of the Vampire State.'

45 Rutten, 'Fresh Killings.'

46 Fratkin, 'The Samburu Laibon's Sorcery and the Death of Theodore Powys in Colonial Kenya.'

valuable than ever before. Whatever the future may bring for Laikipia and Laikipians, the fragmentation of the landscape will hardly become less complex. Nor is it likely that there will be fewer similarly fragmented landscapes elsewhere in the future. Instead, no matter which group one associates with, and which historical experience one is marked by, everyone will need to find new and innovative ways to negotiate their access to these contested lands, if they truly wish to stay there.

Bibliography

Books, Chapters and Articles

Anderson, Benedict. *Imagined Communities: Reflections on the Origin and Spread of Nationalism*. London: Verso, 2006.

Anderson, David. 'Depression, Dust Bowl, Demography, and Drought: The Colonial State and Soil Conservation in East Africa during the 1930s.' *African Affairs* 83 (1984): 321–43.

Anderson, David. *Eroding the Commons: The Politics of Ecology in Baringo, Kenya, 1890s–1963*. Oxford: James Currey, 2002.

Anderson, David. 'Guilty Secrets: Deceit, Denial, and the Discovery of Kenya's "Migrated Archive."' *History Workshop Journal* 80, no. 1 (1 October 2015): 142–60.

Anderson, David. *Histories of the Hanged: The Dirty War in Kenya and the End of Empire*. New York and London: W.W. Norton, 2005.

Anderson, David. 'Managing the Forest: The Conservation History of Lembus, Kenya, 1904–63.' In *Conservation in Africa: Peoples, Policies and Practice*, edited by David Anderson and Richard H. Grove. Cambridge: Cambridge University Press, 1989.

Anderson, David. 'Stock Theft and Moral Economy in Colonial Kenya.' *Africa* 56 (1986): 399–416.

Anderson, David. 'Vigilantes, Violence and the Politics of Public Order in Kenya.' *African Affairs* 101, no. 405 (1 October 2002): 531–55.

Anderson, David and Emma Lochery. 'Violence and Exodus in Kenya's Rift Valley, 2008: Predictable and Preventable?' *Journal of Eastern African Studies* 2, no. 2 (2008): 328–43.

Anderson, David and David Throup. 'The Agrarian Economy of Central Province, Kenya, 1918–1939.' In *The Economies of Africa and Asia in the Inter-War Depression*, edited by Ian Brown. Abingdon, Oxon: Routledge, 2014.

Bachmann, Felicitas. *Smallholders in Laikipia District, Kenya: Land Use Systems and Perceptions of Water Conservation and Agroforestry*. Nairobi and Berne: Laikipia Research Programme, Universities of Nairobi and Berne, 1995.

Barr, Abigail. 'Trust and Expected Trustworthiness: Experimental Evidence from Zimbabwean Villages.' *The Economic Journal* 113, no. 489 (1 July 2003): 614–30.

Beinart, William and Lotte Hughes. *Environment and Empire*. The Oxford History of the British Empire. Oxford: Oxford University Press, 2007.

Berg, Lawrence D. and Robin A. Kearns. 'Naming as Norming: "Race," Gender, and the Identity Politics of Naming Places in Aotearoa/New Zealand.' *Environment and Planning D: Society and Space* 14, no. 1 (1 February 1996): 99–122.

Berger, Peter. *Rainfall and Agroclimatology of the Laikipia Plateau, Kenya*. Berne: Geographica Bernesia and Geographical Society of Berne, 1989.

Berman, Bruce and John Lonsdale. *Unhappy Valley: Conflict in Kenya and Africa*. London: James Currey Ltd, 1992.

Bernard, H. Russell. *Research Methods in Anthropology: Qualitative and Quantitative Approaches*. Lanham, MD: Rowman Altamira, 2011.

Bernard, H. Russell, and Clarence C. Gravlee. *Handbook of Methods in Cultural Anthropology*. Lanham, MD: Rowman & Littlefield, 2014.

Berntsen, John L. 'The Enemy Is Us: Eponymy in the Historiography of the Maasai.' *History in Africa* 7 (1980): 1–21.

Berntsen, John L. 'The Maasai and Their Neighbors: Variables of Interaction.' *African Economic History* 2 (1976): 1–11.

Berry, Sara. 'Debating the Land Question in Africa.' *Comparative Studies in Society and History* 44, no. 4 (2002): 638–68.

Blaikie, Piers M. and Harold Brookfield. *Land Degradation and Society*. New edition. London and New York: Routledge, 1991.

Bollig, Michael. 'Adaptive Cycles in the Savannah: Pastoral Specialization and Diversification in Northern Kenya.' *Journal of Eastern African Studies* 10, no. 1 (2 January 2016): 21–44.

Bollig, Michael. 'Ethnic Conflicts in North-West Kenya: Pokot-Turkana Raiding 1969–1984.' *Zeitschrift Für Ethnologie* 115 (1990): 73–90.

Bollig, Michael. 'Intra- and Interethnic Conflict in Northwest Kenya. A Multicausal Analysis of Conflict Behaviour.' *Anthropos* 88, no. 1/3 (1 January 1993): 176–84.

Bollig, Michael. *Risk Management in a Hazardous Environment: A Comparative Study of Two Pastoral Societies*. New York: Springer Science & Business Media, 2010.

Bollig, Michael. 'Staging Social Structures: Ritual and Social Organisation in an Egalitarian Society. The Pastoral Pokot of Northern Kenya.' *Ethnos* 65, no. 3 (1 January 2000): 341–65.

Bollig, Michael. 'Visions of Landscapes: An Introduction.' In *African Landscapes: Interdisciplinary Approaches*, edited by Michael Bollig and Olaf Bubenzer. New York: Springer Science & Business Media, 2009.

Bollig, Michael and Olaf Bubenzer. *African Landscapes: Interdisciplinary Approaches*. New York: Springer Science & Business Media, 2009.

Bollig, Michael and Carolyn Lesorogol. 'The "New Pastoral Commons" of Eastern and Southern Africa.' *International Journal of the Commons* 10, no. 2 (23 September 2016): 665–87.

Bollig, Michael and Diego A. Menestrey Schwieger. 'Fragmentation, Cooperation and Power: Institutional Dynamics in Natural Resource Governance in North-Western Namibia.' *Human Ecology* 42, no. 2 (1 April 2014): 167–81.

Bollig, Michael and Matthias Österle. 'Changing Communal Land Tenure in an East African Pastoral System: Institutions and Socio-Economic Transformations among the Pokot of NW Kenya.' *Zeitschrift Für Ethnologie* 133, no. 2 (1 January 2008): 301–22.

Bollig, Michael and Michael Schnegg. 'Introduction: Specialisation and Diversification among African Pastoral Societies.' In *Pastoralism in Africa: Past, Present and Future*, edited by Michael Bollig, Michael Schnegg and Hans-Peter Wotzka. New York: Berghahn Books, 2013.

Boserup, Ester. *The Conditions of Agricultural Growth: The Economics of Agriculture under Population Pressure*. London and New York: Faber, 1965.

Botkin, Daniel B. and Edward A. Keller. *Environmental Science: Earth as a Living Planet*. Hoboken, NJ: Wiley, 2003.

Branch, Daniel. *Defeating Mau, Creating Kenya*. Cambridge: Cambridge University Press, 2009.

Branch, Daniel. *Kenya: Between Hope and Despair, 1963–2011*. New Haven, CT: Yale University Press, 2011.

Burrell, Gibson and Gareth Morgan. *Sociological Paradigms and Organisational Analysis: Elements of the Sociology of Corporate Life*. Abingdon, Oxon, and New York: Routledge, 2017.

Carrier, Neil. 'Reviving Yaaku: Identity and Indigeneity in Northern Kenya.' *African Studies* 70, no. 2 (1 August 2011): 246–63.

Chabal, Patrick. *Africa: The Politics of Suffering and Smiling*. London: Zed Books, 2009.

Chimhowu, Admos and Phil Woodhouse. 'Customary vs Private Property Rights? Dynamics and Trajectories of Vernacular Land Markets in Sub-Saharan Africa.' *Journal of Agrarian Change* 6, no. 3 (1 July 2006): 346–71.

Comaroff, John L. and Jean Comaroff. *Ethnicity, Inc.* Chicago and London: The University of Chicago Press, 2009.

Cone, L.W., and J.F. Lipscomb. *The History of Kenya Agriculture*. Nairobi: University Press of Africa, 1972.

Creswell, John W. *Research Design: Qualitative, Quantitative, and Mixed Methods Approaches*. Thousand Oaks, CA: SAGE, 2014.

Cronk, Lee. 'From Hunters to Herders: Subsistence Change as a Reproductive Strategy among the Mukogodo.' *Current Anthropology* 30 (1989): 224–34.

Cronk, Lee. *From Mukogodo to Maasai: Ethnicity and Cultural Change in Kenya*. Boulder, CO: Westview Press, 2004.

Douglas, Mary. *In the Active Voice*. London: Routledge and Kegan Paul, 1982.

Droz, Yvan. 'Si Dieu Veut … Ou Suppôts de Satan? Incertitudes, Millénarisme et Sorcellerie Chez Les Migrants Kikuyu (As God Wills … or Satan's Henchmen? Lack of

Certitude, Millenarianism and Witchcraft among Kikuyu Migrants).' *Cahiers d'Études Africaines* 37, no. 145 (1 January 1997): 85–117.

Droz, Yvan and Beat Sottas. 'Partir Ou Rester ? Partir et Rester: Migrations Des Kikuyu Au Kenya.' *L'Homme* 37, no. 142 (1 April 1997): 69–88.

Duder, C.J. and G.L. Simpson. 'Land and Murder in Colonial Kenya: The Leroghi Land Dispute and the Powys "Murder" Case.' *The Journal of Imperial and Commonwealth History* 25, no. 3 (1 September 1997): 440–65.

Dunn, Kevin C. '"Sons of the Soil" and Contemporary State Making: Autochthony, Uncertainty and Political Violence in Africa.' *Third World Quarterly* 30, no. 1 (1 February 2009): 113–27.

Elden, Stuart. 'Land, Terrain, Territory.' *Progress in Human Geography; London* 34, no. 6 (December 2010): 799–817.

Elkins, Caroline. *Imperial Reckoning: The Untold Story of Britain's Gulag in Kenya*. New York: Henry Holt and Company, 2005.

Essed, Philomena. *Understanding Everyday Racism: An Interdisciplinary Theory*. Newbury Park, CA: SAGE, 1991.

Evans, Lauren A. and William M. Adams. 'Fencing Elephants: The Hidden Politics of Wildlife Fencing in Laikipia, Kenya.' *Land Use Policy* 51 (February 2016): 215–28.

Fairhead, James and Melissa Leach. *Misreading the African Landscape: Society and Ecology in a Forest–Savanna Mosaic*. Cambridge: Cambridge University Press, 1996.

Flury, Manuel. 'Small-Scale Farming and Changes of Land Use in the Highland of Laikipia, Kenya.' *Mountain Research and Development* 8, no. 4 (1 November 1988): 265–72.

Fortmann, Louise. 'Talking Claims: Discursive Strategies in Contesting Property.' *World Development* 23, no. 6 (June 1995): 1053–63.

Foucault, Michel. *The History of Sexuality, Vol. 1, An Introduction*. New York: Pantheon, 1978.

Fratkin, Elliot. 'The Samburu Laibon's Sorcery and the Death of Theodore Powys in Colonial Kenya.' *Journal of Eastern African Studies* 9, no. 1 (2 January 2015): 35–54.

Gadd, Michelle E. 'Conservation outside of Parks: Attitudes of Local People in Laikipia, Kenya.' *Environmental Conservation* 32, no. 1 (March 2005): 50–63.

Galaty, John. 'Reasserting the Commons: Pastoral Contestations of Private and State Lands in East Africa.' *International Journal of the Commons* 10, no. 2 (30 September 2016): 709–27.

Galaty, John and Pierre Bonte (eds). *Herders, Warriors and Traders: Pastoralism in Africa*. Boulder, CO: Westview, 1991.

Galvin, Kathleen A. 'Transitions: Pastoralists Living with Change.' *Annual Review of Anthropology* 38 (2009): 185–98.

Gang, G.Y. *The Middle and Later Stone Ages in the Mukogodo Hills of Central Kenya*. Oxford: BAR Oxford Ltd, 2001.

Gerber, Barbara. *Land Cover and Land Use of Laikipia District, Kenya: Preliminary Map Based on the Interpretation of LANDSAT Images*. Berne: Institute of Geography, University of Berne, 1984.

Geschiere, Peter. *The Perils of Belonging: Autochthony, Citizenship, and Exclusion in Africa and Europe*. Chicago: The University of Chicago Press, 2009.

Geschiere, Peter and Stephen Jackson. 'Autochthony and the Crisis of Citizenship: Democratization, and the Politics of Belonging.' *African Studies Review* 49, no. 2 (2006): 1–7.

Ghai, Yash P., J.P.W.B. McAuslan and Patrick McAuslan. *Public Law and Political Change in Kenya: A Study of the Legal Framework of Government from Colonial Times to the Present*. Nairobi: Oxford University Press, 1970.

Gichuki, F., H.P. Liniger, L. Macmillan, G. Schwilch and J. Gikonye. 'Scarce Water: Exploring Resource Availability, Use and Improved Management.' *Eastern and Southern Africa Geographical Journal* 8 (special issue) (1998): 15–28.

Graham, Maximilian D., William M. Adams and Gabriel N. Kahiro. 'Mobile Phone Communication in Effective Human–Elephant Conflict Management in Laikipia County, Kenya.' *Oryx* 46, no. 1 (2012): 137–44.

Graham, Maximilian D., Benedikt Notter, William M. Adams, Phyllis C. Lee and Tobias Nyumba Ochieng. 'Patterns of Crop-Raiding by Elephants, Loxodonta Africana, in Laikipia, Kenya, and the Management of Human–elephant Conflict.' *Systematics and Biodiversity* 8, no. 4 (2010): 435–45.

Gravesen, Marie and Eric Kioko. 'Cooperation in the Midst of Conflict: Cattle Raids and Land Deals in Laikipia and Narok.' *Africa* 89, no. 3 (August 2019): 562–85.

Gravesen, Marie. 'Twilight Institutions: Land-Buying Companies and Their Long-Term Implications in Laikipia, Kenya.' In *Land, Investment and Politics: Reconfiguring Africa's Pastoral Drylands*, edited by Jeremy Lind, Doris Okenwa and Ian Scoones. Woodbridge, Suffolk: James Currey, 2020.

Granovetter, Mark S. 'The Strength of Weak Ties.' *American Journal of Sociology* 78, no. 6 (1973): 1360–80.

Greiner, Clemens. 'Guns, Land, and Votes: Cattle Rustling and the Politics of Boundary (Re)making in Northern Kenya.' *African Affairs* 112, no. 447 (1 April 2013): 216–37.

Greiner, Clemens, Miguel Alvarez and Mathias Becker. 'From Cattle to Corn: Attributes of Emerging Farming Systems of Former Pastoral Nomads in East Pokot, Kenya.' *Society & Natural Resources* 26, no. 12 (1 December 2013): 1478–90.

Haraway, Donna. 'Situated Knowledges: The Science Question in Feminism and the Privilege of Partial Perspective.' *Feminist Studies* 14, no. 3 (1988): 575–99.

Hardin, Garrett. 'The Tragedy of the Commons.' *Journal of Natural Resources Policy Research* 1, no. 3 (8 July 2009): 243–53.

Hastrup, Kirsten. *A Passage to Anthropology: Between Experience and Theory*. London: Routledge, 1995.

Hayward, Matt W. and Graham I.H. Kerley. 'Fencing for Conservation: Restriction of Evolutionary Potential or a Riposte to Threatening Processes?' *Biological Conservation* 142, no. 1 (January 2009): 1–13.

Herren, Urs J. '"Droughts Have Different Tails": Response to Crises in Mukogodo Division, North Central Kenya, 1950s–1980s.' *Disasters* 15, no. 2 (1 June 1991): 93–107.

Hodgson, Dorothy. 'Becoming Indigenous in Africa.' *African Studies Review* 52, no. 3 (2009): 1–32.

Hodgson, Dorothy. *Being Maasai, Becoming Indigenous: Postcolonial Politics in a Neoliberal World*. Bloomington: Indiana University Press, 2011.

Hodgson, Dorothy. 'Precarious Alliances: The Cultural Politics and Structural Predicaments of the Indigenous Rights Movement in Tanzania.' *American Anthropologist* 104, no. 4 (2002): 1086–97.

Homewood, Katherine, Patti Kristjanson and P. Trench (eds). *Staying Maasai? Livelihoods, Conservation and Development in East African Rangelands*. New York: Springer-Verlag New York, 2009.

Hornsby, Charles. *Kenya: A History since Independence*. London: I.B. Tauris, 2012.

Huber, Martin and Chrisostom J. Opondo. *Land Use Change Scenarios for Subdivided Ranches in Laikipia District, Kenya*. Berne: Institute of Geography, University of Berne, 1995.

Hughes, David McDermott. *From Enslavement to Environmentalism: Politics On a Southern African Frontier*. Seattle: University of Washington Press, 2008.

Hughes, David McDermott. 'Third Nature: Making Space and Time in the Great Limpopo Conservation Area.' *Cultural Anthropology* 20, no. 2 (1 May 2005): 157–84.

Hughes, Lotte. *Moving the Maasai: A Colonial Misadventure*. Basingstoke: Palgrave Macmillan, 2006.

Hughes, Lotte. 'Rough Time in Paradise: Claims, Blames and Memory Making Around Some Protected Areas in Kenya.' *Conservation and Society* 5, no. 3 (2007): 307–30.

Huxley, Elspeth. *White Man's Country: Lord Delamere and the Making of Kenya*. London: Chatto & Windus, 1968.

Häkli, J. 'Re-Bordering Spaces.' In *The SAGE Handbook of Political Geography*, edited by K.R. Cox, M. Low and J. Robinson. Los Angeles: SAGE, 2008.

Igoe, J. 'Becoming Indigenous Peoples: Difference Inequality and the Globalization of East African Identity Politics.' *African Affairs* 105 (2006): 399–430.

Illiffe, John. *A Modern History of Tanganyika*. Cambridge: Cambridge University Press, 1984.

Joireman, Sandra F. *Where There Is No Government: Enforcing Property Rights in Common Law Africa*. Oxford: Oxford University Press, 2011.

Jones, S.B. *Boundary-Making: A Handbook for Statesmen, Treaty Editors and Boundary Commissions*. Washington, DC: Carnegie Endowment for International Peace, 1945.

Juul, Kristine, Christian Lund and Christopher Lund (eds). *Negotiating Property in Africa*. Portsmouth, NH: Heinemann, 2002.

Kanogo, Tabitha. *Squatters and the Roots of Mau Mau, 1905–63*. London: James Currey, 1987.

Kantai, Parselelo. 'In the Grip of the Vampire State: Maasai Land Struggles in Kenyan Politics.' *Journal of Eastern African Studies* 1, no. 1 (2007): 107–22.

Kanyinga, Karuti. 'The Legacy of the White Highlands: Land Rights, Ethnicity and the Post-2007 Election Violence in Kenya.' *Journal of Contemporary African Studies* 27, no. 3 (July 2009): 325–44.

Kinnaird, Margaret F. and Timothy G. O'Brien. 'Effects of Private-Land Use, Livestock Management, and Human Tolerance on Diversity, Distribution, and Abundance of Large African Mammals.' *Conservation Biology* 26, no. 6 (2012): 1026–39.

Kioko, Eric Mutisya. 'Conflict Resolution and Crime Surveillance in Kenya: Local Peace Committees and Nyumba Kumi.' *Africa Spectrum*, 52, no. 1 (2017): 3–32.

Kioko, Eric Mutisya. 'Turning Conflict into Coexistence: Cross-Cutting Ties and Institutions in the Agro-Pastoral Borderlands of Lake Naivasha Basin, Kenya.' PhD diss., Universität zu Köln, 2016.

Klopp, Jacqueline. 'Can Moral Ethnicity Trump Political Tribalism? The Struggle for Land and Nation in Kenya.' *African Studies* 61, no. 2 (1 December 2002): 269–94.

Klopp, Jacqueline. 'Electoral Despotism in Kenya: Land, Patronage and Resistance in the Multi-Party Context.' PhD diss., McGill University, 2001.

Klopp, Jacqueline. '"Ethnic Clashes" and Winning Elections: The Case of Kenya's Electoral Despotism.' *Canadian Journal of African Studies/Revue Canadienne Des Études Africaines* 35, no. 3 (2001): 473–517.

Kohler, Thomas. *Land Use in Transition: Aspects and Problems of Small-Scale Farming in a New Environment: The Example of Laikipia District, Kenya*. Berne: Institute of Geography, University of Berne, 1987.

Kohler, Thomas. 'Landbesitz Und Landnutzung Im Umbruch: Das Beispiel Des Laikipia Distrikts Nordwestlich Des Mt. Kenya (Land Use in Transition: The Example of Laikipia District, Northwest of Mt. Kenya).' *Erdkunde* 42, no. 1 (1988): 37–49.

Kohler, Thomas. *West Laikipia: Report on Small-Scale Farming and How It Could Be Assisted in Development*. Berne: Institute of Geography, University of Berne, 1987.

Kopytoff, Igor. *The African Frontier: The Reproduction of Traditional African Societies*. Bloomington: Indiana University Press, 1989.

Kratz, Corinne A. '"We've Always Done It like This ... except for a Few Details": "Tradition" and "Innovation" in Okiek Ceremonies.' *Comparative Studies in Society and History* 35, no. 1 (1 January 1993): 30–65.

Kuiper, Gerda. *Agro-industrial Labour in Kenya: Cut Flower Farms and Migrant Workers' Settlements*. Cham, Switzerland: Palgrave Macmillan, 2019.

Kvale, Steinar and Svend Brinkmann. *Interview – Introduktion til et Håndværk*. Second edition. Copenhagen: Hans Reitzels Forlag, 2009.

Kyle, Keith. *The Politics of the Independence of Kenya*. Basingstoke and New York: Palgrave, 1999.

LaDuke, Winona. *Recovering the Sacred: The Power of Naming and Claiming*. Boston, MA: South End Press, 2005.

Lane, Paul. 'An Outline of the Later Holocene Archaeology and Precolonial History of the Ewaso Basin, Kenya.' In *Conserving Wildlife in African Landscapes: Kenya's Ewaso Ecosystem*, edited by N. Georgiadis, J. Moss and D. Malleret-King. Washington, DC: Smithsonian Institution Scholarly Press, 2011.

Lane, Paul (ed.). *Landscape and Environmental Change in Semi-Arid Regions of East and Southern Africa: Developing Interdisciplinary Approaches*. Nairobi: British Institute of Eastern Africa, 2005.

Lefebvre, Henri. *The Production of Space*. Translated by Donald Nicholson-Smith. Oxford, UK and Cambridge, MA: Wiley-Blackwell, 1991.

Lentz, Carola. 'Land and the Politics of Belonging in Africa.' In *African Alternatives*, edited by Leo Haan, Ulf Engel and Patrick Chabal. Leiden: Brill, 2007.

Lentz, Carola, and Paul Nugent (eds). *Ethnicity in Ghana: The Limits of Invention*. New York: Palgrave Macmillan, 2000.

Leo, Christopher. *Land and Class in Kenya*. Harare: Nehands, 1989.

Leo, Christopher. 'Who Benefited from the Million-Acre Scheme? Towards a Class Analysis of Kenya's Transition to Independence.' *Canadian Journal of African Studies/Revue Canadienne Des Études Africaines* 15, no. 2 (1 January 1981): 201–22.

Lesorogol, Carolyn K. 'The Impact of Privatization on Land Inheritance among Samburu Pastoralists in Kenya.' *Development and Change* 41, no. 6 (2010): 1091–1116.

Leys, Colin. *Underdevelopment in Kenya: The Political Economy of Neo-Colonialism, 1964–1971*. Berkeley and Los Angeles: University of California Press, 1975.

Li, Tania Murray. *Land's End, Capitalist Relations on an Indigenous Frontier*. Durham, NC: Duke University Press, 2014.

Lind, Jeremy, and John Letai. 'Squeezed From All Sides: Changing Resource Tenure and Pastoralist Innovation on the Laikipia Plateau, Kenya.' In *Pastoralism and Development in Africa: Dynamic Change at the Margins*, edited by Andy Catly, Jeremy Lind and Ian Scoones. Abingdon, Oxon, and New York: Routledge, 2013.

Locke, John. *Two Treatises of Government*, edited by P. Laslett. Cambridge: Cambridge University Press, [1690] 1991.

Lonsdale, John. 'Kenya: Home County and African Frontiers.' In *Settlers and Expatriates: Britons Over the Seas*, edited by Robert Bickers. Oxford and New York: Oxford University Press, 2010.

Luhmann, Niklas. 'Familiarity, Confidence, Trust: Problems and Alternatives.' In *Trust: Making and Breaking Cooperative Relations*, edited by Diego Gambetta. Oxford: Department of Sociology, University of Oxford, 2000.

Luhmann, Niklas. 'Trust and Power,' *Studies in Soviet Thought* 23, no. 3 (1982): 266–70.

Lund, Christian. 'Access to Property and Citizenship: Marginalization in a Context of Legal Pluralism.' In *Legal Pluralism and Development: Scholars and Practitioners in Dialogue*, edited by Brian Z. Tamanaha, Caroline Mary Sage and Michael J.V. Woolcock. Cambridge: Cambridge University Press, 2012.

Lund, Christian. 'The Ethics of Fruitful Misunderstanding.' *Journal of Research Practice* 10, no. 2 (1 July 2014): Article N4.

Lund, Christian. *Local Politics and the Dynamics of Property in Africa*. Cambridge: Cambridge University Press, 2008.

Lund, Christian. 'The Past and Space: On Arguments in African Land Control.' *Africa* 83, Special Issue, no. 1 (2013): 14–35.

Lund, Christian. 'Property and Citizenship: Conceptually Connecting Land Rights and Belonging in Africa.' *Africa Spectrum* 46, no. 3 (14 March 2012): 71–75.

Lund, Christian. 'Twilight Institutions: Public Authority and Local Politics in Africa.' *Development and Change* 37, no. 4 (2006): 685–705.

Lynch, Gabrielle. *I Say to You: Ethnic Politics and the Kalenjin in Kenya*. Chicago: The University of Chicago Press, 2011.

Lynch, Gabrielle. 'Kenya's New Indigenes: Negotiating Local Identities in a Global Context.' *Nations and Nationalism* 17, no. 1 (1 January 2011): 148–67.

Lynch, Gabrielle. 'Negotiating Ethnicity: Identity Politics in Contemporary Kenya.' *Review of African Political Economy* 33, no. 107 (1 March 2006): 49–65.

Lynch, Gabrielle. 'The Politics of Ethnicity.' In *Routledge Handbook of African Politics*, edited by David Anderson, Nicholas Cheeseman and Andrea Scheibler. Abingdon, Oxon: Routledge, 2013.

Lynch, Gabrielle. 'The Wars of Who Belongs Where: The Unstable Politics of Autochthony on Kenya's Mt Elgon.' *Ethnopolitics* 10, no. 3–4 (1 November 2011): 391–410.

Lynch, Gabrielle. 'What's in a Name? The Politics of Naming Ethnic Groups in Kenya's Cherangany Hills.' *Journal of Eastern African Studies* 10, no. 1 (2 January 2016): 208–27.

Løvschal, Mette, Dorthe Døjbak Håkonsson and Irene Amoke. 'Are Goats the New Elephants in the Room? Changing Land-Use Strategies in Greater Mara, Kenya.' *Land Use Policy* 80 (1 January 2019): 395–99.

Malthus, Thomas. *An Essay on the Principle of Population*. London: Printed for J. Johnson, in Paul's Church-Yard, 1798.

McCann, James C. *Green Land, Brown Land, Black Land: An Environmental History of Africa, 1800–1990*. First edition. Portsmouth, NH: Heinemann, 1999.

Mead, Margaret. *Sex and Temperament in Three Primitive Societies*. London and Henley: Routledge and Kegan Paul, 1977.

Meiu, George Paul. *Ethno-Erotic Economies: Sexuality, Money, and Belonging in Kenya.* Chicago: The University of Chicago Press, 2017.

Moore, Donald S., Jake Kosek and Anand Pandian (eds). *Race, Nature, and the Politics of Difference.* Durham, NC: Duke University Press, 2003.

Moore, Sally Falk. 'Law and Social Change: The Semi-Autonomous Social Field as an Appropriate Subject of Study.' *Law & Society Review* 7, no. 4 (Summer 1973): 719–46.

Mungeam, Gordon Hudson. *British Rule in Kenya, 1895–1912: The Establishment of Administration in the East Africa Protectorate.* Oxford: Clarendon, 1966.

Muriuki, Godfrey. *A History of the Kikuyu, 1500–1900.* New York: Oxford University Press, 1974.

Musambayi, Katumanga. 'After the Floods – the Rainbow: Contextualising NARC's Election Victory – Lessons Learnt and the Challenges Ahead.' In *Political Succession in East Africa,* edited by Chris Maina Peter and Fritz Kopsieker. Nairobi: Kituo Cha Katiba and Friedrich Ebert Stiftung, 2006.

Newman, D. 'The Lines That Continue to Separate Us: Borders in Our "Borderless" World.' *Progress in Human Geography* 30, no. 2 (2006): 143–61.

Nightingale, Andrea. 'A Feminist in the Forest: Situated Knowledges and Mixed Methods in Natural Resource Management.' *ACME* 1, no. 2 (2003): 77–90.

Nooteboom, Bart. 'Trust, Opportunism and Governance: A Process and Control Model.' *Organization Studies* 17, no. 6 (1 November 1996): 985–1010.

Nottidge, C.P.R. and J.R. Goldsack. *The Million-Acre Settlement Scheme 1962–1966.* Nairobi: Settlement Department, 1966.

Ochieng, William. *East African Protectorate. A Modern History of Kenya: 1895–1980.* Ibadan: Evans Brothers, 1989.

Ogot, Bethwell A. *Kenya before 1900.* Nairobi: East African Publishing House, 1976.

Ogutu, Joseph O., Hans-Peter Piepho, Mohamed Y. Said, Gordon O. Ojwang, Lucy W. Njino, Shem C. Kifugo and Patrick W. Wargute. 'Extreme Wildlife Declines and Concurrent Increase in Livestock Numbers in Kenya: What Are the Causes?' *PLOS ONE* 11, no. 9 (27 September 2016): 1–46.

Ostrom, Elinor. *Governing the Commons.* Cambridge: Cambridge University Press, 2015.

Oucho, John O. *Undercurrents of Ethnic Conflicts in Kenya.* Leiden: Brill, 2002.

Peet, Richard, and Michael Watts. 'Liberating Political Ecology.' In *Liberation Ecologies,* edited by Richard Peet and Michael Watts. Abingdon, Oxon: Routledge, 2004.

Peet, Richard, and Michael Watts (eds). *Liberation Ecologies.* Second edition. Abingdon, Oxon: Routledge, 2004.

Peluso, Nancy Lee. 'Fruit Trees and Family Trees in an Anthropogenic Forest: Ethics of Access, Property Zones, and Environmental Change in Indonesia.' *Comparative Studies in Society and History* 38, no. 3 (July 1996): 510–48.

Peluso, Nancy Lee. 'Coercing Conservation: The Politics of State Resource Control.' *Global Environmental Change* 3 (1993): 199–217.

Peluso, Nancy Lee and Christian Lund. 'New Frontiers of Land Control: Introduction.' *The Journal of Peasant Studies* 38, no. 4 (1 October 2011): 667–81.

Pestalozzi, P. 'Historical and Present Day Agricultural Change on Mt. Kenya.' In *Mount Kenya Area: Contributions to Ecology and Socio-economy*, edited by Matthias Winiger. Berne: Geographica Bernensia, 1986.

Peters, Pauline. 'Inequality and Social Conflict over Land in Africa.' *Journal of Agrarian Change* 4, no. 3 (2004): 269–314.

Phillips, L. and M.W. Jørgensen. *Discourse Analysis as Theory and Method*. London: SAGE, 2002.

Polanyi, Karl. *The Great Transformation: The Political and Economic Origins of Our Time*. Second edition. Boston, MA: Beacon Press, 2001.

Pratt, Mary Louise. *Imperial Eyes: Travel Writing and Transculturation*. London and New York: Routledge, 1992.

Rasmussen, Jacob. 'Outwitting the Professor of Politics? Mungiki Narratives of Political Deception and Their Role in Kenyan Politics.' *Journal of Eastern African Studies* 4, no. 3 (1 November 2010): 435–49.

Ranger, Terence O. 'The Invention of Tradition in Colonial Africa.' In *The Invention of Tradition*, edited by Eric Hobsbawm and Terence Ranger. Cambridge: Cambridge University Press, 1983.

Ribot, Jesse. 'Theorizing Access: Forest Profits along Senegal's Charcoal Commodity Chain.' *Development and Change* 29, no. 2 (1 April 1998): 307–41.

Ribot, Jesse, and Nancy Lee Peluso. 'A Theory of Access.' *Rural Sociology* 68, no. 2 (2003): 153–81.

Rutten, Marcel. 'Fresh Killings: The Njoro and Laikipia Violence in the 1997 Kenyan Election Aftermath.' In *Out for the Count : The 1997 General Elections and Prospects for Democracy in Kenya*, edited by Marcel Rutten and Alamin Mazrui. Kampala: Fountain Pub. Ltd, 2001.

Rutten, Marcel and Alamin Mazrui. *Out for the Count : The 1997 General Elections and Prospects for Democracy in Kenya*. Kampala: Fountain Pub. Ltd, 2001.

Schlager E. and E. Ostrom. 'Property Rights Regimes and Natural Resources: A Conceptual Analysis.' *Land Economics* 68, no. 3 (1992): 249–62.

Schwarz M. and M. Thompson. *Divided We Stand: Redefining Politics, Technology and Social Choice*. Hemel Hempstead: Harvester Wheatsheaf, 1990.

Shipton, Parker. *Mortgaging the Ancestors: Ideologies of Attachment in Africa*. New Haven, CT: Yale University Press, 2009.

Sheridan, M.J. 'Introduction: The Ecology of Fencing.' *Africa* 78 (2008): 153–156.

Sifuna, Nixon. 'Wildlife Damage and Its Impact on Public Attitudes towards Conservation: A Comparative Study of Kenya and Botswana, with Particular Reference to Kenya's Laikipia Region and Botswana's Okavango Delta Region.' *Journal of Asian and African Studies* 45, no. 3 (1 June 2010): 274–96.

Smith, Adam. *An Inquiry into the Nature and Causes of the Wealth of Nations*. First edition. London: W. Strahan, 1776.

Smith, Patrick D. and Maureen H. McDonough. 'Beyond Public Participation: Fairness in Natural Resource Decision Making.' *Society & Natural Resources* 14, no. 3 (1 March 2001): 239–49.

Sorrenson, M.P.K. *Land Reform in the Kikuyu Country: A Study in Government Policy*. London: Oxford University Press, 1967.

Sorrenson, M.P.K. *Origins of European Settlement in Kenya*. New York: Oxford University Press, 1968.

Sottas, Beat. 'Aspects of a Peasant Mode of Production: Exchange and the Extent of Sufficiency among Smallholders in West Laikipia, Kenya.' *Journal of Asian and African Studies* 27, no. 3 (1 July 1992): 271–95.

Sottas B. and V. Wiesmann. 'Practices of Assistance among Small Scale Farmers of Marura: Direction, Extent and Relevance. Laikipia.' Mt Kenya Papers D10, Laikipia Research Programme. Nanyuki and Nairobi: University of Berne, 1993.

Spear, Thomas and Richard Waller. *Being Maasai: Ethnicity and Identity in East Africa*. London: James Currey, 1993.

Spencer, Paul. *Nomads in Alliance: Symbiosis and Growth Among the Rendille and Samburu of Kenya*. Oxford: Oxford University Press, 1973.

Spencer, Paul. *The Samburu: A Study in Geocentracy*. London and New York: Taylor & Francis, 2003.

Spierenburg, M. and H. Wels. '"Securing Space": Mapping and Fencing in Transfrontier Conservation in Southern Africa.' *Space and Culture* 9, (2006): 294–312.

Straight, Bilinda. 'Making Sense of Violence in the "Badlands" of Kenya.' *Anthropology and Humanism* 34, no. 1 (2009): 21–30.

Taylor, D., P.J. Lane, V. Muiruri, A. Ruttledge, R. Gaj McKeever, T. Nolan, P. Kenny and R. Goodhue. 'Mid- to Late-Holocene Vegetation Dynamics on the Laikipia Plateau, Kenya.' *The Holocene* 15, no. 6 (1 September 2005): 837–46.

Thenya, Thuita. 'Challenges of Conservation of Dryland Shallow Waters, Ewaso Narok Swamp, Laikipia District, Kenya.' *Hydrobiologia* 458, no. 1–3 (1 August 2001): 107–19.

Thompson M. and A. Wildavsky 'A Poverty Distinction: From Economic Homogeneity to Cultural Heterogeneity in the Classification of Poor People.' *Policy Sciences* 19 (1986): 163–99.

Throup, David. *Economic and Social Origins of Mau Mau*. Nairobi: Heinemann, 1988.

Throup, David and Charles Hornsby. *Multi-Party Politics in Kenya: The Kenyatta and Moi States and the Triumph of the System in the 1992 Election*. London: James Currey Publishers, 1998.

Tiffen, Mary, Michael Mortimore and Francis Gichuki. *More People, Less Erosion: Environmental Recovery in Kenya*. First edition. Chichester, NY: Wiley, 1994.

Trotter, R.I., J. Schensul and K. Kostick. 'Theories and Methods in Applied Anthropology.' In *Handbook of Methods in Cultural Anthropology*, edited by H. Russell Bernard and Clarence C. Gravlee. Lanham, MD: Rowman & Littlefield, 2014.

Ulrich, Anne, Chinwe Ifejika Speranza, Paul Roden, Boniface Kiteme, Urs Wiesmann and Marcus Nüsser. 'Small-Scale Farming in Semi-Arid Areas: Livelihood Dynamics between 1997 and 2010 in Laikipia, Kenya.' *Journal of Rural Studies* 28, no. 3 (1 July 2012): 241–51.

Vandergeest, Peter. 'Mapping Nature: Territorialization of Forest Rights in Thailand.' *Society and Natural Resources: An International Journal* 9, no. 2 (1996): 159–75.

Van Zwanenberg, R. *The Agricultural History of Kenya to 1939*. Nairobi: East African Pub. House, 1972.

Waller, Richard. 'Bringing Murder to Court: The Death of Theodore Powys.' *African Studies Association Annual Meetings*. New York, 2007.

Waller, Richard. 'Kidongoi's Kin: Prophecy and Power in Maasailand.' In *Revealing Prophets: Prophecy in Eastern African History*, edited by David Anderson and Douglas Hamilton Johnson. London: James Currey Publishers, 1995.

Waller, Richard. 'The Maasai and the British 1895–1905. The Origins of an Alliance.' *The Journal of African History* 17, no. 4 (1976): 529–53.

Waller, Richard. 'Towards a Contextualisation of Policing in Colonial Kenya.' *Journal of Eastern African Studies* 4, no. 3 (1 November 2010): 525–41.

Wasserman, Gary. 'Continuity and Counter-Insurgency: The Role of Land Reform in Decolonizing Kenya, 1962–70.' *Canadian Journal of African Studies/Revue Canadienne Des Études Africaines* 7, no. 1 (1 January 1973): 133–48.

Wasserman, Gary. 'European Settlers and Kenya Colony Thoughts on a Conflicted Affair.' *African Studies Review* 17, no. 2 (1 September 1974): 425–34.

Wasserman, Gary. *Politics of Decolonization: Kenya, Europeans and the Land*. Cambridge: Cambridge University Press, 2009.

Watkins, O.F. 'The Report of the Kenya Land Commission, September, 1933.' *Journal of the Royal African Society* 33, no. 132 (1934): 207–16.

Watson, Elizabeth E. 'A "Hardening of Lines": Landscape, Religion and Identity in Northern Kenya.' *Journal of Eastern African Studies* 4, no. 2 (2010): 201–20.

Wenneberg, S.B. *Socialkonstruktivisme – Positioner, Problemer og Perspektiver*. First edition. Copenhagen: Samfundslitteratur, 2000.

Yurco, Kayla. 'Herders and Herdsmen: The Remaking of Pastoral Livelihoods in Laikipia, Kenya.' *Pastoralism* 7, no. 15 (19 June 2017).

Court Cases

Environment and Land Court of Kenya, Malindi, Land Case No. 108 of 2011: Kahindi Ngala Mwagandi vs Mtana Lewa.

High Court of Kenya, Nakuru, Civil Suit (HCCC) No. 19 of 1982.
High Court of Kenya, Nyeri, Civil Suit (HCCC) No. 80 of 1983: Wilson Arap Birgen, John Muritu Karumba, Joseph Murithi Maingu, Kaiga Kamau and Koske Maritim vs Lorien Ranching Company Limited.
High Court of Kenya, Nyeri, Civil Suit (HCCC) No. 253 of 1994: Wilson Arap Birgen, John Muritu Karumba, Joseph Murithi Maingu, Kaiga Kamau and Koske Maritim vs Lorien Ranching Company Limited.
High Court of Kenya, Nyeri, Civil Suit (HCCC) No. 248 of 1998: Lorien Ranching Company Limited vs Wilson Arap Birgen, John Muritu Karumba, Joseph Murithi Maingu, Kaiga Kamau and Koske Maritim. (Ruled on 15 March 2015.)

Government Documents

Akuwumi, Hon. Justice A.M. *Report of the Judicial Commission Appointed to Inquire into Tribal Clashes in Kenya*. Nairobi: Government Printer, 2001. https://digitalcommons.law.seattleu.edu/cgi/viewcontent.cgi?article=1009&context=tjrc-gov. Accessed 11 July 2020.
Kenya National Assembly. *Kenya National Assembly Official Record*. Hansard, 2002. https://books.google.co.ke/books?id=6Y9CmdV7yu8C&pg=PT10&dq=Thome+farmers+company+magugu&hl=en&sa=X&ved=0CBsQ6AEwAGoVChMI4LeZ5tIyQIViPEUCh39gQ25#v=onepage&q=Thome%20farmers%20company%20magugu&f=false. Accessed 11 November 2015.
Kenya National Bureau of Statistics (KNBS). *The 2009 Kenya Population and Housing Census*. Nairobi: Government of Kenya, 2009. https://www.knbs.or.ke/2009-kenya-population-and-housing-census-analytical-reports. Accessed 29 September 2017.
Kenya Land Commission (KLC). Report. Evidence and memoranda. Vol. II, Rift Valley Province. Nairobi: Government Printer, 1934.
Kenya Land Commission (KLC). Report. Evidence and memoranda. Vol. II, Rift Valley Province, Part II, Chapter VI. Nairobi: Government Printer, 1934.
Kenya Land Commission (KLC). Report. Evidence and memoranda. Vol. II, Rift Valley Province, Part II, Chapter VII. Nairobi: Government Printer, 1934.
Kenya Land Commission (KLC). Report. Evidence and memoranda. Vol. II, Rift Valley Province, Part II, Chapter VIII. Nairobi: Government Printer, 1934.
Kenya Land Commission (KLC). Report. Evidence and memoranda. Vol. II, Rift Valley Province, Part III, Chapter I. Nairobi: Government Printer, 1934.
Kenya Land Commission (KLC). Report. Evidence and memoranda. Vol. II, Rift Valley Province, Appendix. Nairobi: Government Printer, 1935.
The National Council for Law Reporting with the Authority of the Attorney General. *The Constitution of Kenya*, 2010.

The National Council for Law Reporting with the Authority of the Attorney General. *The Limitation of Actions Act*, Chapter 22, Section 38, 2010.

Republic of Kenya. *Kenya Population Census 1969*. Volume 1. Statistics Division Ministry of Economic Planning and Development. Nairobi: Government Printer, 1970. http://www.knbs.or.ke/index.php?option=com_phocadownload&view=category&id=100:population-and-housing-census&Itemid=1176. Accessed 16 February 2015.

Republic of Kenya. *Kenya Population Census 1979*. Volume 1. Central Bureau of Statistics. Nairobi: Government Printer, 1981. http://www.knbs.or.ke/index.php?option=com_phocadownload&view=category&id=100:population-and-housing-census&Itemid=1176. Accessed 16 February 2015.

Republic of Kenya. *Kenya Population Census 1989*. Volume 1. Central Bureau of Statistics. Nairobi: Government Printer, 1994. http://www.knbs.or.ke/index.php?option=com_phocadownload&view=category&id=100:population-and-housing-census&Itemid=1176. Accessed 16 February 2015.

Media Sources

Barasa, Lucas, and Kennedy Kimanthi. 'President to Hand Out 200,000 Title Deeds.' *The Daily Nation*. 27 February 2015.

BBC Africa. 'Kuki Gallmann's Kenya Safari Lodge Burned Down.' 30 March 2017. http://www.bbc.com/news/world-africa-39442270. Accessed 29 September 2017.

Cruise, Adam and Bibi van der Zee. 'Armed Herders Invade Laikipia's Most Important Wildlife Conservancy.' *The Guardian*, 2 February 2017. https://www.theguardian.com/environment/2017/feb/02/armed-herders-elephant-kenya-wildlife-laikipia. Accessed 12 January 2020.

The Daily Nation. 'Bogus Land Buyers Warned.' 1 July 1980.

The Daily Nation. 'Conservationist Shot at Her Laikipia Conservancy.' 23 April 2017. http://www.nation.co.ke/news/Kuki-Gallman-shot-and-injured/1056-3900476-2j06 2v/index.html. Accessed 2 August 2017.

The Daily Nation. 'Evicted Group in Plea.' 19 February 1994.

The Daily Nation. 'Ex-Governors Pledge to Support Successors.' 22 August 2017. http://www.nation.co.ke/counties/Nakuru-Laikipia-Nyandarua-governors/1107872-4065998-0ce3rsz/index.html. Accessed 30 August 2017.

The Daily Nation. 'Flashback: G.G. Kariuki.' 17 November 2013. http://mobile.nation.co.ke/lifestyle/GG-Kariuki/1950774-2076802-format-xhtml-cdeut2/index.html. Accessed 25 April 2017.

The Daily Nation. '#Frontrow: New Governors Had Better Deliver or Be Ready to Serve.' 22 August 2017. http://www.nation.co.ke/lifestyle/DN2/New-governors-should-deliver/957860-4066692-ppwtsh/index.html. Accessed 30 August 2017.

The Daily Nation. 'Gema Boss Calls for Hard Work at Big Land Ballot.' 30 August 1976.

The Daily Nation. 'Hunting Ban Fails to End Bloodbath.' 26 August 2013. http://mobile.nation.co.ke/lifestyle/Hunting-ban-fails-to-end-bloodbath/1950774-1968130-format-xhtml-7sn4fo/index.html. Accessed 18 April 2017.

The Daily Nation. 'I've Learnt Much, Says Grateful G.G.' 21 December 1988.

The Daily Nation. 'Inquiry Urged into Ownership of Plots.' 16 December 1967.

The Daily Nation. 'Judgement Awaited as Sh7 m Land Closes.' 24 January 1985.

The Daily Nation. 'Land Buyers Warned.' 8 December 1980.

The Daily Nation. 'Lawyers Sit on Public Money.' 27 October 1980.

The Daily Nation. 'Magugu Mastered Art of Political Survival.' 16 September 2013. http://www.nation.co.ke/news/politics/Magugu-mastered-art-of-political-survival-/1064-1509146-n6c636z/index.html. Accessed 19 April 2017.

The Daily Nation. 'Man Shot Dead.' 22 January 1992.

The Daily Nation. 'Pay Up or Lose the Land, G.G. Warns Farmers.' 24 March 1980.

The Daily Nation. 'Politicians, Businessmen behind Cattle Raids: Intelligence Report.' 21 January 2017. http://www.nation.co.ke/news/Politicians--businessmen-fuelling-cattle-raids/1056-3781620-txq5s5z/index.html. Accessed 30 January 2017.

The Daily Nation. 'Sale of Farm Shares Banned.' 15 July 1980.

The East African Standard. 'Squatter System a Menace to White Settlement.' 11 January 1934.

Gettleman, Jeffrey. 'Loss of Fertile Land Fuels "Looming Crisis" Across Africa.' *The New York Times*, 29 July 2017. https://www.nytimes.com/2017/07/29/world/africa/africa-climate-change-kenya-land-disputes.html. Accessed 29 September 2017.

Gikandi, Boniface and Lydiah Nyawira. 'President Uhuru Kenyatta Issues Kihiu Mwiri Titles, Says No More Land-Buying Companies.' *The Standard*, 17 September 2015.

Gitonga, Muchiri. 'Drive Herders back to Samburu, Leaders Demand.' *The Daily Nation*, 19 January 2017. http://www.ipsos.co.ke/NEWBASE_EXPORTS/CARE%20International/161214_Daily%20Nation%20-%20Wednesday_19_c37f6.pdf. Accessed 29 September 2017.

The Home News. 'Commentary: A Wrong Way to Approach Land Issues.' 9–15 September 2004.

The Home News. 'Ethnic Clashes.' 16–31 August 2001.

The Home News. 'From the Diary of a Senior Citizen, with Kigera Theuri: Apartheid in the White Highlands.' 19–24 August 2004.

The Home News. 'Letter to the Editor, Marura Swamp: Game Warden is Wrong.' 14–20 October 2004.

The Home News. 'The Maasai in War Cry.' 29 July–4 August 2004.

The Home News. 'Maasai Land Claim.' 29 July–4 August 2004.

The Home News. 'Marura Swamp in Crisis.' 7–13 October 2004.

The Home News. 'The Samburu–Pokot War.' 1–7 September 2006.

The Home News. 'Shareholders' Demo.' 3 August 2005.

Kenya NTV. 'What Is Ailing Laikipia: Death and Destruction Visits Ranches in Laikipia,' 12 February 2017. https://www.youtube.com/watch?v=2JrOuhmEoMk. Accessed 29 September 2017.

Kimathi, Joe. 'Major rift in KANU Laikipia: Two Rival "Chairmen" Elected to Replace G.G.' *The Daily Nation*, 6 November 1984.

Kiplagat, Sam. 'Even in Old Age Land Tussle Splits Group.' *The Daily Nation*, 12 January 2010.

Leithead, Alastair. 'Are Kenya Ranch Invasions Driven by Drought or Politics?' BBC News. 4 February 2017. http://www.bbc.com/news/world-africa-38866389. Accessed 29 September 2017.

Munyeki, James and Patel Okumu. 'Laikipia Senator G.G. Kariuki Is Dead.' *The Standard*. 30 June 2017. https://www.standardmedia.co.ke/article/2001245479/laikipia-senator-gg-kariuki-is-dead. Accessed 23 August 2017.

Muraya, Joseph. 'Hundreds Flee Their Homes in Latest Wave of Violence between Samburu and Turkanas.' *Capital News*, 9 November 2016. https://www.capitalfm.co.ke/news/2016/11/hundreds-flee-their-homes-in-latest-wave-of-violence-between-samburu-and-turkanas/. Accessed 29 September 2017.

Mwangi, Njeri. 'Court Orders Kones Not to Hold Meeting.' *The Daily Nation*, 28 May 1994.

Mwathi, Moses. 'Mutukanio Shareholders to get Title Deeds – G.G.,' *The Home News*, 27 January–3 February 2004.

Ndirangu, Nicholas. '10,000 Titles Ready.' *The Daily Nation*, 9 March 1992.

Ngugi wa Mbugua. 'Building Castles on Shaky Ground.' *The Daily Nation*, 2 August 1991.

Nyamai, Faith. 'Court Postpones Ruling in Moi Land Case.' *The Daily Nation*, 20 January 2015.

Reuters. 'Britain Rejects Kenya Loans Idea.' *The Daily Nation*, 29 July 1967.

The Star. 'Armed Herders Invade Laikipia Ranch, Harass Elephants as Tourists Watch.' 30 January 2017. http://www.the-star.co.ke/news/2017/01/30/armed-herders-invade-laikipia-ranch-harass-elephants-as-tourists-watch_c1496603. Accessed 2 August 2017.

The Star. 'British Father of Two Shot Dead at Sosian Ranch in Laikipia.' 3 June 2017. http://www.the-star.co.ke/news/2017/03/06/british-father-of-two-shot-dead-at-sosian-ranch-in-laikipia_c1518914. Accessed 2 August 2017.

The Star. 'The Diary of Seven Months of Attacks on Kifuku Farm in Laikipia.' 1 February 2017. http://www.the-star.co.ke/news/2017/02/01/the-diary-of-seven-months-of-attacks-on-kifuku-farm-in-laikipia_c1498811. Accessed 2 February 2017.

The Star. 'Don't Re-Elect Lempurkel, Uhuru Tells Laikipia Voters.' 29 July 2017. http://www.the-star.co.ke/news/2017/07/29/dont-re-elect-lempurkel-uhuru-tells-laikipia-voters_c1606078. Accessed 30 August 2017.

The Star. 'EACC Probes Four Laikipia Land Buying Companies.' 27 August 2016.

The Star. 'Is Rebellion the Next Phase of Laikipia Violence?' 5 June 2017. http://www.the-star.co.ke/news/2017/06/05/is-rebellion-the-next-phase-of-laikipia-violence_c1574344. Accessed 2 August 2017.

The Star. 'Kenya Election Heats up Conflicts over Ethnicity, Laikipia Land.' 7 August 2017. http://www.the-star.co.ke/news/2017/08/07/kenya-election-heats-up-conflicts-over-ethnicity-laikipia-land_c1612075. Accessed 30 August 2017.

The Star. 'Laikipia Clashes Persist as MPs, Cops, Barons Blamed.' 17 November 2016. http://www.the-star.co.ke/news/2016/11/17/laikipia-clashes-persist-as-mps-cops-barons-blamed_c1456695. Accessed 2 August 2017.

The Star. 'Laikipia Farm Invasions Continue.' 15 November 2016. http://www.the-star.co.ke/news/2016/11/15/laikipia-farm-invasions-continue_c1456484. Accessed 2 August 2017.

The Star. 'Laikipia Invasions Are Political, Governor Hopeful Says after Kifuku Ranch Raid.' 21 May 2017. http://www.the-star.co.ke/news/2017/05/21/laikipia-invasions-are-political-governor-hopeful-says-after-kifuku_c1564943. Accessed 2 August 2017.

The Star. 'Laikipia Land Row Ends.' 6 May 2015. https://www.the-star.co.ke/counties/central/2015-05-06-laikipia-land-row-ends/. Accessed 11 July 2020.

The Star. 'Land Invasion Wrecks Laikipia.' 19 January 2017. http://www.the-star.co.ke/news/2017/01/19/land-invasion-wrecks-laikipia_c1489820. Accessed 30 January 2017.

The Star. 'MP Lempurkel Denies Involvement in Suyian Ranch Invasion on Sunday.' 30 January 2017. http://www.the-star.co.ke/news/2017/01/30/mp-lempurkel-denies-involvement-in-suyian-ranch-invasion-on-sunday_c1496907. Accessed 30 January 2017.

The Star. 'Pokot Gunmen Invade Laikipia Conservancy, Kill Wild Animals.' 10 January 2017. http://www.the-star.co.ke/news/2017/01/10/pokot-gunmen-invade-laikipia-conservancy-kill-wild-animals_c1485383. Accessed 30 January 2017.

The Star. 'Residents of Laikipia Are Tired of Violence, Association Says.' 21 August 2017. http://www.the-star.co.ke/news/2017/08/21/residents-of-laikipia-are-tired-of-violence-association-says_c1619801. Accessed 30 August 2017.

Wachira, Patrick. 'Kihika Kimani: The Master Political Clown.' *The Standard*, 6 June 2010. https://www.standardmedia.co.ke/article/2000010993/kihika-kimani-the-master-political-clown. Accessed 19 April 2017.

Wanzala, Ouma. '800,000 Deeds Ready for Issue.' *The Daily Nation*, 12 February 2015.

Grey Literature

Agricultural Finance Corporation. Title deed, David Partridge, 1 July 1963.

Barnes, Juliet. *The Ghosts of Happy Valley: Searching for the Lost World of Africa's Infamous Aristocrats*. Reprint edition. London: Aurum Press Ltd, 2014.

Blixen, Karen. *Out of Africa*. New edition. London: Penguin Classics, 2001.

CETRAD (Centre for Training and Integrated Research in Arid and Semi-Arid Land Development, Nanyuki, Kenya) and CDE (Centre for Development and Environment, University of Berne, Switzerland). Socio-Ecological Database, 2007.

Cresswell, Tim. *Fence*. London: Penned in the Margins, 2015.

East African Women's League. 'Golden Jubilee Scrapbook.' Laikipia Branch, 1968.

Frost, Robert. *North of Boston*. London: David Nutt, 1916.

Gallmann, Kuki. *I Dreamed of Africa*. London: Penguin Books, 1992.

Gavaghan, Terence. *Of Lions and Dung Beetles*. Ilfracombe, Devon: Arthur H. Stockwell, 1999.

Gitanga, John, Tara Hetz, Agnes Maille, Stanley Ngatia and Rebecca Younan. *What Do the Children and Youth of Laikipia Think about Rhinos and Rhino Conservation? An Assessment of the Perceptions on Rhinos and Rhino Conservation from Children and Youth of Laikipia*. Nanyuki, Kenya: Laikipia Wildlife Forum, March 2017.

Graham, Max and Charles Musyoki. 'Wildlife Conservation Strategy For Laikipia County 2012–2030.' Nanyuki, Kenya: Laikipia Wildlife Forum, 2012.

Hardwick, Alfred Arkell. *An Ivory Trader in North Kenia; The Record of an Expedition through Kikuyu to Galla-Land in East Equatorial Africa. With an Account of the Rendili and Burkeneji Tribes*. London: Longmans, Green, and Company, 1903.

Human Rights Watch (HRW). *Ballots to Bullets: Organized Political Violence and Kenya's Crisis of Governance*. Vol. 20, no. 1(A) (March 2006). https://www.hrw.org/report/2008/03/16/ballots-bullets/organized-political-violence-and-kenyas-crisis-governance. Accessed 11 July 2020.

Human Rights Watch (HRW). *Divide and Rule: State-Sponsored Ethnic Violence in Kenya*. New York: Human Rights Watch, 1993. https://www.hrw.org/report/1993/11/01/divide-and-rule-state-sponsored-ethnic-violence-kenya. Accessed 11 July 2020.

Human Rights Watch (HRW). *Multipartyism Betrayed in Kenya: Continuing Rural Violence and Restrictions on Freedom of Speech and Assembly*. Vol. 6, no. 5 (July 1994). https://www.hrw.org/report/1994/07/01/multipartyism-betrayed-kenya/continuing-rural-violence-and-restrictions-freedom. Accessed 11 July 2020.

Huxley, Elspeth. *The Flame Trees of Thika: Memories of an African Childhood*. Edition Unstated edition. New York: Penguin Classics, 2000.

Huxley, Elspeth. *The Mottled Lizard*. English language edition. Harmondsworth and New York: Penguin Books, 1982.

Kariuki, G.G. *Illusion of Power: Fifty Years in Kenyan Politics*. Nairobi: Kenway Publications, 2001.

Kenya Human Rights Commission (KHRC). *Recurrent Ethnic Violence and Claims of Communities Arming ahead of the 2012 General Elections*. Nairobi: KHRC, 2011.

Kes Hillman Smith, A.K., Gordon O. Ojwang and Victor N. Mose. *Systematic Aerial Sample Survey of Laikipia County*. Preliminary report. Nanyuki, Kenya: Impala Research Centre and Laikipia Wildlife Forum, April 2016.

Kinnaird, Margaret, Tim O'Brien and Gordon Ojwang. *Sample Count Aerial Surveys as a Monitoring Tool for Wildlife and Livestock: A Case Study from Laikipia County*. Nanyuki, Kenya: Laikipia Wildlife Forum, 2012.

Kiteme, Boniface and Thuita Thenya. 'Assessment of Ecological Status and Socio-Economic Dynamics of Upper Ewaso Ng'iro Basin Wetlands.' Working paper. CETRAD, 2011.

Mackinder, H.J. 'A Journey to the Summit of Mount Kenya, British East Africa.' *The Geographical Journal* 15, no. 5 (1900): 453–76.

Mburu, John, Michael Odhiambo, Albert Wachira, Njenga Kahiro, Andrew Williams, John Lodisana and John Gachigi. *The Abandoned Lands of Laikipia: Land Use Options Study*. Rumuruti, Kenya: Laikipia Wildlife Forum, The Nature Conservancy and Zeitz Foundation, January 2013.

Merriam-Webster. 'Definition of Fence.' https://www.merriam-webster.com/dictionary/fence. Accessed 19 August 2017.

Merriam-Webster. 'Definition of Self-Interest.' https://www.merriam-webster.com/dictionary/self-interest. Accessed 23 August 2017.

Merriam-Webster. 'Definition of Tenure.' https://www.merriam-webster.com/dictionary/tenure. Accessed 9 August 2017.

Neumann, Arthur H. *Elephant Hunting in East Equatorial Africa*. London: Rowland Ward, Limited, 1898.

Odongo, Judy and Ryan Masila. *Holistic Rangeland Management (HRM): Impact Assessment Report Laikipia*. Nanyuki, Kenya: Laikipia Wildlife Forum; Nairobi: Kenya Markets Trust, 2015.

Powell-Cotton, P.H.G. 'A Journey through Northern Uganda.' *The Geographical Journal* 24, no. 1. (July 1904): 56–65.

Public lecture with Michael Watts, Copenhagen University. 10 September 2015.

Smith, Zadie. *White Teeth*. New York: Vintage International/Vintage Books, Random House Inc., 2001.

Spicer, Paul. *The Temptress: The Scandalous Life of Alice de Janze and the Mysterious Death of Lord Erroll*. First edition. New York: St Martin's Griffin, 2011.

Stigand, Captain C.H. *To Abyssinia through an Unknown Land*. Philadelphia: J.B. Lippincott Company, 1910.

Thomson, J.B. *Joseph Thomson, African Explorer: A Bibliography by His Brother*. London: Sampson Low, 1897.

Thomson, Joseph. *Through Masai Land: A Journey of Exploration among the Snowclad Volcanic Mountains and Strange Tribes of Eastern Equatorial Africa*. Vol. I. London: Low, Marston, Searle, & Rivington, 1887.

Unks, Ryan. *Consequence of Changes in Herding Mobility for Livelihoods and Sustainable Landscapes: A Case Study from Laikipia, Kenya*. Integrative Conservation Research Brief. Nanyuki, Kenya: Laikipia Wildlife Forum; Athens, GA: University of Georgia, 2016.

Wheeler, Sara. *Too Close to the Sun: The Audacious Life and Times of Denys Finch Hatton*. Reprint edition. New York: Random House Trade Paperbacks, 2009.

Whittall, Errol. 'Dimbilil: The Story of an African Farm.' First edition London: Arthur Baker, 1956. In Elspeth Huxley, *Nine Faces Of Kenya*. Random House ebooks, 2011.

Unpublished Sources

Guene, Enid. 'The End of Hunting and Gathering: Identity and Livelihood Transformation among Foraging Communities in Kenya.' PhD diss., Universität zu Köln, forthcoming.

Kanyinga, Karuti. 'The Land Question in Kenya: Struggles, Accumulation and Changing Politics.' PhD diss., Roskilde University, 1998.

Waller, Richard. 'The Lords of East Africa: The Maasai in the Mid-Nineteenth Century (c. 1840–1880).' PhD diss., University of Cambridge, 1979.

Archives in Kenya

Kenya National Archives, Nairobi (KNA)

The following deposits were consulted:

DC Laikipia	District Commissioner, Laikipia
PC Rift Valley Province	Provincial Commissioner, Rift Valley Province

Kenya National Archives, Rift Valley Provincial Archive (Nakuru)

The following deposits were consulted:

DSO Laikipia District administrative files on resettlement schemes, Laikipia

Personal Archive, Papias Mathenge (Ngong)

Letters of correspondence between Advocates and AFC were consulted along with minutes of Directors' meetings in Lorien Ranching Company. The documents are kept by Papias Mathenge in Ngong.

British Institute of East Africa (BIEA)

Minutes of meetings from the Laikipia Farmers Association were consulted. The collections of the minutes can now be found at the British Institute of East Africa.

Archives in the United Kingdom

Weston Library, University of Oxford

Two maps were adapted from G. Per, first published by *Erdkunde* 1978–88. The following aerial photographs were consulted for historical land-use change maps:

1977 Ol Moran: 104/KE/6/123, 104/KE/6/122, V13B/1004/43, V13C/255/38, V13B/1004/44, 104/KE/6/39, 104/KE/7/106.

1969 Lorien: 104/KE/7/99, 104/KE/7/98, 104/KE/7/97, 104/KE/9/42, 104/KE/9/41, 104/KE/9/40, 104/KE/2/132, 104/KE/2/131, 104/KE/2/130.

1969 Thome: 104/KE/9/44, 104/KE/2/134, 104/KE/2/135, 104/KE/9/43, 104/KE/2/133.

Rhodes House Library, University of Oxford (*RH*)

The following deposits were consulted:

Africa.mic.515	Annual Reports, Laikipia District
Africa.mic.515	Annual Reports, Laikipia and Samburu District
Africa.mic.517	Handing-Over Reports, Laikipia District

The National Archive, Kew (*TNA*)

The following deposits were consulted:

CAB 24	Cabinet records, Kenya Land Commission
CO 1054	Correspondence, Kenya; adaptation of map from Moilshaq
FCO 141	Foreign and Commonwealth Office, migrated records, Kenya

Interviews

I conducted interviews in the urban areas of Githunguri, Maralal, Ngong, Nanyuki, Nyahururu, Rumuruti and Nairobi, as well as in the locations of Thome, Lorien and Ol Moran. Moreover, I conducted oral interviews on large-scale conservancies and ranches located in Laikipia East, Laikipia West and Laikipia North. One interview is used with courtesy of Rene Vesper. A total of 80 interviews were conducted. I worked alongside some excellent translators and research assistants: in Thome and surroundings, 'E' and 'H'; in Lorien and surroundings, 'E' and 'J'; in Ol Moran and surroundings, 'H,' 'R' and 'E.' In particular, the research was discussed in detail with the main assistants 'E' and 'H.'

Index

www.ingramcontent.com/pod-product-compliance
Lightning Source LLC
Chambersburg PA
CBHW071432230926
51846CB00001B/207
* 9 7 8 9 0 0 4 4 3 5 1 9 3 *